COLUMBIA COLLEGE LIBRARY
COLUMBIA, MISSOURI

Blue-Collar Workers

Blue-Collar Workers

A Symposium on Middle America

EDITED BY
Sar A. Levitan
CENTER FOR MANPOWER POLICY STUDIES
THE GEORGE WASHINGTON UNIVERSITY

McGRAW-HILL BOOK COMPANY
New York St. Louis San Francisco Düsseldorf London Sydney Toronto Mexico Panama Johannesburg Kuala Lumpur Montreal New Delhi Rio de Janeiro Singapore

Copyright © 1971 by McGraw-Hill, Inc. All Rights Reserved.
Printed in the United States of America. No part of this
publication may be reproduced, stored in a retrieval system,
or transmitted, in any form or by any means, electronic,
mechanical, photocopying, recording, or otherwise, without
the prior written permission of the publisher.

This volume was prepared under a grant from the Ford Foundation.

Library of Congress catalog card number 74-172026

1 2 3 4 5 6 7 8 9 MAMM 7 9 8 7 6 5 4 3 2 1

07-037390-6

This book was set in Times Roman by University Graphics, Inc.
It was printed on Film Kote and bound by The Maple Press
Company. The designer was Christine Aulicino. The editors for
McGraw-Hill Book Company were Herbert Waentig, Nancy
Tressel, and Laura Givner. Frank Matonti and Alice Cohen
supervised the production.

309.173
L579b

Contents

Preface *xiii*

PART ONE. THE CONTINUING CONFLICT

Introduction *3*

1. Is There a Lower-Middle-Class "Problem"? *7*

The Continuity of Class Conflict 7
The Hemmed-in Workers 11
What Is To Be Done? 14
Bringing Ourselves Together 17

2. The Long View *20*

The Search for Perspective 20
Variations 21
Major Transformations 25
Blue-collar Work 30
A Typology of Blue-collar Workers 34
A Look Back and a Look Ahead 44

3. A Profile of the Blue-Collar American *47*

A View through Census Data 47
Trends in Employment and Earnings 51
Geographic Distribution 55
Age 58
Education 64
Industrial Distribution 67
Employment of Wife and Family Income 68
Use with Caution! 71

4. The Problems of Lower-Middle-Income Workers *76*

The Pressures They Face 76
The Economic Squeeze 78
The Workplace Squeeze 87
Environmental-Psychological-Sociological Squeeze 91

PART TWO. ATTITUDES AND INSTITUTIONS

Introduction *97*

5. Blue-Collar Workers and the Future of American Politics *101*

Realignment or Retrenchment 101
New Deal Issues 105
Law-and-order Issues 108
The War 113
Alienation 116
Political Parties 120
Blue-collar Workers and the Future 124

6. Black Demands, White Reactions, and Liberal Alarms *130*

Elements of the Liberal World Outlook 130
Blue-collar Intolerance: Some Contrary Evidence 132
The Southern Experience 140
The George Wallace Question 143

The Sense of Powerlessness 146
Removing Lower-middle-class Strains 150

7. *The Union Member Speaks* *154*

The Viability of Unions 154
Economic Squeeze 157
The Working Conditions 160
The Social Squeeze 165
The Expanding Role of Unions 171

8. *Black and White Blue-Collar Workers and Unions* *176*

Conflict: Present and Potential 176
Development of the Relation 177
Factors Responsible for the Relation 190
Conclusions 200

9. *Making the Good Life: Working-Class Family and Life-Styles* *204*

Working Class or Middle Class? 204
Comfort and Security for the Family 206
Working-class World Views 208
Styles and Goals of Consumption 212
Working-class Morale 219
Politicians, Establishmentarians, and the Working Class 222

10. *Can Workers Transform Society?* *230*

Diversity of Blue-collar Workers 230
Perspectives 236
Short-range Changes 238
Long-term Changes 242
Transforming Policy 246
Counterpressures 248
Joint Actions 250

PART THREE. PROGRAMS AND FUTURE DIRECTIONS

Introduction *255*

11. *The Visible Tax System* *259*

Relative Tax Burdens 259
Visible Taxes 262
Geographic Differentials 275
The Objective Evidence Reviewed 278
Perceptions versus Realities 279
Conclusion 284

12. *Income Maintenance: Who Gains and Who Pays?* *286*

Does Income Maintenance Contribute to Alienation? 286
Is Social Security a Good Buy? 291
Public Assistance: Something for Nothing? 299
Unemployment Insurance and Workmen's Compensation 306
Summary 314

13. *Yearning, Learning, and Status* *318*

What's Bothering the Blue-collar Worker? 318
Education and Mobility: Rising Levels of Education 323
Significance for Blue Collars 324
Avenues to Upward Mobility 325
Labor Market Projections and Educational Requirements 329
Blue Collars and High School 331
Blue Collars and College 333
Adapting the Educational System to New Needs 337

14. *Directions for Action* *342*

15. *Hot under the Blue Collar* *351*

16. *The Blue-Collar Worker Weathers the "Ordeal of Change"* *359*

The Blue-collar Blues Theme 359
Is the Blue Collar Starched? 363
The Blue-collar Burden 367
Mechanisms of Adjustment 373
Changing with the Times 381

Index *385*

THE CONTRIBUTORS

JODIE ALLEN is on the senior research staff of the Urban Institute.

WORTH BATEMAN is Vice-President of the Urban Institute.

MARTHA BUSH is an urban research associate in the Department of Educational Sociology, New York University.

ELI GINZBERG is Hepburn Professor of Economics and Director, Conservation of Human Resources, Columbia University.

RICHARD F. HAMILTON is Professor of Sociology, McGill University.

FRED R. HARRIS, a Democrat, is senior Senator from Oklahoma.

SAR A. LEVITAN is Professor of Economics and Director, Center for Manpower Policy Studies, George Washington University.

RAY MARSHALL is Professor and Chairman of the Department of Economics, University of Texas, Austin.

HERMAN P. MILLER is Director, Population Division, U.S. Bureau of the Census.

S. M. MILLER is Professor of Education and Sociology and Senior Fellow, Center for International Studies, New York University.

DICK NETZER is Dean of the Graduate School of Public Administration, New York University.

LEE RAINWATER is Professor of Sociology, Harvard University.

HOWARD L. REITER is Editor of the *Ripon Forum* and a doctoral candidate in political science at Harvard University.

JEROME M. ROSOW is Assistant Secretary for Policy, Evaluation, and Research, U.S. Department of Labor.

STANLEY H. RUTTENBERG is President of Stanley H. Ruttenberg & Associates and Editor in Chief of *Manpower Information Service.*

ROBERT SCHRANK is a manpower consultant to the Ford Foundation.

LEONARD S. SILK is a member of *The New York Times* editorial staff.

SUSAN STEIN is a research associate, Manpower Assistance Project, New York, N.Y.

ROBERT TAGGART III is a research associate, Center for Manpower Policy Studies, George Washington University.

Preface

Why a book about the blue-collar worker? The easy answer is that this volume attempts to capitalize on the rising interest in hard hats, or middle Americans. A close examination of its contents, however, will indicate that this symposium is a serious effort to examine a major social issue facing the American people in the 1970s. It attempts to analyze the forces and trends that have contributed to revived public interest in the American working class and to examine the nature of the problems they are sharing.

Nineteen social analysts, including public officials, have commented on various aspects of blue-collar life and work; the problems that beset blue-collar people; and how they are treated by American society. Several authors also make a stab at identifying proposed corrective approaches. The contributors include economists, political scientists, and sociologists, in addition to three public servants. And to lend the volume even greater credibility, one of the contributors is less than 30 years old.

The blue-collar citizen is much discussed, but who is he? A major problem in planning the volume was to define the target population. One approach is to include all families with an annual income between \$5,000 and \$10,000. This would encompass roughly the middle one-third of all families in the United States, or some 70 million persons. Income statistics, however, are not a sufficient criterion for identifying the presumably "alienated," "forgotten," or "troubled" Americans, to use some of the more common terms applied to blue-collar workers. Moreover, many people in this income range are obviously not blue-collar workers or even part of the lower middle class. Consider the young college graduate in his first job, the medical intern, or the relatively well-to-do family farmer. Included in the above income range are families whose income is supplied exclusively by the head of the family as well as families who depend on secondary earners. Again, other groups of blue-collar workers earn more than $10,000 annually but may still be considered among "alienated" hard hats and factory workers.

A satisfactory delineation of blue-collar workers proved as elusive as age-old attempts to identify the "working class." Blue-collar workers certainly do not constitute a homogeneous and cohesive group. Therefore, in dealing with the real or imaginary problems faced by the "middle Americans," this volume does not attempt to pigeonhole any segment of the population solely on the basis of income. At best, the income criterion serves as a general indicator of the group under consideration. Each author was asked to delineate the population discussed in his chapter, consistent with a clearly enunciated conceptual framework and the availability of data. This accordionlike approach is a reflection of reality and indicates that the blue-collar population is an amorphous group.

Within this flexible framework, the contributors focus on real or alleged problems of blue-collar workers. Whenever feasible, blue-collar workers are compared both with others in the same income categories and with other major occupational groups.

An effort was made to secure not only interdisciplinary approaches to the blue-collar "problem" but also approaches whose diversity would reflect the complexity of the subject treated. Indeed, the solutions offered in this volume to the ailments of the blue-collar worker range from expanding (in mild doses) some existing social programs to a complete transformation of American society.

Not only do the contributors differ on probable solutions; often they do not even agree on facts. For example, relying heavily upon U.S. Department of Labor statistical series which show that spendable income of American workers has remained relatively stable over the past five years, several analysts infer that the blue-collar worker is victim of an economic squeeze. Other contributors reject this notion because of technical problems inherent in these data.

Another example. Some contributors make much ado of the fact that the average worker's annual earnings are inadequate to provide a modest budget for a family of four, according to Department of Labor figures. Others suggest that there is room to question such an interpretation. By definition, an average family budget means that some will have a lower income. One might also question the realism of a moderate budget which is beyond the means of more than half of American families. Obviously, for the majority of the American people, this budget is a goal rather than a measure of minimum needs, and the different semantics used by a government agency do not change this fact. In most other countries the income needed for this "moderate" budget is within the reach of only a privileged small minority.

There is no single correct answer to these issues. Whether the U.S. Department of Labor income level needed for a moderate standard of living is adequate, or whether the blue-collar worker is being squeezed by the economic system, is a question of values. The editor carefully avoided getting into the line of fire when different contributors disagreed about the interpretation of "facts," and he will leave it to the reader to determine which arguments are most appealing. Here lies the greatest strength of a symposium on a complex subject: it reveals the diversity of views and the difficulties inherent in interpreting facts, let alone suggesting solutions.

Whether there exists a *problem* specific to blue-collar workers is itself unclear. Obviously, the 16 million families headed by a blue-collar worker do not live in uninterrupted bliss. In fact, an observer of any segment of the population would have no difficulty in detecting unrealized aspirations, frustrations, and symptoms of discontent or alienation. Psychiatrists' couches are filled, and the fees paid suggest that the patients are rarely blue-collar workers. *Fortune* magazine, for example, showed that the world is full of problems when it followed up one recent article on "blue-collar blues" with another on "white-collar woes."

Some observers, however, contend that blue-collar workers are more afflicted by problems than are other social groupings. They argue that blue-collar workers are especially disoriented by the radical attitudinal and behavioral changes in American society and the questioning, if not rejection, of long-accepted values. Other contributors believe that, in analyzing the turmoil of American society in recent years, the blue-collar group cannot be treated separately. The vital question is whether the major changes of recent years have downgraded the relative status of blue-collar workers. In sorting out the apparent chaos, the survey researchers may have more satisfactory explanations than the economist or sociologist.

Indeed, economists are at a loss to find a crisis facing the blue-collar worker. To be sure, increases in spendable income since the middle of the 1960s have not kept pace with "normal" expectations. But there is no evidence that the blue-collar worker's share of the total American economic pie has shrunk. And major recent collective bargaining settlements promise that workers will recover the ground lost during the past few years.

It would be difficult, therefore, to make a case that blue-collar workers have been on a treadmill during the rising affluence and tight labor markets of the late 1960s. Like most other Americans, of course, these workers have had to allocate a larger proportion of their incomes to taxes. But the revenues collected by the government are expended on behalf of the citizens, and the middle American seems to reap his share of benefits from total government expenditures. The issue, therefore, is whether blue-collar workers approve of governmental expenditures. Two major controversial areas of government expenditures deserve special attention. The single largest item of federal expenditures goes, of course, for defense or making war. Election results and opinion surveys suggest that blue-collar workers on the whole favor defense expenditures and, indeed, probably support the Vietnam war more actively than does the rest of the population. Another major area of government activity, and an increasingly important one, is outlays for welfare. Most income maintenance programs are based on prior contributions and are strongly supported by middle Americans as well as other groups—though there seems to be considerable dissatisfaction among younger workers with rising Social Security payroll taxes. However, not all income maintenance programs enjoy universal support. Blue-collar workers appear to oppose expanding income maintenance programs and providing special services to the poor while excluding lower-middle-class groups. Perhaps the expansion of antipoverty efforts emphasizing help to disadvantaged people among blacks, Chicanos, and other minority groups is a source of dissatisfaction among blue-collar workers.

Paradoxically, the blue-collar families' quest for rising income may also be a source of alienation. American families depend increasingly upon wives' earnings to sustain and boost the ever-rising standard of living; indeed, more than two of every five married women are employed. Dependence upon wives' earnings is more prevalent among lower-paid blue-collar workers than among more affluent families. Presumably, this could be a cause of discontent among the blue-collar males who find that their earnings are inadequate to support the middle-class standard to which they aspire. But the trend toward working wives is characteristic of all sectors of the American population and may simply reflect a change in life-styles.

If strong feelings of alienation exist among the working-class population, the clues to the underlying changes may be found in overall societal transformations rather than in specific changes in the working class. And the contributors to this symposium differ in their appraisal of whether the working class has been more affected by the changes than other groups. The real or apparent changes in blue-collar status almost inevitably involve political realignment, and here the survey researcher or active politician comes to the fore as an analyst and forecaster of competition for blue-collar votes.

In the remarkable but relatively stable coalition of strange bedfellows shaped by President Franklin Roosevelt, the blue-collar worker has been a major partner for nearly two-score years. Only occasionally has he strayed off the reservation. Though President Dwight Eisenhower succeeded in making inroads into the blue-collar vote, this digression proved to be temporary. The Republican presidential candidates in the 1960s and most lesser candidates were stymied in their attempts to destroy the New Deal coalition, which continued to dominate Congress and other aspects of American political life.

The Republicans' failure to shift large sectors of blue-collar workers into their camp has not been for lack of trying. Over the past decade, they have mounted increasing efforts to break the Democratic coalition and have been most solicitous of Democratic voters who have shown signs of seeking new political allegiances. The effort has paid off in the South where the Republican party has made significant and continuing gains. And blue-collar workers have played an important role in the improved fortunes of the

Republican party. Although racial issues perhaps played a significant role in encouraging Southern workers to defect from the Democratic party, this issue was not enough to undermine their Democratic allegiance in other areas of the country.

In the 1970 congressional elections, the Republicans brought the problems of blue-collar workers to the center of the political arena. They made a major effort to appeal to blue-collar workers, raising "social" issues closely akin to the racial issues which had proved effective in the South and hoping that blue-collar workers would switch again and vote Republican. The apparent aim was to attract voters who defected in 1968 from the Democratic party to Governor Wallace. The effort did not succeed. According to the National Broadcasting Company analysis of the 1970 congressional elections, 69 percent of the blue-collar workers who voted for a major party candidate remained loyal to the Democratic party, and only 31 percent voted Republican. The strategy, as indicated earlier, was more successful in the South, where 43 percent of the blue-collar workers voted Republican. But in the East, Midwest, and West, the Republican share of blue-collar votes ranged between 27 and 30 percent of the total. The NBC findings are supported by a pre-election Gallup poll which indicated that manual workers favored the Democratic party by a 2 to 1 margin over the GOP.

If the NBC analysis holds up under closer scrutiny, it would appear that Republican bids for the blue-collar worker must be backed with more than appeals to their presumed prejudices and bigotry. And Democrats showed that they can play the "social" issues as well as Republicans: everybody who was anybody in 1970 favored "law and order."

It is quite likely that blue-collar workers will continue to be courted assiduously in the future. But recent elections strongly suggest that, barring a charismatic candidate, the Republican party will have to offer inducements more tangible than appeals to prejudice if they are to sway large masses of blue-collar workers to desert the Democratic party.

Such an approach was presumably considered by a Nixon administration task force instructed to delve into the "blue-collar problem." The task force, which included key presidential advisers, considered a broad series of programs that would be of special interest to bluc-collar workers, including federally supported upgrading programs, expanded adult education facilities, improved housing and transportation facilities, and various tax exemptions. While the task force report was released officially prior to the 1970 elections, it was treated only as a working paper, and none of its recommendations received official White House endorsement. The White House faces very real, though not necessarily insurmountable, difficulties in adopting any of the major measures considered by the task force. Any program that would be significant and sufficiently inclusive in its coverage would carry a price tag running into billions of dollars. For example, provision of child care would have great appeal. Possibly as many as a million blue-collar families with working mothers and small children might take advantage of such a program if it were "free" and universally available without stigma. But providing child care is an expensive proposition and, according to government estimates, might cost $1,500 a year for each preschool child and about a third as much for schoolchildren. Obviously, a universal, free child-care program, or even one that was heavily subsidized, would carry a high price tag. It is clear why the Nixon administration, beset by inflationary pressures and rising costs of government, has been reluctant to embrace the expensive programs considered by its own task force.

In contrast, the Democratic party is in an excellent position to hold on to the allegiance of blue-collar workers. Having established credit with disadvantaged minority groups during the 1960s, it can now turn to buttress its position among blue-collar workers even if the process antagonizes upper-class voters. The Democratic-controlled Congress can be used as a vehicle to show that Democrats "care" for blue-collar workers. Not all such legislation would necessarily be costly. For example, "stiff" occupational safety legislation does not require additional government expenditures but does appeal to trade unions. Raising minimum wages diminishes nonunion competition at a direct cost to employers, who are not normally counted among the Democratic faithful. The Democrats can afford to alienate employer groups in order to win points with their traditional constituencies. And as the opposition party, they can make other promises which would be attractive to broader constituencies without having to deliver, at least not before 1973. The Democratic party can even attempt to maintain its Southern contingent by resting on its laurels with regard to civil rights, but without flaunting that record in the South. Though gaining in the Senate, the GOP failed in 1970 for the first time in a decade to make any Southern gains in the House of Representatives and also lost two governorships in that region.

The 1970 elections were not the last joust between the two major parties for the allegiance of that crucial sector in the population. However, predictions that public policy in the 1970s will focus on the problems of the blue-collar workers may prove premature. After all, few would have predicted a decade ago that the problems of the poor would become a major issue of the 1960s. New developments will give life to different tactics, different appeals, and new effects.

This symposium is intended to furnish a better appreciation of the problems of the blue-collar workers and provide a better understanding of their reactions to and perceptions of the evolving issues raised by these problems.

I am indebted to Roger H. Davidson of the University of California, Santa Barbara, for his valuable critical review of the manuscript, and to my colleagues David Marwick and Barbara Ann Pease for editing the drafts submitted by the authors.

This volume was prepared under a grant from the Ford Foundation to The George Washington University's Center for Manpower Policy Studies. In accordance with the foundation's practice, complete responsibility for the preparation of the volume has been left to the editor and the contributors.

SAR A. LEVITAN

Thanksgiving 1970
Washington, D.C.

Blue-Collar Workers

« PART ONE »

The Continuing Conflict

Although no formal poll was taken, the verdict of most of the contributors to this volume seems to be that there is no real blue-collar "crisis." Writing from a broad perspective, Leonard Silk and Eli Ginzberg fail to discern critical new problems facing blue-collar workers as a group. Class conflict has always existed in American society and persists in the present. The current restiveness of blue-collar workers, in the view of these observers, reflects simply a shift to the right and an attempt to seek new alliances rather than any increase in traditional militancy. George Meany, long a leader of American organized labor and possibly the major spokesman of blue-collar workers, has suggested that the American labor movement might "disaffiliate" itself from the Democratic party, which he said had been infiltrated by "leftist" elements. The recession apparently arrested such a movement, if it ever existed, but Silk suggests that the threat to the Democrats might be revived under different circumstances, more propitious to the labor movement.

If there is an increased restiveness among large numbers of American workers, it may be due to the twin factors of rising affluence and resentment of the welfare state. Rising governmental expenditures and the accompanying increased inflation may have created more discontent than the traditional working-class complaints against "the system." Presumably, such discontent is focused on the life-style of intellectuals on the one hand and the poverty-stricken on the other. If this analysis is correct, then the discontent of the blue-collar workers is not very different from that of more affluent middle-class people. Silk sees the present blue-collar worker as beset by a continuation of the historical struggle between Jeffersonianism and Hamiltonianism in American history.

Ginzberg shares this view. Recognizing the diversity among blue-collar workers, he suggests that the long-run trend has been toward improvement of their lot and their ever-greater absorption into the mainstream of American social and economic life. At the turn of this century, manual workers were definitely inferior to clerical workers in social and economic status. While the latter may still enjoy a higher social status, blue-collar workers long ago caught up and even surged ahead economically. With advances in the standard of living, the blue-collar worker remains as mobile occupationally as ever; and expanded public programs, particularly in education, have opened upward mobility for his children to achieve more desired occupations.

Taking a narrower view—circumscribed by data available from the Bureau of the Census—Herman Miller is also unable to find an evolving crisis confronting the blue-collar worker. He compares average income gains of craftsmen and operatives—categories roughly encompassing manual workers—with other major occupational groups. In addition, Census data make it possible to compare advances made by white and black families. The results show that during the decade of the 1960s, married blue-collar workers and their families made relative income gains comparable to those of professional, managerial, and other white-collar workers. As a matter of fact, during the last half of the 1960s, the gains of blue-collar workers were a percentage point or two higher than those of the other occupational groups, and this was the period when the alienation of the blue-collar worker was presumed to have reached its zenith.

Miller recognizes, however, that the gains of manual workers with the largest family responsibilities, those between the ages of 35 and 44, lagged behind those of other major occupational groups. Annual family income of this large group, adjusted for rises in the cost of living but before tax deductions, still rose a respectable 46 percent over the decade. But professional and managerial workers in the same age group received a 70 percent increase in family income, while clerical and sales workers' incomes rose 58 percent. Since man does not live by bread alone, but also by keeping up with the Joneses, the manual worker with a growing family may be casting a covetous eye on the gains made by professional, managerial, and white-collar workers in the same age bracket, and this may be a source of dissatisfaction and frustration. Viewing comparative gains, Miller detects another probable source of frustration in the fact that gains by white manual workers have lagged behind those of black manual workers. Blacks filled one-third of all jobs for craftsmen and operatives added during the 1960s and held by married men; their median annual earnings rose 42 percent during the decade, compared with 25 percent for white workers.

Recognizing the inherent dangers in relying upon averages, Miller suggests that the *relative* greater gains made by other groups may be a source of alienation and frustration among white blue-collar workers. This clue is taken up by Jerome Rosow, who maintains that the lower middle class is indeed being squeezed and that the problems of these workers have been growing. Focusing on the problems of a hypothetical 40-year-old manual worker with growing family responsibilities, Rosow argues that his income gains have not kept pace with rising responsibilities, and in fact that his income is not adequate to fill the needs of a moderate budget, as defined by the U.S. Department of Labor. He finds also that lower-middle-class workers have fewer opportunities in the workplace than they were led to expect, and that many face problems which remain unattended by their employers.

Rosow does not argue that the problems of the $5,000- to $10,000-a-year worker and his family have necessarily been aggravated in the last 10 years. But he does present a persuasive case that the actual life-style of middle Americans is far-removed from the image of affluent America nourished by Madison Avenue and the mass media. Discontent does not stem only from an empty stomach or sheer deprivation. Nor is it necessarily based on objective facts. A person's perception of reality may be just as important a source of alienation as reality itself. Thus, an individual or a group may be troubled because an "inferior" group is catching up or the one right above is achieving greater successes. Average gains in income of blue-collar workers may, therefore, be a very poor barometer for gauging their true feelings.

1. IS THERE A LOWER-MIDDLE-CLASS "PROBLEM"?

by Leonard S. Silk

THE CONTINUITY OF CLASS CONFLICT

"They have been loud in their praise of legally constituted rights; but they have shown an instinctive and implacable distrust of intellectual and moral independence, and have always sought to suppress it in favor of intellectual and moral conformity."[1]

The man who wrote that was referring neither to the law-and-order issue of 1970 nor to the attitude of "hard hats" toward students, professors, hippies, and blacks. He was Herbert Croly, one of the founders of the *New Republic,* and he was writing in 1909 about Thomas Jefferson and his followers, who were largely drawn from the class of workers and farmers. Croly was contrasting the populism of Jefferson with the elitism or establishmentarianism of Alexander Hamilton, whose political philosophy, he said, "was much more clearly thought out than that of Jefferson." Hamilton, Croly wrote,

> has been accused by his opponents of being the enemy of liberty; whereas in point of fact, he wished, like the Englishman he was, to protect and encourage liberty, just as far as such encouragement was compatible with good order, because he realized that *genuine liberty would inevitably issue in fruitful social and economic inequalities.* But he also realized that genuine liberty was not merely a matter of a constitutional declaration of rights. It could be protected only by an energetic and clear-sighted central government, and it could be fertilized only by the

efficient national organization of American activities. For national organization demands in relation to individuals a certain amount of selection, and *a certain classification of these individuals according to their abilities and deserts. It is just this kind or effect of liberty which Jefferson and his followers have always disliked and discouraged.*[2]

To show how unchanging these clashes of philosophy have been since the earliest days of the Republic, one needs only to quote from a letter published in the *New York Times* on October 23, 1970. The letter was written by Martin Duffy of Susquehanna, Pennsylvania, in response to an article by Prof. Edward C. Banfield of Harvard University on "the lower class." Duffy stated:

> Professor Edward C. Banfield's opinions do indeed cause one to doubt the value of higher education. Not that I wish to lump together all professors—as he lumps together the "lower class"—but how can one hold his temper when he reads such nonsense?
>
> Professor Banfield is writing about people, not insects. "The violet smells to him as it doth to me; all his senses have but human conditions." Is he so removed from humanity that he cannot feel his way into another's pain and pride? Is this what cultivating the mind produces?

Banfield, in the letter writer's view, was blithely accepting social and economic inequalities, as the Hamiltonians had always done.

The conflict of Hamiltonianism and Jeffersonianism is a deep and recurrent theme in American political history. One can trace it through the debates over the First and Second Banks of the United States and in the contests over protective tariffs; in the conflicts between the agrarian West and the industrial East, and between the agrarian South and the industrial North; in disputes between farmers and railroads, between small business and big business, and even between labor and management. The genius of Franklin D. Roosevelt in the 1930s was to mask the conflict, at least temporarily, by bringing together "the forgotten men"—the unemployed workers and all those others who feared unemployment, the intellectual, and the Southerner. Roosevelt's masterstroke made the Democratic party the majority force in American politics for almost four decades. Today, in a time of social upheaval, Richard M. Nixon is seeking to bring forth a new majority coalition, including the Southerner, the businessman, and what he calls "the forgotten

American," who is basically the same person as F.D.R.'s "forgotten man." Nixon also calls him a member of the "Silent Majority."

George Meany, president of the American Federation of Labor–Congress of Industrial Organizations (AFL-CIO), raised the hopes of Republican leaders that blue-collar workers can indeed be brought into this new coalition. In the early fall of 1970, Meany declared that trade unionists were "looking less to the Democrats" because, in his view, "the Democratic Party has disintegrated—it is not the so-called liberal party that it was a few years ago. It almost has got to be the part of the extremists in so far as these so-called liberals or new lefts, or whatever you want to call them, have taken over the Democratic Party."

Meany thus appeared to be confirming the thesis of Kevin P. Phillips, the conservative political strategist, that Nixon's "Southern strategy" is actually national in scope, with a strong appeal to "the hitherto Democratic blue-collar workers, hard hats and ethnic (mostly Roman Catholic) conservatives from New York to California."

This shift to the right by blue-collar workers, according to Phillips, is "not simply a question of hostility towards blacks." It also reflects, in his view, "unhappiness with permissiveness and erosion of traditional values, opposition to the principle of federal welfarism and social engineering, and resentment of the anti-Middle American bigotry practiced by the liberal metropolitan intellectual elite."

But the movement of organized labor from the Democratic party to the Republican party is still far from an accomplished fact, especially because of the concern of workers and their leaders over economic issues. Meany himself stopped well short of saying that the AFL-CIO should support the Republicans. Instead, his principle appeared to be a reversion to the traditional policy first developed by Samuel Gompers, the founder of the AFL, that organized labor should reward its friends and punish its enemies. In the fall of 1970, Meany also stated that it would certainly not be outside the labor movement's tradition if AFL-CIO members supported Republicans, and he praised President Nixon for favoring collective bargaining for government employees at every level. Meany's position illustrated what the late Prof. Selig Perlman of the University of Wisconsin called the "job consciousness" of American labor—its dominant concern with such issues as job security, pay and fringe benefits, and working conditions. It should be noted that President Roosevelt drew organized labor to the Democratic party mainly by encouraging union organization and collective bargaining, by increasing job security as well as Social Security, by boosting rates of pay, and by the New Deal's assault on unemployment. With all his discontents about the Democratic party, Meany still was highly critical of the Republicans for increasing the level of unemployment (from 3.5 percent of the labor force when the Nixon administration took office to 5.6 percent in October 1970) in order to check the inflation and still failing to bring inflation under control: consumer prices moved up at an annual rate of about 6 percent during the first 1¾ years of the Nixon administration.

Thus, organized labor in the United States is being pulled in different directions by the crucial issues of the time—the Vietnam war, the upheaval and protests of students on college campuses and many high schools as well, the demands of Negroes for equal rights and access to better-paying jobs formerly reserved for whites only, urban crime and violence, economic stagnation, unemployment, and inflation. Generally speaking, the Vietnam war, student protests, black drive for social and economic equality, and "crime in the streets" have tended to drive blue-collar workers toward the right politically. In some instances, as in the attack of hard-hat construction workers on students demonstrating in Wall Street during the summer of 1970, the blue-collar workers have themselves turned to violence. But the economic issues of stagnation, unemployment, and inflation seem likely to drive the blue-collar workers leftward, or at least to hold them in the Democratic party.

President Nixon has been sensitive to the political cost to his party of rising unemployment and inflation. He had hoped to check inflation without more than a slight rise in unemployment; that was the purpose of his policy of economic "gradualism." But inflation and unemployment proved to be less soluble than the Nixon administration had anticipated and undoubtedly presented the most serious obstacle to the Republican party in capturing greater support from workingmen and -women. But President Nixon sought to offset these economic issues by calling for patriotic support of his Vietnam policy and by stressing his opposition to crime, drugs, pornography, social permissiveness, and student protests. These were all issues on which the President felt that he would have the support of the conservative Silent Majority, including much of the lower middle class.

The worsening economic picture during 1970 appears to have been decisive in strengthening the Democratic party in most industrial states during the midterm congressional and gubernatorial elections. With joblessness rising and real take-home pay shrinking, the "economic issue" apparently outweighed the so-called "social issue" among blue-collar workers. In these circumstances, the love feast between George Meany and the Nixon administration proved to be short-lived. But it may yet prove to be a movable feast, especially under improved economic conditions permitting blue-collar workers to resume their movement up the economic and social scale.

THE HEMMED-IN WORKERS

The rising income of blue-collar workers during the postwar years has made them more conservative—and anxious. During a Labor Day interview in 1970, George Meany asserted that trade unionists were disturbed about the Democratic party because, he said, it is too far to the left and "our members basically believe in the American system, and maybe they have a greater stake in the system now than they had 15 or 20 years ago, because under the system and our trade union policy they have become middle class."

Workers making 30 cents an hour could be quite radical, said Meany, "but you have people who are making $8,000 or $9,000 a year, paying off mortgages with kids going to college." In fact, special tabulations done for this study show that in 1969 the median income of white families headed by blue-collar workers had reached $10,700—a 30 percent increase in constant dollars from 1960.[3]

The change in the financial status of blue-collar workers, said Meany, makes for a very different situation when it comes to calling workers, with heavy fixed obligations, out on strike; he suggested that this might even cause the strike to atrophy as a means of bringing pressure on employers for higher pay and better working conditions.

To be sure, the AFL-CIO president does not speak for all trade unionists, and obviously not for all American workers, more than two-thirds of whom are not union members. Some trade unionists are more militant than Meany, and many workers—both organized and unorganized—are still closer to the poverty line than the middle class. Nevertheless, the emergence of a working class that is to such a large degree middle-class is posing a new set of political, economic, and social problems with which the nation is just starting to grapple.

Moving up in the world seems to have intensified rather than calmed certain discontents of the blue-collar workers. A generation ago, during the great organizing drive of the American labor movement, blue-collar workers could say, with G. K. Chesterton, "And we were angry and poor and happy, and proud of seeing our names in print." Today, after three decades of economic growth, the workers' plaint should go, "Still we are angry, but now we are middle-class and unhappy, and longing to see our names in print." For the workers feel that they have again become, as Nixon says, "forgotten Americans," and they want more attention paid to their grievances.

But what are the real grievances of the blue-collar workers?

Even though many of them have moved up the income ladder, the "gut issue," as Meany said, still is the pocketbook issue. Many workers (like other Americans) feel that inflation is making them poorer despite higher dollar earnings. But is this really so? Overall data indicating that real per capita income has declined slightly since 1965 are misleading, because they lump part-time and female labor with full-time male workers, thereby understating the rate at which the average income of blue-collar family heads has been rising. In fact, since 1965, the average white married man employed in a blue-collar job has had a 15 percent increase in his annual income, measured in constant dollars. During the entire decade of the 1960s, white men in blue-collar jobs had real gains of 25 percent—about the same as whites had in other occupations. With more wives working and more men moonlighting, family incomes of white workers rose still more dramatically during the 1960s.

But that gain in average family income, which lifted so many into the middle class, may have come at the cost of heightened personal and social strains. Moonlighting is certainly a source of tension for many, and so is the far greater participation of wives in the labor force. Particularly for women with children living at home, the double responsibility of a job away from home and of rearing a family and taking care of cooking, cleaning, and other household chores can be a source of serious tension. A further source of tension or concern among white blue-collar workers may have been the even faster progress of Negroes in income and employment. Not only did Negroes narrow the income gap during the 1960s, but they also succeeded in increasing their share of blue-collar jobs, especially in manufacturing.

Both the greater competition for jobs and the narrowing of the income gap between whites and blacks undoubtedly offended some whites; expressions of resentment were widespread. These attitudes doubtless had much to do with the support of many blue-collar workers for George Wallace of Alabama during the presidential campaign of 1968 and help to explain why proponents of the "Southern strategy" for the Republican party feel that it is a Northern and working-class strategy as well.

Relative income may be more important to the ego and self-esteem than absolute income. The social reformer's dream of greater equality of incomes may intensify social bitterness and bigotry as the gap between white and black income is narrowed, even though the absolute real income of both groups rises.

It is even possible that many white workers feel less secure with higher incomes—and middle-class values—than they did before. As Meany stressed, they have taken on large debts: they have acquired homes and real estate that represent the largest share of their assets, and they fear that they will sustain huge losses in property values if there is "block busting" in the neighborhoods and Negroes move in. Thus, worries about debts and financial equity feed into the anxieties of lower-middle-class whites about open housing and integrated neighborhoods, and these anxieties are further aggravated by fears of crime, drugs, sexual license, and violence. Many white workers who feel that they have finally succeeded in moving up a bit in the world are fearful of community changes that will wipe out the middle-class economic values that they have struggled so hard to achieve—by working overtime, by moonlighting, by having their wives go to work, and by going heavily into debt.

Similar threats to their social values turn many blue-collar workers bitterly against demonstrating students, hippies, and opponents of the Vietnam war—all of whom they tend to lump together. For them the "greening of America," in Prof. Charles A. Reich's arresting phrase, seems like social degeneration and subversion. During the election of 1970, leaders of the Republican party sought to turn these social anxieties into political assets.

The grievances of the blue-collar workers thus appear to be of two basic types, economic and social. The *economic* pressures result from both inflation and unemployment or threats of unemployment and reduced hours of work. For the many blue-collar workers who are middle-aged, these economic pressures are intensified by the fact that, while their capacity to earn reaches a plateau in their forties, family expenses keep rising as they acquire debts, as their children grow and seek to get college educations, and as their parents age. The *social* pressures are intensified as they feel that they are looked down upon by richer and better-educated whites above them, and pressed by blacks and other minority groups coming up from below them. Many white workers feel frustrated, hemmed in, neglected, and despised in a generally affluent society by their inability to make it. For many, their feelings of social inferiority are intensified by a sense that they are the *victims* of bigotry that is directed at them because they are Italian, Polish, or of some other nationality which they believe the upper classes regard as low, vulgar, ignorant, or stupid. Their resentments are intensified by their feeling that the manual work they do, which is often exhausting, backbreaking, and frustrating, receives so little social esteem. Many feel dissatisfied with the rewards—psychological and social as well as economic—of their jobs. Some observers maintain that a lack of pride and satisfaction in blue-collar work is producing shortages of skilled hands, with inflationary consequences both because the supply of labor to many difficult and demanding manual occupations is reduced and because workers in such jobs translate their deep resentments into exorbitant wage demands.

WHAT IS TO BE DONE?

What can be done about the economic and social grievances of the blue-collar workers or the lower middle class generally?

It is not difficult to think of long lists of measures that the government might take to improve the lot of this group in the population. A task force of the Nixon administration studying the problems of the blue-collar worker concluded that the four main areas for concern are: *upgrading,* that is, helping workers to get better jobs; *income,* getting more money to lower-middle-class families not just by upgrading the jobs of the husbands but also by making it easier for wives to work, or possibly in other ways; *expenses,* finding ways to relieve the workingman's budget through subsidized housing, transportation, recreation, education, and various kinds of tax relief; and *social issues,* including efforts to raise the low status of blue-collar work, improve the urban environment, and correct inadequate health and medical facilities. More specifically, the task force proposed job training programs for workers and their wives and children; child-care services for working wives, not just for welfare mothers; more adult education in high schools and community colleges; government assistance to make it easier for children of blue-collar workers to go to college; more tax breaks for those in the $5,000 to $10,000 income class; public relations programs, such as awards to skilled workers and special postage stamps, to give more status to blue-collar jobs; improved recreational facilities, more parks, improved local transportation, better disability protection, better housing, and other social benefits.

A study group of the American Jewish Committee similarly suggests that the federal government should try to meet the needs of lower-middle-class white Americans in two major directions: first, "fulfilling our government's obligations to a large population of taxpayers no longer capable of adequately meeting economic, social, child rearing, communal and intergroup relations needs because of urban decay and metropolitan disorder"; and, second, "offering, interpreting and delivering programs in such a way as to depolarize racial and other intergroup tensions in our metropolitan centers." Again, this is translated into a long list of specific measures to raise real income by reducing taxes on the lower middle class, providing tax benefits for parents who send their children to private schools and colleges, encouraging discount buying through government support for cooperatives, and subsidizing interest rates for home buyers or the rents of tenants. At the same time that taxes are reduced, the study group would increase social services and health services, improve public education, expand job and manpower programs, provide more financial support for housing, guarantee homes in racially changing neighborhoods against loss of value, expand the Model Cities program, sponsor "urban fairs," provide "impacted aid" to support local services, and encourage private entrepreneurs, public agencies, and voluntary organizations to build "new towns." The group also called for more effective law enforcement, programs to improve community and intergroup relations, and more research on social policy in order to find better ways to reduce group tensions and hostility.

But all such proposals for increasing the after-tax incomes and social benefits of the lower middle class run up against one basic obstacle: 40 percent of all American families—including 70 million family members—have incomes between $5,000 and $10,000 a year. It is simply not possible to provide a significant increase in social benefits for these 70 million people without increasing taxes, including the taxes they themselves must pay. If their taxes are to be cut, then the taxes of others must be raised all the more.

Certain specific programs could and should be targeted at the low end of the lower middle class. The Family Assistance Plan (FAP) of the Nixon administration, which ran up against such heavy resistance in Congress, would help those just above the poverty line, the so-called "working poor." But without huge increases in funds, running into many billions of dollars, FAP cannot do much for the vast majority of the lower middle class.

The problems of this third of the nation cannot be solved in isolation from those of the rest of the nation, including unemployment, underemployment, inflation, a strained federal budget, the level and distribution of income and taxes, urban congestion and decay, air and water pollution, crime, choked transportation, the inadequacies of public education and the heavy costs of college education, strained race relations, problems of mental and physical health, as well as war and threats to national security. At bottom, the blues of the blue-collar workers (and the lower middle class generally) are the blues of America, and the solutions to their problems must be national.

In fact, there is nothing uniquely American about these problems; they are found in varying degrees in all advanced industrial societies. In Great Britain, for example, Anthony C. Crosland has set forth what he regards as the primary goals for the Labour party during the 1970s. They include:

> First, an exceptionally high priority, when considering the claims on our resources, for the relief of poverty, distress and social squalor. . . . Second, a more equal distribution of wealth, not because redistribution will make all the workers rich, but to help create a more just and humane society; third, a wider ideal of social equality, involving not only educational reform, but generally an improvement in our social capital so that the less well-off have access to housing, health and education of a standard comparable, at least in the basic decencies, to that which the better-off can buy for themselves out of their private means; and fourth, strict social control over the environment to enable us to cope with the exploding problems of urban life, to protect our countryside from the threat posed by more industry, more people and more cars, and to lessen the growing divergence between private and social costs in such fields as noise, fumes, water pollution and the rest.

Crosland adds that these environmental goals are another aspect of social equality, "since the rich can largely buy privacy and protection from these intrusions; only social action can give the less well-off the same protection."

But a quite different sort of approach can be made in responding to the problems and anxieties of the lower middle class: for instance, the racist approach of a George Wallace in the United States or that of an Enoch Powell in Great Britain. Still more frightening must be the realization that Adolf Hitler found the mass base of support for his Nazi party in the lower middle class.

Concerns about improving the quality of life are not limited to any one political party in Britain, the United States, or other Western democracies. The heart of the political issue in our time, indeed in all times, is determining the priorities of the social and economic problems to be placed on the national agenda, and deciding on the allocation of resources and the mixture of public and private means for solving those national problems.

BRINGING OURSELVES TOGETHER

We cannot say, however, that there is no such thing as a "blue-collar problem" or "lower-middle-class problem." Its essence seems to be a drawing apart of the people at the bottom of the society and those who have moved up into the lower reaches of the middle class. Although this split is made more dramatic and obvious in the United States because of the sharp cleavage between blacks and whites, it can be found in other advanced industrial societies. In Sweden, for instance, after the setback of the Social Democratic party in the September 1970 election, Prime Minister Olof Palme said that he was greatly concerned about the dangers of a split in his own country between "hard-hat workers" and the poor, similar to that taking place in the United States. Referring to Vice President Agnew's contention that there is a shift to the right in the world, Palme admitted:

> There are complaints about people living on welfare. There are complaints about law and order, a general vague sense of discontent. There are complaints against demonstrations and anarchists and people with long hair, people with beards, and all that. . . .

But he appealed for unity among the various social groups:

> It is a terribly dangerous situation because the split widens. One recurring point of my speeches during the elections was that we must never come to a situation where we talk about *we and they,* but only *we.* That is a basic philosophy of solidarity this movement has. We should never allow this type of gap to arise, and I tried to say to my people that people receiving social benefits are not special people—they are usual people who have come into a special situation as left-overs or drop-outs of a highly technocratic society.

Palme added that conservatism about modern art or life-styles is not so important, "but if it becomes a conservatism that turns against the poorer section of the community, you are in great danger for the future."

In the American scene, there are signs that this lower-middle-class group may be turning against not only the poor and the Negroes but also liberals and intellectuals. However, it is extremely difficult to make any sure statements about the attitudes of this group and its state of discontent; indeed, it is difficult even to define the group. A Conference on Blue-Collar Alienation sponsored by the Ford Foundation on January 22, 1970, agreed that "disaffection *does* exist within a large segment of the white working class, a segment that has been alternately ignored and attacked, and in whose name very little in the way of positive action has been forthcoming." The conferees noted that "this segment, while not easily definable, crosses ethnic, cultural, economic, and social lines. The disaffection, while not reducible to a 'common thread,' is more than superficial and involves social and psychological as well as economic variables."

However great the difficulties of definition may be, there is reason to fear that the hostility of large numbers of white workers toward the poor and the black, and toward intellectuals, may pose a serious danger for this democratic society. Alienation may lead white workers to raise walls against others and turn our cities and suburbs into bitter and militant enclaves. And the danger exists that the lower middle class may seek an escape from its tensions and fears and frustrations by supporting reactionary and repressive political movements.

If this nation is to move ahead socially, it urgently needs the kind of political and trade-union and community leadership that will lessen the alienation and hostility of groups within our society. Americans need to know one another better and to draw closer as a people, while respecting each other's individuality and cultural identity.

The tension between Jeffersonianism and Hamiltonianism seems unending in American life. We are at our best as a people when these philosophies achieve a kind of dynamic equilibrium within our political parties and within our nation as a whole. The so-called "blue-collar problem" seems to me to present us with a very old issue in a new guise.

NOTES

1. Herbert Croly, *The Promise of American Life,* Dutton, New York, 1909, p. 44. (Reprinted 1963.)
2. Ibid. (italics added).
3. The tabulations were subsequently published as U.S. Bureau of the Census, *Current Population Reports, Occupation and Earnings of Family Heads in 1969, 1965, and 1959,* ser. P-60, no. 73, Sept. 30, 1970.

2. THE LONG VIEW

by Eli Ginzberg

THE SEARCH FOR PERSPECTIVE

This chapter explores ways of analyzing the position of the large group of blue-collar workers in our industrialized society. Rather than distilling substantive findings, we will seek perspective.

In the 1930s the dean of the School of Business at Columbia University, Roswell C. McCrea, called attention to an interesting transformation that had occurred in his youth. In McCrea's earliest years in Norristown, Pennsylvania, the town clerk was at the top of the middle sector of the occupational hierarchy—below the lawyer, the minister, and the physician, but above the skilled worker and the farmer. Only a small minority of the population had learned to read and write well enough to be trusted with public records. But before McCrea was out of his adolescence, the pay and prestige of the clerk had dropped several notches because of the widespread increase in literacy. By the time McCrea left home to go to college, the craftsman had moved up into the position formerly held by the clerk and was receiving equivalent pay.

Economists know that in a dynamic economy changes in demand and supply affect the distribution of rewards. But economists have paid insufficient attention to the rewards of different occupational groups. How does a society determine what different workers contribute? Here is one hurdle for occupational analysis. A second problem relates to the time dimension. How the members of a socioeconomic group feel about their circumstances and conditions depends on their background, their current position, and their estimate of the future. However, this kind of analysis requires a time span of about 100 years, the decades during which a person's father and the person himself reach a maximum level of occupational achievement and the additional period before his sons reach theirs. Since the United States is still a few years away from its bicentennial, 100 years represents half its history and in any case is a long time period to compress into a single analytical framework. It is well to bear this in mind in striving for broader generalization about blue-collar workers.

Another observation is that if the group under study consists of as significant a proportion of the total population as blue-collar workers do, their attitudes and behavior might not be unique but might reflect overall societal changes. For example, it is conventional to refer to the economic insecurity and political conservatism of blue-collar workers. Let us grant for the moment that these attributes are characteristic of them. But since these traits also characterize many white-collar workers, the fact of their prevalence among blue-collar workers adds little to our understanding of the group.

The search for perspective to which this chapter is addressed starts with a cross-sectional analysis of the variations which characterize blue-collar workers and their families. Next we will review the major transformations that have occurred in American society during this century as they have affected the relative position of the blue-collar group. Then we will delineate the specific transformations that have occurred in the working lives and earnings of blue-collar workers. And we will conclude by distilling a limited number of observations growing out of the long view.

VARIATIONS

If we define blue-collar workers as all workers who are not classified as white-collar, domestic workers, farmers, or farm laborers—that is, if we combine the Census categories of craftsmen, operatives, service workers (other than household), and laborers (other than farm)—the composite group accounts for nearly half of the nonagricultural labor force. We will use this definition, for the several subgroups here included display crucial points of similarity, such as their social background and educational preparation, how they work, the environments in which they work, the way in which they are paid (primarily by the hour), the people with whom they associate on and off the job, and their broad orientation to life and values.

Any schema of occupational analysis must be sensitive to the income range: the greater the spread within a category, the less useful is the occupational categorization. The broadened "blue-collar" group outlined above has a substantial spread in income. The lowest fifth of full-time, full-year workers earn under $5,000 annually; the top fifth earn more than $12,000. Thus, a minority of blue-collar workers are unable to earn enough to lift their families out of poverty, even if they work full time, full year; yet others are able to enjoy a comfortable standard of living. The majority are distributed more or less evenly between the low and high earners.

But not all income is earned by the head of household. It is important whether the wife of a blue-collar worker is also in the labor market, working part time or full time, for the standard of living of a family depends to a significant degree on whether the wife is a supplemental earner. In approximately two of every five blue-collar families, the wife is a supplemental earner and contributes about 30 percent of total family income.

Whether the wife is able to work, and whether the husband's income or the combined incomes of husband and wife permit the family to enjoy a satisfactory standard of living, depend on the number of dependent children. Once again, the variability is marked. Within the age group 35 to 44, about one in three blue-collar families has either two or three children, while the third with the largest number have an average of four or five.

The amount of formal education that a person acquires reflects a composite of his family background, his aspirations, and his aptitude for school, not to mention other factors, such as the size of the community in which he is reared. While more than a quarter of all male blue-collar workers between the ages of 25 and 64 have had eight or fewer years of elementary school, a somewhat higher proportion (about one-third) are high school graduates, and a small minority (about one in ten) have attended or graduated from college.

A college man thinks and lives differently from a grammar school graduate, and allowance must be made for the fact that both are represented in the blue-collar group.

Additional characteristics in which blue-collar workers differ from those employed in other major occupational groups are sex, race, and ethnic background. There are relatively more blue-collar workers among men (55 percent) than among women (33 percent), reflecting the heavy concentration of women in clerical and sales positions. And because white workers have easier access to the higher occupational categories, there are relatively fewer blue-collar workers among whites (44 percent) than among nonwhites (66 percent). In addition, a disproportionately large number of white blue-collar workers are foreign-born or have one or two foreign-born parents. Since blue-collar workers differ according to race, sex, and country of birth, and since these factors presumably affect styles of working and living, they also must be taken into account in analyzing the blue-collar group as a whole.

Another important differentiating characteristic of blue-collar workers is their membership in trade unions. Just under half are members, in contrast to the low rate of 8 percent for white-collar workers. But our primary concern is to note the variation in trade-union membership within the blue-collar group. The spectrum stretches from the strongly organized craft unions in construction, through the strong industrial unions in automobile, steel, rubber, and other mass-production industries, to the relatively weak union organizations among certain service employees, such as restaurant workers. Finally, there are approximately 18 million blue-collar workers who have no trade-union affiliation. To the extent that a worker's wages, job security, work satisfaction, and style of living are influenced by his membership in a union, we must allow for these differences in the affiliation patterns of blue-collar workers.

There is another important difference among blue-collar workers. We must distinguish among: the skilled man who makes tools and dies or repairs critical parts of airplane motors; the operative whose work is controlled by the movement of a conveyor belt, such as the well-paid male worker on an automotive assembly line or the low-paid female worker engaged in packaging materials; and the chef's assistant or the hospital orderly. If the work that a man does, independent of the income which he earns, makes a difference in how he sees himself and his adjustment to the world about him, then assuredly one cannot talk about *the* blue-collar worker!

Let us now shift in our search for variation from the workplace to the nonwork environment. The press reports periodically on confrontations between blue-collar workers living in ethnic enclaves in New York, Chicago, Detroit, and other large cities, and minority groups, particularly blacks, who seek to rent or purchase property in these established neighborhoods. A major source of discontent among white blue-collar workers stems from such "invasions" by outsiders who threaten their property values, educational and religious infrastructures, and way of life. Confrontations and conflicts are occurring with increasing frequency, and it is reasonable to see them as responsible for changes in the attitudes and behavior of many blue-collar workers.

But the following caveats are in order: many among the challengers of the status quo are themselves blue-collar workers although they are black; except for the color problem, there is nothing new in such neighborhood conflicts. However, while many confrontations have occurred and will doubtless continue to occur in the metropolitan centers of the North and West, millions of blue-collar workers live in communities which are free of racial conflict and where, because of demographic and housing patterns, it is unlikely that such conflicts will develop.

Of the nation's thirty largest cities, Negroes compose less than 10 percent of the total population in six; the proportion is above 40 percent in another six, including Washington, D.C., where Negroes are 70 percent of the population. In the face of such striking variations in black-white population ratios, it would be wrong to generalize about the pervasiveness and inevitability of neighborhood conflicts in which white blue-collar workers fight the encroachment of minority groups.

The need for caution is increased when allowance is made for the prevailing differences in life-styles between blue-collar workers in small- or medium-sized communities and those in metropolitan centers; between those who live in the South and those in the North or West; between those living in high-income and those in low-income states. The region of the country and income level of the state in which they live will have an effect on how blue-collar workers think and act.

Thus, it is difficult and often impossible to deal with blue-collar workers as a homogeneous category for social analysis in the face of the substantial differences which exist among them in the earnings of the head of household, in family income, in size of family, in education, in sex, race, and ethnic characteristics, in skill level, in trade-union membership, and in the size and type of city in which they live.

Despite these substantial variations, blue-collar workers might still be dealt with as a group if they could be distinguished from white-collar workers according to the foregoing indices. However, we tentatively conclude that because variations among white-collar workers also are substantial, it is difficult to compare meaningfully the two groups. The overlaps are too many and extend over too wide a range of the total distributions.

MAJOR TRANSFORMATIONS

We are now ready to review some of the major changes in American society during the present century that may have influenced the present status and future prospects of blue-collar workers. But before we speculate about these influences, let us review the principal transformations.

During the early years of this century, large numbers of immigrants arrived annually with only one occupational option. They entered the labor force at the bottom. As a consequence the native born were pushed up the occupational scale. In 1933 a leading industrialist remarked that the country would be facing less trouble on the labor front if immigration had not been cut off.[1] In his view, the new aggressiveness of the trade-union movement was a direct reflection of the growing dissatisfaction of native-born workers. For the first time, many native-born workers were at the bottom of the occupational ladder. Since the early 1930s more and more blue-collar workers have come from the ranks of the native born; individuals who had been taught since birth the American ideal that opportunity was open to everybody and that if a man worked hard, he was entitled to a share of the good things in life, were able to find only low-paying jobs. These workers felt that, at the very least, they had a right to better jobs than those with weaker claims, such as foreigners, Negroes, and women.

During this century the United States has made ever-larger investments in education. The typical student used to leave school at the end of elementary school; today he is a high school graduate. The college man no longer is the raccoon-coated, tippling son of an upper-income family; he is often a commuting student from a modest-income home. Instead of one in twenty of the age group completing college, the current proportion is one in five.

This vast expansion, especially in higher education, has been associated with new occupational and career paths. At the turn of the century a man who got a job in a steel mill or on the railroad could hope to advance regardless of his educational background. He merely had to outdistance his competitors. But that is no longer the case. Occupational achievement is predetermined: even an able man is unlikely to obtain a preferred job unless he has a college degree. He is unlikely to make the jump from the factory floor into the ranks of management.

Another change in the educational-occupational arena has been the rapid increase in white-collar employment, both overall and in the professional and managerial categories. During the half century between 1910 and 1960 the total labor force increased from about 37 to 70 million, or about 90 percent. Meanwhile white-collar employment grew about four times as fast, and professional and managerial manpower expanded almost as rapidly; but the number of blue-collar workers rose more slowly. The "manual and service"—our blue-collar category plus domestic workers—experienced approximately an 80 percent increase in the half century between 1910 and 1960: a doubling in the number of foremen and skilled workers and approximately an 80 percent increase in semiskilled workers, laborers, and service workers.[2] These few selective data indicate that the growth of the blue-collar sector was less rapid than the growth of the other groups.

Another transformation that must be noted is the substantial decline in agricultural employment and the concurrent pressures for young people and adults from rural communities to obtain alternative employment. In 1910, the farm labor force amounted to 11.5 million, or about 30 percent of the total labor force. A half century later the agricultural labor force accounted for 5.1 million out of 70 million, or approximately 7 percent. This represented a shrinkage of about 80 percent in five decades. A great many people lost their farms, left them voluntarily, or drifted away from agriculture to seek employment in an urban environment. Most of them ended up in the blue-collar ranks, initially as laborers or semiskilled workers and later in skilled occupations.

There was also a radical change in the role of women in employment. Prior to World War II, it was customary for the daughters of blue-collar workers to work until they married or until they had a child. They then withdrew from the labor market, and unless their husbands were injured or died, they were not likely to reenter it. But after the war more and more married women have worked on a continuing or intermittent basis. In 1940 about one in seven married women was in the labor force; currently the proportion is approximately two in five. The significance of women's earnings to the rising standard of living of the American family is underscored by the finding that, for families with incomes above the median, the wages and salaries earned by wives account for about one-quarter of the family's total income; among families with lower family income, the earnings of women account for about one-sixth of total family income.

Because blacks account for a disproportionate number of present-day blue-collar workers, it is important to trace the extent to which their occupational distribution has changed during this century. In the half century between 1910 and 1960 the total black labor force increased from about 4.7 million to 6.9 million, or approximately 70 percent. According to Hiestand's calculations, black blue-collar workers more than doubled, increasing from about 2.2 to over 4.7 million. During these years the number of blacks in farming declined from 2.3 million to about 750,000.

The United States radically changed its manpower policy when in the early 1920s it curtailed the number of immigrants permitted to enter the country. The foreign born had always been an important source of blue-collar workers, but after 1924 their importance declined rapidly. It was not immediately clear who the new recruits for blue-collar employment would be, but with the rapid expansion of employment in the early 1940s the answer was forthcoming: married white women and blacks born and raised in the South who relocated in the North and West.

This century has also witnessed an accelerated drift toward urbanization. More and more of the nation's population lives and works within the boundaries of metropolitan areas, either in the core city or on the periphery, in the fast-growing suburbs. And, as noted earlier, major tensions have arisen from the pressures exerted by the rapidly expanding black population in the North against ethnic groups of blue-collar workers in settled areas of the city.

The inevitability of these conflicts and their heightened intensity have reflected the strenuous and generally successful efforts of most suburbs to remain lily-white; the shortage of low-cost urban housing in the post-World War II years; housing segregation within city limits; and the relatively lower incomes of Negroes, which reduce their options with regard to where they can live, even when they have freedom to rent or buy.

Another pervasive influence upon the lives of Americans during this century has been the steady and pronounced trend toward family limitation. But as frequently happens in matters of social change, significant differences in timing occurred in the adoption of the new approach by different groups. For several subgroups of blue-collar workers, the acceptance of birth control has come relatively late. Among both native and foreign born who were practicing members of the Catholic Church, religious teachings slowed their acceptance of the new techniques.

Forces beyond Catholic dogma operated to reinforce the tendency of blue-collar workers to have large families. Since a major inflow into the blue-collar ranks were former white and Negro farmers and farm laborers, from a background in which large families were the norm, time had to pass before they adopted the practices of the city-bred. As a result large families were prevalent among many first-generation blue-collar workers earlier in the century.

One might question the significance of family size for the life-styles of blue-collar workers. Briefly, we can note the following: a family's standard of living depends, first, on the number of people among whom the family's income must be divided. Secondly, whether the wife is able to make a significant contribution to family income depends very much on the number of young children in the home. For instance, among families in which the husband earns between $7,000 and $10,000, wives who have no young children to care for are twice as apt to work (46 percent) as women with preschool children at home. The prospects for children of blue-collar workers to attend and complete college and professional school are reduced when there are many children in the family because higher education, even when supported by government, always involves considerable out-of-pocket expenditures.

Another phenomenon of relatively recent date should be considered at this point. Although Americans have always purchased their homes on credit, it was the automobile that transformed their consumption habits. In 1929, Prof. E. R. A. Seligman of Columbia University completed his two-volume work on consumer credit, a study subsidized by General Motors. The venerable professor demonstrated that it was not morally or economically unsound for consumers to purchase high-priced items on credit, paying for them out of wages to be earned in the future. Today most families purchase their cars, television sets, washing and drying machines, refrigerators, freezers, and air conditioners on credit. Consumer indebtedness has grown in the two decades since World War II from $6 billion to $86 billion, or at an annual rate of over 14 percent, more than twice as fast as the growth of all financial assets.

This implies that the material improvement and well-being, while grounded in gains in real income, has been substantially reinforced by recourse to credit financing. As long as the labor market remains tight and jobs are plentiful, a large and growing indebtedness can be carried by consumers without difficulty. But once the economy turns downward and the employment situation weakens, as in this country during 1969, then many jobs become insecure and some workers encounter difficulties in maintaining their installment payments.

This brings us to a final major transformation in American society: the marked changes in mass communications. We know less than we need to know about the ways in which movies, radio, and television have affected both the expectations and the behavior of different social groups. But on the basis of the imperfect knowledge at hand, we can postulate that they have had a deep and lasting impact on the value structure of Americans and have generated and reinforced mass desire for high-level consumption. This means that blue-collar workers, like many other groups, experience a continuing gap between their current income and the standard of living which they see constantly portrayed and to which they aspire.

We have now completed our selective review of the major social changes which have characterized American society in the present century, leaving their mark on the blue-collar group as well as on the nation as a whole. We will withhold until the concluding section our judgments about the differential impact of these changes on the blue-collar group. We will first consider the experience of blue-collar workers in the economic sphere, particularly with respect to the characteristics of their work and remuneration.

BLUE-COLLAR WORK

A person's job has long been, and continues to be, perhaps the best clue to the life he leads and the opinions he holds. Significant changes in the conditions of employment have occurred during recent decades. During the earlier decades of the century the American economy was characterized by a considerable degree of seasonality. It was the exceptional blue-collar worker who worked full time, full year. In the 1920s a group of forward-looking large companies, such as Kodak, Procter & Gamble, and General Electric, and smaller ones, such as Hormel, Hickey-Freeman, and Dennison, experimented with ways of reducing and eliminating the seasonality of employment. Their efforts were washed away in the turbulence of the Great Depression.

Although seasonality has not been eliminated—even the strong United Automobile Workers have not been able to win a guarantee of annual hours of work—a significant proportion of *male* blue-collar workers are employed full time, full year. This is true for three out of four of the more than 10 million craftsmen and foremen and two out of three of the almost 11 million operatives and kindred workers who worked during 1968. Among the remaining 8 million service workers and laborers, the proportion who worked regularly varied from about two-fifths to over half. During this century, then, blue-collar workers have experienced significant gains in their reduced vulnerability to layoffs resulting from seasonal production and employment.

A second important change on the employment front has been the substantial reduction in the average number of hours worked per week. One of the causes of the major steel strike at the end of World War I was that men had to work 84 hours a week when they changed shifts. A 60-hour week was widespread. A great many workers, after a hard day's work, would go immediately to the nearest saloon, where they would drink themselves into forgetfulness, and then stagger home to eat and fall exhausted into bed. This was their pattern—day in and day out.

While the conventional hours of work for blue-collar workers have not been much reduced from the early post-World War II norm of 40 per week, some exceptions should be noted. As early as the late 1940s movie projectionists in the New York City area were working four days on with three days off, then three days on with four days off, or an average of 28 hours weekly. More recently, the Electrical Workers Union (Local 3) in New York City succeeded in negotiating a basic 25-hour week. Nevertheless, most electricians work more, and they earn overtime when they do. In negotiating the new norm, Harry Van Arsdale, the head of the Local, wanted to ensure that a skilled worker could earn enough in a 5-hour day to support himself and his family in at least modest circumstances. These are by no means the only substantial reductions from the 40-hour norm, though they probably represent extremes.

In contrast to the industrial nations of Western Europe, the United States moved slowly to enact labor legislation aimed at controlling accidents and occupational diseases. The dominant ideology sought to keep the government out of employment relations; the 48 states were reluctant to take action in areas new to them; and, perhaps most important, immigrants—considered expendable by the public—were filling the least desirable jobs. These factors reduced the pressure for social intervention. For instance, among railroad crews at the turn of this century, about one of every hundred men suffered fatal injuries each year! But the passage of time brought governmental reforms which, together with preventive actions by management, led to a marked reduction in fatalities and injuries in the workplace. We still lose over 14,000 workers annually through fatal accidents, and another 800,000 are injured seriously enough to lose time from work; but during recent decades much of the risk to limb and life has been removed from the work setting.

A related development has been the marked improvement in other aspects of the work environment. For instance, great advances have occurred in temperature control. More and more workplaces are able to establish and maintain a comfortable temperature throughout the year. However, too little attention has been paid to the importance of this factor in speeding the industrial development of the South. Similarly, the cleanliness and orderliness of the areas where employees work, eat, and rest have been substantially improved. Nevertheless, there is still substantial room for improvement: one needs only to note the difficult working conditions of such high-wage earners as the men who tend the steel furnaces or such low-wage earners as those who work in commercial laundries or as dishwashers in restaurants and hotels.

Most workers learn to make their peace with their physical surroundings. More difficult, however, is acceptance of a situation of inferiority from which they cannot escape. And that is exactly the position in which most blue-collar workers found themselves early in this century. The story is told of a Pennsylvania employer in the early 1900s who dismissed his entire work force of more than 1,000 in the morning and rehired all but a few in the afternoon. He wanted to teach them that he was the boss. As late as the 1930s the Secretary of Labor was able to talk to the steelworkers at Homestead only from the steps of the federal post office; the U.S. Steel Corporation owned all the other land.

The first half of this century saw a rapid increase in unionization, particularly among blue-collar workers, with the result that today approximately half belong to a trade union, in contrast to a quarter of the labor force as a whole. Unions helped to reduce the powerlessness of the workers. First and most importantly, workers were no longer subject to arbitrary dismissal. As they acquired seniority, they came to "own" their jobs. Unless the employer went bankrupt, the worker's job was his as long as he could do the work. Next, the workers came to exercise ever more control over the rules which governed how they should work, how much they were required to produce, how quickly, and according to what standards. Moreover, the union saw to it that as a better job became available, the employer was no longer able to pick a favorite and reward him; he had to offer the job to the man with the greatest seniority. Only if that man failed to bid could the employer approach the next man on the list.

In these and in a great many other ways, the union was able to reduce or eliminate many vulnerabilities. Many blue-collar workers were no longer industrial slaves but were participants in an employment relation which gave them a feeling of security about their job, enabled them to play a part in determining how they worked, and left them free to plan their off-the-job activities.

These were changes of extraordinary importance, and their reach went beyond those who held union membership. Many large employers, seeing the success of the unions in organizing blue-collar workers, decided to match and even exceed the benefits that unions were securing for their members in the hope of keeping their employees from joining up.

Another development of importance to blue-collar and other workers for which unions can take considerable, but not exclusive, credit relates to the vast expansion of fringe benefits. Currently, only slightly more than three-quarters of gross payroll costs for blue-collar workers in manufacturing consists of straight-time pay. Another 5 to 6 percent represents legally required contributions by the employer for Social Security, unemployment insurance, and workmen's compensation. The remainder, approximately 15 to 20 percent of gross payrolls, is accounted for by overtime, vacations, holidays, sick leave, and employer contributions to private pension plans.

This bundle of benefits has gone far to remove some of the worst insecurities that used to confront blue-collar workers: the uncertainty of what would happen if they, or members of their family, were to require hospitalization; if they became unemployed or disabled; or if, because of age, they were no longer able to work. Although the blue-collar worker and his family are not now protected against all exigencies resulting from loss of earnings, we should not minimize the importance of the changes that have been introduced. The best-protected among blue-collar workers are eligible for supplemental unemployment benefits which enable a man who is out of work to receive up to 90 percent of his regular wages; he is entitled to three or four weeks of vacation a year; he is eligible for three months of vacation after 15 years of employment; and he can retire with three-quarters pay at the end of 25 or 30 years of service or when he reaches 65. So far these benefits accrue to only a minority of all blue-collar workers, but they indicate a trend.

Although it is not likely that any single blue-collar worker has benefited from all the foregoing advances—the reduction in seasonality of employment, the reduction in the hours of work, protection against industrial accidents and disease, improved conditions of work, the supports supplied by the unions, greater control over his job, and improved fringe benefits—almost every blue-collar worker has enjoyed some of these gains. If he compares the conditions under which he began to work and those which govern his present employment, he cannot fail to note that in almost every respect he has made substantial gains in his role as a worker.

A TYPOLOGY OF BLUE-COLLAR WORKERS

The analysis up to this point has drawn attention to the following: first, marked variations exist among blue-collar workers as a result of differences in such fundamentals as race, sex, education, family structure, and income characteristics; second, the difficulties of disentangling the major changes that attend the conditions of life in the United States and their differential impact on blue-collar workers; and third, the substantial changes that occurred in the world of work during the past seven decades of this century and left their mark on all blue-collar workers but not to the same degree.

The blue-collar group, then, embraces workers of different backgrounds, accomplishments, and aspirations. It includes some men who carry memories of the Great Depression, when no jobs were available, no matter how hard they tried to earn enough to feed themselves and their families. But the great majority have known only the conditions of post-World War II prosperity, and some of these entered the labor market during the longest expansionary period in the recorded history of the American economy (1962–1969).

Some are at the top of a seniority list; this means that, short of an economic catastrophe, their jobs are secure and they can look forward to the best assignments in the years ahead. However, many others hold low-paying jobs which are not unionized; they cannot feel optimistic about the future with regard to work, income, or deferred benefits.

Some workers have limited the size of their families, whereas others are struggling to earn enough to give their five children a reasonable start in life. Men with different family responsibilities see the present and the future differently.

The families from which blue-collar workers come are another important element in analyzing blue-collar typology. The basic wage rate in the repair shops of American Airlines in Tulsa averages about $5.25; for a 40-hour week, this comes to a gross pay of $210 weekly, without additions for seniority, lead job, or overtime. For the worker who was born and brought up on a neighboring marginal farm and whose father never cleared more than $2,000 a year, his job at the Tulsa base is a big step up. The same job means something different, however, to the Tulsa-born man whose father was a fireman on the Southern Railway. At best this job has enabled him to maintain a standard of living for his family comparable to that which his father had maintained. The same Tulsa job represents a step down for the son of an Atlanta dentist who began engineering school, dropped out, and after moving from job to job for some years, finally settled into his present groove.

It is not possible to talk meaningfully about a man's adjustment to his work, his life, and the society of which he is a part without some knowledge of his background, his present circumstances, and his aspirations. But social analysis can proceed only on the basis of simplifications. No categorical scheme can be responsive to the entire range of variability. Therefore, we will present our simplified typology in the hope that an analysis of it will prove illuminating. We have developed the following three types: *the mobile, the immobile,* and *the vulnerable.*

The Mobile

As has been implicit in our analysis, how a person feels about his current position depends on how he measures himself. He can look backward; he can look around; he can look forward.

If he looks backward, he is likely to assess his present position from the vantage of his father's. Has he moved up—in terms of the work he does, the income he earns, and the way he lives—from the standards that prevailed in his parents' home? In this assessment, he is likely to make allowance for the fact that over the period of a generation there has been a general upward trend in the occupational and income structure.

On the basis of this criterion of generational improvement, one must conclude that a significant proportion of white, native-born American blue-collar workers, particularly craftsmen and foremen who were born into farm families or whose fathers had been laborers, will see themselves as mobile. They have moved several notches up the occupational-income scale. This is borne out by Blau and Duncan's work as well as that of other investigators.[3]

The same finding of upward mobility describes the vast majority of blue-collar workers who were born abroad or who are the offspring of foreign-born parents. Our knowledge of the socioeconomic origins of immigrant groups, particularly those who arrived in this country prior to the passage of the immigration actions of the 1920s, indicates that a disproportionate number came from rural backgrounds or had marginal urban attachments, which helps to explain in large measure why they were interested in immigrating. Once again, it is reasonable to say that those offspring of immigrants who achieved skilled status or a family income over $10,000 must be placed among the mobile.

Perhaps the clearest case of upward mobility is the black. Myrdal, writing in the early 1940s on the basis of the experience of the 1930s, was deeply concerned about the economic future of the Negro population. He noted that most of them were marginal farmers in the Southeast, a region where agriculture was declining, and that they had achieved a very low rate of penetration into the more preferred blue- and white-collar occupations. The route up for the Southern Negro in the 1930s was to get on public assistance, preferably in the North.

There has been a steady movement of Negroes out of the lower occupational groupings into categories of craftsmen and operatives. By 1969, about one of every five Negro workers belonged to this sector of the labor force. More striking is the fact that during the 1960s the blacks' rate of increase in the preferred craftsman category was four times that of whites. By 1969, the underrepresentation of blacks in the operative category had been reversed, and among craftsmen and foremen the difference between whites and blacks had narrowed to 4 percentage points (11 versus 7 percent). Unquestionably discrimination against blacks continues to be embedded in every sector of American life—in education, health, housing, and employment—but the foregoing figures suggest, and other data and analyses confirm, that powerful forces are working to improve the occupational and income status of the blacks. A large number of blacks are still mired in poverty, but a larger number are leaving it.[4]

To round out the picture, a few words should be added about women blue-collar workers. Many blue-collar families are in the middle-income range, or somewhat above, by virtue of the fact that the wife is a supplemental earner. In about one-third of the white families and over two-fifths of the Negro families the earnings of the wife account for approximately 30 percent of total family income. Since men tend to marry women from their own social class, we find that, by working, many women who came from families of modest circumstances have helped to raise their connubial family's status. Specifically, about 18 percent of all wives who work do so as operatives, and another 15 percent are employed as service workers outside of private households; in short, one of every three working wives is a blue-collar worker. Another third are employed as clerical workers, and most of the remainder are in professional, sales, or domestic work.

Reference must be made to one other group of women, those who are heads of families. Approximately one of every ten families is headed by a woman, and in only a very small number is there sufficient income to enable the family to maintain a reasonable standard of living unless the head is regularly employed. Since few women are employed as craftsmen or foremen; since the average earnings of full-time, full-year female operatives is below $4,000; and since female service workers generally earn below $3,500, blue-collar employment does not provide opportunities for upward mobility for most women heads of households.

Using the first of our three criteria, which compares the socioeconomic status of blue-collar workers today with that of their parents, we are led to conclude that a high proportion can be classified as mobile. This is particularly so in the case of native-born whites who came from low-income farm families; for most blue-collar workers of foreign extraction; and above all for the vast majority of Negro blue-collar workers. There is no way to quantify the numbers who meet this criterion, but from the parameters that we do control we can conclude that they represent a significant proportion of all blue-collar families.

How mobile is the blue-collar worker under our second criterion? How extensive are his opportunities during the course of his working life to move up the occupational and income scale? In the absence of adequate longitudinal studies, a gap that Herbert Parnes is beginning to close, we must rely on qualitative assessments.

We know that a high proportion of those who complete apprenticeship eventually leave the ranks of blue-collar workers to join the ranks of management or to enter business for themselves. This has been the pattern in manufacturing, and many building contractors have advanced through apprenticeship. This route has been used by many in the past and will probably be utilized in the same way by many in the future.

A second route that has long been used by blue-collar workers who seek to improve their position is the direct transition from worker to employer status: for example, the waiter who opens his own restaurant, the mechanic who becomes the owner of a repair shop, the truck driver who becomes a small fleet owner, the taxi driver who buys his own cab and later several more, and the bartender who buys a bar. Although there is no certainty that such a shift will result in a net improvement for the ambitious blue-collar worker—the mortality rate for small businesses runs high—the fact remains that this route enables many to raise themselves by their own bootstraps (though often with financial assistance from their relatives).

Another approach which is increasingly coming to the fore involves the considerable number of workers who after 20 years in the military or in civilian employment are able to retire at half pay, often based upon their earnings during their last years. Many are blue-collar workers, such as mechanics, drivers, protective service workers, cooks, and repairmen. With substantial retirement pay and often other benefits as well, these blue-collar workers are able to do quite well by taking a similar job in a new environment. Others shift into a new occupational category, such as sales or managerial.

Still another route lies in gaining access to a higher-paying job, such as skilled construction work or long-distance truck driving. The men who succeed in obtaining such preferred blue-collar jobs generally have few complaints. They know from their own experience and from that of other workers that they are relatively far up the income scale.

This brings us to the last and by far the most widespread system for mobility: the progression provided in internal labor markets which are characteristic of many large corporations. A man is hired at the bottom, usually as a laborer or semiskilled worker. With time, he has the opportunity to move up, by bidding for training and a better job. In the steel industry a beginner may be able to earn no more than $7,000; the top men who are responsible for determining when the furnaces are to be tapped can earn, including wages and bonuses, up to three times that sum. From the identification of the diverse routes that are available to blue-collar workers, particularly men, to improve themselves from their starting position, it becomes apparent that there are a great many opportunities. Of the total of about 35 million blue-collar workers, about 25 million are males. Some 10 million are classified as craftsmen and foremen, and for the most part these are jobs with above-average income and status. In addition there are two other major subgroups who have above-average income and status: the high-earning operatives (long-distance truck driver) and those who have passed into a managerial or entrepreneurial status. Conventional wisdom notwithstanding, there are many mobile blue-collar workers, according to the criterion of opportunity to advance in the labor force.

Our third criterion is the prospect of improvement for children of blue-collar workers. Definitive data are scarce. Nevertheless, we can find a few facts and figures which will provide at least a basis for speculation and extrapolation.

There are two routes along which the offspring of blue-collar workers move ahead. The first is through the help they receive in gaining access to preferred employment opportunities. The classic illustration is the craftsman who smooths the way for his son into the apprenticeship program operated by his union. While racial prejudice undoubtedly plays a part in the long-term efforts of many craft unions to keep blacks and other minority group members out of apprenticeship and journeyman programs, such a defensive posture is often more rooted in a desire to help their own.

Moreover, parental help is not limited to the fields where formal apprenticeship prevails. The young man whose father is a foreman, a lead man, or simply a respected long-term employee will definitely be preferred as a "hiree." And if the firm practices promotion from within, he has a good start. If he remains with the company and fails to make the transition into management, he may end up no better off than his father. Nevertheless, his father was responsible for his good start.

The other way up the mobility ladder is through education. If parental income is a determinant of educational attainment, the sons and daughters of higher-income blue-collar families are in a preferred position to go to junior or senior college, especially if the family has only one or two children. In this connection it is well to note the rapid expansion which has been taking place in junior and senior colleges (branches of state universities) within commuting distance from the homes of many blue-collar workers. These new institutions have greatly reduced the cost of a young person's acquiring an associate or baccalaureate degree.

Among other factors that influence whether or not a young person goes on to college are the level of education that his parents have achieved and his own interest in and capacity for study. In these respects, children of blue-collar workers are at a relative disadvantage because so many of their parents have not had much schooling and tend to place a low value on educational achievement. Parenthetically, this withholding, or even negative, attitude toward education on the part of many high-earning white blue-collar workers does not seem to be shared by black parents. who appear to be more concerned that their children go to college.[5]

We see, then, that many blue-collar workers have reason to be optimistic about their children because they will be able to assist them to get a preferred opening job or, by enabling them to go to college, make the transition into a higher occupational and income status.

On any of the three criteria, and particularly on the three combined, the verdict is now in. Many blue-collar workers are mobile in the sense that they are relatively better off than their fathers; they themselves have had opportunities to advance even to the extent of entering managerial or entrepreneurial ranks; and they have reason to believe that their children will be able to continue to move up the socioeconomic scale, particularly if they graduate from college.

The Immobile

Having set out the considerations that led us to conclude that a high proportion of all male blue-collar workers can be classified as mobile, we can now consider the factors that lead us to classify others as immobile.

To begin with, a considerable proportion of present-day blue-collar workers are themselves the offspring of blue-collar workers. The initial presumption is that they are immobile. Whether they are in fact or not depends on where they are, in relation to their fathers, within the blue-collar hierarchy. If a man's father was a laborer and he himself has become a foreman in a major company, we can classify him as mobile, even though there has been no generational shift in occupational status—only a shift within the broad blue-collar category. But if there is no intraoccupational improvement, or if there has been some slippage, it is sensible to classify such a person as immobile. Moreover, most children of blue-collar workers, except those whose fathers are at the top of the income scale, will not move up and out through the educational route. Some will, but the majority will not.

It is impossible on the basis of currently available statistics to estimate the proportion of all blue-collar workers who should be classified as immobile, but the number must be sizable. Included are the large number of second-generation workers in the North and South employed in the manufacturing plants of a single company that offers the principal source of a community's employment. Consider next the large number of first- and second-generation blue-collar workers in heavy industry whose fathers held similar jobs, and the numerous construction workers and other craftsmen who were fortunate enough to have fathers who smoothed their way so that they too could become journeymen.

If we disregard the question of intraoccupational mobility, we can state that because relatively few blue-collar workers had fathers who were in white-collar occupations, all blue-collar workers today (except for those who came off the farm) are the sons, and in many cases the grandsons, of blue-collar workers. Again, setting aside intraoccupational mobility and using the criterion of family origin, a significant proportion of present-day blue-collar workers must be considered immobile.

We will now evaluate briefly the mobility of the females who head about one in ten of all households, many of whom are employed full time, full year as blue-collar workers. While women constitute more than one-fourth of all blue-collar workers, they are grossly underrepresented among the higher-earning foremen and craftsmen, amounting to only about 3 percent.

The median earnings of women who work full time, full year as operatives or workers average, as we noted earlier, between $3,500 and $4,000. With such modest earnings these heads of households must be placed in the immobile group. If more information about their backgrounds were available, a few might be classified as mobile; this would apply, for example, to an operative whose parents had been migrant workers and who is earning $4,000 annually. Because we do not have the data to make firm estimates, we can merely point to the problem and leave its magnitude undefined. But we can conclude that most regularly employed blue-collar female workers who are household heads are immobile.

The Vulnerable

This brings us to our last category, the vulnerable. Who are they, and why do we use the term "vulnerable" to describe them? Most people seek to achieve a level of work and income at least comparable to that of their parents' home. They feel uncomfortable, unhappy, or frustrated if they fail to achieve this level. Thus, we include within the vulnerable category all blue-collar workers whose fathers were white-collar workers. If the sole criterion were relative income, some blue-collar workers are not in fact in a worse position than their white-collar fathers. In fact, they may be better off. But income is not the whole of the matter. Take, for instance, a worker on the Detroit assembly line whose father was pastor of a church in a small Southern community or who was the principal of a small elementary school. With regard to income, the automotive worker is relatively better off; and yet he is likely to feel that he has slipped on the socioeconomic scale.

Blau and Duncan provide us with data for estimating the proportion of blue-collar workers who can be classified as vulnerable on the score of generational slippage. Their data reveal significant slippage into the blue-collar category from white-collar occupations.[6]

A second approach is to consider the number of blue-collar male workers who work full time, full year, but still do not earn $5,000—a modest figure indeed for a man who must support a family. Among males, about 13 percent of all craftsmen and foremen, 24 percent of operatives, 37 percent of service workers, and 39 percent of laborers fall below this arbitrary level. Among women who have to take care of themselves and their dependents, half of the operatives who work full time, full year earn under $4,000; half of the laborers under $3,500; and half of the service workers under $3,200.

Of all fully employed male blue-collar workers, one in four was unable to earn $5,000 or more; and among women heads of households who work regularly, the proportion who failed to meet the $5,000 standard is more than three of four.

If a person who works full time, full year is unable to support himself and his dependents at a reasonable level above the poverty line, he is likely to be dissatisfied and consider himself a failure. The foregoing data do not begin to reveal the full range of vulnerability and failure. There are many additional male and female blue-collar workers who are heads of households and who are *not* employed full time, full year; most of them fall below the poverty line.

Another insight into the vulnerability of blue-collar workers can be gained by assessing the prospects that face their children. Young people who do not finish high school will be in a poor competitive position, and one must observe that a high proportion of all noncompleters come from blue-collar families. This means that even some blue-collar workers who have done quite well—and who would be ranked as mobile in terms of their own achievements—would, in terms of what is likely to happen to their children, be classified as vulnerable. Many of their children will not find a good job from which they will be able to advance and earn a decent wage.

In summary, then, considerable numbers of blue-collar workers must be classified as vulnerable—because they have moved down the occupational scale, or because they are unable to earn enough to enable their families to live much above the poverty level, or finally because their offspring are unlikely to make a satisfactory economic advancement.

If figures were available to fill out our simple three-generational category schema, the totals would exceed 100 percent of all blue-collar workers. The explanation is the nonexclusiveness of the components that are included in the matrix. A man can be classified as mobile according to the criterion of improvement over the status achieved by his father; the same man can be called immobile in terms of the limited progress that he himself has been able to achieve; he can also be assessed as vulnerable in terms of the potential achievement of his children. There are eight other possible combinations, but only three would place a man exclusively in one category—mobile, immobile, or vulnerable. Here is a further reason that social scientists should exercise caution before they generalize about the past progress, present status, and future prospects of blue-collar workers.

A LOOK BACK AND A LOOK AHEAD

This social analysis is selective, as all social analyses must be. We have not considered all the forces which impinge on the lives of blue-collar workers and have had major impact on some. We have not considered, for instance, the impact of rapid changes in technology on bituminous coal miners, packinghouse workers, firemen on steam locomotives, and longshoremen, many of whom had their livelihoods eroded from under them as a consequence of technological breakthroughs. We note this omission to emphasize that any broad historical treatment of a large group will omit or underemphasize forces that have had a particular impact on specific subgroups.

The impact of technology was not our only omission. With the exception of a period of less than two years in the late 1940s, the United States has had recourse to compulsory military service for three decades, during which most of the young blue-collar workers of the last generation and many of their sons have seen active service. Some were killed, more were injured, and all were affected in varying degrees by their military experience. A significant proportion broadened their horizons as a result of this experience, and large numbers acquired skills.

A final factor that we skirted but that left its mark on many offspring of blue-collar workers has been the substantially enlarged public expenditures for post-secondary education and training, particularly the growth of community and senior colleges. Having stressed the importance of the education-training route for occupational mobility, we should note that the period since World War II has witnessed many broadened opportunities for the children of blue-collar workers, and others, to go to college.

In calling attention to these omissions—technological change, military service, and the expansion of higher education—we moved a step closer to even more important omissions that can be subsumed under the term "discontinuities," three of which have cut deeply into our national fabric: the reappraisal of our national power, the racial revolution, and the revolt of youth.

These discontinuities have affected blue-collar workers in much the same manner as they affected the American people at large. There is every reason to believe that blue-collar workers, like all of us, have been deeply shaken by the advent of the atomic age, the unsuccessful war in Vietnam, and the mounting evidence of the limits of American power. They, like most other Americans, have been shaken also by the racial revolution. But there is little evidence to suggest that blue-collar workers have more or less racial prejudice than other groups in American society. This we do know, however: we have made more progress in opening up employment opportunities for Negroes than we have in desegregating our schools or our neighborhoods. If blue-collar workers had not acquiesced in the reduction of job discrimination, our civil rights efforts would be even further behind than they are.

Finally, most blue-collar workers are distressed by, and some are hostile to, some aspects of the revolt of youth. But it would be a venturesome analyst who would seek to prove that the reactions of blue-collar workers are markedly different from those of the rest of society.

What then do we conclude from this long view? First, American society continues to be characterized by considerable flexibility, which enables many people to move to a higher occupational class and permits others to improve their position considerably even if they remain in the class into which they were born.

Second, the last three decades have enabled a high proportion of Negroes to make striking advances in their occupational and income status, both absolutely and relatively, by moving into, through, and out of the blue-collar category.

Third, many families who remain in the blue-collar category have been able to move into the upper quartile of the income distribution as a result of the wife's ability to supplement her husband's income.

Fourth, because of the low wage scales typical of the fields in which most women are employed, it is difficult for women heads of blue-collar households to earn an adequate income to support their dependents.

Fifth, a significant number of male heads of blue-collar households, even when they work full time and particularly when they work part time, are not able to lift their families out of poverty.

Sixth, whether or not the children of blue-collar workers will be able to improve their status will depend in large measure on whether they earn a college degree.

It must be recalled that blue-collar workers account for almost half of all nonagricultural workers. It is almost as difficult to generalize about time as about the employed population as a whole. If we limit ourselves to one cautious conclusion about the past, it is that during the first seven decades of this century the transformations in American society and the economy have enabled most blue-collar workers to achieve a position that is relatively better than that of their fathers.

As we look ahead, we see many unsettling and unresolved problems facing the American people. Blue-collar workers, like most other members of the public, reflect in their attitudes and behavior the uncertainties, tensions, and conflicts which surround and frequently engulf us all. But as our long view has sought to demonstrate, it is dangerous to treat blue-collar workers as a homogeneous group. In looking ahead, the cautious estimate would be to see some improving their position, some standing still, and yet others retrogressing.

One generalization can be safely ventured: If the United States solves some of its problems in the years ahead, the outlook for blue-collar groups will be favorable. If the nation falters, the blue-collar groups will be in serious trouble. But if the nation is not to falter, the blue-collar group must play its part in solving the nation's problems, and in this process it will alleviate its own.

NOTES

1. Eli Ginzberg, *The Illusion of Economic Stability,* Harper, New York, 1939, p. 53.
2. Dale L. Hiestand, *Economic Growth and Employment Opportunities for Minorities,* Columbia, New York, 1964, p. 8.
3. Peter M. Blau and Otis Dudley Duncan, *The American Occupational Structure,* Wiley, New York, 1967, *passim.*
4. Eli Ginzberg and Dale L. Hiestand, *Mobility in the Negro Community,* U.S. Civil Rights Commission, 1968.
5. Eli Ginzberg, *Career Guidance,* McGraw-Hill, New York, 1971.
6. Blau and Duncan, op. cit., p. 32.

3. A PROFILE OF THE BLUE-COLLAR AMERICAN

by Herman P. Miller

A VIEW THROUGH CENSUS DATA

This chapter provides a comparison of the social and economic profile of the married blue-collar worker with that of other groups in the population both today and over time.* It is based primarily on Census statistics—the 1/1,000 sample of the 1960 Census, the March 1966 Current Population Survey, and the March 1970 Current Population Survey—which are very limited for an analysis of the thesis that blue-collar workers are alienated, troubled, or forgotten Americans. These data can show how the demographic composition of blue-collar workers has changed over time and how it compares at a given point in time with other groups in the population with respect to age, education, regional and metropolitan area residence, and earnings. They can show also the extent to which the wives of bluc-collar workers work and contribute to family income in comparison with other groups in the population. They permit us to test a limited range of hypotheses which deal almost entirely with economic changes. Admittedly the problem of blue-collar alienation, if it exists, is far deeper than that. Gus Tyler of the International Ladies' Garment Workers' Union stated recently that "the mood today . . . is compounded of economic

*The opinions expressed are those of the author and do not necessarily represent those of the Bureau of the Census.

frustration, personal fear and political fury. It has been produced by the erosion of living standards that have been marginal at best in the 1960s, by the incompetence of government in dealing with social problems, and by the disorders and violence disrupting American life."[1] Only the economic factors described in Mr. Tyler's evaluation can be tested using Census data, and even these factors can be explored only cursorily. For example, we can measure the changes in earnings of blue-collar workers, but we cannot measure the change in their sense of job security resulting from the pressure of blacks to enter into unions and occupations from which they were once excluded. We can measure changes in the numbers employed in blue-collar jobs, but we cannot measure the increase in the fear that jobs will be eliminated because of technological change. The troubled feelings of blue-collar workers may be due more to anticipated economic loss than to that which has already taken place.

Despite their limitations, the Census data can contribute to our understanding of the feelings and behavior of blue-collar workers. Men are likely to feel threatened if those they regard as below themselves in social status are catching up and if those who are ahead of them are pulling away. It is undoubtedly true that a person's perception of his well-being and his needs is only partly a function of the amount of income he has; it is related also to the circumstances of others around him. A deterioration in *relative* economic or social status can more than offset substantial absolute increases.

The blue-collar workers are compared with the following groups: white professional and managerial workers, white clerical and sales workers, white service workers and nonfarm laborers, all employed nonwhite married men in blue-collar jobs. These data permit the analysis of earnings differentials for the decade 1959 to 1969 as well as for 1959 to 1965 and 1965 to 1969. It should be of particular interest to compare income changes during the latter half of the decade of the 1960s, when tight labor markets existed, with those which took place during the first half of the decade.

In March 1970, there were 43.4 million husband-wife families in the United States. About one-third (14.3 million) were white families headed by a man employed as a craftsman or an operative. These are the men who form the control group in this chapter—the so-called "troubled Americans." As in any occupation, the group includes some men with very low earnings owing to illness, prolonged unemployment, or entry into a new occupation, as well as some men with very high earnings. If the control group were restricted to men who earned between $4,000 and $12,000 in 1969, the number would be reduced by 3.1 million, or about one-fifth of all husband-wife families headed by a blue-collar worker.

There is little difference between the characteristics of all blue-collar workers and those with earnings of $4,000 to $12,000 (Table 1). It was therefore decided to use the entire group rather than just those within the limited income range on the assumption that

TABLE 1
DISTRIBUTION OF WHITE CRAFTSMEN AND OPERATIVES WHO ARE HEADS OF HUSBAND-WIFE FAMILIES BY EARNINGS IN 1969 AND SELECTED CHARACTERISTICS

Characteristics	*Total*	*Husbands with earnings of $4,000–$11,999*		
		Total	*$4,000–$7,999*	*$8,000–$11,999*
Number (in millions)	14.3	11.2	5.8	5.4
Residence				
Total	100%	100%	100%	100%
North and West	72	72	66	78
In metropolitan areas . .	50	49	41	57
In central cities	18	18	17	19
Outside central cities	31	31	24	38
Outside metropolitan areas	23	23	26	21
Urban	9	9	10	9
Rural	14	14	16	12
South	28	28	34	22
In metropolitan areas . .	13	14	14	13
In central cities	5	5	6	5
Outside central cities	8	8	8	9
Outside metropolitan areas	15	14	20	9
Urban	4	4	5	3
Rural	11	11	15	6
Labor-force status and earnings of wife				
Total	100%	100%	100%	100%
Wife not in labor force . .	56	55	53	58
Wife in labor force	44	45	47	42
Median earnings of wife	$3,465	$3,418	$3,392	$3,459

TABLE 1, *continued*
DISTRIBUTION OF WHITE CRAFTSMEN AND OPERATIVES WHO ARE HEADS OF HUSBAND-WIFE FAMILIES BY EARNINGS IN 1969 AND SELECTED CHARACTERISTICS

Characteristics	*Total*	*Husbands with earnings of $4,000–$11,999*		
		Total	*$4,000– $7,999*	*$8,000– $11,999*
Industry				
Total	100%	100%	100%	100%
Construction	17	15	15	14
Manufacturing	49	51	49	53
Transportation	8	8	7	9
Trade	10	10	12	8
Service	7	6	8	5
Other	9	10	8	11
Family income in 1969				
Total	100%	100%	100%	100%
Under $2,000	1	...	...	...
$2,000 to $3,999	3	...	...	...
$4,000 to $5,999	8	7	14	...
$6,000 to $7,999	16	18	35	...
$8,000 to $9,999	20	24	20	28
$10,000 to $11,999	19	23	15	32
$12,000 to $14,999	18	16	10	22
$15,000 and over	16	12	6	18
Median income	$10,731	$10,066	$8,052	$11,370

the figures for the larger group could be analyzed in greater detail before encountering serious problems of sampling variability.

There are some important differences between the characteristics of the 5.8 million blue-collar husbands with earnings of $4,000 to $8,000 and the 5.5 million with $8,000 to $12,000; but there is no logical basis for restricting the analysis to either group or to any other earnings subgroup that could be devised. There is a striking geographical difference between the two earnings groups, reflecting in part regional differences in the pay and price structure. About 78 percent of the higher-paid blue-collar workers reside in the North and West as compared with 66 percent of the lower-paid men in the same occupation group. Much of this difference is due to the fact that a larger proportion of the lower-paid men live in the rural South. It is of particular interest that about the same proportion of the families in both income groups reside in central cities.

TRENDS IN EMPLOYMENT AND EARNINGS

More of the lower-paid men had working wives. About 47 percent of the men with earnings between $4,000 and $8,000 in 1969 had wives in the labor force as compared with 42 percent of the men with earnings between $8,000 and $12,000. Both groups of working wives had about the same median earnings—$3,400 a year.

Blue-collar workers are often described as alienated, troubled, and forgotten Americans who are badly in need of aid. They may indeed feel that way, but they have made great economic advances during the past four decades.

During the 1930s millions of men and women in factories and mills joined newly formed industrial unions. With workers in established craft unions and the coal mines, they engaged in prolonged, bitter, and often violent struggles with management that were reported daily in headlines and made household words of the names of John L. Lewis, Sidney Hillman, and Philip Murray. By the end of World War II the blue-collar unions had become a part of the recognized establishment in American life, and since then they have made substantial gains in income and standards of living. The working wife became an integral part of this pattern and made it possible for record numbers of families to buy homes in the suburbs.

Along with material goods like air conditioners, freezers, and second cars, higher education for the children became more prevalent. At present over one-third of the children of blue-collar workers attend college.[2] By 1969, the median annual income of white families headed by blue-collar workers was $10,700, up 30 percent from the $8,200 (measured in dollars of 1969 purchasing power) received by these families at the beginning of the decade. This increase of 3 percent per year in real family income is about equal to the productivity gains recorded during the past decade.

The success of blue-collar workers can be seen most clearly in their own expressed attitudes. Various opinion surveys show that union members (two-thirds of whom are blue-collar workers) now see themselves as part of the solid majority and not as a group that is alienated or that is struggling to establish its identity. In a 1968 Harris poll, 82 percent of union members said they have as good a chance to get ahead as other people, and about two-thirds said that the leaders of the nation really care about what happens to people like themselves.[3]

These are hardly the symptoms of alienation or deep dissatisfaction. On the contrary, surveys on many different subjects, such as Vietnam, civil rights, the poverty program, and admission of Red China to the UN, show that the opinions of union members are very similar to those held by the general public. For example, in April 1968, 59 percent of the general public and 64 percent of union members favored more vigorous prosecution of the war. With regard to Negroes, about 61 percent of all people and 69 percent of union members said, "Negroes are moving too fast."[4]

By contrast, most black people do feel alienated. In surveys conducted by Louis Harris, about 60 percent of blacks say, "What I think doesn't count much," and about the same proportion say, "The people running the country don't care what happens to me."[5] The people who voted for George Wallace in 1968 show about the same degree of alienation as blacks.

The notion that blue-collar workers are caught in an economic squeeze is based primarily on Labor Department statistics on gross weekly earnings for workers on private nonagricultural payrolls, which, after adjusting for inflation, rose from $87 in 1965 to $90 in 1969.[6] When taxes are taken into account, these figures show a slight drop in earnings during this period. But this measure has some serious shortcomings for the particular problem under consideration. It includes both men and women and part-time as well as full-time workers. For many purposes it is more appropriate to examine changes in the earnings of men who are family heads.

Moreover, the Labor Department figures lump together the earnings of blacks and whites. For some purposes that would be fine. In the present case, however, it would be preferable to show separate statistics for each group because people who speak about the Silent Majority or troubled Americans refer to the white middle-class family man who might be a construction worker, a plumber, an electrician, a mechanic, a semiskilled factory worker, a farmer,

TABLE 2
MEDIAN EARNINGS OF MARRIED MEN, BY OCCUPATION GROUP AND COLOR: 1959, 1965, AND 1969
(IN CONSTANT 1969 DOLLARS)

Color and occupation group	*Median earnings*			*Percent change*		
	1959	*1965*	*1969*	*1959–1969*	*1959–1965*	*1965–1969*
White						
Blue-collar workers.	$6,408	$6,998	$ 8,025	25	9	15
Professional and managerial workers.	8,658	9,686	11,074	28	12	14
Clerical and sales workers.	6,678	7,366	8,333	25	10	13
Service workers and laborers. .	5,150	5,513	6,259	22	7	14
Nonwhite						
Total employed	3,714	4,561	5,934	60	23	30
Blue-collar workers.	4,213	5,032	5,979	42	19	19

or even a man on a pension. Census data show that during the past decade, the median earnings (in constant dollars) of white married men in blue-collar jobs increased 25 percent. This gain was about the same as that received by white men in other occupations but considerably less than the gain received by nonwhite married men, whose average earnings rose 60 percent overall and 42 percent in blue-collar jobs. Most of the gains by white men in blue-collar jobs were received since 1965, whereas the gains received by nonwhites were more evenly spread throughout the decade (Table 2). The earnings data reported by the Census Bureau do not take taxes into account. The analysis by Dean Dick Netzer in this volume suggests that earnings, net of taxes, have not increased much since 1965 for white men employed in blue-collar or other occupations.

In the North and West blue-collar workers who were white had about the same relative gains in earnings during the decade as non-whites. In the South, however, the earnings gap between the two groups was narrowed considerably. White married men in the South who were blue-collar workers had an average increase in earnings of 28 percent between 1959 and 1969 whereas nonwhite men in comparable occupations had an average increase of 56 percent. Despite the change, however, white men who were blue-collar workers in the South averaged $7,100 in 1969 as compared with $4,800 for nonwhites.

In addition to the changes in earnings of married men, there were significant changes in occupational distribution between 1960 and 1970. The number of married men in blue-collar jobs increased 7 percent for whites and 46 percent for nonwhites. The number of white men employed in professional and managerial jobs also rose sharply from 7.8 million to 11.4 million, a gain of 46 percent (Table 3).

When the pieces are put together, it hardly seems appropriate to label blue-collar workers as economically "squeezed." They are not falling behind other groups economically. They had the same increases in earnings as other workers during the past decade.

The striking new economic fact is that there has been a very large increase in the number of black workers in blue-collar jobs; and blacks in most occupations, though starting from a much lower base, have had far greater relative gains in earnings than whites. The white man in a blue-collar job today is much more likely to find himself working side by side with a Negro than he was 10 years ago, and many of these Negroes are earning as much as he does.

Union men have about the same attitudes as the average American on most major social issues. Their stronger negative reaction

TABLE 3
OCCUPATION DISTRIBUTION OF MARRIED MEN, BY COLOR: 1960 AND 1970

Color and occupation group	*Number of workers (thousands)* 1960	*Number of workers (thousands)* 1970	*Percent change*
White			
Blue-collar workers	13,343	14,285	7
Professional and managerial workers	7,797	11,394	46
Clerical and sales workers	4,339	4,310	−1
Service workers and laborers	3,006	2,986	−1
Nonwhite			
Total employed	2,660	3,060	15
Blue-collar workers	972	1,417	46

to Negro gains (69 percent compared with 61 percent of the entire population) may stem from the fear of economic competition from black workers.

Much is also made of an alleged incompatibility between the earnings and family needs of blue-collar workers during their life cycle. Although it may be true that most blue-collar workers have little opportunity for promotion or advancement, it does not follow that they reach a plateau in earnings. Although the man on the assembly line may have no place to go in terms of occupational advancement, his income, adjusted for changes in purchasing power, generally continues to grow at the rate of 3 percent or more per year because of productivity gains. In addition, many wives of blue-collar workers enter the labor force once their children enter school. The added income provided by a working wife helps defray many of the expenses which begin to mount during the latter stages of the family cycle.

Many white men employed in blue-collar jobs have reason to be fearful of the economic competition they are beginning to encounter from black workers. There may be little the government can do for them other than to pursue policies that will provide full employment in an expanding economy. More and better training programs, which would improve occupational skills and increase the options available to operatives and craftsmen, would surely be a step in the right direction.

Blue-collar workers are now represented by strong unions which can bargain effectively for greater job security. The white man who is sure of his job is less likely to feel threatened by Negro competition than the one who fears that his job may be eliminated or that he may be thrown out of work for other reasons.

But in the final analysis, white workers in some trades and in some parts of the country will simply have to accept the fact that they can no longer enjoy the monopoly position they once had. They will have to accept a change in the status of the Negro, and either they will do so gracefully or it will be forced upon them.

GEOGRAPHIC DISTRIBUTION

We turn now from overall trends in the employment and earnings of blue-collar workers to an examination of their social and economic characteristics. White married men in blue-collar jobs are geographically distributed in virtually the same fashion as the general population. About half of all blue-collar workers live in metropolitan areas of the North and West, mostly in the suburbs rather than the central cities. An additional one-fourth live in the smaller cities and rural areas of the North and West, and the remaining one-fourth live in the South, where they are about equally divided between metropolitan and nonmetropolitan areas.

White-collar workers tend to be more metropolitan and suburban than blue-collar workers. About 75 percent of white clerical and sales workers and 69 percent of professional and managerial workers live in metropolitan areas as compared with only 63 percent of the blue-collar workers and service workers and laborers. In each of the occupation groups, most of the white workers residing in metropolitan areas live in the suburbs. Nevertheless, large numbers continue to live in the central cities. About 23 percent of all white families headed by blue-collar workers live in central cities as compared with 24 percent of those headed by professional and managerial workers and 31 percent of those headed by clerical and sales workers.

Nonwhite married men in blue-collar jobs have about the same residential distribution as other nonwhite workers. Somewhat more than half of them reside in the North and West, for the most part in the central cities of that region. An additional one-fourth reside in metropolitan areas of the South, and the remaining one-fifth live in small towns and rural areas of the South.

The most striking change in the residential distribution of workers since 1960 is the movement from central cities to the suburbs. The proportion of white married men in blue-collar jobs residing in the suburbs of metropolitan areas increased from 35 percent in 1960 to 39 percent in 1970. Among professional and managerial workers the increase was from 39 percent to 46 percent; the proportion of clerical and sales workers residing in the suburbs rose from 38 percent to 43 percent.

Income gains for white workers during the past decade were very similar in different parts of the country and among different occupation groups. Median earnings of white workers increased about 25 percent in each of the four occupation groups for which data are presented. The rate of growth was about the same in the South as in the rest of the country, and it also did not vary much between metropolitan and nonmetropolitan areas. Although the level of earnings in the rural South lagged behind the rest of the nation, the relative gains in this area tended to be higher than elsewhere.

Nonwhite workers in all parts of the country had greater relative gains in earnings than white workers. Between 1959 and 1969 the median earnings of nonwhite married men increased 60 percent overall and 42 percent for those employed in blue-collar jobs. The relative gains for nonwhites were greatest in the South, where annual earnings in blue-collar jobs increased 56 percent as compared with only 30 percent in the rest of the country. Despite this change, in 1969 nonwhites in blue-collar jobs in the South earned about 80 percent as much as nonwhites in the same occupation in the rest of the country. Part of this difference is accounted for by the lower prices in the South. The earnings differential between white and nonwhite blue-collar workers was also considerably greater in the South than in the rest of the country. Nonwhite men employed in blue-collar jobs in the South earned only about 67 percent as much as whites in these occupations in 1969. Ten years earlier they earned about 55 percent as much as the whites. In the Northern and Western states, nonwhite blue-collar workers earned about 85 percent as much as whites in 1959 and 1969.

Overall, gains in earnings appear to have been somewhat greater during the latter half of the decade than during the first half. This change was undoubtedly associated with the full employment conditions generated by the war in Vietnam, which gained momentum after 1965. The pattern of change, however, differed greatly between the South and the rest of the country, and between whites and nonwhites. Blue-collar workers in the North and West had an average increase of 13 percent in earnings between 1959 and 1965 and again between 1965 and 1969. Professional and managerial workers also had about the same rate of increase in both halves of the decade; clerical and sales workers had a lower rate of increase during the last part of the decade. In contrast, nonwhite married men in the North and West had gains of only 8 percent overall during the first half of the decade and 26 percent during the last half. The corresponding increases for nonwhite men in blue-collar jobs were 10 and 19 percent respectively. It does appear, therefore, that the earnings of nonwhite workers in the Northern and Western states forged ahead during the latter half of the decade. The contributing factors here were undoubtedly the war in Vietnam and the intensification of the campaign for equal employment opportunities.

In contrast to the changes observed in the Northern and Western states, white workers in all occupations in the South made far greater gains during the last half of the decade than during the first half. The gains for nonwhites in the South were also somewhat greater during the last half of the decade, but the difference from the first half was not nearly as pronounced for nonwhites as it was for whites.

AGE

White and nonwhite married men in blue-collar jobs have about the same age distribution as white-collar workers, but they are somewhat younger than service workers and laborers. The median age is 42 years for white men in blue-collar jobs, 43 years in white-collar jobs, and 45 years for service workers and laborers. About one-fourth of the service workers and laborers are over 55 years old. This proportion is significantly larger than that found in any of the other occupations. It reflects the fact that many older men lack the education and training needed to hold better jobs in today's economy, and that many older men who do have the training are forced to retreat to less-skilled work as they are hit by the infirmities of old age and by the unwillingness of employers to give them the same opportunities as younger men.

The variation of earnings with age for 1969 is shown for each occupation group in Table 4. It is important to recognize that these figures show the variation in pay at a given point in time; they should not be interpreted as tracing the pattern of earnings over a working lifetime. It would be entirely incorrect to assume from these numbers that blue-collar workers reach their peak earnings at age 35 and remain at a plateau for the next 20 years. Other evidence indicates that because of gains in productivity, the earnings of men in most jobs continue to increase until they are close to retirement.

Beginning salaries are somewhat higher in blue-collar jobs than in other occupations. In part this difference is due to the fact that

TABLE 4

MEDIAN EARNINGS OF HUSBANDS BY AGE, OCCUPATION GROUP, AND COLOR: 1959 AND 1969
(IN CONSTANT 1969 DOLLARS)

Year and age of head	White				Nonwhite	
	Craftsmen and operatives	*Professional and managerial workers*	*Clerical and sales workers*	*Service workers and laborers*	*Total employed*	*Craftsmen and operatives*
Median earnings: 1969						
Total	$8,025	$11,074	$8,333	$6,259	$5,934	$5,979
Under 25 years	6,178	6,061	5,730	4,981	5,229	5,321
25 to 34 years	8,222	10,107	8,563	7,141	6,219	6,222
35 to 44 years	8,479	12,142	9,366	7,245	6,939	6,629
45 to 54 years	8,462	12,049	8,742	6,815	6,278	6,256
55 to 64 years	7,891	11,077	8,127	5,645	5,014	5,134
65 years and over	4,166	6,648	3,625	1,900	1,780	*
Percent change: 1959–1969						
Total	25	28	25	22	60	42
Under 25 years	28	20	16	29	94	*
25 to 34 years	29	31	29	26	57	41
35 to 44 years	24	26	29	25	59	39
45 to 54 years	29	26	26	32	73	47
55 to 64 years	30	23	26	22	58	40
65 years and over	−13	−4	−24	−28	−23	*

* Base less than 75,000.

many men in white-collar jobs are just beginning their careers at age 25, whereas most blue-collar workers have already had several years of work experience by that time. The earnings of blue-collar workers are higher than those of service workers and laborers in each age group, and they are below those of professional and managerial workers in each age group above 25 years. Clerical and sales workers also tend to have somewhat higher earnings than blue-collar workers in most age groups.

White workers between the ages of 25 and 64 had gains in earnings ranging between 25 and 30 percent in all the occupations for which data are shown; the earnings of older workers declined in each occupation. Nonwhite workers had gains of about 60 percent or more in each age group below 65. Nonwhites in blue-collar jobs had gains of about 40 percent in most age groups.

By comparing the earnings in each occupational group in 1959 with the average earnings in 1969 for the appropriate age groups, we can obtain a *very rough* measure of the variation of earnings with age for a decade (Table 5). It must be emphasized, however, that such figures can be very misleading, particularly for the younger age groups, because they are based on the erroneous assumption that the married men employed in each occupation group in April 1960 were still married and employed in the same occupation group in March 1970. The problem can be seen most dramatically in the figures for professional and managerial workers. In April 1960, about 1.8 million white married men 25 to 34 years old were classified as professional or managerial workers. In March 1970, 3.2 million white married men 35 to 44 years old were classified in these occupations. Instead of decreasing slightly over the decade because of deaths, as would be the case in any true cohort, the number of men in this group increased 75 percent. Thus, we know for certain that the earnings data shown in Table 5 and the income data in Table 6 do not measure the changes over a decade for the same group of men, and there is reason to question whether this is even approximately the case for some age groups and some occupations. Nevertheless, it may be of interest to examine the relations shown by these data, keeping in mind the limitations described above, as well as the fact that the relations reflect the labor market conditions at two particular points in time and might be different under other economic conditions.

TABLE 5

MEDIAN EARNINGS FOR SELECTED COHORTS OF MARRIED MEN BY OCCUPATION GROUP AND COLOR: 1959 AND 1969
(IN CONSTANT 1969 DOLLARS)

Color and occupation group	*Cohort of 1926–1935*			*Cohort of 1916–1925*			*Cohort of 1906–1915*		
	25–34 in 1960	*35–44 in 1970*	*Percent change*	*35–44 in 1960*	*45–54 in 1970*	*Percent change*	*45–54 in 1960*	*55–64 in 1970*	*Percent change*
White									
Blue-collar workers	$6,393	$ 8,479	33	$6,854	$ 8,462	24	$6,547	$ 7,891	21
Professional and managerial workers	7,728	12,142	57	9,652	12,049	25	9,601	11,077	15
Clerical and sales workers. . .	6,639	9,366	41	7,243	8,742	21	6,929	8,127	17
Service workers and laborers.	5,677	7,245	28	5,818	6,815	17	5,170	5,645	9
Nonwhite									
Total employed	3,962	6,939	75	4,378	6,278	43	3,626	5,014	38
Blue-collar workers	4,428	6,629	50	4,759	6,256	32	4,271	5,134	20

Table 6

Mean Family Income for Selected Cohorts of Married Men by Occupation Group and Color: 1959 and 1969

(In constant 1969 dollars)

Color and occupation group	Cohort of 1926–1935			Cohort of 1916–1925			Cohort of 1906–1915		
	25–34 in 1960	*35–44 in 1970*	*Percent change*	*35–44 in 1960*	*45–54 in 1970*	*Percent change*	*45–54 in 1960*	*55–64 in 1970*	*Percent change*
White									
Blue-collar workers.	$7,570	$11,053	46	$ 8,685	$12,165	40	$ 8,998	$11,336	26
Professional and managerial workers.	9,614	16,361	70	12,443	18,086	45	13,809	17,680	28
Clerical and sales workers . . .	8,486	13,385	58	10,220	14,825	45	10,644	13,321	25
Service workers and laborers	6,648	9,609	45	7,397	10,901	47	7,442	9,411	27
Nonwhite									
Total employed.	5,433	10,198	88	6,099	9,775	60	5,638	9,122	62
Blue-collar workers.	5,785	9,484	64	6,328	9,681	53	6,231	8,374	34

Perhaps the most striking fact is that, in all occupations, both whites and nonwhites made greater gains between the ages of 30 and 40 (the midpoints of the 25–34 and 35–44 year age groups) than later in life. This is not surprising in light of the fact that younger workers are more mobile than others in the labor force. They are not tied down as much by family responsibility, home ownership, seniority, and other factors which reduce mobility. They are, therefore, more likely to move into new areas and new industries where wages tend to be higher and opportunities for rapid advancement are greater. Conversely, having been in the labor force a relatively short time, they are less likely to be trapped in declining industries where incomes may be dropping despite the overall growth of the economy. Having been exposed to more modern methods of education and training, these new entrants into the labor force also tend to be better trained than men who have been employed for a decade or more. Finally, employers may prefer younger workers even when they have the same ability as older workers because of their interest in growth potential. For these and other reasons, this evidence regarding the differential impact of economic growth for different age groups, based on the experience during the past decade, seems reasonable despite the limitations of the data.

Individual earnings are the return to the worker for his services in the labor market. When related to various personal characteristics such as age, sex, color, residence, education, and occupation, individual earnings represent the amount that employers are willing to pay for a given type of labor at a given point in time. For some problems, particularly for questions relating to welfare, family income rather than individual earnings is the appropriate measure. For example, if we are concerned with the ability of different kinds of workers and their families to maintain an adequate level of living, the appropriate measure would be family income rather than the earnings of the family head. Table 6 presents the same data as Table 5—with all the same limitations—except that the figures shown are family incomes rather than individual earnings.

For each occupation and for each age group, family income rose proportionately more than the earnings of the head during the past decade. This difference primarily reflects the overall increase in the employment of wives. Blue-collar husbands increased their earnings 33 percent between the ages of 30 and 40, whereas family income for this group rose 46 percent during the same period. Similar changes took place in each occupation group. Another important relation suggested by Table 6 is that there is no diminution in the rate of growth in family income between the ages of 40 and 50, whereas the earnings of the family head appear to grow at a diminishing rate beyond the age of 40. The probable reason for this difference is that married women begin to return to the labor force in large numbers after the age of 40, when most of their children are in school.

EDUCATION

As might be expected, blue-collar workers have more schooling than service workers and laborers but far less schooling than white-collar workers. About half of all white men in blue-collar jobs have completed high school or have had some college training, as compared with 87 percent of the professional and managerial workers and 79 percent of the clerical and sales workers.

Blue-collar workers, like most other groups in the population, have shown a marked increase in years of schooling during the past decade. The major change is a considerable reduction in the proportion who did not go beyond elementary school (down from 40 percent in 1960 to 26 percent in 1970) and an increase in the proportion who are high school graduates (up from 26 percent in 1960 to 41 percent in 1970). There was no significant change in the proportion of blue-collar workers with college training.

The gains in education for nonwhite married men were similar to those experienced by whites. In 1960, about 58 percent of all employed nonwhite men had terminated their schooling by the eighth grade. This proportion dropped to 35 percent in 1970. The proportion of nonwhite high school graduates and men with some college training roughly doubled during this period. The gains in educational attainment for nonwhite blue-collar workers were similar to those experienced by other workers except that there was no change in the proportion with college training (Table 7).

In blue-collar jobs, as in nearly all other kinds of work, there is a very close association between years of schooling and earnings (Table 8). White married men who did not go beyond the eighth

TABLE 7

PERCENT DISTRIBUTION OF HUSBAND-WIFE FAMILIES BY YEARS OF SCHOOL COMPLETED, OCCUPATION GROUP, AND COLOR OF HEAD: 1960 AND 1970

Number and years of school completed by head	*White*				*Nonwhite*	
	Craftsmen and operatives	*Professional and managerial workers*	*Clerical and sales workers*	*Service workers and laborers*	*Total employed*	*Craftsmen and operatives*
1970						
Number (in thousands)	14,285	11,394	4,310	2,986	3,060	1,417
Percent	100	100	100	100	100	100
Elementary	26	6	8	36	35	38
High school: 1 to 3 years	25	7	13	20	23	28
4 years	41	28	44	34	27	28
College: 1 to 3 years	7	19	22	8	8	5
4 years or more	1	40	13	1	7	1
1960						
Number (in thousands)	13,343	7,797	4,339	3,006	2,660	972
Percent	100	100	100	100	100	100
Elementary	40	11	16	52	58	58
High school: 1 to 3 years	27	12	20	24	20	24
4 years	26	23	35	19	15	14
College: 1 to 3 years	5	18	18	5	4	4
4 years or more	2	36	11	1	3	1

TABLE 8

MEDIAN EARNINGS OF HUSBAND BY YEARS OF SCHOOL COMPLETED, OCCUPATION GROUP, AND COLOR OF HEAD: 1959 AND 1969

(IN CONSTANT 1969 DOLLARS)

Years of school completed by head	White				Nonwhite	
	Craftsmen and operatives	*Professional and managerial workers*	*Clerical and sales workers*	*Service workers and laborers*	*Total employed*	*Craftsmen and operatives*
Median earnings: 1969						
Total	$8,025	$11,074	$ 8,333	$6,259	$5,934	$5,979
Elementary	7,064	7,117	6,436	5,121	4,560	4,993
High school: 1 to 3 years	8,014	8,493	7,452	6,200	5,979	6,378
4 years	8,592	10,102	8,330	7,569	6,678	6,793
College: 1 to 3 years	8,773	10,890	8,753	7,162	7,285	6,909
4 years or more	9,665	12,368	10,655	*	9,912	*
Percent change in median earnings: 1959–1969						
Total	25	28	25	22	60	42
Elementary	22	10	15	16	47	38
High school: 1 to 3 years	22	13	19	13	38	27
4 years	26	22	23	25	32	33
College: 1 to 3 years	22	24	20	23	28	*
4 years or more	10	22	25	*	50	*

* Base less than 75,000.

grade earned about $7,100 in blue-collar jobs in 1969; those with an average of two years of high school earned about $8,000; high school graduates earned $8,600. The relatively small number of blue-collar men who were college-trained had even higher incomes. The same general pattern was found in other occupational groups, for nonwhites as well as whites, and in 1959 as well as in 1969.

Although the relation between earnings and education is understandable among professional and managerial workers or even among clerical and sales workers, it is not quite so apparent why the blue-collar man with two years of high school should earn about $1,000 more per year than the man who never went beyond the eighth grade, or why the high school graduate should earn about $600 more per year than the man with only two years of high school. A small part of the difference may be due to what men learn by staying in school longer. More plausibly, the willingness to stay in school longer reflects greater native intelligence and learning ability, which is translated to better performance on the job when the student enters the labor market. Finally, the greater earnings of high school graduates reflect the commercial value of the diploma. Many employers give preference to high school graduates. A worker with a diploma is more likely to find regular employment with a large firm; and even if he is paid the same hourly rate as the less educated worker, he is likely to have more continuous employment and will have higher earnings as a result. The high school diploma also paves the way for many apprenticeship and training programs which further increase occupational skills and earnings.

INDUSTRIAL DISTRIBUTION

The industrial distribution of blue-collar workers has not changed much during the past decade. Manufacturing industries are by far the largest employers of blue-collar workers. About one-half of the total work in these industries. The construction industry ranks next in importance with about 17 percent of the total. Among nonwhite men in blue-collar jobs, there has been an increase since 1960 in the proportion employed in manufacturing industries and a drop in the proportion engaged in the service trades. The proportion employed in construction, transportation, and trade did not change significantly.

Although hourly rates of pay are relatively high in the construction industry and these jobs are often regarded as promising careers for school dropouts and other uneducated young men, particularly blacks, the figures show that blue-collar workers in transportation and manufacturing industries earned more than those in construction. In 1969, white men in blue-collar jobs earned $8,500 in transportation, $8,200 in manufacturing, and $8,000 in construction. The averages for blacks in these same industries were $6,400, $6,300, and $5,000, respectively.

Among whites, blue-collar workers employed in construction jobs had somewhat larger increases in annual earnings over the decade than those employed in other industries, but the difference was not striking. The earnings of white construction workers rose 31 percent as compared with 29 percent in transportation, 25 percent in manufacturing and service industries, and 22 percent in trade. Nonwhite blue-collar workers had gains of 40 percent or more in all industries except manufacturing.

EMPLOYMENT OF WIFE AND FAMILY INCOME

Most married men are aware of the importance of the wife's contribution to family income. About 40 percent of them derive this awareness from the fact that their own wives are working; and many of those whose wives are at home cannot afford the vacations, automobiles, color television sets, and other luxuries enjoyed by their more fortunate coworkers. Table 9 provides a good indication of the contribution of the working wife to family income. The "family income" column shows the number of husband-wife families at each income level in 1968. This column is obtained by classifying each family by the combined income of all its members. The "husband's income" column shows the distribution that is obtained by classifying each husband by his own income. This table shows that the number of families at the "$15,000 and over" income level would be cut in half if families were classified by the income of the husband alone, rather than by the income of the entire family. While it is true that the income of all relatives—not just that of the husband and wife—is counted in family income, the fact is that wives are the most important supplementary contributors to family income.

TABLE 9
FAMILY INCOMES COMPARED TO HUSBANDS' INCOMES: 1968
(NUMBERS IN THOUSANDS)

Total money income	*Husband-wife families listed by*	
	Family income	*Husband's income*
Total	43,800	43,800
Under $3,000	3,300	6,100
$3,000 to $4,999	4,700	6,300
$5,000 to $6,999	6,100	8,500
$7,000 to $9,999	10,800	11,800
$10,000 to $14,999	11,800	7,800
$15,000 and over	7,100	3,500

SOURCE: Herman P. Miller, *Rich Man, Poor Man,* Thomas Y. Crowell, New York, 1971.

Men at all income levels have working wives; but those who are at the bottom of the income scale and can most use help are not as fortunate as men in the middle-income ranges. Only one-third of the men with earnings under $1,000 have working wives; the proportion is only slightly higher for men in the $1,000 to $2,000 income bracket. The main reason their wives work less than others is that they are older: about half of them are beyond the age of 50. The proportion of working wives rises gradually with income and reaches a peak at the $5,000 to $7,000 income level, at which nearly half the wives are in the labor market. Beyond this point on the income scale there is a gradual reduction in the labor-force participation of women. But even at the $10,000 to $15,000 income level, 35 percent of the wives were working in March 1969; 26 percent were employed at the $15,000 to $25,000 level and 18 percent at the very highest income level (Table 10).

The general relations described above appear in the statistics for each of the occupational groups. In the case of white men employed in blue-collar jobs, about 44 percent had working wives. This proportion was slightly greater than the worker rate among the wives of professional and managerial workers (41 percent) and service workers and laborers (43 percent), but below that of clerical and sales workers (49 percent). Since the earnings of clerical and sales workers with working wives are higher than those of blue-collar workers, it seems likely that the higher worker rates among the white-collar workers are more attributable to their better educa-

TABLE 10
PERCENT OF WIVES IN THE LABOR FORCE IN MARCH 1969 AND MEDIAN AGE OF WIFE, BY EARNINGS OF HUSBAND IN 1968

Earnings of husband	*Percent of wives in labor force*	*Median age of wife*
$1 to $999 or loss	33	55
$1,000 to $1,999	38	50
$2,000 to $2,999	42	41
$3,000 to $3,999	44	39
$4,000 to $4,999	45	38
$5,000 to $5,999	47	39
$6,000 to $6,999	47	39
$7,000 to $7,999	45	39
$8,000 to $9,999	41	39
$10,000 to $14,999	35	40
$15,000 to $24,999	26	42
$25,000 and over	18	45

SOURCE: Herman P. Miller, *Rich Man, Poor Man,* Thomas Y. Crowell, New York, 1971.

tion and training than to financial reasons. Aside from the increase in worker rates among wives in each occupational group since 1960, the relation between the earnings of husbands and labor-force participation of wives was about the same at the end of the decade as it was at the beginning.

Nonwhite wives have far higher worker rates than do white wives (Table 11). Although nonwhite men in blue-collar jobs have higher incomes than white men employed as service workers and laborers, the worker rate among nonwhite wives (57 percent) was far higher than the rate for white wives. Nonwhite men in blue-collar jobs whose wives are employed have higher earnings ($6,300) than those whose wives are not employed ($5,700). The reverse is true among white men, for those with wives in the labor force had average earnings of $7,700 in 1969, and those whose wives stayed at home averaged $8,300. Since the need for additional income is undoubtedly greater among men with lower earnings, their wives probably have good reasons for not working. It is possible that they have more small children or other family responsibilities, or that they are not as well trained or educated for employment as those nonwhite women who are in the labor force.

USE WITH CAUTION!

The study of alienation and other troubled feelings belongs more in the domain of the social psychologist than the economic statistician. Blue-collar workers are subject to the same sources of anxiety as most other Americans. Their personal fear has increased along with racial tensions and the rise in urban crime and violence. They are frustrated by the involvement in the prolonged war in Vietnam. They are angry and confused because many young people are challenging established values. In a very real sense, the blue-collar blues are the blues of all Americans in the seventies. These workers, however, may also have special problems of an economic nature. Their take-home pay is being eroded by inflation and higher taxes. They are experiencing economic competition from lower-paid workers in minority groups who were formerly excluded from many higher-paid jobs; and many feel insecure in their jobs because of anticipated technological change.

The Census data that have been presented here provide few insights into the noneconomic sources of anxiety that are troubling blue-collar workers and other Americans, and they leave much to be desired in explaining the economic sources of anxiety. One important limitation is that the figures for 1960 are from the decennial census whereas those for 1965 and 1970 are from the Current Population Survey (CPS). Differences in the procedures used to collect and process the data in these two sources could have some effect on the results. Although the income data in the Census and CPS are in close agreement, there are some considerable differences in the number of workers reported in some occupational groups.

The income concept used in the Census data—income before taxes—also limits the utility of the data for economic analysis. It is true that taxes are a form of involuntary expenditure, and according to the best evidence available, families at the middle-income levels receive about as much in benefits from the government as they pay in taxes to the government. Nevertheless, it is easy to understand why workers who look at their take-home pay feel that their gains in earnings are considerably less than the Census figures show. But even if data on income after taxes were available, they might not throw much light on blue-collar blues. Families at each

TABLE 11

DISTRIBUTION OF HUSBAND-WIFE FAMILIES, BY EARNINGS AND LABOR-FORCE PARTICIPATION OF WIFE AND BY SELECTED OCCUPATION GROUP AND COLOR OF HEAD: 1960 AND 1970

Labor-force participation of wife	*White*				*Nonwhite*	
	Craftsmen and operatives	*Professional and managerial workers*	*Clerical and sales workers*	*Service workers and laborers*	*Total employed*	*Craftsmen and operatives*
1970						
Total	14,285	11,394	4,310	2,986	3,060	1,417
Wife in labor force:						
Percent	44	41	49	43	57	57
Median earnings of wife in 1969	$ 3,465	$ 3,932	$ 4,107	$3,167	$2,996	$2,828
Median earnings of husband in 1969	$ 7,732	$ 9,807	$ 8,043	$5,954	$6,264	$6,204
Wife not in labor force:						
Median earnings of husband in 1969	$ 8,299	$11,899	$ 8,665	$6,489	$5,554	$5,715
Mean family income in 1969	$10,731	$15,755	$12,547	$9,147	$9,066	$8,695
1960						
Total	13,343	7,797	4,339	3,006	2,660	972
Wife in labor force:						
Percent	33	30	36	34	43	45
Median earnings of wife in 1959	$ 2,818	$ 3,404	$ 3,307	$2,613	$1,594	$1,647
Median earnings of husband in 1959	$ 6,082	$ 7,456	$ 6,295	$5,079	$3,722	$4,085

Wife not in labor force:						
Median earnings of husband in 1959	$ 6,566	$ 9,309	$ 6,915	$5,186	$3,706	$4,337
Mean family income in 1959	$ 8,236	$12,074	$ 9,615	$6,891	$5,529	$5,984
Percent Increase: 1960–1970						
Total	7	46	—1	—1	15	46
Wife in labor force:						
Percent	33	37	36	26	33	27
Median earnings of wife	23	16	24	21	88	72
Median earnings of husband	27	32	28	17	68	52
Wife not in labor force:						
Median earnings of husband	26	28	25	25	50	32
Mean family income	30	31	31	33	64	45

income level in the middle-income ranges pay about the same share of their income in federal, state, and local taxes. Why, then, would blue-collar workers feel they are suffering disproportionately from the increase in tax burdens? High taxes are not uniquely troublesome for blue-collar workers. They are a problem that affects all American families.

Another limitation of the data is that they are presented as averages, and averages can be misleading. When blue-collar workers are compared with white-collar workers, there is a tendency to assume that we are dealing with homogeneous groups, when in fact the groups are quite diverse. It is entirely possible that middle-income workers in different occupations are more alike in their feelings and attitudes than higher-paid and lower-paid workers within the same occupation group. The available statistics show that *on the average* blue-collar workers had about the same gains as other workers during the past decade. A more refined analysis might show considerable occupational variation around this average, and it could lead to conclusions different from those presented here. The data needed for such an analysis are available from the 1970 Census results, but they had not been published at the time of writing. It is hoped that the very tentative conclusions presented here will be tested on the basis of the more detailed data.

The variation of earnings with age in the various occupations is a very important question that cannot be adequately answered with the data at hand. A comparison of the average earnings in each occupation group in 1959 with the average earnings in 1969 for the appropriate age groups provides a *very rough* measure of the variation of earnings with age for a decade. But such figures can be misleading, particularly for the younger age groups, because they are based on the erroneous assumption that men do not change their marital status or their occupation during a decade.

Perhaps the most we can say at present is that during the past decade, white married men employed in blue-collar jobs have had about the same relative changes in earnings and in several other characteristics as white married men employed in other broad occupations. Their median earnings, *before taxes,* increased 25 percent, about the same as that of white married men in other occupations. This gain, however, was considerably less than that received by nonwhite married men, whose median earnings rose 60 percent overall and 42 percent for blue-collar workers.

In addition to the changes in earnings of married men, there were significant changes in occupational distribution between 1960 and 1970. The number of white married men who were blue-collar workers increased 7 percent, from 13.3 million to 14.3 million, whereas the number of nonwhites employed in these occupations rose 46 percent, from slightly less than 1.0 million to 1.4 million. The increased employment of nonwhite men as blue-collar workers and the reduction in the earnings disparity between whites and nonwhites in this occupation may be a source of special concern to many whites in these occupations.

NOTES

1. Quoted in the *Washington Post,* May 31, 1970.
2. U.S. Bureau of the Census, *Factors Related to High School Graduation and College Attendance, 1967,* ser. P-20, no. 185, July 11, 1969.
3. Louis Harris, "The Currents of Social Change," speech at a meeting sponsored by the Conference Board in New York City, Mar. 24, 1970.
4. Derek C. Bok and John T. Dunlop, *Labor and the American Community,* Simon and Schuster, New York, 1970, pp. 62–63.
5. Ibid., p. 61.
6. *Economic Report of the President,* 1970, p. 214.

4. THE PROBLEMS OF LOWER-MIDDLE-INCOME WORKERS

*by Jerome M. Rosow**

THE PRESSURES THEY FACE

American workers expect that steady, full-time, conscientious job performance will pay off in an acceptable quality of life for themselves and their families. Unfortunately, however, large numbers are getting less than a satisfactory return from the system.

Millions of full-time workers are finding themselves in a three-way squeeze: their paychecks don't stretch across their basic needs; they are unhappy on the job and can't break out; they find their total life pattern unrewarding.

These represent three very basic pressures that could be called the economic squeeze, the workplace squeeze, and the environmental-psychological-sociological squeeze.

These squeezes affect particularly those persons who are members of families whose income is above the poverty line but below what is required to meet moderate family budget needs. Generally, the total family income is between $5,000 and $10,000. This group is a particular slice of the American workingman, an occupational and income cross section rather than a totally representative slice of all workingmen.

* As Assistant Secretary of Labor for Policy, Evaluation and Research, Mr. Rosow directed the preparation of a report on "The Problems of the Blue-Collar Worker" that was submitted to the White House by a Cabinet-level task force. The views expressed in this article do not necessarily represent official government policy.

Millions of workers, of course, work in high-wage firms, enjoying craftsman status and earnings; get their wages supplemented by their wives' wages; receive many fringe benefits; and live in the suburbs. According to a 1968 survey by the University of Michigan Survey Research Center, 63 percent of all workers would strongly recommend their job to a good friend, and 61 percent, given a fresh choice, would pick the same job. While the nation is justifiably proud that millions of workers are in this situation, this does not diminish concern for millions of other steady workers who face these three very basic problems. These workers are the focus of our discussion.

Approximately 20 million families—80 million individuals—have an income that puts them above the poverty line but below what is required to maintain a moderate income budget. Some, who are in this situation only temporarily, can anticipate increased earnings plus the job and living conditions to which they aspire, but most people in this group, given current conditions, are permanently confined to the income, job, and living conditions that now bind them.

It is impossible to estimate the number of workers whose earnings lag behind their family income needs or, indeed, the number who are able to maintain their standard of living by moonlighting or relying on their wives' earnings. Available information indicates that at the age of peak earnings about 45 percent of all male heads of families earn between $5,000 and $10,000. This number includes those whose families are either smaller or larger than the four-person family, whose budget needs are estimated to be about $10,000 at the period of peak need. Moreover, some of the families whose heads have attained this income presumably started out with incomes below the level required to maintain a reasonable standard of living but have been able to progress to it.

Included are relatively young workers in low-wage industries with small children, high expectations, and no way to increase their income, as well as middle-aged workers in relatively high-wage industries whose family budget needs, owing to the higher costs of older children, have outdistanced paycheck increases and opportunity for promotions. Tedious tasks, few fringe benefits, and unsafe conditions often make up the environment of the workplace. Crime, pollution, and mediocre schools often make up the environment of the home neighborhood. The majority are white, but three out of four nonwhites in the labor force are blue-collar workers; this indicates that disproportionately large numbers of nonwhite workers face problems stemming from lower-middle-income or blue-collar status. In 1969, 37 percent of all nonwhite families and 34 percent of all white families were in the $5,000 and $10,000 income category. Of course, on the average, most black families are still not nearly as well off as white families: the median income of all nonwhite families was $6,190, while that of all white families was $9,794. But the point is that both these groups have essentially "working class" economic and social problems related to wage, tax, and government benefit structure for the nonpoor.

The head of the household in the lower-middle-income group is usually a blue-collar worker, but many are in white-collar and service jobs. More are nonunion than union members, more are low-skilled than highly skilled.

These are the people about whom we are concerned: lower-middle-income; looking toward a middle-class life; but achieving at best a low-quality substitute.

The extent to which a worker and his family are affected by the three-way squeeze differs because economic, workplace, and environmental-sociological-psychological factors vary. Most lower-middle-income workers are not at the lower extreme pictured in Chart 1. Neither are most enjoying the benefits of the favorable extreme. The majority fall somewhere in the middle.

THE ECONOMIC SQUEEZE

The economic squeeze is caused essentially by three factors: the wage-budget situation, the tax situation, and, of course, inflation.

The wage-budget squeeze occurs when income fails to keep pace with the increased budget needs of growing families. A 40-year-old worker, for example, is likely to be supporting a wife and two children (one in high school). Ten years earlier he had a wife and one preschool-age child. To maintain the same standard of living for his growing family, he must have increased his income by about 6 percent a year. But his real earnings will have increased during his working life only about as much as average productivity has increased (unless other factors change). Assuming productivity

CHART 1.

THE LOWER-MIDDLE-INCOME WORKER

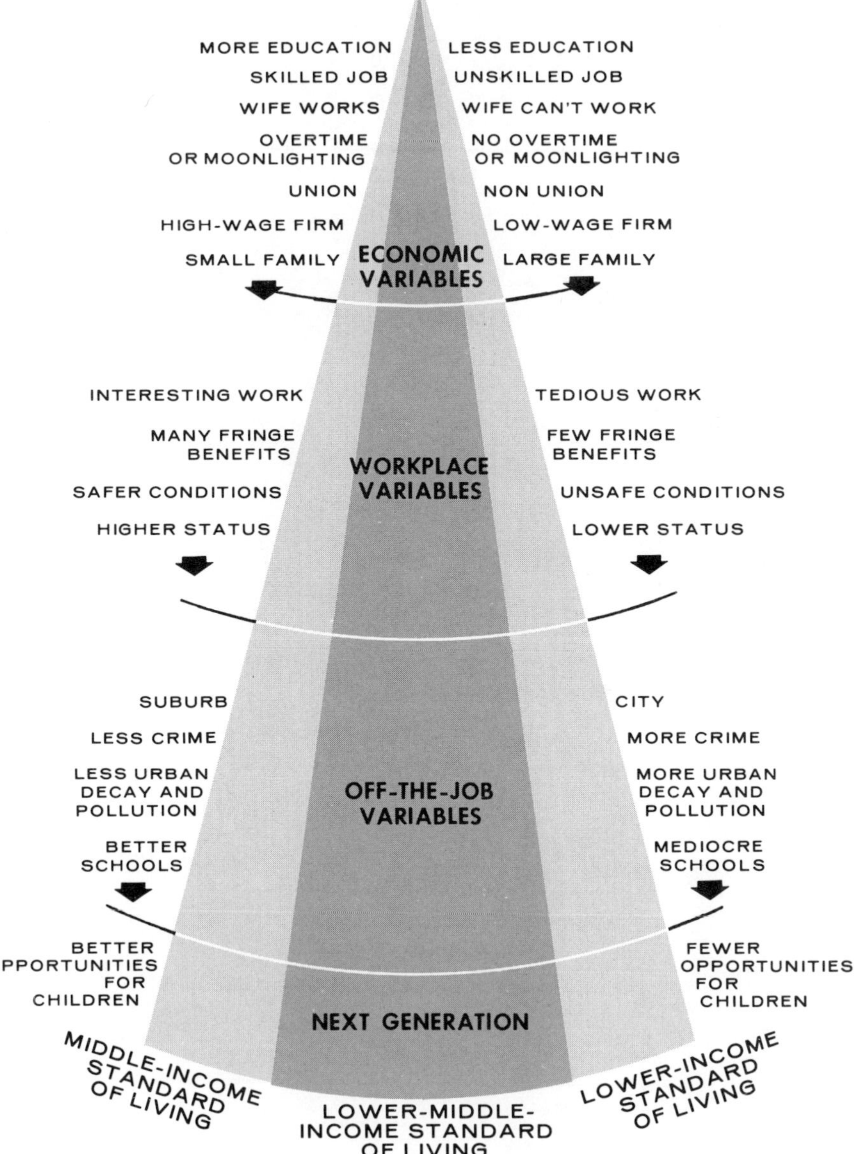

MOST WAGE EARNERS

CHART 2

ECONOMIC SQUEEZE

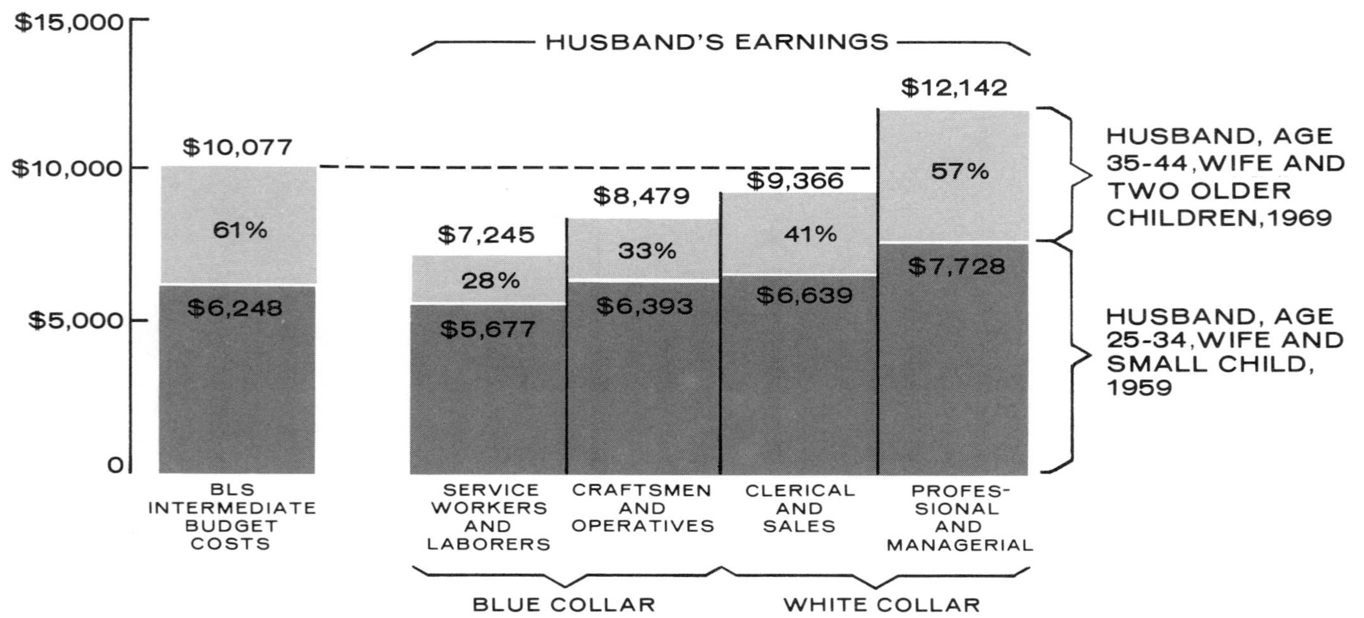

SOURCE: BUREAU OF LABOR STATISTICS; AND CURRENT POPULATION REPORT, "CONSUMER INCOME," BUREAU OF THE CENSUS, SERIES P-60 NO. 73. DOLLARS ARE 1969 DOLLARS.

increases 3 percent a year, he cannot maintain his former standard of living unless he gets promoted or finds way to supplement his earnings.

A moderate family budget, as designated by the Bureau of Labor Statistics (BLS), indicates that this change in family size and composition requires a 61 percent increase in real family income, more than double the 10-year pay increase that workers in all occupational categories (except managerial and professional) can expect from the sum of general wage increases and promotions. This conclusion is drawn from Chart 2, which compares earnings of a 25- to 34-year-old cohort in 1959 with the same cohort 10 years later. It assumes that the later cohort has a standard BLS four-person family with two children, one at least 6 to 15 years old, and that the earlier cohort has a smaller, younger family, with one child under 6. The BLS budget equivalents for these two families were translated into dollar terms. (The chart actually underestimates budget costs, since the average United Sates family has three children, not two.)

The BLS moderate budget figure is generally used to denote a "middle-class" standard of living. About half of this figure is comprised of expenses considered necessary for health and well-being, in terms of food, housing, and other items. The other half of the expenses is based on "typical" spending of families in a certain middle-income bracket (Table 12). Although a moderate budget figure is used in this discussion, it is important to note that even the BLS *low* budget figure requires a 60 percent increase in income to maintain a low living standard with a larger family. The millions of workers below the median earnings figure, who have geared themselves to lower than moderate budgets, increase their earnings at a 3 to 4 percent rate and thus also have difficulty keeping up with their lower budget standard.

The difficulties of the 40-year-old worker may be compounded later in life when one or more children are in their late teens and ready for college, or when the worker must help support aging parents. At that point family budget costs are at their peak, while the worker usually has reached a plateau in his capacity to earn.

After years of dependable job performance, many workers thus find themselves worse off economically than when they started their working lives. This is a sad situation—in stark contrast to the American dream and our world of rising expectations.

TABLE 12

ESTIMATED DISTRIBUTION OF MODERATE BUDGET COSTS FOR A FOUR-PERSON FAMILY,* URBAN UNITED STATES AVERAGES, 1969

	Dollars	*Percent*
Total budget	$10,077	100.0
Total family consumption	7,818	77.6
Food	2,288	22.7
Housing	2,351	23.3
Other†	2,179	21.6
Taxes‡	1,735	17.2
Personal income	1,348	13.4
Social Security	387	3.8
Other costs§	524	5.2

* Family consists of employed husband, age 38, wife not gainfully employed, a girl 8, and a boy 13.
† Includes cost for transportation, clothing, personal care, medical care, reading, recreation, education, tobacco, and alcohol.
‡ Property taxes and sales taxes are included in family consumption.
§ Includes cost for gifts and contributions, life insurance, and occupational expenses.
SOURCE: U.S. Bureau of Labor Statistics.

How Workers Deal with the Economic Squeeze

To beat the economic squeeze and close the gap between income and budget needs, the worker generally tries one or a combination of measures. Some draw on savings or other unearned income; some go into debt; some seek to increase earnings by getting a promotion, changing employers, moonlighting, or having their wives work. The mix varies with the potential in each area and the determination to maintain one's standard of living. These measures yield varying results in easing the economic squeeze.

Few workers have the option of drawing on nonwage income. Only about 10 percent of adjusted gross income reported to the Internal Revenue Service by persons in the $5,000 to $10,000 group was not in the form of wages or salaries in 1968. By contrast, the figure for the $15,000 and over group is 37 percent.

Few workers having savings on which to draw. As a result, many go into debt—a strategy of dubious benefit, despite the theory that it may help to beat inflation. The $5,000 to $10,000 group had the heaviest consumer debt in 1968, according to the University of Michigan Survey Research Center. In the $5,000 to $7,500 class, only two of five families were entirely free of debt, aside from home mortgages. Most debts were fairly substantial: two of five families owed more than $500, and one in ten owed more than $2,000. One of every five families spends 10 to 20 percent of their annual income paying off these debts, and one in seven families needs to allocate more than 20 percent of their income for this purpose.

Next to houses, automobiles represent the largest single debt item of American families. Eighty percent of the families in the $5,000 to $10,000 income group have a car, and more than a quarter of the families in the $7,500 to $10,000 group have more than one. Observers may classify two-car ownership as an economic achievement. However, at a cost of $900 a year per car, they represent a burden. The almost total reorientation of social, leisure, and work life around the automobile and the decline in the quality of public transportation indicate that a car may be more a necessity than a luxury, more a burden than an achievement.

A promising way to beat the budget gap is promotion to a higher-paying job. But a combination of factors limits the opportunity of this group for promotions. Most obviously, upward movement may be restricted by limited education and limited opportunities for educational advancement.

Moreover, mobility patterns in firms and industries are restrictive. A study by E. F. Shelley & Co. of 11 major industries estimated that one-third of all nonsupervisory jobs were dead-end. According to a recent survey, two-thirds of all workers say they never expect a promotion in their present job. Firm-sponsored training is available to only two of five workers, and corporations are often unwilling to advance "older" workers in their forties.

Of course, some of these workers are able to improve their job status by staying in one firm. But the average worker changes six times during his lifetime—often as the only way to advance. In one sense this high mobility is evidence of the problem of the American worker. Job change requires strenuous effort and initiative, and generally the worker receives little, if any, aid in coping with it. He lacks a detailed, free flow of information about other jobs. The Employment Service does not offer complete job listings; private employment agencies, which sometimes offer choice job openings, are often beyond his economic reach.

Moonlighting is one of the more successful techniques for dealing with the economic squeeze. Studies show that moonlighting increases with family size, and is higher for lower-middle-income groups than for those income groups above them: 9 percent for males earning $5,000 to $7,500 compared to 6 percent for those earning $10,000 and over. Adjusting for nonreporting, one can assume that at least 15 percent of lower-income men moonlight as a means of closing the income gap. This means an average of 13 hours extra work per week. Moonlighting, however, is limited by the availability of jobs, the physical stamina of the individual, and the willingness of the worker to give up leisure time and family activities.

An obvious solution to the budget squeeze is for the wife to work, and in the past decade the proportion of working wives has grown from one-third to two-fifths. The highest percentage of working wives is in the $5,000 to $10,000 group. In families in the $5,000 to $7,000 class with preschool-age children, some 36 percent of the wives work to meet the intense economic squeeze.

More than one-half of the lower-middle-income wives who are working have school-age children. Many of those who are not working indicate that lack of child-care facilities is preventing them from entering the job market. Private day-care facilities for preschool children are expensive, and afterschool supervision for school-age children who are too young to be left on their own can be difficult to arrange. Government-subsidized child-care centers, such as those under Head Start and WIN programs and those to be set up with enactment of the Family Assistance Program, are targeted to "the poor" and *not* available to this group. Nor do government tax policies on child care give much relief. At present, families with incomes of $6,900 or above cannot deduct child-care expenses.

Other barriers facing wives who want to work are transportation problems, the limited number of jobs that pay enough to make child-care expenses worthwhile, and the limited availability of part-time jobs. Of course, with their limited educational qualifications, many working wives hold low-paying jobs with little or no status. All too often it is an uphill effort for these women to work.

Taxes

Federal tax reform, enacted in the late 1960s, will provide some relief when fully operative but will not completely bridge the budget gap. In 1973, when the new federal tax law takes full effect, a married couple with two children and total family income of $8,000 will pay $263 less than now. This still leaves the family with a deficit of more than $1,500, assuming the BLS moderate budget, even if prices remain stable until 1973. The tax relief is noteworthy, but unfortunately the tax burden remains for these families, who represent 40 percent of the American population. On the other hand, tax reduction would create other revenue problems for the country as a whole.

Even under the new tax law, deductions for dependents provide more at higher income levels than at lower or moderate levels (the $750 deduction is a tax savings of $125 for the person in the 16 to 17 percent bracket and $300 for the person in the 40 percent bracket). Moreover, the size of the tax deduction has no relation to the age of the children, even though budget costs for older children are more than for younger. This deserves further consideration.

Lower-income workers have increasingly felt the burden of Social Security and state and local taxes. A major part of state and local taxes, now representing about one-third of all taxes collected, take the form of state sales taxes and local property taxes, both of which are largely regressive and strike heavily at the lower-income worker. Forty-five states now have general sales taxes; 10 of these raised their rate in 1969. Thirty-eight states have broadened personal income taxes, and many states assess incomes above $5,000 at rates of 5 to 8 percent. In many states the top tax rate applies over $5,000. These and Social Security taxes have continued to grow in recent years. Workers earning about $7,000 a year have felt the maximum impact of the rise in Social Security taxes.

The Income Picture and the Next Generation

Whether a young person completes secondary school and whether he goes on to college appear to be strongly related to family income. By the late 1960s, about 75 percent of all youths were graduating from high school and about six in ten of the graduates were enrolling in post-secondary schools. These overall figures obscure the differences between youths from lower-middle- and upper-income

CHART 3.

HIGH SCHOOL DROPOUT RATES VARY BY INCOME

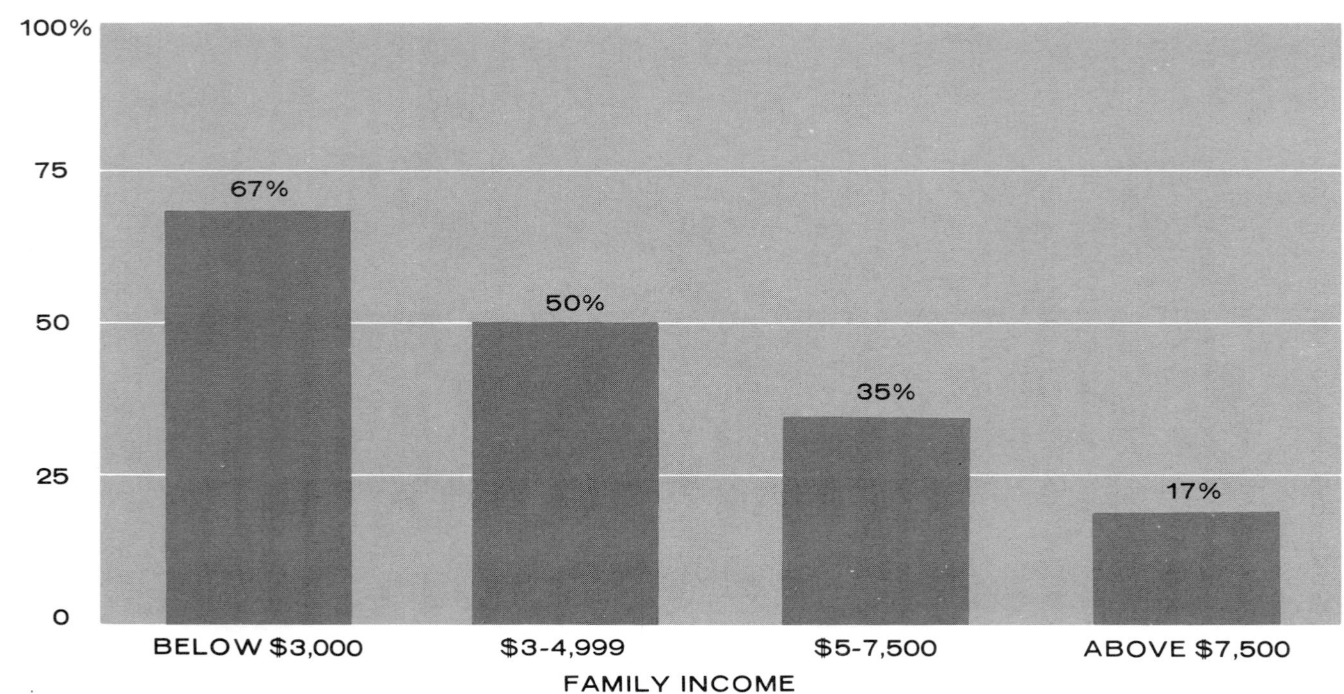

SOURCE: U.S. OFFICE OF EDUCATION, PERCENT OF DROPOUTS AMONG YOUTH 16-21, WHO DID NOT GO ON TO COLLEGE, OCTOBER, 1965.

families. Probably 30 percent of lower-middle-income youth do not finish high school—far more than the percentage of upper-income youth who drop out. Among those 16- to 21-year-old youths who in 1965 did not go on to college, the proportion of dropouts to high school graduates was twice as high among the children of families earning $5,000 to $7,500 as it was for those from families earning more than $7,500 (Chart 3).

The factors, financial and otherwise, that produce dropouts tend to be more pronounced in lower-income groups. In many cases, an inappropriate combination of students and school environment induces the young person to leave school. For example, students whose personal style of culture conflicts with the predominantly middle-class culture of many public schools are more likely to drop out. Typically dropouts come from lower cognitive ability groups, and they include those who tend toward manipulative, manual, or artistic skills rather than toward the verbal and book-oriented. In addition, adult models more often than objective counseling shape the educational and career decisions of young people. Lower-income youth are less likely than higher-income youth to have contact, either at home or in the neighborhood, with college-educated adults.

Although the gap between the proportion of upper-income and lower-middle-income youth who plan to attend college is narrowing, college attendance is still heavily related to family income (Chart 4). Consequently, large numbers of the next generation within these families are not going to "make it," showing as they do strong tendencies to follow in the economic footsteps of their parents.

THE WORKPLACE SQUEEZE

How a worker feels about his workplace depends naturally on his expectations, the nature of his particular job, and the atmosphere of his work environment. The worker in the lower-middle-income bracket is as likely as other workers to have rising expectations about his workplace, but he often works in a world apart from those in higher-income brackets. Typically, the workplace setting of a blue-collar worker in the lower-middle-income bracket contains

CHART 4.

UNEQUAL COLLEGE OPPORTUNITY

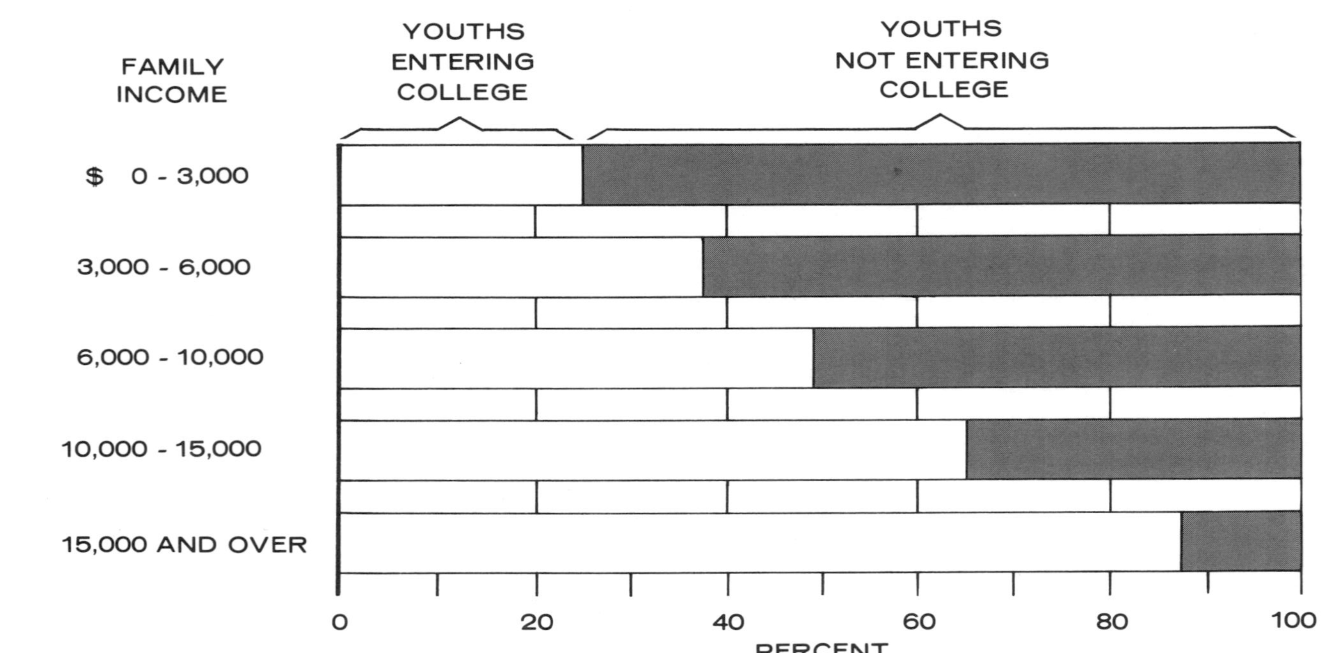

SOURCE: U.S. OFFICE OF EDUCATION

fewer of the elements that make for job satisfaction than the workplace of a white-collar worker, even at the same income level. Typically, the blue-collar worker is lower on the job satisfaction scale than a white-collar worker.

Job challenge, or "interesting work," was rated by workers as the single most important aspect of job satisfaction in the pioneering survey of workingmen, undertaken in 1968 by the University of Michigan Survey Research Center (SRC). Seventy-three percent ranked this "most important" while only 64 percent stressed good pay. Of course, interesting work means different things to different people; but it is generally agreed that repetitive tasks that restrict personal freedom and limit decision making are not interesting. Yet this is the nature of many lower-middle-income jobs.

Studies support what psychiatrists and psychologists have been saying: the amount of personal freedom and autonomy on the job is related to overall mental health. An in-depth study[1] of automobile workers found that mental health varies consistently with the level of jobs held. Thirty percent of the factory workers said they were often worried or upset, compared to 10 percent of white-collar workers. Fifty percent of repetitive production workers, compared to 25 percent of white-collar workers, answered negatively when asked whether "you can do much to make your future what you want it to be." As a *Fortune* article on blue-collar workers pointed out, younger workers—much more than their fathers' generation—expect to participate in the decision-making processes in their job world and often react negatively in terms of job performance and job attendance when they are not satisfied with working conditions.[2] With the sharp rise in labor-force participation of 25- to 34-year-olds during the 1970s we can anticipate growing problems.

Promotion opportunities are strongly related to job satisfaction and mental health, according to the Michigan survey. The survey showed that workers' perceptions of the fairness of the promotions at their place of employment had a sizable and consistent relation to job satisfaction and mental health measures.

The Michigan report did not analyze these workers' responses by income level; it can be assumed, however, that lack of promotion opportunities is a major source of dissatisfaction among workers in the lower-middle-income group. In fact two of three workers indicated that they "never" expect to be promoted from their present jobs. Their occupational future is a cul-de-sac.

Top job-related problems as ranked by workers in terms of frequency and importance in the SRC survey are the following:

Sizable or great problem	Percent of all workers reporting
Health and safety hazards	17.5%
Inadequate fringe benefits	16.7
Inadequate income	16.5
Transportation problems	13.9
Unpleasant physical conditions	12.5
Inconvenient or excessive hours	11.5
Race discrimination (black workers)	11.1

Many more lower-income than upper-income workers cited as major problems inadequate income, inadequate fringe benefits, and unpleasant working conditions. The concern of lower-income workers with income level corresponds with the wage-budget squeeze of this population. Fringe benefits, also a major item of concern among lower-income workers, were broken down in the survey by percentage of work force whose employer provided certain benefits. The survey found that among all workers:

28 percent did not receive medical, surgical, or hospital insurance coverage
38 percent were not covered by a life insurance policy
39 percent were not included in a retirement program
41 percent of the women workers were not entitled to maternity leave with full reemployment rights
61 percent did not have available to them employer-sponsored training

In terms of people, the results of the SRC survey indicate that American workers generally expect that working entitles them to more than a paycheck, that the lack of these extras is a source of worker concern, and that millions of workers—primarily in lower-income categories—are not receiving these benefits.

Unpleasant working conditions are not, of course, always related to income level. But the preponderance of lower-income workers who cited unpleasant working conditions as their major problem is not surprising. A $5,000 to $10,000 worker is much less apt than the man in a higher-income bracket to be encouraged to share his ideas about how a job should be performed. This is so because upper-income personnel have higher skills and individual work assignments which allow better command of their workplace.

Projections indicate that the economy is moving toward more white-collar and service jobs. That such jobs will be available to a larger number of workers and are touted as more "challenging" than blue-collar jobs may add to the dissatisfaction of those who feel locked out of jobs that include these factors.

For black workers, a feeling of discrimination adds to the workplace squeeze. Of the 155 black workers included in the Michigan survey, 17.4 percent reported some form of job discrimination, mainly in promotions or assignments; and of this group, about two-thirds indicated that this was a sizable or severe problem. The survey results probably understate the total extent of job-discrimination feeling among black workers because of the exclusion of the unemployed. Also, discrimination on the job often is not perceived where workers are in fact completely segregated along racial lines, e.g., in all-black work crews.

ENVIRONMENTAL-PSYCHOLOGICAL-SOCIOLOGICAL SQUEEZE

Workers in the lower-middle-income bracket live intimately with the major environmental problems of the nation. These conditions combine with sociological and personal factors to produce an environmental-psychological-sociological squeeze.

Those who live in the suburbs may get some relief from the tension of a less than satisfactory job when they go home to well-manicured lawns and quiet patios. But millions of lower-middle-income workers, more blue- than white-collar, still live in the city. To many, going home merely means substituting one set of problems for another. Off-the-job hours are likely to be spent in neighborhoods that show signs of urban decay and reduced city services, where the sense of community is sometimes eroded by freeways and urban renewal, and where air and noise pollution from traffic and industry are greater than in the suburbs. This is hardly the place to relax and get away from job frustrations.

Home ownership, part of the stereotyped payoff for steady, hard work, is less and less within the reach of workers with these incomes. According to the Department of Housing and Urban Development, the average single-family house now costs $27,000 and requires an annual income of $14,000 to buy and maintain.

Crime and fear of crime hit hard at millions of workers, both black and white, who live in the center or outer ring of the city. They create legitimate psychological pressures and inhibit nighttime excursions to movies or social events that might ease internal tensions. According to the report of the National Commission on the Causes and Prevention of Violence, the violent-crime rate increased 100 percent between 1958 and 1968. Black workers and their families suffer the effects of crime almost three times as often as whites.

A steady worker whose paycheck does not reach far enough, whose work life is uninspiring, and whose home environment is both drab and frightening may understandably view with some resentment the money and effort devoted to helping someone else out of a squeeze.

Some of the resentment is unrealistic because it is based on exaggerated and incorrect notions of the amount of aid given to the poor. However, some resentment is understandable. Workers with wages just a notch above welfare payments, who live in minimum housing or need training to increase the size of their paychecks, are excluded from government programs that subsidize social benefits. Parents of children attending mediocre schools see their tax dollars providing extra help to ghetto schools attended by someone else's child. Parents whose sons do not receive special attention from the prestige colleges read that such colleges are making special efforts to recruit and give financial aid to black students, no better prepared for entrance to such schools than their own children.

Despite this resentment, job integration, along with integration in public places, has been successful—more successful than efforts in housing or schools. The substantial economic and job gains by minority groups in the last five years have been generally unaccompanied by outbreaks of violence in offices and plants. By contrast, integration of schools and neighborhoods has met much greater resistance. This augurs well for continued efforts to expand economic job opportunity for minorities as one of the most meaningful integration measures.

Those newly arrived at any situation are likely to feel insecure: by immigrants or sons of immigrants, racial progress is sometimes seen as a threat; blacks just entering middle-class economic status without extra help may resent antipoverty efforts.

Those whose jobs are ignored or even slighted by society also may feel insecure: our culture dramatizes diploma-accredited professional experts in the field of science and technology but neglects—or sometimes stigmatizes—the millions of skilled and unskilled workers who transform the ideas of scientists and the plans of engineers into tangible goods and services. Many skilled blue-collar jobs, such as auto mechanics, demand more knowledge and are more interesting than some white-collar jobs; yet schools and the media pass along relatively little information that would draw young people to these fields.

The result is that young people look upon many jobs in the $5,000 to $10,000 bracket as a last resort; those already in these jobs press for higher wages, motivated by psychological as well as economic needs, or hope to find for themselves or for their children another way to make a living. Fathers hesitate to describe their work to their own sons and are often ashamed to hold themselves as models to their own children. Also resulting are chronic and inflationary shortages and exacerbation of racial friction when black youth refuse to take "dirty" blue-collar jobs (although they may be well-paying) offered by a "white society."

Limited education often reduces a worker's leverage to command a paycheck that permits him to buy a house outside areas of high crime and pollution or to change to a job that society applauds. There is also evidence that educational limitations make it difficult to surmount ethnic viewpoints and prejudices. Educational level plays a role in how objectively and constructively one tries to deal with problems as complex and interwoven as those faced by the $5,000 to $10,000 income group. How can we expect these people, living on the razor's edge of life, to be full of understanding and sympathy for minorities or the poor?

[Mr. Rosow's proposed program for the lower-middle-income worker is presented in Chapter 14.]

NOTES

1. Arthur Kornhauser, *Mental Health of the Industrial Worker,* Wiley, New York, 1965.
2. Judson Gooding, "Blue-Collar Blues on the Assembly Line," *Fortune,* July 1970.

« PART TWO »

Attitudes and Institutions

Because aggregate economic data and overall averages or medians are a poor gauge of the working class's "real" feelings, an examination of the way they feel deep down in their hearts must rely upon opinion surveys. Such studies can explore specific group attitudes and can be secured with a minimal time lag. Nonetheless, attitude surveys are not always a dependable basis for social theories and programs. Survey responses can be easily misleading because the views of respondents may be fickle, and also because both questions and answers normally leave a great deal to interpretation and, therefore, misinterpretation.

The chapters by Howard Reiter and Richard Hamilton offer ample proof of the difficulties of relying upon attitudes surveys. Using different surveys of essentially the same population, the two analysts discover different sets of "facts" about the attitudes of the groups surveyed and, not surprisingly, reach different conclusions about the objective data.

Given this caveat concerning the use of attitudinal survey data, Reiter and Hamilton also display wide areas of agreement. Although they differ on details, both conclude that the presumed racism, bigotry, and conservatism of the blue-collar worker is primarily a figment of the imagination of certain commentators and is not reflected in the views expressed by their carefully selected samples of blue-collar workers. Despite their general agreement about the mood of America's manual workers, Reiter and Hamilton use different crystal balls to gaze into the future and offer different sets of prescriptions to alleviate working-class ailments.

The extent of a given group's alienation depends very largely upon its perception of the power that the members have in society, and the extent to which institutional arrangements protect their rights and advance their aspirations. Perhaps the most important institution serving blue-collar workers is the trade-union movement. Relying on his conversations with union members, Stanley Ruttenberg concludes that unions have well served the blue-collar worker and are indeed the main link between workers and the mainstream of American economic and social life. Ruttenberg maintains that the unions have helped channel blue-collar workers into this mainstream. Collective bargaining, according to this view, not only has improved the economic lot of its members but also has given them a sense of power and "belonging."

While sharing Ruttenberg's enthusiasm for the positive contributions of unions, Ray Marshall focuses on an area of union conflict; the result is that the shining armor of unions comes out somewhat tarnished. A major function of unions has been to control jobs. Whites, who have traditionally held the more desired of these jobs, are understandably reluctant to share their hard-won gains with blacks who are demanding an ever-larger share of all jobs controlled by unions. Marshall favors equality of blacks and whites in American life, including trade unions, and he would also provide institutional arrangements to help black workers to qualify and compete effectively for preferred jobs; but he shares with many trade unionists their opposition to preferential treatment for blacks to compensate for past discrimination, placing them in jobs for which they do not qualify. Marshall argues that this would perpetuate inequality and would not be, in the long run, the most effective means of serving black workers.

Other contributors do not share the enthusiasm of Ruttenberg and Marshall for the achievements of trade unions. They bemoan the fact that unions have become defenders of the status quo in society, having lost the idealistic fervor which characterized them in the 1930s. Critics insist that the labor movement is chiefly concerned with furthering the interests of its own members and displays inadequate interest in societal goals. Friends of the labor movement, even when agreeing with the attacks, question why unions should act differently from other interest groups in society and why union leaders should relinquish their own values in favor of opposing views. For example, no matter how critical one may be about George Meany's ardent support of the war in Vietnam, no evidence has been presented that the majority of AFL-CIO membership does not support his views.

What is most important in the present context is that unions have admittedly served their membership well, though they may have limited opportunities for nonmembers, particularly blacks.

Possibly the role of unions is not as pervasive as Ruttenberg suggests. In Lee Rainwater's description of working-class life-styles, for example, unions do not seem to play an important role. Indeed, Rainwater's analysis seems to attach little significance to the views of other contributors that blue-collar workers have experienced cataclysmic changes, and he rejects the claim that the rising standard of living of American workers has obliterated many of the class distinctions between blue-collar workers and the lower middle class. He maintains that while the working class has been changing, lower-middle-class life-styles also changed and class distinctions have, therefore, not been altered. Rainwater's conclusions also indicate that the entry into the labor force of an increasing number of blue-collar wives has affected very little the life-style of the American working class. If Rainwater's conclusions are correct, concern about the changing political loyalties of the American working class may be unwarranted.

S. M. Miller is not as sanguine as Rainwater about the distinctiveness of the American working class. Miller sees great diversity in the American working class, ranging from fat cats, hardly distinguishable from middle-class Americans, to those who are counted among the working poor. Unlike Rainwater, Miller is concerned that this diverse and mercurial working class, or at least large segments of it, might fall prey to the blandishments of right-wing politicians and thus destroy the political coalition established by F.D.R. Miller does not say why such development would be disastrous to the American working class or for that matter why the breaking up of Roosevelt's coalition should be avoided. He takes it on faith not only that the F.D.R. coalition should be buttressed and strengthened but also that the interests of the American working class depend upon the continuation of the old coalition which would dedicate itself, possibly with some new allies, to the transformation of American society.

5. BLUE-COLLAR WORKERS AND THE FUTURE OF AMERICAN POLITICS

*by Howard L. Reiter**

REALIGNMENT OR RETRENCHMENT

Early in August 1970 a Republican Secretary of Labor told a partisan audience, "I find these working people are squarely behind the Administration on two really big things—first, scaling down the war, and second, taking a firm approach to crime and unrest at home." He went on to say that, against the GOP, "They've really got only one big issue—the economy."[1]

Several days later, the president of the AFL-CIO told a group of reporters that "our people are looking less to the Democrats . . . in so far as these so-called liberals or new lefts, or whatever you want to call them, have taken over the Democratic Party." He then noted "that the law and order issue affects our people the same as it does the most conservative people in the country. But I don't say that that is the big issue. I still think that the biggest issue with our people is the economic issue."[2]

Here, summarized by two men who would traditionally be expected to stand poles apart on every issue, is the conventional wisdom of blue-collar politics in the 1970s. Almost before the ink was dry on President Nixon's inaugural address, Kevin Phillips, a campaign aide, produced a book arguing that the white working class would soon desert the Democratic party.[3] Subsequent works

*I am indebted to William Schneider of the Harvard University Government Department Data Center for technical advice and to Miss Laura Rosen for editorial assistance.

by Samuel Lubell[4] and by Richard M. Scammon and Ben J. Wattenberg,[5] while taking exception to Phillips's confidence in the certainty of Republican gains, affirmed that the Democrats were indeed in danger of losing many voters over "law and order" issues.

On the other hand, there are those who believe, with Michael Harrington, that "if the peace movement could overcome some of its middle-class prejudices about unions . . . we would have a very good chance to start rebuilding a majority coalition during the next several months."[6]

Who is right? Is the workingman a bigoted war hawk, eager to forget the legacy of F.D.R., or have we been underestimating the depths of his liberalism? Is the wave of the future for the blue-collar worker the goals of Spiro Agnew or the dream of Robert Kennedy?

There is only one sure way to cut through the morass of generalizations and guesses about the political instincts of blue-collar America, and that is to look at national survey data. Only in this way can we ascertain, not how George Meany or someone's hypothetical machinist or construction worker thinks, but how the mass of American blue-collar workers actually appraise the political situation.

The survey data that will be used here are those of the Survey Research Center at the University of Michigan in Ann Arbor.[7] The SRC polls a nationwide sample every two years, and the literally hundreds of questions asked of each respondent provide the opportunity to analyze many issues in depth. We will be looking at their most recent survey as of this writing, taken in the autumn of 1968.

In this chapter, we are concerned with several major questions pertaining to the political views of blue-collar workers. These are:

(1) What does the blue-collar worker think about traditional bread-and-butter issues like Social Security and federal aid to education? Is the appeal of liberal Democrats as strong as it once was?

(2) What does the blue-collar worker think about so-called law-and-order issues? Does he advocate a hard-line, authoritarian approach to society's problems? Is the white worker a racist, or is he willing to give black people an equal role to play in American life?

(3) What does the blue-collar worker think about the war in Vietnam? Is he willing to escalate in order to win, or does he want to bring the soldiers home without a military victory?

(4) Is the blue-collar worker alienated from our political system? Does he trust the government and see it as receptive to his ideas and solicitous of his needs?

(5) Finally, what chance is there of the blue-collar worker deserting the Democrats and becoming a Republican?

Because the category "blue-collar worker" is so broad, we are limiting it in this study to the lower-middle-income members of the white race making an annual income from $4,000 to $8,000 in 1968. The lower-income group was chosen because of the well-known fact that as Americans earn more, they tend to become more conservative on many bread-and-butter issues, and this is often reflected in a switch to the Republican party. If we discover that blue-collar workers are turning Republican, but only because they earn more, this will hardly be a sign of fundamental political change; after all, if their income declines next year, they may revert to their former Democratic affiliation. But if we discover that even lower-income blue-collar workers are becoming conservative and Republican, this means that income is no longer a major determinant of one's party affiliation. And because so much of our investigation will be concerned with racial questions, we are limiting the investigation to blue-collar whites.

This group is the basis of much of the stereotyping of blue-collar workers that has been written for the last couple of years. Lower-middle-income blue-collar whites are the backbone of the backlash, we are told, the most antiblack, anti-intellectual, antipeacenik element of the population. Fortressed in their decaying city tenements and modest suburban developments, they fear and hate the encroaching blacks who occupy the next lower rung on the social ladder.

Because "lower-middle-income blue-collar workers of the white race" is such an awkward expression, we will call them simply the "Target Group." But there is an analytical problem with our Target Group, and that is that they are *both* blue-collar *and* lower-middle-income. If we discover, for example, that the Target Group is racist, is it because lower-middle-income groups are racist, or because *blue-collar* lower-middle-income groups are racist?

The only way to find out is to compare the Target Group with people who make the same income but are not blue-collar workers. Then, if we find that both groups are equally racist, we know that such racism is a lower-middle-income phenomenon. But if, on the other hand, the blue-collar group is more racist than the other lower-middle-income group, then it is likely that the racism is a blue-collar phenomenon.

And so we are going to look also at white workers who earn an annual family income of from $4,000 to $8,000 but are employed in occupations other than blue-collar. It is tempting to call this group "white-collar," but because it includes some service workers, farmers, and fishermen in addition to white-collar workers, we will call this group the "Equivalent Income Group." Furthermore, we will sometimes be comparing both these lower-middle-income groups with the population at large. This will show whether, for example, their degree of racism is part of a national consensus.[8] And finally, in some cases we will look back to the SRC data of 1960, to see whether there have been any significant changes in the attitudes of these groups since that time. But because dollar incomes were generally lower in 1960 than in 1968, we must change our income definition of the lower middle class. In 1960, our Target and Equivalent Income Groups earned a family income of from $3,000 to $6,000. In both years, the Target Group earned more than the lowest quarter of the population and less than the highest 40 percent.

To study the Target Group is to answer some questions not merely about one segment of the American people, for the answers to some profound questions about the future of American politics depend to a great extent on what blue-collar workers do.

(1) It is a fact that every major governing coalition in American history—the Jeffersonians, the Jacksonians, the Republicans from the Civil War until the Great Depression, and the Democrats since then—has made strong appeals to the urban proletariat. This was most obvious in 1896, when the workers were lured to the Republicans' "full dinner pail" for a generation, and in 1932, when they swung to the Democrats' New Deal for another generation. And most analysts today, when predicting the American political future, put the working class squarely in the majority of whatever coalition is on top. If they go Republican, Phillips may well get his lasting Republican majority.

(2) Also, any major revolution in American politics, right or left, is likely to include blue-collar workers in its vanguard. For if we face a fascist revolt, it is likely to be a combination of nationalism and economic populism, similar to the George Wallace movement (or what Seymour Martin Lipset terms "Peronism"),[9] with a strong working-class appeal. Or, if our future is to be Red, and to adhere to Marxist orthodoxy, the proletariat will lead it.

By studying blue-collar politics, then, we may learn a great deal about the future of American politics nationally.

NEW DEAL ISSUES

Most of the prophets of political change allege that the coalitions which characterized the New Deal and Fair Deal periods are breaking up. In particular, they say, the workingman is no longer vitally interested in the kinds of causes that provided the cement for the Democratic majority—including Social Security, aid to education, the farm subsidy program, union power, and Medicare.

How well are these New Deal and post-New Deal issues mobilizing the concern of the worker? Before investigating this question, it is important to sketch briefly some relevant features of the Target Group: its class consciousness, its union membership, its employment status, and its home ownership patterns.

First, it should be noted that class consciousness is alive and well in America. More than three of four workers in the Target Group were willing to call themselves "working-class," as opposed to less than half the Equivalent Income Group and only a little more than half of the general population. The self-identification of the Equivalent Income Group with the middle class, even though they earn no more than the Target Group, will prove relevant later on. Furthermore, while 17 percent of the Equivalent Income Group has shifted from "working class" to "middle class" identification since 1960, there has been very little change in the Target Group.

As one might expect, more than 40 percent of the Target Group belong to unions, while less than 10 percent of the Equivalent Income Group do (and about one-seventh of the whole population).

But other economically relevant facts wash out differences between the Target and Equivalent Income Groups. Four of every five in both groups were employed when the poll was taken in late

1968, and about three of five owned their own homes. This last figure is equal to the national average, but it does not necessarily mean a decent living standard: to rent an apartment on Manhattan's Park Avenue may require more money than owning a house elsewhere. But this high rate of home ownership may mean that workers are adopting middle-class values (even when they do not identify with the middle class) as they own property.

Certainly this economically below-average group was not impressed with the importance of economic issues; only 11 percent of the Target Group referred first to an economic issue when asked, "What do you personally feel are the most important problems the government in Washington should try to take care of?" This should not be too surprising, since the economy was doing relatively well in 1968 and was not a dominant campaign issue, but it is interesting that the Target Group is somewhat less interested in these issues than the rest of the population is: 19 percent of the total population referred to an economic issue as the most important problem for the federal government. In contrast, 10 years ago the Target Group was considerably *more* interested in economic issues than the rest of the population was.

In their views on economic issues, lower-middle-class blue-collar whites either do not differ from the rest of the population or else are a bit more *conservative* on most important questions relevant to New Deal issues (Table 13). On only one issue does the Target Group stand out as more "liberal": it is more likely to look with favor on labor unions, which is hardly surprising, given the large number of Target Group union members. Note also in Table 13 that the only issue on which the Target Group is willing to give a liberal verdict is medical care. The low support for federal aid to education may be reflective of the fact that only 28 percent of the Target Group have children in public schools, and also of the extent to which the issue suggests school integration to many parents.

As for economic mobility, 16 percent of the Target Group felt that their families' financial situation had worsened from 1960 to 1968, while a majority (56 percent) saw no change at all. Their economic prognosis, both for their own families and for the economy, tended to be a bit less optimistic than other groups', although on the whole no group was overwhelmingly pessimistic. It seems possible that a person's economic forecast might affect his views on

TABLE 13
VIEWS ON NEW DEAL ISSUES

	Target Group	*Equivalent Income Group*	*Total population*
Federal aid to education:			
In favor	23%	27%	31%
Opposed	58	51	46
Other responses	19	22	23
Federal government's power			
Too powerful	43	47	38
Not too powerful	27	24	32
Other responses	30	29	30
Federal medical assistance			
In favor	53	42	54
Opposed	22	35	25
Other responses	25	23	21
Federal job and income security			
In favor	32	21	34
Opposed	55	51	44
Other responses	13	27	22
Attitude toward big business			
Favorable	52	42	48
Neutral	31	34	34
Unfavorable	15	23	15
Other responses	3	1	3
Attitude toward labor unions			
Favorable	55	34	45
Neutral	27	32	30
Unfavorable	14	34	22
Other responses	4	1	3

issues; for example, someone who thinks that times will get worse may be more likely to favor a guaranteed income. Our data, however, show that within the Target Group there was no relation between a person's sense of economic mobility and his views on the issues presented in Table 13.

Finally, we might ask what meaning the standard political terms "liberal" and "conservative" have for workers. Each respondent was asked to rate liberals and conservatives on a scale from 0 to 100. Most of the Target Group chose a "neutral" score of 50 in both cases, signifying mixed feelings, neutrality, or lack of knowledge of what "liberal" and "conservative" mean. But those who committed themselves were more likely to give liberals an unfavorable rating, while the population at large gave them a slight edge on the favorable side. As for the conservatives, they received many more favorable than unfavorable scores from both the Target Group and the population at large. We may conclude that among workingmen liberals are hardly popular figures. (The Equivalent Income Group is more favorable than the Target Group to *both* liberals and conservatives.)

We must conclude that lower-middle-income blue-collar whites were rather conservative on New Deal bread-and-butter issues in 1968. But as the economic situation has deteriorated in many parts of the country, with continuing inflation, it would not be surprising to see the blue-collar worker take renewed interest in economic issues, as he did in 1960, and from a liberal point of view. And if this is the case, it would be an ominous sign for Republicans, for GOP fortunes fluctuate with the employment picture. But if the blue-collar worker continues to relegate economic concerns to the back burner, the Democrats will have to court him on other issues.

LAW-AND-ORDER ISSUES

When political analysts cite the declining interest of the blue-collar worker in bread-and-butter issues, they usually go on to say that these issues are being replaced by a cluster of issues known as "law and order"—such as race relations, crime, dissent, patriotism, and permissiveness. A third of all the groups under scrutiny here cited such an issue as the nation's most important in 1968; in 1960, practically no one did. Some liberals have claimed that "law and order" is a "code word for racism," and so we shall begin by looking at the blue-collar worker's attitudes toward black people, and then go on to his views on authority and dissent.

The Kerner Commission set the tone for apocalyptic statements on race relations in America with its oft-quoted statement that "Our Nation is moving toward two societies, one black, one white—separate and unequal."[10] Andrew Hacker claims that "white America does not want to deploy its resources toward redeeming the black citizenry."[11] About the least pessimistic account is Samuel Lubell's:

> In all my interviewing since 1950, I have found that the main concern of most white voters has never been racial justice. Always the balance of sentiment has swung to the course of action that seemed to them to offer the best prospect for racial peace.[12]

Whatever the analysis, the usual claim is that blue-collar whites are among the least liberal of their race when the subject is racial. This is often attributed to the fact that as blacks move into Northern cities, out of the ghettos, and finally out of the cities, they come into contact first with lower-income blue-collar whites. More than one politician has made the cry that this group, and not the "limousine liberals," has felt the brunt of integration.

But our data show that our Target Group is *not* more likely than other white Americans to live in an integrated environment or send their children to integrated schools. By all measurements the Target Group almost exactly parallels all other whites in their degree of exposure to black people. The same proportions of all groups reported all-white neighbors, local schools, coworkers, fellow shoppers, and friends. The notion of a lower-class white cadre manning the bastions of white society against black encroachment is absolutely unsubstantiated by these respondents' own perceptions.

In order to analyze the Target Group's attitudes on racial issues, we should first see what they think about black people in general. Table 14 shows that they are, on the whole, favorable toward Negroes in the abstract, although somewhat less so than other whites. They are more inclined than other whites to think that Negroes have not made much progress in recent years, but half of them think that Negroes have made a lot of progress. More than other whites, they think that civil rights leaders have been moving too fast.

Civil rights advocates may be disheartened by the views of these groups about some of the important racial issues of the day (Table 15). On most issues, whites are opposed to federal activity to ensure equal rights for the black man. On only two issues do liberals far outnumber conservatives in the Target Group: on equal accommodations and open housing. Federal action to ensure equal accommodations does not have the support of more than half of any group, and the results may have been biased by the fact that the interviewers prefaced the question by noting that Congress had already

TABLE 14
HOW WHITES VIEW BLACK PEOPLE IN GENERAL

	Target Group	*Equivalent Income Group*	*All whites*
Attitude toward Negroes			
Favorable	52%	60%	57%
Neutral	33	29	29
Unfavorable	12	10	11
Other responses	4	1	3
"How much real change do you think there has been in the position of the Negro in the past few years?"			
A lot	50%	54%	49%
Some	27	34	35
Not much at all	22	10	15
Other responses	2	2	2
"Do you think that civil rights leaders are trying to push too fast, are going too slowly, or are they moving about the right speed?"			
Too fast	76%	72%	67%
About right	18	18	24
Too slowly	1	7	4
Other responses	5	3	5

passed such a bill. Respondents may have been more willing to endorse a *fait accompli,* sanctioned by Congress, than some of the other issues. The open-housing results must be viewed with some care, also because respondents were asked how strongly they felt about the issue. Less than half of those in the Target Group who favored open housing felt strongly about it, while nearly all the opponents did so. Opponents of open housing seem far more likely to take action on the issue than proponents; certainly the experience of many communities suggests that this is the case.

But when asked about desegregation in general, the greatest number of whites took a middle course. This suggests that Lubell may have hit the nail on the head when he indicated that whites tend to be neither very segregationist nor very integrationist, but just interested in peace. Also note that only on the housing and desegregation issues is the Target Group noticeably less favorable to black aspirations than other whites.

Frequently stereotypes of the blue-collar racist include "ethnicity," a euphemism for Catholic nationality groups. Indeed, one recent study of Connecticut city dwellers shows quite marked differences between members of various ethnic groups,[13] and so we compared Target Group Protestants with Catholics on the issues in Table 15. (There was only one Jew in the Target Group.) On the issues of desegregation and school integration, the Catholics turned out to be *more liberal,* and there were few differences on the other issues. (Practically none of the Catholics had children enrolled in parochial schools, and so their greater preference for school integration cannot be explained away by that line of reasoning.) Differences between the two religious groups were significantly reduced, however, when Southerners were removed from the sample; apparently the religious differences were the result of the fact that many more Protestants than Catholics were from the South.

To measure blue-collar attitudes toward the other aspect of law-and-order issues, authority and dissent, we turn to several questions

TABLE 15
VIEWS OF WHITES ON RACIAL ISSUES

	Target Group	*Equivalent Income Group*	*All whites*
Federal equal-employment efforts			
In favor	31%	30%	34%
Against	51	52	46
Other responses	17	18	20
Federal school-integration efforts			
In favor	31	38	34
Against	53	42	47
Other responses	16	21	20
Federal equal-accommodations efforts			
In favor	48	47	50
Against	38	40	35
Other responses	14	14	15
Open housing			
In favor	54	63	66
Against	31	27	23
Other responses	15	10	11
Desegregation			
In favor	22	32	33
In between	53	46	47
Against	19	16	16
Other responses	6	6	5

relating to authority figures in society and various acts of protest and civil disobedience. These questions were not asked in the context of any particular issue, such as civil rights or the war in Vietnam. The first two, measuring attitudes toward policemen and the military, employed the same 0-to-100 scale used to measure attitudes toward groups discussed earlier—big business, labor unions, liberals, conservatives, and Negroes. The Target Group tends to be more respectful of authority and less tolerant of protest than the Equivalent Income Group or the whole population. There were practically no differences between men's and women's attitudes on these questions in the Target Group (Table 16).

These findings are no proof of "working-class authoritarianism."

TABLE 16
VIEWS ON AUTHORITY AND PROTEST

	Target Group	*Equivalent Income Group*	*Total population*
Attitude toward policemen			
Favorable	86%	88%	83%
Neutral	10	8	10
Unfavorable	1	3	4
Other responses	4	1	4
Attitude toward the military			
Favorable	81	72	76
Neutral	12	16	14
Unfavorable	3	11	7
Other responses	4	1	3
Protest meetings or marches, approved by local authorities			
Approve	8	19	19
Depends	22	15	25
Disapprove	62	62	48
Other responses	8	4	8
Refusing to obey a law considered unjust			
Approve	8	17	15
Depends	25	25	21
Disapprove	61	53	55
Other responses	7	4	10
Obstructing the government as a last resort			
Approve	3	5	8
Depends	8	19	17
Disapprove	83	70	65
Other responses	7	7	10

Our data suggest that lower-middle-class blue-collar whites seem more respectful of established authority and less tolerant of protest and civil disobedience than other groups—even other whites in the same income bracket.

Why this greater respect for authority in the blue-collar group? One explanation might be that they are far less educated than other groups: 38 percent graduated from high school, as opposed to 74 percent of the Equivalent Income Group and 58 percent of the general population. But even when we compare how respondents of different educational levels answered the questions, education seems to explain the difference between the Target and Equivalent Income Groups only on the question about protest meetings or marches. About 40 percent of high school graduates, regardless of occupation, approved of them, but only 25 percent of those who never completed high school did.

Within the Target Group, there were no important differences between those optimistic and those pessimistic about the state of the economy or their family fortune; nor were there any important differences between Catholics and Protestants.

We can conclude by stating that while white Americans tend to be less than ardent civil rights advocates, and Americans in general strongly support authority figures and oppose protesters, lower-middle-income blue-collar whites are somewhat more conservative than other groups. Nothing we have examined—income level, race, religion, education, or economic outlook—other than their blue-collar occupations explains this rightward trend. But it is also clear that, on these issues, blue-collar America is not far from the mainstream.

THE WAR

Analyzing public opinion about the war in Southeast Asia is like trying to carry on a conversation on a crowded city street with horns blaring, jackhammers screaming, and pedestrians shouting to each other. So many issues are involved that it is difficult to isolate the one or two most revealing.

For example, does a person who says, "I support the President," do so because he likes the President's policy, or because he believes that he has a duty to support the President—any President—in time of war? And if the same person says, "I oppose antiwar protesters," is it because he supports the war, or because he dislikes hippies and thinks that all protesters are hippies? And perhaps the most baffling response of all is "Either escalate all the way or pull out now; just get the war over with." What are we to make of *this* answer? Hawk or dove?

The fact that our poll data are from 1968, when President Johnson was still in office and before Vietnamization and the Cambodian invasion of 1970, may strike some readers as a weakness. But if we are careful, we can probe the overriding question: whether our Target Group is more inclined toward a military solution or negotiation. This question is not necessarily tied to patriotism, party loyalty, or dissent.

The Target Group then did and probably still does take an active interest in developments in Vietnam. About 40 percent of them, like 40 percent of the Equivalent Income Group and 40 percent of the total population, first mentioned the war in response to the question, "What do you personally feel are the most important problems the government in Washington should try to take care of?" It should be noted that no other single response came close to that number. In addition, 63 percent of the Target Group said that they had paid "a good deal" of attention to what was going on in Vietnam, a slightly higher proportion than either the Equivalent Income Group or the total population. Less than 6 percent said they were paying "not much" attention.

On the war, the Target Group is apparently more hawkish than the rest of the population. In response to the question, "Which of the following do you think we should do now in Vietnam?" nearly half—48 percent—of them chose the alternative, "Take a stronger stand, even if it means invading North Vietnam." Only 32 percent of the general population and 41 percent of the Equivalent Income Group took this stand. And on a scale with "immediate withdrawal" at one end and "complete military victory" at the other, 51 percent of the Target Group put themselves on the hawkish side of the scale, in contrast with 38 percent of the Equivalent Income Group and 35 percent of the total population.

This hawkishness carries over into other foreign policy fields as well. The Target Group was more likely than other groups to oppose talks with Communist leaders, to oppose trade with Communist nations, to oppose admitting Communist China into the United Nations, and to favor getting the Communist government out of Cuba. Are we then to conclude that these blue-collar workers are hawkish *because* they are blue-collar?

Despite the popular image of the militaristic hard hat, many public-opinion polls indicate that manual workers and lower-income groups *in general* are more dovish than the rest of the population. But after a very intensive study of public attitudes toward the Vietnam war, a team of political scientists concluded in 1967:

> Variables of social status—occupation, income, or education—do not relate to policy preferences on the Vietnamese war. . . . Two differences among social groups do stand out, however. One is the difference between men and women, with women more in favor of de-escalation; and the other between whites and Negroes with the Negroes more in favor of de-escalation.[14]

There is an easy way to test this conclusion on our own data, and that is to isolate the male members of our Target and Equivalent Income Groups (all are of the white race) and all male whites in the population at large. The result is that the differences among the groups are drastically reduced when sex and race are "held constant" by eliminating females and nonwhites.

Now that we have confirmed that sex and race are the main determinants of attitudes toward the war, we can see some of the reasons behind some of our earlier findings: (1) Manual workers and low-income groups are more dovish than the rest of the population in many public-opinion polls because of the disproportionate number of black people in both groups. (2) Our Target Group, all-white and 85 percent male, turns out to be hawkish. (3) Our Equivalent Income Group, also all-white but only 38 percent male, is generally less hawkish than the Target Group. And so, while it is clear that lower-middle-income blue-collar workers of the white race are rather hawkish on the war issue, it is not so much because of their occupation or income as because of their race and sex.

Until now, we have been looking at blue-collar attitudes on substantive issues, and we have discovered that although this group tends to be more conservative than the rest of the population on economic, law-and-order, and war issues, there were few truly dramatic differences. Now we will turn to questions about the workability of the political system, and see whether the blue-collar worker believes the system is giving him a fair shake. These are the crucial questions, for they hold the key to the role that the blue-collar worker will play in America's political future.

ALIENATION

In a representative political system such as ours, authority requires popular consent, which in turn must be based on a feeling that the system is working properly and that all major groups are fairly represented in the government. When large numbers of people feel that they are not being represented fairly, and that the system is prejudiced against their receiving fair representation, they may respond by militant protest, "dropping out" of politics, or resorting to new forms of political action. Clearly, the events of the last few years have shown what difficulties our nation faces when large groups of people—blacks, students, Wallace voters, hard hats—feel that they are not getting their fair share from the system as it presently stands.

In this context, it is vital to discover the extent of blue-collar alienation, both to understand this group's views and to discover their potential for disruption. We shall do this in two parts: first, to see how they view the government and whether they have developed organizations outside the government to deal with their concerns; and second, to see how they view the political parties. Then we will be able to assess what use they are likely to make of traditional avenues to power.

One symptom of total alienation is a lack of interest in politics. On this score, the blue-collar workers do not seem to differ much from the general population, although they vote less. While only a small minority of all groups surveyed do more than vote, the Target Group does not stand out significantly from the population at large, though they were less interested in politics or the 1968 campaign than the Equivalent Income Group.

But while other groups seemed to be a bit *more* interested in the 1968 campaign than the 1960 campaign, the Target Group's interest *dropped.* This is our first clue as to long-term trends within this group.

The survey in 1968 included a series of questions testing people's faith in the political system. Again and again, the Target Group stands out in its malaise. When these questions were asked, the interviewer stressed that the respondent was not being asked to evaluate any particular party or administration, but rather to comment on government in general. Whereas the Target Group was considerably more alienated than the general population, the Equivalent Income Group was considerably *less* alienated; we are seeing in the Target Group a blue-collar and not a lower-middle-class phenomenon. The belief that government is run for the benefit of a few, perhaps the most damning indictment of a democratic system, runs particularly strong in the Target Group. We can only speculate whether the "few" refers to Wall Street or the NAACP.

But the most revealing figures of all are those for questions asked both in 1960 and 1968, and they show that while the national trend is toward less faith in the political system, the rate of increasing alienation is much higher in the Target Group than elsewhere. This is reflected in the fact that while differences among the three groups were slight in 1960, the Target Group stood out in 1968. The most difficult question to interpret in Table 17 is the statement that "Voting is the only way that people like me can have any say about how the government runs things." In an age of increased protest against government policies in many areas, many people apparently changed their minds about this subject, but the Target Group changed less than the others. Two-thirds of them still see voting as their only input into the political system.

The Target Group's deeper level of alienation is also reflected in the answers to the question, "Suppose a law were being considered by your city government that you considered very unjust or harmful. What do you think you could do about it?" While only 28 percent of the Equivalent Income Group and 36 percent of the total population could think of nothing, 46 percent of the Target Group were unable to state a course of action.

Several of these questions measuring alienation were tested to see whether the significant differences between the Target and Equivalent Income Groups could be explained by different educa-

TABLE 17
ALIENATION IN 1960 AND 1968

	Target Group	*Equivalent Income Group*	*Total population*
"People like me don't have any say about what the government does."			
Agree—1960	24%	25%	27%
—1968	52	34	42
"Voting is the only way that people like me can have any say about how the government runs things."			
Agree—1960	78%	74%	72%
—1968	67	51	58
"Sometimes politics and government seem so complicated that a person like me can't really understand what's going on."			
Agree—1960	53%	56%	57%
—1968	87	66	71
"I don't think public officials care much what people like me think."			
Agree—1960	21%	21%	24%
—1968	55	36	44

tion levels; they could not. The same questions were tested to see whether differences within the Target Group were related to differences on the authority/protest questions, the economic outlook questions, or religion. The only significant difference was that Protestants were more likely than Catholics to think that the government is run for a "few big interests looking out for themselves." But this difference, like the one cited above between Catholics and Protestants, was reduced when Southerners were omitted.

In the absence of a pervasive faith in the political system, has the blue-collar worker developed strong interest groups (besides labor unions) to advance his concerns? Traditionally, sociological studies have shown that the blue-collar worker is less a joiner than his white-collar counterpart.[15] In the last few years, there has been little published research in this area. One recent study was by Prof. Harold J. Abramson of the University of Connecticut, who found that 65 percent of white-collar respondents in a survey of Connecticut city dwellers belonged to one or more voluntary associations, as opposed to only 42 percent of the blue-collar respondents.[16] While it would be risky to generalize from Professor Abramson's exact figures (for there are probably many more established associations in the old cities which he surveyed than in younger cities or suburbs), his findings indicate that the gap between blue-collar and white-collar participation in organizations has not narrowed in recent years.

The survey we are using affirms this. While almost everyone reported a religious affiliation, only 27 percent of the Target Group said that they attend church regularly, contrasted with 47 percent of the Equivalent Income Group and 38 percent of the general population. And almost no one in any group suggested that he would work through established nongovernmental institutions to fight a proposed municipal law he considered unjust or harmful.

These are sobering findings. They document graphically how disillusioned the blue-collar worker has become with the American political system in eight years. In 1960, they were indistinguishable from other population groups under consideration; today, they stand out as by far the most alienated.

And they have lost faith not only in the government, but in the legitimate private means that Americans have always used to influence government. When asked how they would fight the hypothetical proposed local law, the answers most frequently given by all categories were to contact public officials alone or work through informal groups. The voting booth, the political party, the ongoing civic or interest group occurred to very few people as a means of waging political warfare at the grass roots. Perhaps most sobering of all is the fact that nearly half of the blue-collar sample simply could not think of any way to wage such a fight.

Surely self-perception is an important factor here. Members of the Equivalent Income Group are not wealthier than those in the Target Group, and yet they feel much more comfortable about American institutions. The key is probably that they consider themselves middle-class, and therefore in the mainstream of the American system. In 1960, many more people in this group called themselves working-class, and their degree of alienation was much closer to the Target Group's.

But while class identification may explain the low level of alienation in the Equivalent Income Group, it does not explain why the Target Group, whose class consciousness has not changed much, is far more alienated now than 10 years ago. Whatever the cause, this loss of faith in American institutions has profound implications for the nation's political well-being.

POLITICAL PARTIES

Blue-collar class consciousness has not changed much since 1960, and the workingman's attitudes toward our parties can be gauged from his views about their proper role, differences between the major parties, party identification, and how he voted in 1968, when there was not only a choice between Democrats and Republicans, but also a candidate opposed to both major parties.

What are our parties supposed to do for the American voter? In a healthy party system, parties presumably will seek out voter opinion, present a reasonable choice among candidates, and provide a link between the citizen and his government. But the 1968 survey data reveal a good deal of popular skepticism about our parties, especially in the Target Group. That group was considerably more likely than others to feel that the parties do not make the government more responsive, keep their promises, or seek out voter opinion. These findings are consistent with those showing alienation about the rest of the political system. It is also relevant to point out here that nobody in the Target or Equivalent Income Group thought of using political parties to fight a proposed local law.

Even more revealing is the large number of blue-collar workers who perceive no difference between the major parties on various issues. Fortunately, many of these questions were asked both in 1960 and in 1968 (Table 18). On most issues, *more* people in the whole population and the Equivalent Income Group saw differences between the parties after eight years. As for the Target Group, on some issues *fewer* workers saw differences between the parties after eight years; on others, more workers saw differences, but the rate of increase was less than that of the general population or the Equivalent Income Group. (This latter condition existed in the case of the two racial issues.) On every issue, many more in the Target Group than in the other groups saw no difference between the parties in 1968. On other questions, blue-collar workers were more likely than other groups to see no difference between Wallace and the major parties, and less likely to feel that either party would make a difference for one's family's economic situation.

Another measure of change can be found in the reason that each respondent gave first for favoring a particular presidential candi-

TABLE 18
PERCEIVED DIFFERENCES BETWEEN THE PARTIES, 1960 TO 1968

	Target Group	*Equivalent Income Group*	*Total population*
No difference on the issue of:			
Federal government's power—1960	25%	28%	19%
—1968	34	21	25
Federal job security—1960	24	36	27
—1968	42	21	25
Federal school aid—1960	36	39	33
—1968	36	32	28
Equal employment—1960	54	46	43
—1968	42	26	29
Medicare—1960	32	28	30
—1968	25	15	20
School integration—1960	51	46	46
—1968	41	32	30
No important differences between the parties cited			
—1960	44	58	50
—1968	55	40	46

date. Some responses can be grouped under the heading "voting for or against the man": examples are "Nixon's more honest," "Humphrey will help the little man," or "Wallace is no good." Other replies can be grouped under the heading "voting for or against the party": for example, "I'm voting for Nixon because he's a Republican," or "The Democrats always get us into wars." In general, people were more likely to vote "for or against the man" and less likely to vote "for or against the party" in 1968 than in 1960. Particularly the blue-collar Target Group has switched more than the other groups to "voting for or against the man."

Next, we can observe the trend in party identification (Table 19). The nation as a whole has seen a slight drift away from the Republican party (with Democrats and Independents sharing the ex-Republicans) and a very mild trend toward greater independence from parties. The Equivalent Income Group displays a similar moderate shift away from Republicanism (mainly into the Independent category) and a moderate trend toward greater independence in general. But in the Target Group, we can see a massive shift away from

TABLE 19
PARTY IDENTIFICATION IN 1960 AND 1968

	Target Group	*Equivalent Income Group*	*Total population*
Democrats—1960	57%	39%	44%
—1968	44	41	48
Republicans—1960	22	30	29
—1968	25	25	23
Independents, etc.—1960	20	20	27
—1968	31	34	29
Not very strong partisans—1960	40	34	38
—1968	45	36	39
Strong partisans—1960	40	36	35
—1968	24	30	31

the Democrats, with almost all the dissidents bypassing the GOP and becoming independents. And the trend away from strong party allegiances is even greater.

This is truly significant, and shows the practical outcome of all the trends toward alienation that we have seen. There is no question that the chief casualty of these trends has been the Democratic party; but it is equally clear that the Republicans have failed to benefit from the Democrats' losses. If anything, the blue-collar worker seems to be saying, "A plague on both your houses." Like the black man, he is unwilling to commit himself to either party but will cast his ballot for the highest bidder. If this is so, then the candidacy of George Wallace, opposed to both parties and appealing to the lower class, could not have been better timed for the Target Group.

Wallace did rather well in the Target Group (as compared to his showing in the general population); Nixon had considerable success with the Equivalent Income Group; and Humphrey made the greatest gains toward the end of the campaign in the Target Group (Table 20). But on Election Day, the Target Group gave a plurality of its votes to Nixon, because a greater proportion of Nixon supporters than Humphrey supporters went to the polls. Indeed, in all groups, but especially in the Target Group, Nixon supporters were more likely to vote than Humphrey or Wallace supporters were. This suggests that perhaps they were motivated by a strong turn-the-rascals-out attitude, combined with the knowledge that Nixon, and not Wallace, was the only candidate who had a realistic chance to turn them out.

Within the blue-collar Target Group, how did Nixonites, Humphreyites, and Wallaceites differ on the issues? There were almost no differences on alienation and authority/protest questions; the only difference was that people who gave the military a relatively low rating tended to vote for Wallace. This may surprise those who see the Wallace movement as militaristic; indeed, it may surprise Wallace himself, who chose a hawkish Air Force general as his running mate. It suggests that the blue-collar Wallace voter may have been more populist than conservative.

The real differences came on bread-and-butter and racial issues. Proponents of Medicare, federal aid to education, equal-employment programs, equal-accommodations legislation, open housing, and desegregation voted, logically, for Humphrey. Wallace voters were more liberal than Nixon voters on economic issues and were more likely than Nixon voters to favor equal-employment programs; on other racial issues they were more conservative than the Nixonites. Those who opted for the middle of the road on the desegregation question went to Nixon.

Thus, it would appear that, despite blue-collar alienation from parties and the rest of the political system, the blue-collar voter behaved rather rationally in the voting booth in 1968. (A "rational" voter is one who votes for the candidate who best represents his views.) Liberals supported Humphrey, moderates and conservatives went to Nixon, and those who were conservative on most racial

TABLE 20
CANDIDATE PREFERENCES IN 1968

	Target Group	*Equivalent Income Group*	*Total population*
Humphrey	40%	34%	46%
Nixon	40	55	43
Wallace	20	11	11
Change in popularity in last few weeks of campaign			
Humphrey	+13	+9	+7
Nixon	+1	+2	+3
Wallace	−2	−3	−2

questions but liberal on bread-and-butter issues opted for Wallace. While Wallace did comparatively well in the Target Group, most alienated voters nevertheless stayed with the major-party candidates. Apparently, elections are probably a poor indicator of alienation, because the campaign and the voting-booth choice have a sobering effect on antiestablishment voters.

Those Democrats who rejoiced at working-class waverers' last-minute reconversion to Humphrey in the fall of 1968 would be wise to heed the warning that these surveys convey. The workingman is becoming more and more estranged from his Democratic affiliation, even if he can be lured back now and then on Election Day. Relatively speaking, in 1968 the big winner in the Target Group, despite Humphrey's late gains, was Wallace.

But if Democrats may fall prey to false security, so may Republicans. Blue-collar workers are *not* entering the GOP, and they are tending more and more to vote for the man and not the party. A colorful conservative like Ronald Reagan or Spiro Agnew might win their votes, as Dwight Eisenhower did in the 1950s; but as with Eisenhower, they are unlikely to translate the man's personal popularity into blue-collar allegiance for his party.

Without a Wallace on the ballot, the worker will probably vote for the highest bidder, as we suggested above. The issues on which the bidding is based will probably depend on the circumstances and the candidates in each case. But it seems plausible to assert that the blue-collar worker is not at some temporary junction on the road from one party to another; rather, he is on the way to an independent limbo, isolated from all parties.

BLUE-COLLAR WORKERS AND THE FUTURE

As the turbulent decade of the 1960s drew to a close, blue-collar America stood out as profoundly alienated from American political institutions, despite a lack of pessimism about the economy and despite views on issues that did not differ much from the American mainstream. What does this augur for the fate of blue-collar politics, and American politics in general?

The political activity of any group results from an interaction between its attitudes—its values, stands on issues, and perceptions of the world—and the social structure in which it finds itself. But to say that attitudes are translated by the medium of the social structure into actions would be too simple, for it ignores the crucial "feedback" effect in which the social structure affects the attitudes. In other words, attitudes are not formed in a vacuum but are shaped to some extent by the social surroundings; and those surroundings also play a large role in determining how attitudes turn into actions.

To understand the role that blue-collar workers are to play in American politics, we must first clarify what we characterize as their alienation from American institutions. Are they disillusioned merely with the current state of affairs, or does their disaffection go deeper to a reaction against basic American values? Are they likely to turn against the Bill of Rights, against representative government, against the political theory that lies behind the Constitution of the United States?

It seems plausible to conclude that blue-collar workers are no more likely than any other Americans to spurn these values. While they are more prone to oppose various forms of dissent than are other Americans, this reaction against the turmoil of the 1960s does not seem to be linked with a more general antagonism to American values. Most of them voted in 1968, and most of the voters did stay with the established parties. While civil libertarians may properly fear popular tolerance of wiretapping, no-knock laws, preventive detention, and other manifestations of a preference for security rather than liberty, blue-collar workers are about as tolerant of such measures as other groups. These measures are often seen as a way to preserve "the American way of life," even if that "way" implies less concern for the Bill of Rights than Americans exhibited 180 years ago.

Perhaps it should be noted that many of the signs of blue-collar alienation may be not pathological but rather the result of a realistic assessment of the current state of affairs. It may simply be true that there is not "a dime's worth of difference" between the parties on most issues, or that the federal government is indeed too remote from the grass roots to be responsive to popular desires. Too much of the writing about the working class depicts alienation as an irrational, mischievous phenomenon rather than a logical response to a plausible view of political reality.

Blue-collar alienation thus seems focused on the failures of government in the 1960s rather than on the failures of the American political philosophy. The social structure in which this attitude is expressed is, as we have seen, relatively devoid of voluntary associations. The blue-collar worker remains a comparative nonjoiner, except for his labor union. And most blue-collar workers in the lower-middle-income category do not even hold union cards.

There are two major implications of the lack of voluntary associations in the blue-collar worker's life. One is that this void may itself be a major cause of his alienation. In an atmosphere of declining partisanship, politically concerned workers need a vehicle to voice their resentments and lobby for their goals. George Wallace may have provided a temporary answer to this need. But in general, there is no substitute for an ongoing spokesman group, and this may be why the worker feels that his needs go unrepresented and unanswered in government. The other is that the paucity of organizations representing the worker in part determines the forms of activity he is likely to adopt. He may vote for the antiestablishment candidate like Wallace, or he may engage in militant, even violent, protest, such as the bitter conflicts over open housing in Milwaukee or the ferocious attacks on peace demonstrators in Manhattan. Dropping out of politics altogether will probably not be a popular recourse among blue-collar workers; they are just as interested in politics as the rest of the population, although more alienated from specific political institutions. Especially with the lack of alternative organized activities to absorb their energies, they will seek expression of their keen political interest in ways outside normal political channels.

A good way to observe the importance of organized groups is to view the experience of blacks in recent years. No less than blue-collar workers have they eschewed traditional partisan ties. While it is true that blacks have voted almost unanimously for the Democrats in the last two presidential elections, there are signs that they are tied to the party less by tradition than by momentary self-interest. For example, John Conyers, Jr., of Detroit, who has replaced Adam Clayton Powell, Jr., as the foremost black spokesman in the House, was the first black congressman to win his seat by opposing the entrenched Democratic/labor leadership in his district. In 1966 Spiro T. Agnew himself captured the black vote in Maryland because his Democratic gubernatorial opponent was accused of being a Wallaceite.

Beyond their declining partisanship, black voters have been at least as resentful of their underdog status in American politics as blue-collar whites are. This resentment on the part of blacks flared up in several major urban riots in the late 1960s; but even without a sudden and massive national commitment to meeting black demands, rioting in major cities seems to have subsided. The most critical reason is probably the proliferation of community-power and black-power organizations which monopolize the energies of militant blacks and channel their desires into organized, institutional behavior. It is these organizations that have displaced the political party as the major vehicle for black political aspirations. If similar groups were to develop for blue-collar whites, presumably they would feel less need to voice their frustrations in violent and bitter ways, and they would change as the blacks did.

But providing interest groups tailored to working-class needs is time-consuming, and in the meantime there is a critical need for leadership to draw blue-collar America back into a position of faith in the American political system. This requires, above all, a sense that America's leaders care about the workingman's needs. Such an attitude of concern is difficult to develop, for clearly it cannot be evidenced by a set of programs like the New Deal.

Nor is it appropriate to pander to every whim of the workingman. The typical liberal refrain after protests by blacks and student militants was, "They're trying to tell us something; let's see what they want." As time went on, and much of the populace discovered that they were unable or unwilling to meet all the demands, a reaction set in. Many of the same politicians who are urging resistance to black and student demands are quite willing to accede to the workingman's less noble instincts, notably with reference to civil rights and dissent. For the President of the United States to welcome to the White House union leaders who encouraged attacks on peace demonstrators and who have been implicated in criminal activities, as Mr. Nixon did in early 1970, is surely not a healthy way to demonstrate concern for blue-collar aspirations.

Neither is there a clear sign that such tactics will be effective. What the worker needs is politicians who will act not like politicians but like statesmen. As party ties diminish and the worker is increasingly observant of the candidates' quality, the candidate who coyly plays politics with blue-collar concerns is likely in the end to lose blue-collar allegiance. Indeed, blue-collar workers will vote for the highest bidder, but only if the bid looks sincere.

Leadership is needed in the unions, too. The AFL-CIO should have a leader who is not content to sit back and comment on change but tries to shape change. Unions are the logical source for the encouragement of working-class interest groups, especially for the majority of blue-collar workers who are not unionized. It is in the interest of union leaders to deal with change, too; despite the virtually unanimous support of union leaders for Humphrey in 1968, large numbers of the rank and file deserted the Democrats. This makes the credibility of union leaders all the more tenuous.

It is unlikely that responsible leadership or viable organizations will arise suddenly to reintegrate the blue-collar worker into American political life. We will probably face more years of alienation, absence of institutional alternatives to the political parties, and various forms of militant protest by the working class. Political parties will continue to lose their grip on the voters; in a future not like the 1930s, when a predominantly Republican electorate became a predominantly Democratic electorate, we are likely to have a predominantly nonpartisan electorate. And blue-collar workers will stand in the forefront of the emerging independent majority.

NOTES

1. Remarks of Secretary of Labor James D. Hodgson to the Republican Governors Conference, Lake of the Ozarks, Missouri, Aug. 12, 1970.
2. "Meany Fears Left Seizing Democrats," *Washingtcn Post,* Aug. 31, 1970.
3. Kevin P. Phillips, *The Emerging Republican Majority,* Arlington House, New Rochelle, N.Y., 1969, pp. 463–464.
4. Samuel Lubell, *The Hidden Crisis in American Politics,* Norton, New York, 1970.
5. Richard M. Scammon and Ben J. Wattenberg, *The Real Majority,* Coward-McCann, New York, 1970.
6. Michael Harrington, "A Radical Strategy—Don't Form a Fourth Party; Form a New First Party," *New York Times Magazine,* Sept. 13, 1970, p. 133.
7. The data utilized in this study were made available by the Inter-University Consortium for Political Research.
8. In all, 1,673 people were interviewed. The Target Group consists of the 105 of them who fit our description and were interviewed both before and after the election; the Equivalent

Income Group numbers 146. Chi-square statistical significance tests were used throughout the study in distinguishing these three groups from one another.

9. Seymour Martin Lipset, *Political Man,* Anchor Books, Garden City, N.Y., 1963, pp. 173–176.
10. *Report of the National Advisory Commission on Civil Disorders,* Mar. 1, 1968, p. 1.
11. Andrew Hacker, *The End of the American Era,* Atheneum, New York, 1970, p. 107.
12. Lubell, op. cit., p. 72.
13. Harold J. Abramson, "Ethnic Pluralism in the Connecticut Central City," Institute of Urban Research, University of Connecticut, Storrs, August 1970.
14. Sidney Verba et al., "Public Opinion and the War in Vietnam," *American Political Science Review,* June 1967, p. 331.
15. Richard F. Hamilton, "The Behavior and Values of Skilled Workers," and Murray Hausknecht, "The Blue-Collar Joiner," in Arthur B. Shostak and William Gomberg (eds.), *Blue-Collar World,* Prentice-Hall, Englewood Cliffs, N.J., 1964.
16. Professor Abramson graciously provided me with these unpublished findings; other parts of his study are published in Abramson, op. cit.

6. BLACK DEMANDS, WHITE REACTIONS, AND LIBERAL ALARMS

by Richard F. Hamilton

ELEMENTS OF THE LIBERAL WORLD OUTLOOK

Liberal social scientists have portrayed the American scene as one fraught with the imminent danger of backlash. The black population, no longer accommodating and quiescent, has been demanding equality and, even more, compensation for past crimes against their people. Influential whites have reacted by yielding to these demands as well as they could, paying off here, passing special legislation there, making some highly visible appointments to fend off one thrust, creating some jobs in response to another, and indulging in unusual judicial leniency to forestall a third.

In the liberal litany, these responses are undertaken by enlightened and fundamentally decent upper- and upper-middle-class populations, who are affluent, educated, and secure in their social positions. After years of indifference and neglect, these confident and tolerant upper and upper middle classes are now yielding to black demands. Their willingness to make amends is limited only by the minor inconvenience of a costly war which, together with sundry additional "commitments" to "world affairs," momentarily prevents the diversion of resources toward this new end.

All this does not occur in a vacuum. Mute observers of this scene, the white lower middle class and the white working class, have watched and waited. Unlike the upper middle class, these groups—so it is said—do not display the openness and tolerance that come from security and affluence. Although they no longer live on the margin of existence, theirs is a recent achievement. If they are members of white ethnic minorities, they have just barely "made it" and are not about to give up hard-won gains of position and status. They have received no special benefits, no special reparations. In many instances, they have "paid the costs" of the upper- and upper-middle-class generosity. It is, after all, working-class neighborhoods that are being integrated; it is the schools in those neighborhoods that are being integrated; it is these workers' jobs that are "threatened" by fair-employment practices.

The struggle for jobs is possibly the key ingredient in this complex of events. White skilled workers will attempt to hold onto their jobs and to preserve new openings for their children. White operatives, laborers, and service workers, lacking the "sure thing" of the skilled workers, will be exposed to a fierce competition for scarce jobs.

Thus the poorest, the least secure, least educated, and least tolerant whites are thrust into close physical proximity to blacks, and it is here that backlash is most likely. Black moderates, to be sure, are allied and working with the white upper and upper middle classes for "responsible" social change. The black militants, on the other hand, are making extreme and, in the short run, unrealizable demands. Their protests, their marches and demonstrations, and their violence or threat of violence have paved the way for the current reaction from white "middle America."

The Vietnam war adds further complications and strains. The effects of the war are more serious for white middle America than for the upper middle class. The war takes the sons of middle America and returns dead and wounded. War-induced inflation erodes incomes; counterinflationary policy creates unemployment. Mixed into this already tense and explosive situation are the increasingly bizarre and unfathomable protests of white radicals—protests which appear to challenge everything that white middle America has learned or stood for. These developments also contribute to the welling reaction.

After the customary reference to the tragedy of Weimar, one then turns to the lesson that "responsible" leaders should let up on the demands, at least for the moment, taking some of the pressure off the white workers and lower middle class. In the long run, with the liquidation of the Vietnam enterprise and with stable economic growth, there will be enough of everything to satisfy all groups. In the short run, however, the imminent threat of civil war can be averted only by following the strategy of present restraint and gradual change.

It would be impossible in this short space to comment on all the claims of this interpretation, but a key to the assumed dynamic is the assertion that intolerance is greatest among the poorer working-class whites and that tolerance is greatest in the upper middle and upper classes. Rather than taking this on faith, it would seem worthwhile to examine some relevant evidence.

BLUE-COLLAR INTOLERANCE: SOME CONTRARY EVIDENCE

Much of the evidence presented in support of this claim is anecdotal, depending on flagrant instances of brutality. These include, for example, the open-housing marches in Chicago and Cicero in the summer of 1966; Father Groppi's marches to the south side of Milwaukee in the summer of 1967; and the action of the hard hats against Vietnam demonstrators in the Wall Street area in May 1970. Such scenes can misrepresent things. The ugly scenes on the south side of Milwaukee involved a maximum of 8,000 persons, most of them spectators; yet the area within a radius of about 15 blocks contained a population of more than 150,000. The number of counterdemonstrators, in short, constituted only a very small minority of the area's population. The arrest records indicate that a large proportion of the counterdemonstrators were not even from the area. Moreover, a check done at that time by the *Milwaukee Journal* found a majority of the area's residents in favor of open housing.

A fair amount of survey evidence allows a more accurate assessment of the sentiment within the various class segments. The evidence, as we shall see, provides some surprises.

For the purpose of this inquiry, we have taken only married respondents in households whose head is economically active. This procedure controls for a number of extraneous factors from the very start. We will not have to worry, for example, about whether or not a given result is due to the disproportionate presence of middle-class widows.

Males are classed as manuals or nonmanuals; and wives are classified according to their husbands' occupations. Although frequently discussed, a precise definition of the terms "upper" and "lower middle" classes is a rarity; most analyses proceed with rule-of-thumb judgments. Some social scientists have used the U.S. Census categories "professional, technical, and kindred" and the "managers, officials, and proprietors" as their "upper middle class" and have taken sales and clerical workers as their "lower middle class." This procedure confuses things because the professional category includes many low-paid occupations (teachers and clergy) and also many semiprofessional and "technical" workers. The "managers, officials, and proprietors" category presents a similar problem with its combination of General Motors executives and candy-store proprietors. The sales category, especially on the male side, is by no means exclusively "lower middle class" because it includes real estate and stock brokers and insurance salesmen among others. To examine the cluster of traits discussed—affluence, security, higher education—it seems safer to divide the nonmanual ranks by income rather than by the usual combination of categories. In the 1968 studies used in this chapter, we distinguish nonmanuals living outside the South whose annual family income is $12,000 or more from those with less income; in the South, to adjust for the lower incomes there, we have used a $10,000 figure.

The manual category has been divided into two groups, the skilled (craftsmen) and all others (operatives, laborers, and service workers). This division also provides a rough separation of the manuals in terms of their relative income levels, job security, and education. Two additional adjustments have been made. Foremen have been removed from the manual ranks (from the category craftsmen, foremen, and kindred) and classed with the nonmanuals. The same has been done with independent artisans.

Since most cross-sectional samples do not include significant numbers of persons we could call upper-class, the analysis here will be restricted to comparisons of the two working-class and two middle-class segments.

Before examining the data, it should be noted that the attitudes of the general population do not cluster in the same ways as those of intellectuals. One often finds equalitarian answers to some questions and the opposite responses to others. There is, moreover, some evidence that shifts occur over time in opposite directions, greater tolerance being found in one area of concern and less in another. Rather than viewing these as irrational, confused, or uncrystallized orientations, we can more sensibly interpret them as reactions of the general population to their existential conditions and to formal or informal educational experiences. This is not to say that the certain clusterings of attitudes are good or bad; it merely suggests the error of interpreting the attitudes of the general public from the conventional perspectives of the upper-middle-class intelligentsia.

The principal survey we will examine is the 1968 election study of the University of Michigan's Survey Research Center (SRC).* The study contains four questions asking about the rights of blacks. Three of these probe into specific topics of job rights, schooling, and public facilities, asking whether the federal government ought to guarantee equal treatment. These questions combine two concerns, equality and the federal government's role. Some people indicate that they favor equality but object to the government's role as guarantor. The responses indicate a minimum expressed sentiment which is both for equality in a given area and for government intervention to guarantee it. The fourth question does not involve this particular difficulty, asking only about the principle of equal-housing opportunities. Additional questions drawn from other studies will be discussed later. Since the circumstances inside and outside the South are markedly different, we will make separate analyses, beginning with non-Southern regions.

The basic findings may be summarized very simply: outside the South, only very small differences in attitude exist between the four groups we have delineated (Table 21). The upper middle class, despite claims of their unique virtue, have attitudes very similar to those of the less-skilled blue-collar group. In point of fact, the blue-collar group is slightly more favorably disposed to equality

---

*I wish to thank the directors of the Survey Research Center and of the Inter-University Consortium for Political Research for making the 1968 and other studies available for this purpose. I also wish to thank the local distributors, the University of Wisconsin's Data and Program Library Service, and its director, Alice Robbin, for assistance in aiding this effort.

TABLE 21
CIVIL RIGHTS ATTITUDES OF NON-SOUTH WHITES BY CLASS, 1968
(MARRIED WHITE RESPONDENTS, HEAD ECONOMICALLY ACTIVE)

	Percent in favor (of those with opinions)			
	Operative, laborer, service	*Skilled*	*Lower middle*	*Upper middle*
Government should see that Negroes get fair treatment in jobs	49	44	43	45
Government should see that Negroes can go to any hotel or restaurant	67	62	64	65
Government should see to it that white and Negro children go to the same schools	55	40	48	47
Negroes have a right to live wherever they can afford to	82	88	85	82

than the upper middle class in three of the four items. In the fourth item there is no difference.

On the basis of these results, it would be difficult to support a claim either of a special intolerance of the manual or lower middle class or of the special virtue of the upper middle class. All the differences are small. Those which might support such claims are countered by others going in the opposite direction. The rough equality of tolerance in the four subgroups also suggests that education does not have the impact that is so often and so easily assumed. The upper middles, who have much more formal education than the other three groups, are clearly not different in their tolerance levels from those less benefited. This evidence indicates, in short, that "class" is not a significant factor in accounting for proequality or antiequality attitudes.

Also of some interest in Table 21 is the absolute level of proequality sentiment. The housing question, which is not encumbered with consideration of a government role, shows more than four-fifths of all groups affirming the principle of equality. Where a government role is involved, the proequality levels are lower, ranging from roughly 45 to roughly 65 percent.

It is useful to ask about the composition of these four population groupings. Some of the respondents were born and raised in the South and, as one would expect, they are less favorably disposed to government initiatives and housing equality than those reared outside the South. The Southern-reared individuals are somewhat concentrated in the lower-status categories. By itself, however, this disproportionate presence of ex-Southerners among the "poor whites" has only a very limited impact on the result. Religion is a factor of some greater significance. The non-Southern Jews in this sample accounted for 13 percent of the upper middle class and 2 percent of the lower-middle segment; and Jews are found to be more favorable to equal rights than other groups. Thus the upper middle class as a whole gained some edge in relative tolerance because it contained a relatively large and liberal Jewish population. When only Catholics and Protestants (and the few "others") who were reared outside the South are considered, the relative tolerance of the upper-middle-class segment drops, as might be expected. The impact of these additional two factors was not very great; but controlling for these factors yielded a result which went even more against the belief that workers are intolerant and the middle class, in particular the upper middles, are especially tolerant.

A comparison with the results of the Survey Research Center's 1964 study indicates some changes over the four-year period. The results show opposing trends. With respect to the job question, none of the four groupings showed any significant change in outlook. Attitudes toward school integration deteriorated sharply in three of the groups. On the open-housing question, by comparison, there was improvement in attitude on the part of all four segments.

The shift in attitudes toward school integration might initially be cited as evidence of the much-discussed working-class backlash. To be sure, skilled workers showed a major shift in attitude, with their approval of government action declining from 68 to 40 percent. The decline in lower-middle-class approval is also consistent with expectations. But at the same time, a decline in support also appears in the upper middle class, and, to confuse matters further, there is a small increase in approval for government action among the less-skilled blue-collar workers.

Opposite tendencies are found with respect to the open-housing question. Here skilled workers showed a marked increase in tolerance, shifting from 71 to 88 percent approval over the four years; unskilled workers also showed an increase. For all practical purposes there was no change within the upper middle class.

It is difficult to say what is operating here. Perhaps a long-term trend toward tolerance is under way, but with a reaction in one area of significant public concern, the school question. This could be a case of backlash stimulated by actual or pending integration; or alternatively, it might be stimulated or legitimated by the efforts of various political leaders. In any event, the evidence indicates the "segmented" character of the reaction. And the reaction indicated here includes the upper middle class but does not include the unskilled blue-collar worker.

A more comprehensive National Opinion Research Center (NORC) study conducted in 1963 allows some elaboration on these findings.[1] In this case we took non-South whites and divided them simply into manual and nonmanual categories. The two groups exhibited essentially no differences in their responses to questions about schools, public transport, neighborhood, Negro intelligence, jobs, parks and restaurants, and voting. In general, however, the closer or more intimate the contact, the greater the opposition to integration. Thus neighborhood integration received less support than integration of schools, parks, or public transport. When it was a question of bringing a Negro home to dinner, the level of approval declined even further; when it was a question of intermarriage laws, the level of support was still lower. In these latter instances some class differences did appear. Forty percent of the blue-collar workers, for example, opposed laws against intermarriage, in contrast to 58 percent of the white-collar group.

The opposition to black-white marriages is strongest in smaller communities and least in the large cities; it is also strong in the older generations and relatively weak in the younger. It would appear that it is part of an older, small-town, or rural heritage. It seems likely that the routine processes of demography will considerably reduce this source of opposition in the course of time.

Some of the responses appear to be contradictory. Some 70 percent said it would not make any difference if a Negro with the same income and education were to move into the neighborhood. And yet about half thought that whites had a right to keep Negroes out of their neighborhoods. The positions, strictly speaking, are not contradictory: though it would not make any personal difference to some respondents, they would, nevertheless, approve the "right" of other whites to keep out blacks. Such a position is different from committed opposition to equality. At best, one could fault it as a kind of laissez-faire position which is indifferent to the human lives and feelings that are involved.

A second National Opinion Research Center study, in April 1968, provides similar findings. Again, a high level of tolerance is found with respect to schools and jobs. More than four-fifths say that the native intelligence of Negroes and whites is the same. The same proportion say that a Negro of the same income and education in the block would make no difference to them. Although manual workers are not as tolerant as nonmanual workers, the differences in the non-South population were not very large. If controls were made for religion and for the region in which the respondents were reared, even these small differences might disappear.

More intimate social relations, once again, yield different response patterns. A question dealing with the right to keep Negroes out shows a lower level of approval and a larger class difference (18 percentage points). A similar class difference appears with respect to a question about pushing where not wanted. Here again, the responses to these questions stand in sharp contrast to the high level of tolerance toward a Negro of the same income and education moving into the neighborhood. The same explanation seems likely, namely, that the one response represents a personal position and the other a laissez-faire attitude.

There is a still larger class difference in this study in the responses to the question about laws against intermarriage, this being the largest difference (28 percentage points) to be found for the non-South in any of the studies reviewed here.

Six of the seven NORC questions reported on thus far are exact repeats of those used in the 1963 study. In the nonmanual ranks the shift in responses to all six questions between 1963 and 1968 was toward increased tolerance. In the manual ranks the pattern was not clear. There were some increases in tolerance, most notably in the response to the question about a Negro moving into the neighborhood; but in other cases there is either little change or, in two instances, slight declines, the latter with respect to Negro intelligence and the question about pushing where not wanted.

One point is unambiguous about these NORC results: no evidence in these studies indicates a *massive* reaction. In response to only two of the questions is there any suggestion of a reaction. Both of these occur in the manual ranks, one change amounting to five percentage points and the other to seven. Otherwise the pattern is one of either immobility or improvement in outlook. The most substantial evidence in support of the backlash claim, that based on the Survey Research Center's school-integration questions, is contradicted by the evidence from these NORC studies. Both manuals and nonmanuals in these studies showed increases in the percentages agreeing that whites and Negro students should go to the same schools. If there were a reaction of the size and the importance discussed in the alarmist literature, it certainly ought to be indicated in surveys such as these. Large and consistent changes in attitudes should be indicated in all, or at least many, of the areas touched on by these questions.

The 1968 study has a range of additional questions, one of which is of some interest. The reduced tolerance for more personal levels of integration is strikingly indicated by the responses to the question which asks about a teen-age son or daughter dating a Negro. Only 6 percent of the blue-collar respondents said they would not object; but the level of equalitarian sentiment is not very different in the middle-class ranks, where only 13 percent would not object.

The most important points, in summary, are the following:

A high level of tolerance, of equalitarian sentiment, is indicated among the non-Southern white population with respect to jobs and public facilities. Here there are no important differences in the levels of tolerance of manual and nonmanual workers. In other areas, where more intimate social contact is involved, there are both a lower level of tolerance and also some class differences, with the manuals somewhat less tolerant than the nonmanuals.

One serious instance of a counterequalitarian tendency appeared, along with two minor reactions. The first of these instances was countered by the evidence from another set of studies. The reaction, moreover, did not appear in the "proper" location inasmuch as it extended to the upper middle class and excluded the less-skilled manuals. The evidence presented here, in short, does not substantiate the claim of a major reaction. The best evidence that can be offered in support of such a claim are a few fragmentary findings which, at the same time, run counter to other evidence, which shows either no change or else improvement in the outlooks.

The major areas of struggle which presumably have stimulated the presumed backlash have been jobs, education, and housing. It is important to stress that in these areas there are both high levels of tolerance and, for all practical purposes, no class differences. Thus the key assumption of the alarmist speculation does not appear to be valid. The class differences in tolerance appear in areas which have not been in the forefront of public discussion. Nor have they been, to this point, areas of serious or open contention.

THE SOUTHERN EXPERIENCE

Thus far we have considered the class-tolerance relation only outside the South. Conceivably, the relation might be different in the South. The claims about the propensities of Southern poor whites are so familiar that they need no repetition here. Again, however, one may put the question, is it so?

The basic results from the 1968 study are more surprising even than those for the non-Southern respondents. In general the most tolerant groups prove to be the poor and upper-middle-class whites. While the poor whites are presumed to be engaged in a bitter struggle over jobs, the data here show that half of them approve government intervention to support Negro job equality. And they are more approving than the upper middle class are (Table 22). Similar patterns appear with respect to the government's role in guaranteeing equal access to public facilities and public schools. As for the open-housing question, just over half the poor whites approve the equal-opportunity suggestion, a level which is somewhat below that of the upper middle class. In all these comparisons, the skilled workers and the lower middle classes appear to be the least tolerant groups; and in most cases the differences between these groups and the others are relatively large.

TABLE 22
CIVIL RIGHTS ATTITUDES OF SOUTHERN WHITES BY CLASS, 1968
(MARRIED WHITE RESPONDENTS, HEAD ECONOMICALLY ACTIVE)

	Percent in favor (of those with opinions)			
	Operative, laborer, service	*Skilled*	*Lower middle*	*Upper middle*
Government should see that Negroes get fair treatment in jobs	50	22	19	44
Government should see that Negroes can go to any hotel or restaurant	47	13	38	52
Government should see to it that white and Negro children go to the same schools	35	14	20	34
Negroes have a right to live wherever they can afford to	55	37	49	67

There are some interpretative questions which ought to be considered before proceeding further. One should raise the "Southern equivalents" of those questions considered with respect to the non-South findings. A considerable proportion of the South's population was reared outside the South, and they tend to bring more moderate attitudes with them to their new locations. However, movement into the South tends to be disproportionately by the upper middle class; some 22 percent of the South's upper middle class was reared outside the region. Taking only Southern-reared respondents, one does find a disproportionate drop in the tolerance of the upper middle class, but the basic pattern remains very much the same: groups at the extremes of the class structure seem to be relatively tolerant, and the skilled and the lower middle classes seem to be intolerant.

The responses of the poor whites—operatives, laborers, and service workers—are clearly at variance with conventional expectations. This result might be dismissed as sampling error, except that other studies have yielded results which follow along similar lines.[2]

There were no clear trends between the 1964 and 1968 surveys indicated in the responses of Southern respondents. Support for government-guaranteed job equality rose impressively (24 percent) among the less-skilled blue-collar workers and moderately among the upper middle class. These changes were countered by sharp declines among the skilled and the lower middle class. The school-integration question shows another pattern of responses, with small increases in tolerance of the manual groups and small decreases among both nonmanual groups. Support for open housing increased by approximately 20 percentage points among all groups except skilled, where there was a small decline. It would be a mistake to place great faith in any single shifts, because the number of cases involved is very small. Nevertheless, if there were a substantial reaction occurring, it should be indicated in the overall picture; that is, there should be a preponderance of significant negative shifts. As it is, four of the six shifts in the Southern blue-collar ranks were positive, and the largest percentage changes were positive. In the nonmanual ranks there were three positive and three negative shifts, and again the positive changes were somewhat larger.

The NORC study of 1963, with its extended range of questions, does offer some evidence for the received hypothesis about class differences. With a single minor exception, Southern white workers are shown in the study to be less tolerant than the Southern white middle class. In general, as was noted outside the South, where closer contact is involved, the level of tolerance declines.

It is difficult to make any simple summary statement about such diverse results. Some comparisons show no difference, while a number of them do support the received hypothesis. To choose the most conservative reading of the data, one would accept the evidence of the 1963 NORC study which shows clear and, with one exception, consistent support for the received hypothesis. The same tendency was evidenced in a 1968 NORC study although in this case there were more instances of "no difference" than in 1963. The 1968 SRC study found the greatest tolerance at the extremes of the class structure. The safest summary of the evidence for the Southern states would be to suggest *limited* support for the received hypothesis about blue-collar intolerance.

Turning to consideration of the trends as indicated by those questions contained in both NORC studies, one again finds only feeble support for the backlash hypothesis and a fair amount of evidence suggesting the opposite. In the blue-collar ranks, there is an increased tolerance as indicated in the responses to four of the six questions. (The greatest changes occurred with respect to the school-integration and the equal-intelligence questions.) There were slight declines in tolerance registered within the middle class in response to five of the six questions; four of these were very slight. With respect to school integration, there was a significant increase in equalitarian sentiment.

Outside the South, the following conclusions appear to be in order: (1) no clear evidence of class differences exists in the areas of public concern and controversy, that is, in questions about jobs and public facilities; (2) class differences tend to appear in responses to questions concerning closer contacts and private social life; (3) no clear and consistent evidence supports the backlash hypothesis. Most of the evidence points, instead, in the opposite direction, toward an increased tolerance.

In the South, there is: (1) Some evidence of class differences in the areas of public concern and controversy. But contradictory evidence exists, including findings of unusual tolerance among the less-skilled blue-collar workers. The evidence here, in short, is neither clear nor consistent. Unlike the non-South findings, however, there is some support for the received hypothesis. (2) Evidence of consistent class differences in response to questions about closer social contacts. (3) No clear and consistent evidence in support of the backlash hypothesis. Once again, more evidence points in the opposite direction.

THE GEORGE WALLACE QUESTION

Attitudes are one thing, so it is said, and behavior another. In this context, the aphorism means that when "the chips are down," the real, or underlying, predispositions of the blue-collar workers will come through. The George Wallace candidacy of 1968 provides a convenient test of this hypothesis. Wallace spoke clearly and directly in a language which would be readily understood and appreciated by the increasingly uneasy blue-collar workers. As we now know, many of them did vote for Wallace. Theodore H. White summarized the matter as follows:

> George Wallace in 1968 was different. His vote [unlike Dixiecrat Strom Thurmond's in 1948] was *not* a sectional vote. . . . No less than 4.1 million [of his 9.9 million] votes came from the Northern and Western states: and these were, overwhelmingly, white workingman votes. Despite all the influences of the media, all the pressure of their labor leaders, all the blunders and incompetence of the Wallace campaign, they had voted racist.[3]

Once again, it is useful to raise a simple question: Is this true? Although the Wallace vote did have greater territorial spread than Thurmond's, it was still very much concentrated geographically: more than half of his total came from the 11 states of the Confederacy, which provided only a quarter of the 1968 votes. Another 9 percent of his vote came from border states where historically there has been considerable Southern influence. Thus, we must once again examine the results separately by region.

Was it the white workingman who voted for Wallace? Outside the South the result, as indicated by the Survey Research Center study, was as follows: the Wallace percentage among non-Southern blue-collar workers was 9 percent; among white-collar workers it was 8 percent. There was, in short, essentially no difference between the two groups. The study also asked the nonvoters which of the candidates they preferred, that is, for whom they would have voted had they chosen to participate. A recalculation to include the nonvoter preferences makes little difference in the result. These results, in short, prove to be remarkably consistent with the evidence on the attitudes: outside the South there was no significant difference between manuals and nonmanuals either in attitude or in the vote for Wallace.

To maximize the number of cases for analysis, we combined the responses of voters and nonvoters who reported a preference for one of the three presidential candidates. When we take a more detailed look at the result, using the four categories delineated earlier, we find slight differentiation within the blue-collar rank, the Wallace percentage being somewhat greater among the less-skilled workers (Table 23). Moreover, the upper class was just as susceptible to the

TABLE 23
SUPPORT FOR WALLACE BY CLASS AND REGION, 1968
(MARRIED WHITE RESPONDENTS, HEAD ECONOMICALLY ACTIVE)

	*Percent for Wallace**			
	Operative, laborer, service	*Skilled*	*Lower middle*	*Upper middle*
Non-South	12	7	9	9
South	33	48	32	13

* Includes both those who voted for Wallace and those nonvoters who preferred Wallace.

Wallace appeal as the lower middle category. When we controlled for the disproportionate number of ex-Southerners and Jews among non-Southern manuals by taking only white Protestants and Catholics reared outside the South, even those slight differences indicated in Table 23 disappeared.

The pattern in the South is more in keeping with conventional expectations. Here Wallace had the support of nearly half of the skilled workers and a third of the less-skilled and the lower middle class. The upper middle class turned out to be very moderate, or at least so it would appear. Most of the indigenous Southern white upper middle class voted for Nixon in 1968. A majority of these Nixon voters took intolerant positions with respect to government intervention to guarantee job equality and school integration. Yet a majority took a tolerant position toward integration of public facilities and open housing.

Some partial explanation for this distribution of attitudes is available. Taking the indigenous population, that is, the Southern-reared whites, one finds that intolerant attitudes are strongly centered in the small towns and rural areas. The Wallace vote also happens to be centered in the smaller communities, although the pattern is not as clear as in the case of the attitudes. Thirty-seven percent of those in the small towns favored Wallace and 40 percent of those in the middle-sized cities, but only 18 percent of those in the large cities.[4]

It is impossible with the materials at hand to say why the Southern small towns have the outlooks they do. It might be the influence of fundamentalist sects preaching the inferiority of Negroes. It might be a result of competition for jobs, though rural blacks tend to be located in different areas from the majority of the rural whites, thus making direct continuous competition difficult. (Blacks were located in the lowland plantation areas, whites in the uplands and the hill country.)

Whatever its sources, this intolerance does appear to originate in the small town and rural locations. The manual population of the South is overwhelmingly found in these areas; more than half of those in the 1968 study, for example, were living in communities of less than 2,500 persons. The same is true of the lower middle class. It must also be kept in mind that we are discussing here the indigenous Southern white populations. Those reared outside the South, who tend to be considerably more tolerant than the indigenous groups, are located overwhelmingly in the middle-class ranks of the larger cities.

One indication of the erosion of the small-town hostilities appears in examination of the attitudes of small-town people who are now located in larger communities. Among the people who grew up in small towns, those still located in small towns are the least tolerant, those in middle-sized communities next, and those in large cities most tolerant. Of course, it is possible that the tolerant small-town people move out and the intolerant ones stay. Although there may be some tendency in this direction, it seems unlikely that such self-selection would explain this entire result.

THE SENSE OF POWERLESSNESS

Some of the claims in the liberal repertory do gain support, although even here the received portrait contains some serious inaccuracies. One of these is the assumption of a widespread sense of alienation among the blue-collar groups. Roughly half of the blue-collar workers report that they cannot understand politics, and a similar proportion feel that public officials do not care about people like them (Table 24). A larger proportion, just over half of those outside the South and approximately three-quarters of those in the South, say that voting is the only way they have to influence events. Only a minority feel that they have "many ways" to influence policy. Perhaps the most striking finding is the high percentage who say that they "don't have much say" about how things are run.

The sense of alienation is somewhat less in the lower middle

TABLE 24
ALIENATION BY CLASS AND REGION, 1968
(MARRIED WHITE RESPONDENTS, HEAD ECONOMICALLY ACTIVE)

	Percent "alienated" (of those with opinions)			
	Semiskilled, laborer, service	*Skilled*	*Lower middle*	*Upper middle*
Non-South:				
Can't understand politics	45	44	38	29
Public officials don't care	45	44	33	29
Voting only way to influence	57	55	45	34
Don't have much say	79	75	70	64
South:				
Can't understand politics	47	67	43	28
Public officials don't care	42	53	51	27
Voting only way to influence	72	82	62	42
Don't have much say	77	94	74	62

class. The differences, as compared to the manuals, however, are not very large. When we divided this group by family background, taking those who were of farm or manual parents on the one hand and those from middle-class families on the other, we found the former to be very much like the blue-collar group and the latter considerably more likely to report that they understand events and have "many ways" to influence them. (Many in this latter group are probably only temporarily in the lower middle class. They are young, just out of college, and en route to upper-middle-class positions.)

Because of some important changes from earlier studies in the wording of questions, we cannot say definitely whether this sense of powerlessness is "new" (a response to the recent insurgencies) or a more or less constant part of the social and political landscape.

It is possible to link both the sense of alienation and intolerance with support for the Wallace candidacy. For this purpose, the two blue-collar groups were combined with the lower middle class to allow a sufficient number of cases; outside the South the groups are similar enough in their tolerance, their alienation, and the Wallace support to justify this procedure. The two occupational categories were divided into those who felt they did not have much say in how things were run and those who did think they had some say. Each of these groups was then further divided by pro and con attitudes toward federal enforcement of school integration. As might be expected, the groups who feel they have little say in affairs tend to be somewhat less tolerant than those who feel they do have influence. As would be anticipated, Wallace supporters came largely from that segment which feel they "don't have a say" and also oppose federal government intervention in school-segregation matters.

This finding indicates that the liberal view is at least partially correct in its assessment of the source of the Wallace support. The view is wrong in two ways, however, concerning the extent of the presumed reaction. First, all ranks of the non-South population display a considerable quantity of tolerance. Among the tolerant groups, the Wallace appeals gained an insignificant response. The other error involves the response of that small minority which both feels alienated and is intolerant. Only about one of five such persons reacted as predicted, that is, favored Wallace.

A second area in which the liberal theorizing has some validity concerns antiwar protesters. The evidence as of October 1968 left no doubt about the existence of an immense and widespread hostility toward the protesters. This was the case despite a majority sentiment for deescalation of the war. Such hostility is found in almost all the social groups we have discussed. The strongest sentiment in favor of the protesters, taking only those with opinions, appeared among the Jews, Negroes, and college-educated.[5]

The long and the short of the story, at least as indicated by the evidence of late 1968, is that the protest was neatly encapsulated within two pockets of the population, the blacks and the college-educated. Even in these cases, attitudes favorable to the protesters were not a majority sentiment. Perhaps sentiment in favor of the protesters has changed over time in such a way that within the two pockets they may now have gained majority status. But it does not seem likely that there has been any similar transformation in the outlook of the rest of the population—given the increasingly bizarre form of the protests and the improbability that these events could be understood by any distant observer.

The lessons appear to be simple: at least outside the South, the white working-class population is not as vicious as some have portrayed it. They were no more responsive to the Wallace appeal than the middle-class populations. In the South the situation is different. Wallace's blandishments were widely accepted. Even this one clear instance of support for the received theorizing is somewhat complicated. The reaction occurs, as it turns out, mainly in the small towns and rural areas. The Southern white working class is more likely than other nonfarm categories to be located in, or to have come from, those settings. In short, the reaction appears to have its origins in the special heritage of the small towns of the South rather than the contemporary dynamics of black-white relations. The greater tolerance of the small-town workers who have moved to the cities suggests the orientations are not fixed but are capable of being reformed.

In putting the above findings into a larger context, one should not forget the impressive changes in attitudes toward Negroes in recent decades. A comparison of studies which asked identical questions in 1942, 1956, and 1963 revealed, with insignificant and fragmentary exceptions, an immense and continuous shift toward more favorable attitudes. Another study with evidence through 1965 found the same trend.[6] Our own comparisons of the responses to NORC questions in 1963 and 1968 indicate a continuation of the trend, and the odd bits of evidence which have appeared since then do not reveal any clear and systematic reversal of it.

Liberal alarmism stems from two main sources. Ignorance of this long-term trend is the first. A rather striking misperception of the relative prevalence of tolerant or intolerant attitudes is the second. This latter misperception is shared by the population in general. For example, the 1968 respondents were asked whether they favored segregation, integration, or something in between. Outside the South approximately one respondent in ten favored pure segregation, a ratio which was roughly the same in all four class segments (Table 25). The respondents were also asked how they thought most people "in this area" felt on the subject. Roughly two-fifths of the respondents thought that most or all of the people in the area favored strict segregation. It is clear that the amount of segregationist sentiment is wildly exaggerated.

These distortions may have some important consequences. Those who support segregation may be more outspoken and aggressive in

TABLE 25
ATTITUDE TOWARD SEGREGATION AND PERCEPTION OF ATTITUDES BY CLASS AND REGION, 1968
(MARRIED, WHITE RESPONDENTS, HEAD ECONOMICALLY ACTIVE)

	Class			
	Semiskilled, laborer, service	*Skilled*	*Lower middle*	*Upper middle*
Non-South:				
Percent personally favoring strict segregation	10	13	10	8
Percent thinking most or all people in area favor strict segregation	47	44	42	41
South:				
Percent personally favoring strict segregation	35	42	27	7
Percent thinking most or all people in area favor strict segregation	66	63	53	50

the presentation of their claims, feeling that they speak for a large portion of the white population. Contrarily, the opponents of segregation may be intimidated and hesitant to speak out, being convinced of enormous opposition to their position. Political leaders, thinking there was considerable and possibly growing segregationist sentiment in the population, may be hesitant to take the lead against those institutions. And those leaders so disposed would feel encouraged to continue their play with "code words" and "Southern strategies."

REMOVING LOWER-MIDDLE-CLASS STRAINS

Despite the diverse character of the white reactions, the trend in recent decades has been steadily in the direction of tolerance. The available evidence does not indicate anything that one would label as backlash, that is, a sizable reversal in this trend. As public opposition to the war has grown, opposition to the antiwar protest, the more bizarre variety at any rate, has hardened. Obviously a considerable amount of anxiety is present in the society and, as indicated here, a sense of powerlessness very widespread.

Although the evidence indicates no antiblack reaction, it would be foolish to make declarations about what may occur in the future. If things were to get worse, if white workers were to be further victimized by the war, by inflation, and by unemployment, they might react as predicted. The case of the New York City hard hats makes clear that a little "outside agitation" can easily generate a moderately capable striking force, one which will have a fair amount of public sympathy.

Given this threat, it would seem the better part of reason to work to relieve the sources of tension. Such efforts could, and presumably should, be at the heart of a liberal program. If there is an imminent threat of civil war, as the liberal spokesmen say, and if that is caused by competition for jobs, they should work to eliminate that source of strain. Rather than pleading helplessness, they should design a program to achieve full employment, so that people do not have to compete for jobs. Many European countries have led the way and have been operating for years at full employment, bringing in tens of thousands of foreign workers; meanwhile in the United States, a 4 percent unemployment rate is "acceptable."

If one is serious about improving the human condition, about reducing the stresses in the lives of blue-collar workers and the lower middle class, one could work to reduce expensive and inflationary "services," especially those involved in so-called "defense efforts."

An anxious, hand-wringing stance will not suffice. The liberal presentation which argues that the society is constrained by a set of inherent, technical necessities is based on false "realism." The discussion of inherent or necessary "strains" which must be suffered by major subgroups is largely pretense. To say that one is concerned with the human condition but cannot intervene to affect any of the factors causing the problems is not a very credible assertion. This is especially so when the major "policy implication" is an urgent request to relax the pressures for just and legitimate demands.

In the present context that argument has been presented with more than the usual urgency. Relax the pressures, it is said, or else you will generate a formidable reaction, one which we (your friends) will not be able to contain, a reaction which will end up giving you nothing. The reaction, it is said, is already here, present on the scene; people who were once either favorably disposed to the new demands or at least neutral are now opposed. This particular argument does appear to be supported in the evidence made available here. The evidence does indicate a reaction against the antiwar protesters, against demands and forms of protest which the average person finds more and more difficult to comprehend. A mass public reaction against the black demands, however, is not indicated, the trend here being generally favorable.

What this all comes to is the suggestion that the liberal alarms involve a misreading of what is, to be sure, a very complicated reality. The major impact of this misreading is to immobilize. There is another option suggested by the alternative reading of the evidence presented in this essay. One is not up against a wall of threatening oppostion. There are many things to be done to improve the condition of blacks and whites. There are immense amounts of misused resources which, if properly directed, could reduce or end the major stresses and strains. There is, in short, no justification for immobility.

NOTES

1. Some of the results from this study have been reported in Donald J. Treiman, "Status Discrepancy and Prejudice," *American Journal of Sociology,* May 1966, pp. 651–664. I wish to express my appreciation to him for making the data from this study available for my analysis.
2. A similar result appears in the response to the fair-employment question contained in the 1968 NORC study. The tolerant percentage among the less-skilled blue-collar workers in the South was 86; for the skilled, 71; for the lower middles, 74; and for the upper middles, 79. Other similar findings appeared in the Survey Research Center's 1956 study. These results are reported in Richard Hamilton, *Class and Politics in the United States,* Wiley, New York, forthcoming, chap. 11.
3. Theodore H. White, *The Making of the President: 1968,* Atheneum, New York, 1969, pp. 368–369.
4. Small towns are those of fewer than 2,500 inhabitants; middle-sized communities are those of 2,500 to 49,999 persons; large cities are those of 50,000 or more. Included in the last category are suburbs of the largest metropolitan communities. This pattern of the greater intolerance in the smaller communities is found only in the South.
5. Evidence on this subject is reported in Philip E. Converse and Howard Schuman, "Silent

Majorities and the Vietnam War," *Scientific American,* June 1970, pp. 17–25; Philip E. Converse, Warren E. Miller, Jerrold G. Rusk, and Arthur C. Wolfe, "Continuity and Change in American Politics: Parties and Issues in the 1968 Election," *American Political Science Review,* December 1969, pp. 1083–1105; and John P. Robinson, "Public Reaction to Political Protest: Chicago 1968," *Public Opinion Quarterly,* Spring 1970, pp. 1–9.

6. Herbert Hyman and Paul B. Sheatsley, "Attitudes toward Desegregation," *Scientific American,* July 1964, pp. 16–23; and Mildred A. Schwartz, *Trends in White Attitudes toward Negroes,* National Opinion Research Center, Report No. 119, Chicago, 1967.

7. THE UNION MEMBER SPEAKS

*by Stanley H. Ruttenberg**

THE VIABILITY OF UNIONS

"I think they've done beautiful. Yes, the best we could." This was the answer given by a young trade unionist recently to a general question on union performance in improving wages and working conditions for its members. Some might argue that this expression of confidence is misplaced, but in the light of a recent informal survey, it is not atypical. The question was asked as part of a series of discussions held with union members in the Baltimore area in the late summer of 1970, in an effort to find out just how they are reacting to the current flurry of official and journalistic concern over the average worker and his problems.

A precise definition of this concern remains elusive, and indeed appears to change with each new entrant into the debate. Sometimes it is the blue-collar worker who is discussed, sometimes the lower-middle-income group. The group has been vaguely defined as the "forgotten" American. It has also been specifically limited to white male family heads who work in certain skilled or semi-skilled occupations. But whatever the definition, there can be no question that union members make up a substantial portion of the group being considered.

*Although I am responsible for the contents and conclusions in this report, it could not have been completed without the invaluable assistance of my associates Jocelyn Gutchess and Alan Adams.

It should be obvious that any discussion of workers and their problems must be concerned also with the labor movement. Union members account for approximately 30 percent of all nonagricultural, nonsupervisory wage and salary workers; they are, by definition, workers who have problems. Their decision to organize into a collective force means they are determined to seek solutions to those problems. Collective bargaining is the institutional device to find such solutions. Problems, of course, are not restricted to union members, but the labor movement does provide an opportunity for redress that is not readily available to the isolated, unorganized worker. Insofar as the problems of the organized worker are work-related, they are part of the labor movement's agenda—an agenda that expands as the problems do.

Many today contend that workers are faced with problems not only in their work but in other areas, and that the resulting discontent and malaise have become a national problem demanding official government attention, if not political exploitation. A recent White House task force report on blue-collar workers identified three so-called "squeezes" facing the blue-collar worker: (1) the economic squeeze, (2) unsatisfactory working conditions, and (3) a social squeeze. The first relates to the well-documented fact that the hourly wage rate and take-home pay of the average worker have not kept pace with inflation. Indeed, real spendable income has actually declined since 1965 for nonsupervisory workers. The second squeeze involves the question of job satisfaction: how workers feel today about their work and working conditions. The third area relates to the general dissatisfaction among lower-middle-income groups that is allegedly demonstrated by the Wallace vote, the Agnew response, and hard-hat demonstrations.

Evidence of uneasiness and discontent in our society is not, of course, limited to the blue-collar worker and his white-collar cousin. It shows up in student unrest and rebellion, minority-group pressures for recognition, militancy of blacks and others, the women's lib movement, the increase in and acceptance of draft evasion, desertion from the Armed Forces, and even the drug scene. Together these manifestations raise serious questions about the efficacy of our institutions for dealing with the postindustrial or "techtronic" age.

An underlying assumption of a successful democracy is that its institutions are adaptable, that they can be used to correct deficiencies and alleviate inequities that appear in the system. Institutions need not be barriers to change in a democratic society. They can and should themselves become instrumental in bringing about change. The labor movement is a prime example of how an institution can bring about social change; it has certainly performed this function in the past. As this report will demonstrate, there is good reason to believe that it can and will continue to remain a force for progressive change in the future.

A second assumption in this study is that any pervasive disaffection of the average worker not only is a serious national problem but, in the long run, is directly related to the individual's effectiveness as a worker and is therefore a proper labor-management concern. As one worker described it, "he [workers in general] has become *so* frustrated with his job, and this is causing many, many emotionally disturbed people, the alcoholic, the absentee, the hostility." Another said, "I feel if the employer would make us *comfortable,* they would get better production out, more work out of us."

To test the vitality of the labor movement and our thesis that the institutional framework of the labor movement and the collective bargaining process provide a proper and indeed a necessary vehicle for resolving the problems that affect workers today, my associates and I spent some time in the summer of 1970 talking to groups of union members and officers in the Baltimore area.

We wanted to find out how union people felt about the rash of public statements being made on their behalf; how they viewed the performance of the unions in meeting the challenge posed in the three "squeezes"; and especially how they felt about the use of the collective bargaining process to resolve problems, not only in the traditional areas of economic concern and working conditions, but also in areas of social or community concern. In brief, can the labor movement adapt itself to the new pressures and new issues which are confronting it today?

This report does not pretend to be based on a scientific study or systematic sampling of union members' attitudes. It is essentially impressionistic; but enough agreement appeared among our discussants to suggest that what we heard may be fairly representative of the thinking of union members. Group and individual discussions were held with members of the Retail Clerks; the Meat Cutters; the Steelworkers; the Shipbuilders; and the American Federation of State, County and Municipal Employees (AFSCME). The groups included rank-and-file members, shop stewards, business agents, organizers, and AFL-CIO City Central Body representatives. Most of those with whom we spoke were men; most were heads of families. Older and middle-aged workers predominated, although some younger workers also took part. A majority were white, except in the case of the AFSCME, of which most were black.

The discussions took place in union halls, in the evening, after work, or, for some participants, before the night shift began. Those who came, came voluntarily. They had something to say. Perhaps because of the setting, there was a bias toward the labor movement, but what emerged very clearly was the strength of the labor movement. Those who think trade unionism, along with the institution of collective bargaining, is a fading or anachronistic institution will find little support in this report. The faith and fealty that union members give to their union seem strong and enduring—not only among older members who fought the fierce battle for union recognition and survival during the twenties and thirties, but also among younger members.

The interviews were informal and unstructured. Each one usually began with a discussion of the economic squeeze, moved on to problems of job satisfaction, and ended with some consideration of social and community problems. A constant theme was the issue of the proper role of the union and the labor movement in meeting these challenges. Some conclusions can be drawn, but first let the members speak for themselves.

ECONOMIC SQUEEZE

The administration report on the blue-collar worker describes the economic squeeze facing the worker today as a twofold problem: first, wages are not keeping up with the increased cost of living; and second, for the typical worker's family, obligations escalate as he and his children grow older. The report contends that precisely when the children of the blue-collar worker reach their teens and family budget costs are at their peak, two things happen to the bulk of middle-income male breadwinners. They reach a plateau in their capacity to earn by promotion or advancement; at the same time expenses continue to rise to meet such costs as home ownership, college education, new cars and household equipment, and support for aging parents. Union members tend to agree that money is the number one problem, but not for the reasons stated in the administration report. They put the blame primarily on inflation, and secondly on an unfairly increased burden of taxes: "We feel that we should get more money for the work we do." "Just keeping up is rough."

The union people did not complain about increased family obligations, college education costs, or inadequate opportunities to advance or increase earnings. As one said, "There can only be so many chiefs." In that they are perhaps more realistic about their situation than the scholars and politicians studying them. And they do not generally regard themselves as caught in a treadmill. Indeed, although they agreed that things were frequently bad, they did not feel powerless to improve the situation. They looked with confidence to the union to protect their interest and promote their welfare. On the need for additional money they had this to say:

> As far as the economic conditions are concerned, we have two points of view. Number one, it appears like we're always in the process of attempting to catch up with the cost of living. So our number one item that is most important to us is to really not even improve, but remain stable, merely by meeting, by increased wages, the increased cost of living. Number two, we have another aspect and that is, it's not only a question of wanting to maintain the level of our standard of living. We want to increase it. We want to make a little bit of improvement. Today we may be satisfied with a piece of linoleum on the floor. But tomorrow we might want to have a little rug. I don't think that's so much for a blue-collar worker to want. And this is what they do want. Right now we feel we're going back; we're going down and down and down. The costs are rising. We're not even able to keep up with the cost of living.

> The way I see it—most of the things I have now, I'm trying to buy. I feel the pinch. I'm not against pensions, but I'd like to have more money now so I can make it to have a pension.

In addition to the expressed need for more money just to keep on the same level, many of the trade unionists felt that the tax burden had become too onerous and was unfairly distributed.

> Our people think the tax has gotten higher than the salaries.
>
> Like me, I'd rather have my taxes; they keep the pay.
>
> The blue-collar worker pays more in taxes, because he's the guy who is living in the city where there have to be more services.

If most adult male blue-collar workers feel a double squeeze—in that they are faced with rising family obligations at the same time that earning capacity has leveled off—the workers we talked to were not aware of it, or did not consider that a problem. Indeed, their personal health loomed as much more important than the problem of sending children to college or taking care of older parents. As one worker put it, "When you get older, you have the additional costs of the breakdown of your body, the upkeep of your body."

Asked if the rising of the general standard of living had made his life more difficult, he answered:

> That's like asking how do you feel now that instead of having a privy out in the backyard, you've got plumbing in the house. This is something that you take for granted. This is not a better way of living. The kind of increases we expect to have is in the manner which we are able to meet our responsibilities, with having less pressure put on us.

It is apparent that an obligation to provide college education for one's children was not among the pressures felt by most workers. This is a middle-class or upper-middle-class value, perhaps not shared by the average blue-collar worker. They want the opportunity for higher education to be available, but it appeared that in their view the utilization of that opportunity is the youth's responsibility, not theirs, and should be taken care of either by scholarships or by work-study programs. The expectation that a parent should pay for his son's education is probably more typically an upper-middle-class attitude and is not as widespread among the lower-middle-income group. Interestingly enough, there was considerable support for free education through college for all who had the ability or interest. "Schooling should be free all the way through. I can't see a free education for elementary school, junior high and up through high school, but once you graduate from high school, you're cut off."

It is obvious that in order to make ends meet, many blue-collar workers become two-income families, with the wife working as well as the husband. This is not a satisfactory situation as far as they are concerned.

> The way we think, a man should be able to make enough money to take care of things, so that his income doesn't have to be supplemented by his wife *having* to work. This is the whole thing in a nutshell.

> This is one of the roots of evil in this country. Kids running around, because their parents are both out working. Something's got to be done.

So as far as union members are concerned, the primary problem is still the economic one. "It's always wages." However, this is a problem which they feel confident of meeting through the union; they always have met it, and they feel certain that they always will.

THE WORKING CONDITIONS

Discussing the second squeeze—job satisfaction, working conditions, and possibilities for advancement—most workers again expressed confidence that the union, through the collective bargaining process, was an effective instrument for taking care of their problems. The problems themselves, and they do exist, more often concerned the area they defined as benefits than real dissatisfaction with the job. Health benefits, safety measures, pensions, vacations, sick leave, and free medicines and drugs ranked high among their concerns in improving working conditions. Opportunities for advancement and training and education programs were a secondary concern, except in the case of the public service employees, whose long history of inadequate opportunity has resulted in a different set of values and priorities.

Boredom, lack of challenge in the job, was not as significant a factor as has generally been believed. On the other hand, discrimination by employers, whether on the basis of race or age, or in favor of the disadvantaged to compensate for past deficiencies of the social system, was resented, for most workers thought it contributed to an unsatisfactory work situation.

On the question of boredom, the workers with whom we talked showed that pride in their jobs was considerably greater than is popularly believed, although they admitted there could be dissatisfaction with some routine jobs. As one worker said, "It's like after you've been President of the United States, what is there? After you're a top mechanic, what else is there?" Or "I've got to challenge what people say about things being so boring. At least in our industry. It's not like a fellow at Fisher Body, or Chevrolet. To me, that would drive me crazy. I couldn't take that."

They agreed that workers reach a plateau. With the faster pace of advancement that characterizes many work situations today, this poses a problem, particularly for the young or middle-aged workers. There comes a time when a worker can go no further. One older work commented:

> You get up the ladder so far, someone's gonna have to die for you to get further. A young fellow today, he gets dissatisfied much more quickly. Youth hates seniority, especially where it is strong. In the industrial places, where seniority is God Almighty, youth is opposed to this.

Describing how the middle-aged worker feels when there appears to be no room for advancement for him, one worker said:

> We got a lot of members, full time, in that age group—30–35—that have *had* it. Eight years' service, six years as a retail clerk. They leave and come back. They leave and try—driving a truck, working in a factory, working in a steel mill. They'll work five or six jobs. Three years they're gone; two years they're gone. These guys will tell you when they're back in our industry. They hadn't found themselves a home. They'll work with us six years, top rate of pay. They're not satisfied. They've got to find another way. *Would that be true 15 years ago?* No. *Is the 35-year-old fellow more willing to take a chance than he used to?* Because he's got nothing to lose. He thinks the grass is greener on the other side of the fence. And it ain't. But he's got more guts than he used to. He's more adventuresome.

Union members generally felt that the company had a responsibility to improve job satisfactions, and that many things could be done. However, they felt also that the unions had an equal responsibility—a responsibility that was not always met. "We've failed miserably in some things—in getting workers involved in participation." Union members felt that increased health benefits, paid vacations, and sick leave would contribute to job satisfaction. Unions have bargained successfully for company-paid medical insurance programs, though it is interesting to note that most of the programs began with the company paying only half of the insurance premiums, with the percentage gradually increasing to 100 percent. Such programs by the company were recognized as a good trade-off for additional wage increases, although as one trade unionist repeatedly reminded us, "There's only so many ways you can cut the pie." Special programs under which union members receive medicines and drugs at discount prices from participating pharmacies were also popular, as were employer-paid programs for eye and dental care.

The issue of discrimination or unequal treatment of employees by the employer came up frequently in the discussion as a source of job dissatisfaction. By and large, older union members are disturbed when young workers, reaping the rewards of the battles already fought and won, take these benefits for granted. However, the older union members also recognize that this was bound to happen and do not really want their sons to have it as hard as they did. No doubt the generation gap is a source of discontent and uneasiness for many workers, with the distrust of youth which pervades society generally spreading to the workplace. But talking about today, one worker said:

> I wouldn't want to see it ever reach a point where we were faced with what we had back in the thirties. Admittedly it's bad today—it's too easy for the kids today, but I don't think the alternative should be what we had in the mid-thirties.

> I've been down there [in the shop] almost 14 years, and it took me all those years to get to be a first-class welder. I'm not in a rut. I would like to get higher, but it's not paying off, all those years. You get a person that comes in off the street, and he works only a year. He sees that I'm making so much money, and he says, "Boy, I want that job." But he doesn't know that it took me 14 years to get my job. Well, I think that he should work at it the way I did. Maybe not as long, but the way I did.

> It's the youth and the things that go with it. The lack of discipline. The "hell with it" attitude that creates the griping and the bad feeling that there is between young fellows and the older ones. It rubs the wrong way—to see these young guys walk around as if someone ought to hand them something.

> But I don't blame these young fellows for wanting to advance. There's no sense in waiting for 14 or 15 years, if you can get it in 2.

Race as such did not appear to be a problem among the groups with whom we talked. Workers generally felt strongly that opportunity for employment should be equal. White workers did not resent it when recently hired blacks moved up faster than they did, if the blacks had ability and could do the job. "When a guy does first-class work, he deserves first-class pay." But special treatment for the disadvantaged was resented, particularly when absence or tardiness was excused for black but not for white workers:

> With the hard core, this is where the resentment is. Management has been wrong all these years. And now they're making up for it. That's where the resentment is. A guy works two weeks and takes off, and he don't get cut [his pay]. I took two days off a couple of months ago, and I got cut three days.

> In our shop, they [the disadvantaged hired with government support] miss time terrible. And they don't get two or three days off like the regular workers would.

To cope with this problem, the union members thought that the union had a responsibility to educate the new people coming in and help them understand the work situation.

On the other hand, the elimination of discrimination in the work situation, according to a group of black workers with whom we spoke, had resulted in markedly better work performance for the benefit of the employer and, in this case, the public. One worker said that since black workers had been given equal opportunity for advancement in a public service department five years ago, "Things have changed. The work has improved. You don't have the abuse of sick leave and vacation like you did in the past."

Aside from fringe benefits and equal treatment, clearly considered legitimate concerns for the union and important factors in increasing job satisfaction, we addressed ourselves in these discussions to two other issues: (1) education and training programs as they relate to employment advancement, and union and management responsibility for such opportunities, and (2) the desirability and/or utility of providing recreational programs in a labor-management context to improve the work situation.

As far as recreation was concerned, most of the union members believed that this was more a personal responsibility than a union or company responsibility. They agreed that such an issue might be put on the bargaining table, but not in the immediate future.

> There are a number of things on the agenda that are a whole lot more important. Such as the wage scale, meeting the cost of living, number

one. Number two, the retirement plan. There's gonna be a continual need for more things along the line of pork chops.

If salaries don't level off [to keep up with the cost of living], you're not going to get the recreational programs, the leisure-time fund—because people'll always want to make more money. People, for as long as I can see, are going to want to make more money per hour so that they can take care of their own needs. As far as to sit down at negotiating time on recreation, it would never happen. We'd do it ourselves.

One worker was asked how he felt about the establishment of a leisure-time fund (with the employer paying the major share of the cost), from which employees would be entitled to draw to develop their own recreational interests such as travel, continued education, sports, or other leisure activities. "It is a hell of a good idea," he replied. But even this worker felt that such a development was a long way in the future.

The question of education and training, however, brought a different reaction. The most interesting comments came from members of the State, County and Municipal Employees, who expressed a strong preference for additional training and education paid for by the employer, as opposed to additional wages. This is not to say that they rejected increased wages; but this group, hemmed in by rigid Civil Service rules, job classifications, and statutory position qualifications, saw an educational program as the best, if not the only, way to get an increase in earning capacity.

"The system keeps us in a low pay range. We intend to agitate or any other method we have to use to make these [advancement] opportunities available to our people. This is what we're dedicated and obligated to do." "We see this as a continuing thing all the way through," a union leader answered when asked whether upgrading should be a one-time or open-ended arrangement. His particular union has set up its own training programs on occasion to prove that upgrading works and has then subsequently bargained successfully for employer-supported programs. Asked whether he would make these things an issue with the city or state on the collective bargaining table, he replied:

Yes. Training makes better employees and better service. For 25 years, they [his members] have been getting the work done but the employers say "you don't qualify." But every day you're doing the same thing.

You're doing the job. But for some technical reason you don't qualify, because you don't have a degree, or because you didn't pass a Civil Service test. These people have been robbed for years. So we're saying [to the city], since you don't feel the people are qualified, we'll work with you. Let's train them.

These unionists made it very clear that they would accept training instead of wages if that trade-off was required.

You'd take 10 or 15 cents an hour and put it into a training program rather than put it into wages? Right, right. Because when you get the 10 cents or 15 cents, what are you talking about? It won't amount to more than 3 or 4 cents after taxes and deductions. But if you train these people, then you know, you're giving them the opportunity to earn a better salary. This is what we're [the union] all about.

We know that people in lower jobs have to have an increase in salary—in order to have something to live on. But, we feel that if we put part of this on salary and the other part into some type of training program, now, maybe everybody won't make it, but the bulk of the people will make it, and everybody will have an equal opportunity at it.

THE SOCIAL SQUEEZE

Workingmen and -women do not see themselves as different from other people in what they want for themselves or what concerns them in the community and the nation.

The blue-collar workers are just as much concerned as anyone else about the conditions that exist today. The crime, the dope problem, the juvenile delinquency, civil rights; about anything you can imagine. And also with their civic duties. We are normal people as far as that is concerned. We do have a civic pride, and we do participate.

The interviews sought not so much to investigate the social issues that concerned the union members as to determine the extent of union responsibility for handling these issues on behalf of the workers. Opinion was divided along three major lines. Some thought that the responsibility lay primarily in the political arena. This is, of course, the traditional approach of the labor movement through its national and international unions and the AFL-CIO. In addition in each city and state, a central labor council carries the responsibility for promoting the workers' general, social, and economic interests through state and local government. For the most part, this activity is divorced from the collective bargaining process, where only directly work-related issues are laid on the bargaining table. The principle is, of course, that the union can bargain for only those things over which it can exert some leverage and for which it is willing to strike. Our discussion went to the question of whether this concept should or could be changed, whether the union itself could or would want to extend its leverage to improve the general conditions under which workers lived. Is it possible or desirable to use the strike weapon to deal with such issues as housing, pollution, improved education, mass transportation, or improved city public services?

Discussion on this topic was always lively, and there was no universal agreement on the issue. Opinion divided roughly into three major categories: those who felt that such issues were not a labor-management problem and should be dealt with in the political arena; those who felt that if management were involved at all, it would have to be on a cooperative basis working with the union and other groups in a joint community effort; and those who thought that this kind of issue might eventually—and in the case of one union immediately—be a proper subject for collective bargaining.

The traditionalists (and their numbers were not confined to the older trade unionists) had this to say:

> Social issues—like crime, law and order, pollution—I don't think employers would be susceptible to bargaining on community issues. When you sit at a bargaining table with a group of employers, you're discussing what the employer is going to give to the membership; not about pollution, housing, and so forth.

> When you bargain, every issue you try to bargain into, there [the contract] has to be strong enough that if the company won't give it to you, you can take issue with them. We bargain the best economic contract we can possibly get for the membership.

> This is the kind of thing that has to be handled in the political arena.

> In these areas we have an interest, but it's with the city government, the state. Our interest is in putting pressure on the city and the state.

The way to handle problems like that isn't between the company and the union, but the companies should pay what they ought to in taxes to solve their part of the problems.

Even those who expressed the least enthusiasm for the idea of unions' taking up social issues directly with employers, however, admitted that "it might some day come to this," particularly where government programs and legislation had paved the way. As an example they pointed to the passage of federal Social Security legislation, which enabled unions to bargain with employers for pension plans to supplement the federal system, something which was unthought of in the early days of the labor movement.

Objections to making social issues a part of the collective bargaining process were based primarily on a practical appraisal of the union's strength.

You mention some of these civic things that we ought to be involved in. And yet the tragic fact is that we've got to devote all of our energies just to keep building the organization and centering our attention on the economic things between us and the company. Sure, if we had a stable industry, and we could build continuously at the same pace, then we could go off on some of these things. But too much of our energy is spent on just scrambling to keep up.

Some union members preferred the political route for pressing their interests on social and economic matters. Like all the workers to whom we talked, they felt very strongly that there must be social improvement for all citizens in the country, particularly since it is the worker who more often than not got the short end of the stick. Describing the housing situation, for example, one worker explained:

Because he [the blue-collar worker] has got to live and wants to live close to his job, he's living in deteriorating, pretty dilapidated areas. He's living in the older portions of the city—the closet thing to the ghetto areas. They've tried [to keep up their homes], but they're living in a neighborhood that's bound to become—in the next few years—just unlivable. And because they're living in those areas, they're subject to a lot of vandalism; a lot of hoodlums that patrol the streets. It's unsafe to go out on the street.

It was also very clear that most union members felt that employers have an obligation to work with them toward improvements in the community.

> I feel that companies ought to be very glad to enter into any kind of program that's going to make for better citizens, for the simple reason that it's from those better citizens that they're going to have to draw their future employees.
>
> And besides, it eases the burden of their present employees to know that their kids are being taken care of, that they don't have to worry about drugs, school, walking the streets, and getting shot.
>
> There are things the company and the union ought to work together on.

In most communities, labor and management do, of course, work together in various civic endeavors, such as the Community Chest, scouting, and clean-up campaigns. This is a pattern which trade unionists feel is worthwhile, and they would like to continue and strengthen such efforts. However, cooperative effort between employers and unions is not fully trusted as the final solution to workers' problems.

> You know what the trouble with all these areas is? Why the worker feels bad about it? It's whenever they set up commissions to look into the evils of housing, or urban renewal, or anything else. Who do you find on these commissions? You find Joe Blow, who's vice president or on the board of this company. You find Mr. Smith, who's from this other bank. You find another guy who's got $48 million in a Swiss bank and I don't know how much he's got here. You find a guy who's got 14 percent interest in Caesar's Palace. These are the kind of people you find on commissions. You don't find the kind of guy who can bring to the commission a worker's point of view, which to me is more important because that worker has more to lose, and more to gain."

Indicative of this distrust of management's ability to resolve community, social, and economic problems were the comments of one worker who felt that the public education system should give more attention and credit to the labor movement as an important institution in our democracy:

> One thing that real gripes me: Before the teachers became organized, all you every heard a kid [in school] say was "I want to be a management trainee." Everybody wanted to be either a doctor, or a lawyer, or a manager-trainee. I think the school, the public education system, has

to start teaching a little bit more about other than management training and business courses. Why not have courses about labor unions in the school? My nephew is a junior in college and still doesn't know the first thing about unions. I think the school system has got to give equal time to labor.

In addition to relying upon cooperative efforts, the groups with whom we talked seemed to support a larger role for unions, including use of the collective bargaining process, in bringing about social improvement. Because members were well aware of the trade-offs involved in such an event, they did not foresee such activities in the immediate future; but they saw it as an eventual possibility.

I think the time will come when that will happen. What we'll have to do, however, is the same thing that we're doing now with pensions and all these other things. We're going to have to strike that happy medium that will appeal to all people. These things are going to come.

What we have said is that we do expect new things, but we do not expect such things immediately. We want to make additions, but we still have a lot of things that we're working on.

I think that the company sooner or later, and it's going to come to that, is going to have to get involved in these things which make up the life of the worker. Where he lives, his medical care, and all of these type of things.

Some social areas, they believed, were more susceptible than others to the collective bargaining process. In general, these were areas that could be related more or less directly to a particular situation. Pollution by a particular company, for example—in contrast to issues of environmental control in the broad sense—was thought to be an area for the bargaining process. On the other hand, "mass transportation—hell, we ought to have it. But, first, we have to protect ourselves" through higher wages and improved living standards.

I think there's one thing unions could take a hand in, in a lot of plants. They could make their influence felt for the betterment of the entire nation. And that's with pollution. Now there I think a union can exert pressure to nudge a company to get something done, about dumping all those wastes, acids, and that sort of thing into rivers, that destroy them. That's something that could be very responsive to pressure from unions. This could be fresh ground to break.

> Definitely on pollution. We're going to get down to it.

Health care was another area of general agreement on the propriety of union involvement. Most workers felt that it would be possible and appropriate to push for improved community services, not only for the workers and their families but for the broader community as well. Some efforts have already been made in this direction with the union successfully pushing for discount pharmaceutical stores in the inner city.

In all the discussions some time was spent talking about housing, particularly about the possibility of using collective bargaining to improve worker housing. It was suggested that pension funds (usually employer-financed but administered by trustees) could be invested in low-cost housing which would benefit the community as a whole. This kind of idea appealed to the members, although in most cases the pension funds were newly established, and, therefore, workers were more concerned about their adequacy. Members were also enthusiastic about such things as employer-provided day care, although, as one member was careful to point out, day care is essentially an economic issue because it can result in increased family earnings by making it possible for the wife to work.

Understandably, employees in the public sector were more enthusiastic than those in the private sector in seeing ways in which the union could use collective bargaining to bring about better social conditions for the community as a whole.

> We feel that we have an obligation in the community, whether it's sanitation, or education, or housing. And, of course, in politics, which is our lifeline. And we do participate. We're trying to get the city to start an education program for the citizens of the city. To let the citizens know that this is co-op, between the workers and the citizens.

Perhaps one reason why the public employees were more willing to put their jobs on the line to obtain general community improvements was that in Baltimore most of the public employees are black, and many are from the central city. Like most large urban areas, the central city is shockingly deficient in providing services for its citizens. In this case, therefore, the union interest is the clearly consistent community interest, and vice versa. To the question "Is it a citizen responsibility or a union responsibility?" the answer was "It involves us twice—it's a dual responsibility."

This union has already successfully used its influence to obtain improved service for the community and not merely for the workers it represents. There have been several instances, but one is especially interesting. A few days before the beginning of the school term, the city board of education announced that it would not provide aides on public school buses as it had before. Involved were 50 bus aides whose job was to ride the buses to help young children, especially handicapped children who are transported to special classes around the city. The union felt so strongly about this action on the part of the board that it threatened to strike the bus drivers, who were organized (the aides themselves were not organized), unless the aides' positions were restored. The threat was successful; the aides were reinstated before school opened. Obviously, a steelworker could not strike his employer on the same issue. But most of the union members agreed that there were work-related situations where they might strike to bring about better conditions. As one union officer summed it up:

> So what we're really trying to say is that if we expect to do anything, it's got to be attacked from all levels, including collective bargaining. It's got to be attacked from every possible angle in order to gain what we're trying to gain.

THE EXPANDING ROLE OF UNIONS

Unions have long been the bastion of the blue-collar worker at the workplace—at once the aggressor for his economic interests and the defender of his employment rights. That they have served him well through the institution of collective bargaining is a view strongly supported by our interviews with local union members and officials in Baltimore.

Even while citing their priority need for higher wages to meet rising living costs and more extensive fringe benefits to meet medical and other expenses, these union members attest to gains they have made through collective bargaining contracts. They feel frustrations on the job, but at the same time point to the improvements in working conditions already won in negotiations. Even the broader issues not directly involved with the job, such as education and training programs away from the work site, are beginning to break through the surface.

If collective bargaining is labor's stock in trade, it is obviously viewed as a growth stock with a future as well as a past. That it has not solved all the problems of the blue-collar workers is quite apparent; but it has provided a means for seeking to resolve them, and the results have been impressive. Having this source of collective strength and the machinery to assert it gives the blue-collar worker an outlet to find a relief from his disaffections that others do not have. Through prior gains the labor movement has helped to minimize these disaffections. As a consequence, the blue-collar union member and the black militant or the youth who sees no relief through established institutions are in different frameworks. The blue-collar worker is not about to explode, nor is he about to discard the labor movement, which is a source of his power.

Our discussions with union members holding jobs in both private and public organizations clearly revealed that the major concern of the blue-collar worker, whatever his job, is economic. His prime goal is to establish an adequate standard of living and to escape the treadmill that one union member described as "attempting to catch up with the cost of living."

But while the blue-collar worker's problems may be primarily economic, they are not solely that. Indeed, these problems are quite obviously becoming broader as the worker seeks more satisfaction and rewards on the job. He is becoming increasingly concerned about working conditions, chances for promotion, and the factors such as education and training that will enhance his prospects for upgrading.

"There's only so many ways you can cut the pie," as one trade unionist kept repeating. But many of the blue-collar workers we interviewed were ready to take some of the economic pie and cut it up for some items not directly related to wages and fringe benefits. From the total package, they were willing to apply some of their earned income to issues which would yield less immediate gain but would pay off in the long run.

In the Baltimore city institutions, for example, the unanimous feeling of the social workers who represented the wide spectrum of skills was a willingness to apply some of the cents-per-hour in a contract toward more education. Of course, this response is related directly to the civil service strictures requiring specific educational attainments to advance on the job; but it is an indication of the broadening scope of collective bargaining. It was clear from the interviews that the union members are prepared to utilize the bargaining process increasingly as a means for achieving broader ends and not merely for pure economic issues.

The flexibility of collective bargaining has long been apparent. Two decades ago, health and welfare and pension benefits were strangers to the bargaining contract; so also were supplemental unemployment benefits. Now they are accepted as basic contract ingredients. Longer vacations are now being extended into sabbatical leave for senior workers, and scholarship funds are being negotiated for the children of union members. The trend continues, and the list of issues in the negotiated contract continues to lengthen. As new job situations arise, the labor movement brings them into focus at the bargaining table. It has displayed a capability to adjust to new situations and indeed, through the process of collective bargaining, has helped to bring about change and not just respond to it.

The problems of the blue-collar worker today, of course, are not just work-related. Like other people, he is beset by social and community problems, though because of his place on the social spectrum he is perhaps more directly threatened than most. Because of his reliance on the labor movement to solve his problems, it may be inevitable that he will turn to unions to help solve these other problems that do not stem directly from the job. He is no less affected by community conditions because they are not directly the responsibility of his employer. Concerns over inadequate education for himself and his children are becoming more prevalent. He is worried about substandard housing and pollution and crime. But more than being just disturbed, he now talks of doing something about them.

Social and community issues are hardly unfamiliar to the labor movement. But for the most part these subjects have been tackled through the forums of labor federations at the national level and through state and city central labor bodies. Their thrust has been via the legislative route, and the solutions have been primarily embodied in new laws. Nevertheless, such political activities are not without cost to the union member. He is well aware that his dues support labor's lobbying efforts, and he is conditioned to help paying the freight. This could make it easier when the time comes to trade off pennies for noneconomic benefits in negotiations.

These lobbying activities are not isolated from collective bargaining. The negotiated contract frequently can be a source to supplement legislation, for example, Social Security payments enhanced by union-negotiated pensions. This double-barreled thrust could well become the pattern for the future.

The labor movement is unlikely to rely exclusively on either approach, but when community conditions directly affect him, the union member appears ready to make some of them a matter for collective bargaining. Particularly in the central city, where the union member is likely to be most prominently represented, it is in his direct interest to have adequate transportation, to walk along safe streets, and to have adequate care for his children in day-care centers. More and more it appears that the collective bargaining process may well be used to gain supplementary forms of employer-paid benefits: perhaps extra police protection around the plant, partial tuition payments for education, payments to help offset costs of child care. Even pollution, where it directly relates to the union member—either because the environmental damage is caused by his employer or because it affects his own home environment—could well become a bargaining issue, as one interview indicated. Noise pollution at the plant is already a subject of negotiations.

To the blue-collar worker, the problems are not just where he works. They also pertain to where, and how, he lives. Increasingly, he views benefits earned on the job as a way to pay for the activities he pursues away from the job. One example is the relatively new contract benefit, extra vacation payment above the regular paycheck to pay for travel costs and other expenses. It may be a lengthy step, but in time this could turn into something like the leisure-time fund from which workers could draw to finance a favorite recreational activity.

The findings from our interviews in Baltimore clearly indicate a restiveness on the part of local union members mingled with faith in the collective bargaining process. While the workers with whom we talked were heterogeneous in income and industry, there appeared to be a general agreement that the collective bargaining process may well be used increasingly in the future to resolve "restiveness" off, as well on on, the job. As the scope of problems broadens in the future, the labor movement could provide the vehicle for finding solutions.

To be sure, these findings are necessarily tentative and drawn from limited contacts. But a thread of uniformity runs through the interviews that bears further investigation in other regions and among other unions and industries: this is the premise that collective bargaining will remain the process to help the blue-collar worker achieve his expanding goals.

8. BLACK AND WHITE BLUE-COLLAR WORKERS AND UNIONS

by Ray Marshall

CONFLICT: PRESENT AND POTENTIAL

Public concerns seem to focus on particular problems for a time and then swing, pendulumlike, to others. During the 1950s and 1960s, attention was devoted to the problems of Negroes and other minorities, with very little apparent concern for white manual workers. However, now that white blue-collar workers have given evidence at the polls and in public demonstrations that they are dissatisfied with public policies, including those espoused by their unions, government officials have become concerned for this group.

A major point of conflict between black and white manual workers has been the control of jobs by unions. Historically, the labor organizations have been controlled mainly by whites, except for a few all or predominantly black organizations like the Brotherhood of Sleeping Car Porters. Moreover, since most immigrants were workers seeking to establish themselves in the American system, white ethnics have given strong support to the American labor movement. Historically, these white-controlled unions have been used to ration scarce job opportunities to particular groups of white workers, especially the better jobs in the railroad, printing, and construction crafts.

As Negroes migrated out of the rural South, they began to challenge the unions' racial restrictions. Negro demands for job opportunities became particularly strong during World War II and resulted in a steady series of government programs to improve their lot, culminating in the Civil Rights Act of 1964 and antipoverty and manpower legislation of the 1960s. Many white unionists now think that the government has gone too far in promoting job opportunities for Negroes at the expense of whites. Since white unionists are a strong political force, some observers are afraid their reactions will impede additional progress in equal-employment-opportunities programs, aggravate race conflicts, and split the Negro-labor political coalitions formed during the 1930s. Some even see a danger of a sharp swing to the right in the American labor movement.

An examination of the historical relation between black and white manualists in the American labor movement provides some insight into the basic causal relation at work.

DEVELOPMENT OF THE RELATION

The AFL

The main labor federation in American labor history before the 1930s was the American Federation of Labor (AFL), organized in 1886. From its inception, Samuel Gompers and other AFL leaders were committed to organizing workers without regard to race or religion. This policy seems to have been followed steadfastly until about 1895, when the Machinists were admitted to the federation by the subterfuge of transferring the race bar from their constitution to their ritual.

Ideologically, the AFL never abandoned its opposition to excluding Negroes from its affiliated unions, but Gompers apparently surrendered to the reality of racial discrimination among the federation's members. While he continued to emphasize that the better part of economic good sense was to organize workers regardless of race, creed, or color, he finally decided that it was better to organize whites and Negroes into segregated locals than not to organize them at all.

As a consequence, the AFL's affiliates followed a variety of racial practices ranging from complete exclusion to almost complete acceptance of Negroes. Although the exact number is not known with certainty, in 1930 there were at least 26 national unions which formally barred Negroes from membership. Many other unions barred Negroes by various informal means, including agreements not to sponsor Negroes for membership; refusal to admit Negroes into apprenticeship programs or to accept their applications (or simply to ignore their applications); general "understandings" to vote against Negroes if they were proposed (for example, as few as three members of some locals could bar applicants for membership); refusal of journeyman status to Negroes by means of examinations which either were not given to whites or were rigged so that Negroes could not pass them; exertion of political pressure on governmental licensing agencies to ensure that Negroes failed tests; and restriction of membership to sons, nephews, or other relatives of members. Most of the unions which barred Negroes from membership by formal means were in the transportation industry, whereas those which used informal exclusion were mainly in the building and printing trades.

A number of unions which did not wholly bar Negroes organized them into auxiliary locals, an arrangement which was usually adopted in lieu of formal exclusion and which was sometimes the next stage following the elimination of formal restrictions. An intermediate stage between outright exclusion and auxiliary locals frequently was the organization of federal locals for Negroes. These locals were affiliated directly with the AFL. The difference between segregated locals and auxiliaries was that the segregated locals had separate charters and equal status with white locals, though this distinction was often more theoretical than real because the whites in fact bargained for the Negro locals. Segregated locals existed throughout the country, but most of them were in the South. In some cases, segregation was insisted upon by the Negroes as a condition for joining. Segregation also was imposed because of community pressure or local laws against integrated meetings. Indeed, about the only union with a long history in the South which did not establish segregated locals was the United Mine Workers, whose members were isolated and relatively impervious to community pressure. Even so, seating in United Mine Workers' (UMW) union locals was often segregated, and in some cases in Alabama it remained segregated as late as 1965; and the miners frequently were attacked in the South because of their integrated meetings.

In view of these circumstances, it was perhaps natural for Negro leaders to ally themselves with powerful employers, especially some big companies with headquarters outside the South, who were willing to work with Negro leaders like Booker T. Washington in order to obtain a steady supply of cheap, nonunion labor. In his famous Atlanta Exposition address in 1895, Washington advised Negroes to shun politics and to acquire the necessary skills to meet the competition of whites. He explained the proemployer sentiments of Negroes as follows:

> The average Negro who comes to town does not understand the necessity or advantage of a labor organization which stands between him and his employer and aims apparently to make a monopoly of opportunity for labor. . . . [He is] more accustomed to work for persons than for wages. When he gets a job, therefore, he is inclined to consider the source from which it comes.[1]

Antiunionism among Negroes extended to unions which admitted them, and although the extent to which Negroes were used as strikebreakers probably has been exaggerated, Negroes did play an important role before the 1930s in breaking strikes in such industries as meat-packing, steel, coal and ore mining, automobiles, and railroads. White workers also were extensively employed to break strikes in these industries, but Negroes were more conspicuous and far more resented by the strikers.

Negro-AFL relations were, to say the least, strained by the time of World War I, and both Negroes and union leaders considered the other side to be at fault.

The AFL's racial practices were thus products of a complex constellation of social, economic, and political forces. Industrialization, urbanization, and Negro migration probably were the most important factors tending to change race relations in unions as well as in the whole society. The industrialization of the United States and of the South after the 1880s caused many Northern employers to look to the South for a source of cheap manpower to run the mines, factories, and steel mills. The steady flow of Negroes out of the rural South was stimulated by wars and other events. War not only increased the demand for labor but, by halting immigration from abroad, reduced the available supply of unskilled white labor. The demand for Negro labor continued during the 1920s as employers turned to Negro strikebreakers to buttress their antiunion, open-shop movements, and as congressional action permanently diminished the flow of immigrants. These developments wrought a virtual transformation of the Negro population. In contrast to only 12 percent in 1910, by 1964 more than half of all American Negroes lived outside the states that had made up the Confederacy, and 90 percent of employed Negroes worked outside agriculture.

The urbanization of the Negro population had important consequences for race relations. It increased the Negro's political power, especially in the North, where Negroes could vote and where their political power was enhanced by two-party political systems. The urban environment also tended to raise the Negro's aspirations and caused greater demands for equal education, civil rights, and job opportunities. Moreover, migration brought the Negro increasingly into conflict with white workers and their unions. Race riots erupted in the North as employers imported Negroes as strikebreakers, as cheap labor, or as a way of averting unionization of their companies. There were particularly bitter race riots in East St. Louis and Chicago in 1917 and 1919.

The expansion of union membership during World War I brought the unions face to face with the Negro problem. Some unions responded by organizing Negroes on an equal basis with whites; but where they would not, the AFL followed its policy of chartering locals affiliated directly with the federation. This policy proved quite unsatisfactory, because the AFL usually conceded to the interests of international unions and did not adequately represent the Negroes in these federal locals. The Negro federal locals in jurisdictions covered by discriminating railroad unions asked the AFL either to require these discriminating unions to admit Negroes or to grant national charters to the federal locals. These demands went unheeded, however, as the international unions responded by organizing Negroes into auxiliaries, an arrangement which was bitterly opposed by the Negroes, who were thus denied equal representation. Although some Negroes remained in the auxiliaries as a condition for retaining their jobs, others rejected this inferior status and refused to join the union. The auxiliaries also proved unsatisfactory to the unions because they could neither present a united front in collective bargaining nor collect dues from Negroes in their jurisdictions who, in spite of their unequal status, nevertheless benefited from the unions' collective bargaining activities.

Another factor tending to change the racial practices of the AFL and its affiliates was the growth of organized Negro opposition to union discrimination. Two of these organizations, the National Association for the Advancement of Colored People (NAACP) and the National Urban League (NUL), frequently called upon the AFL to eradicate racial discrimination.

A number of Negro labor organizations fought discrimination from within the labor movement. By far the most important of these was the Brotherhood of Sleeping Car Porters (BSCP), which had an influence in the Negro community and in the labor movement far out of proportion to its size. The leader of the BSCP, A. Philip Randolph, became a symbol of the Negro fight for recognition within the trade unions.

The CIO

The Congress of Industrial Organizations (CIO) was formed as a result of what its leaders thought was the AFL's failure to take full advantage of the favorable organizing climate of the 1930s. The AFL responded to the CIO's challenge by extending its membersip to older jurisdictions and by launching organizing drives in new fields.

It was this rivalry that caused the AFL and its affiliates to relax some of their racial restrictions. The CIO adopted an equalitarian racial position from the beginning. One reason for this position was the CIO's desire to appeal to the large numbers of Negroes in the steel, automobile, mining, packing, rubber, and other mass-production industries. No CIO leader better understood the importance of equalitarian racial policies for successful unionism than the United Mine Workers' John L. Lewis, who provided much of the initial financial and leadership support for the CIO. The UMW long enjoyed a favorable reputation among Negroes in both the North and the South because of its steadfast refusal to sanction discrimination even in the face of vigorous opposition in the important Southern coal areas.

The CIO's racial policies also were influenced by its industrial structure, which gave its leaders a much different outlook from that of the craft-oriented leaders of the AFL. Industrial unions have very little control over the racial compositions of their membership because they do not control jobs; they attempt to organize workers who are already employed. Craft unions, on the other hand, have the ability to determine whom the employer hires because they often control the supply of labor. Industrial unions therefore have less opportunity for discrimination. The industrial unions also tended to have broader objectives than the craft unions. A narrow job-oriented organization is likely to discriminate against Negroes or other groups if its leaders feel that discrimination strengthens the economic position of the members. On the other hand, an organization like the CIO, which has broad social objectives, will appeal to the Negro community for political support in helping to achieve these objectives.

These several considerations help to explain why the CIO adopted a nondiscrimination policy and made vigorous efforts to gain a favorable image among Negroes. These efforts included financial contributions to organizations such as the NAACP and to Negro churches and newspapers; the adoption of equalitarian racial resolutions; the establishment of a Committee to Abolish Racial Discrimination to help implement its policy; and the service of its leaders in official positions in such organizations as the NAACP and the National Urban League. The NAACP and the NUL were convinced of the genuineness of the CIO's policies and urged Negroes to join its affiliates. This position did not go unopposed within the black community, because some of the proemployer Negro leaders strongly objected to Negroes' joining unions. But the potential power of the CIO and the New Deal programs which helped Negroes greatly reduced the influence of antiunion Negro leaders.

The cooperative relation between the CIO and the Negro community proved mutually beneficial. The NAACP actively campaigned for CIO unions, and the CIO gave financial support to civil rights organizations and civil rights causes.

The foregoing is not meant to imply, however, that the CIO automatically followed equalitarian policies and received Negro support while all AFL locals discriminated and were shunned by Negroes. Some CIO locals barred Negroes from membership, and others permitted segregated locals; and Negroes either segregated themselves or were segregated by whites in many, and perhaps most, of the "integrated" CIO unions in the South.

But the most serious problem for Negroes and CIO unions was

segregated seniority lines, which restricted Negroes to certain menial and disagreeable jobs. These seniority arrangements were not entirely the responsibility of the unions, of course, but few CIO unions actively tried to abolish job segregation in the South. And the problem was not restricted to the South, for CIO members struck in Detroit and other Northern cities during World War II, when Negroes were hired or upgraded to formerly all-white jobs. It should be noted, however, that the CIO's national affiliates almost invariably cooperated with employers in putting down these racial strikes, and there appears to have been considerable upgrading of Negroes outside the South during World War II.

The AFL-CIO

At the time of the AFL-CIO merger in 1955, race relations in America were undergoing momentous changes. These changes were caused in large measure by a continuation of trends brought about by the transformation of the Negro population from one which was predominantly rural and Southern to one which was mainly urban and Northern. As Negroes moved to urban areas, their need for better education increased along with their aspirations and their political power.

In some ways, however, the Negro's position deteriorated in the North. Although Negroes had inferior positions in the South, they were able to develop institutions—schools, churches, professional and fraternal organizations, and unions—which they controlled within the limits imposed by institutionalized segregation. The Southern Negro community also produced its own civil rights organizations and business and professional leaders, and although Negroes were relegated to inferior occupational positions, they had some good jobs within the Negro community.

In the North, on the other hand, Negroes had few institutions which they controlled; the church began to lose its influence; predominantly Negro schools were controlled by white principals and teachers; and whites held many of the better jobs in the Negro communities. Indeed, even civil rights organizations were controlled more by white liberals there than in the South. Negroes probably also were frustrated because they did not understand Northern whites as well as they had understood Southern whites. Northerners freely condemned discrimination in the South but resisted integration and fled to the suburbs as Negroes moved in.

The merger also coincided with ideological and political attacks on unions from a number of quarters. These attacks did not come entirely from labor's traditional enemies, but also from many intellectuals who supported the civil rights movement. Some of these intellectuals had backed unions during the 1930s but became increasingly critical of what they considered the labor movement's willingness to deal with the "establishment" rather than fighting to change it. These critics considered discrimination to be related to the labor movement's other defects. Intellectuals of the extreme left, for example, consider racial discrimination to be a part of class oppression created by the capitalist system. Since the labor movement openly supports the capitalist system, according to their view, it is not meeting its responsibilities to either black or white workers because only militant or radical reorganization of the system will solve the country's fundamental economic, political, and social problems. Realizing the importance of history to ideology, some of these critics emphasize the racist views of Samuel Gompers and other labor leaders. Since the labor movement has become a fundamental part of the American capitalist system, left-wing critics hope to gain Negro support for their programs by establishing a close association between the AFL racism, capitalism, and the AFL-CIO.

Many radicals, having traditionally emphasized black separatist movements, encouraged the growth of black-power ideas stimulated by ghetto conditions. The Negro's sense of frustration, powerlessness, and rejection in the ghetto produced a resurgence of black nationalist feeling, especially among Negro males, whose frustration was compounded by unemployment and underemployment, and by welfare systems which (up to 1961) allowed benefits for women and children only if no able-bodied man was present. It is therefore not surprising that many young Negro males resorted to militancy and revolutionary rhetoric in order to protest their conditions.

Relations between the AFL-CIO and the Negro community were also influenced by the fact that two-thirds of the official positions of the merged organizations, including the presidency, went to the AFL, which was never able to overcome its unfavorable image in the Negro community and never had close relations with civil rights organizations. Furthermore, the AFL-CIO Executive Council admitted two unions, the Brotherhood of Locomotive Firemen and the Brotherhood of Railway Trainmen, even though they still had race bars in their constitutions. Negro-labor relations were exacerbated by a number of widely publicized cases of legal action against discriminating local unions in Northern cities with large Negro concentrations. At a time of increasing unemployment among Negroes, there was a growing conviction that union discrimination in apprenticeship training and upgrading within plants was at least partly responsible for the Negro's economic plight.

These developments, therefore, produced strained relations between the AFL-CIO and the Negro community, and these manifested themselves in a number of ways. One of the most significant was the tension in the working relation which had been established between the NAACP and other Negro organizations and the CIO. The NAACP's victories in school desegregation cases increased its prestige in the Negro community, but the changes taking place in race relations made it difficult for it to continue to work closely with organizations, like the AFL-CIO, which were considered by increasing numbers of Negroes to be discriminatory. Also, the NAACP's position of leadership enabled it to rely more on Negroes and less on unions and liberal whites for financial support. At the same time, however, the NAACP was being challenged in the Negro community by younger and more militant leadership. These developments made it inevitable that the NAACP would become increasingly critical of unions.

Opposition to the AFL-CIO also came from an organization of Negro trade unionists within its own ranks and the formation of Negro caucuses within the various international unions. In 1960, for example, following vigorous debate over race matters in the 1957 and 1959 AFL-CIO conventions, A. Philip Randolph of the Brotherhood of Sleeping Car Porters and other Negro union leaders formed the Negro American Labor Council (NALC), which sought, among other things, to fight discrimination from within the labor movement.

The attacks on the labor movement by the NAACP and other organizations were not restricted to the craft and railroad unions, which had the longest and worst records of discrimination. For example, Herbert Hill, labor secretary of the NAACP, launched a vigorous attack against the International Ladies' Garment Workers' Union (ILGWU), long regarded as one of the staunchest allies of Negro rights. Hill accused the ILGWU of barring Negroes from positions of leadership in the union and from higher-paying jobs. Although the ILGWU was defended by the NALC and A. Philip Randolph, the NAACP fully supported Hill in this conflict. Significantly, the NAACP Board of Directors restated Hill's charges against the ILGWU and concluded that "the union cannot live on its past glories. It must face the reality of its present practices and move to eradicate inequalities."[2]

In spite of continuing friction between the Negro community and the AFL-CIO, the New Deal coalition of union, liberal, and civil rights forces persisted throughout the 1960s. This alliance was continued partly because of mutual dependence of Negroes and unions. Moreover, the AFL-CIO's decisive support of civil rights legislation strengthened its position in the Negro community. The publicity given to racial discrimination and the undeniable fact that widespread discrimination existed in craft unions, on the railroads, and in the building, printing, and skilled machinists' trades changed the AFL-CIO's posture from one of defensiveness to one of advocating measures to eliminate discrimination.

The breach which developed between the AFL-CIO and some Negro leaders in the years following the merger of these federations had thus been partially closed by the late 1960s. One important factor that improved Negro-union relations was the realization by many civil rights and labor leaders that their common objectives and common enemies were more important than the factors that divided them. Few civil rights leaders doubted the value of the AFL-CIO's help in achieving the Negro's political objectives or questioned the union's sincerity in its attempt to implement its civil rights policies. It became increasingly clear, moreover, that the AFL-CIO's power over its affiliates was rather limited and that the main problem of discrimination was at the local and national union levels. The federation's relations with the Urban League and the Negro American Labor Council seemed especially improved by 1966, when the former entered into an agreement with the AFL-CIO to undertake a program to enhance the job and promotion opportunities of Negroes, and the latter announced that it was shifting from its earlier position of attacking the AFL-CIO to one of alliance and cooperation. The AFL-CIO's relations with the NAACP were also improved, although there was considerable mistrust and mutual antipathy between the association's labor secretary and the federation's leaders.

Conflict over Policy

Partly as a result of the Negro-labor political coalition, a number of measures were adopted during the 1960s to promote Negro employment opportunities. Especially important were the Manpower Development and Training Act (MDTA) of 1962, the Civil Rights and Economic Opportunity Acts of 1964, and subsequent amendments which were designed primarily to help the disadvantaged. Also in 1964, the National Labor Relations Board extended the "duty of fair representation" imposed on unions which won bargaining rights under the National Labor Relations Act to include elimination of racial discrimination. Prior to that time, the Labor Relations Act did not prohibit racial discrimination as such. Moreover, the federal government applied new concepts to the enforcement of antidiscrimination provisions in government contracts during the 1960s. An especially significant concept was the idea of affirmative action, applied to government contractors. The underlying rationale for affirmative action was the conviction of government officials that the mere elimination of discrimination would lead to relatively limited advances by Negroes. Contractors were therefore required to take affirmative action to ensure that Negroes were recruited for jobs or upgraded into positions from which they had previously been excluded.

A key factor creating conflict over the affirmative action concept, however, was its lack of operational precision, because no one could say exactly how many Negroes should be hired or admitted to unions. In order to give the idea more precision, those entrusted with the enforcement of the equal-opportunity provisions of government contracts often implied that employers and unions were expected to meet certain racial quotas based on the proportion of Negroes in the general population. This led many unions and white workers to feel that the federal government was determined to promote the advancement of Negroes by giving them preferential treatment compared with whites.

One of the most important controversies over preferential treatment in the building trades came in the summer of 1969, when Assistant Secretary of Labor Arthur Fletcher issued an action plan for government contractors in the Philadelphia construction industry. Under this plan, builders were required to "set specific goals of minority manpower utilization" which met standards determined by the local Office of Federal Contract Compliance (OFCC) and contracting agency representatives. Although Fletcher's memorandum declared that the specific goals were "not intended and shall not be used to discriminate against any qualified applicant or employee," the "Philadelphia plan" was widely criticized by contractors and unions as requiring quotas and preferential treatment.

In spite of these objections, the Labor Department imposed the Philadelphia plan and vigorously defended the concept which it embodied. Indeed, the basic idea was extended to contractors in other industries by a general order. Union leaders objected to the Philadelphia plan on a number of grounds, one of which was that it was imposed upon unions by the federal government. The unions would have preferred an extension of the "outreach" concept, by which unions and community organizations agreed to fill a certain number of positions through special outreach organizations whose function was to recruit, tutor, and place Negroes in apprenticeship and journeyman positions. Moreover, the union leaders argued that the Philadelphia plan would not ensure that blacks got jobs in the construction industry because contractors could merely move black workers from nonfederal jobs to federal jobs in order to meet the OFCC's requirements. These union leaders emphasized that in the construction industry it was much more important to be attached to the labor market than it was to be attached to a specific job. Following this principle, unions, contractors, and civil rights organizations in Chicago developed the "Chicago plan," based on outreach and voluntary negotiation concepts. For its part, the Labor Department did not object to such plans and, indeed, seemed to prefer them; but it was convinced that pressure such as that imposed by the Philadelphia plan was necessary in order to get unions and contractors to adopt voluntary plans.

The picture of white trade-union attitudes toward civil rights matters that emerged at the end of the 1960s was one of considerable complexity. White trade unionists obviously were increasingly hostile to many of the programs designed for the disadvantaged. There also was some evidence that white trade unionists were very much concerned about neighborhood integration. However, it is not clear to what extent these attitudes were determined by racial considerations and to what extent they were a reflection of economic forces. For example, many white workers have considerable investments in their homes and feel that neighborhood integration would cause a deterioration in real estate values. Moreover, neighborhoods in transition seem to be characterized by high crime rates inflicted to some degree on the families of white manualists, although blacks themselves clearly bear the heaviest burden of rising crime rates. As many observers have emphasized, therefore, it is too simple to brand the white manualist a racist because he is concerned about adequate police protection or real estate values. The blue-collar worker is particularly concerned when this charge is made by upper-income whites who have moved to the suburbs.

The actions of higher-income whites raise considerable doubt about the finding that racial prejudices tend to decline with higher incomes and education. Perhaps the higher-income and better-educated whites express more liberal attitudes on race because they have more economic power to avoid the disagreeable consequences which might follow from race conflict. Lubell, for example, considers the movement of better-income whites to the suburbs of considerable significance in aggravating the racial strife in Northern cities:

> It would be difficult to organize a process more surely calculated to aggravate racial strife within the city as lopsided black concentrations account for an increasing share of a declining population; the whites left generally tend to be older and poorer families who cannot afford to move. In most Northern cities, they usually are factory workers either from Southern or border states or Catholics descended from Italian, Polish, Hungarian, Czech, Slovenian, and other eastern European elements who tend also to have strong community ties.[3]

Lubell's conclusions confirm earlier studies which find a strong relation between the degree of one's attachment to his neighborhood and rejection of neighborhood integration. Dietrich Reitzes, for example, found that rejection of Negroes in the neighborhood did not apply to barring their involvement in union activities and the acceptance of Negroes at work.[4]

FACTORS RESPONSIBLE FOR THE RELATION

Attitudes of White Workers

How important is race in the constellation of factors producing dissatisfaction by white manualists in general and union members in particular? We do not have enough information to answer this question. We do know something about the relative progress of white manualists during the 1960s, although we do not know the extent to which the relatively greater progress made by black manualists was responsible for the white manualists' discontent.

Some observers claim to see evidence of a white backlash in voting behavior. It is sometimes argued, for example, that union support for George Wallace in the 1968 presidential election was a positive indication of racial bias. If this were true, an opinion survey conducted by Louis Harris on November 2, 1968, indicated less "prejudice" among union members who earned less than $3,000 per year than among those who earned $15,000 or more per year, as indicated by the following comparison of votes for George Wallace by income:

	Percent of group voting for Wallace		
Income level	*Total*	*Union members*	*Others*
Under $3,000	14%	4%	15%
$3,000 to $4,999	14	9	14
$5,000 to $6,999	16	17	15
$7,000 to $9,999	13	15	11
$10,000 to $14,999	11	11	11
$15,000 and over	7	20	5

These responses show that union members in the $5,000 to $10,000 income bracket gave greater support to George Wallace than did nonunion people in the same income group. If it indicated racial bias, this survey also would seem to support the conclusion that prejudice declines with income; however, the union responses clearly differ from the nonunion responses, because Wallace received relatively few union votes from those with less than $5,000 income and relatively many from those with over $15,000 annual income. Nevertheless, these results are inconclusive because they have not been controlled for nonracial factors which caused union members and others to vote for George Wallace.

On direct questions relating to race, there is some evidence that union members on the whole were slightly more favorable to the passage of the Civil Rights Act of 1964, as indicated by the following results of a Gallup poll taken December 31, 1963, which asked, "Would you like to see Congress pass the Civil Rights Act (1964)?"

	Nonunionists (3,214)	*Union members (575)*
Yes	59%	64%
No	32	28
Not sure	8	10

A later poll taken by Louis Harris (April 15, 1968) tested union and nonunion workers' response to the question, "Have Negroes tried to move too fast?"

	Total	*Union members*	*AFL-CIO*	*Teamsters*
Too fast	61%	69%	63%	66%
Too slow	9	6	6	4
About right	20	18	24	11
Not sure	10	6	7	19

These figures suggest that many union members who favored the Civil Rights Act of 1964 also thought, perhaps as the result of riots and demonstrations between 1964 and 1968, that Negroes had tried to move too fast. This too is far from conclusive because the responses are not controlled for other factors (such as income, education, and region) which might have influenced attitudes about the rate of racial progress.

Since a great deal has been written about the so-called "backlash" among white ethnics, it is instructive to examine some race attitudes by ethnic and religious groups. In a Harris poll conducted in March

1970, about half the people of Anglo-Saxon extraction thought blacks had pushed too fast for equality as compared with the following percentages of Americans from other ethnic groups: Irish, 37 percent; Italian, 42 percent; Polish, 44 percent. However, since regional characteristics are not controlled and since people of Anglo-Saxon extraction predominate in the South, where attitudes are less favorable to racial equality, it is possible that other ethnic groups might be more hostile to Negroes in the North than Anglo-Saxons were. The following proportions of persons of various religious faiths thought that blacks were pushing too rapidly for racial equality: Protestants, 51 percent; Catholics, 47 percent; Jews, 22 percent.

Without further disaggregation, these data suggest that minority ethnic groups are less, rather than more, opposed to the Negroes' efforts to achieve racial equality. We also have some fragmentary, though consistent, evidence that blacks and whites have vastly different conceptions of the causes of the Negro's inferior economic position. As a general rule, Negroes are likely to give heavy weight to discrimination while whites are likely to stress the Negro's inadequate preparation and qualifications for jobs. For example, Ferman concluded after a review of management experiences in 20 companies that "most whites felt that Negroes have the same job opportunities as anyone else and deny that prejudice or discrimination operate in the case of Negroes."[5] Although few whites studied by Ferman thought Negroes should be denied equal job opportunities, most thought the solution to the Negro job problem was to have Negroes help themselves through more education and training and better motivation.

It is unfortunate that we do not have more information about union members which controls solely for union membership. Although the information available suggests that union members do not differ markedly in their attitudes from the communities in which they live, more information would probably support the following conclusions with respect to the attitudes of union members:

(1) Union members on the whole would probably be more favorably disposed to equal rights for Negroes than nonunion members if we could control for other factors. This assumes that the equalitarian positions taken by most international unions and the AFL-CIO have had positive effects on the attitudes of union members, as suggested by their relatively favorable attitude toward the Civil Rights Act of 1964.

(2) Union members have less resistance to integration on the job than they do to social and residential integration, a rather consistent finding to be explained in greater detail below.

(3) The union member's commitment to racial equality varies with the strength of his loyalty to the union and the importance of the union for his job control. Other things equal, younger workers with stable jobs will show more hostility to Negro job aspirations than older union members, because younger members are less likely to attribute their conditions to the union and are more likely to feel threatened by Negro job demands and taxation for social programs which are beneficial to Negroes. People with strong commitments to their unions are more likely to favor racial equality on the job than people with limited commitments are. This would seem to stem from the realization that a common front by all workers strengthens collective bargaining. However, the union's response to Negro demands also will depend on such other factors as the structure and objectives of the union, its geographic location, and the cultural and ethnic homogeneity of union membership.

(4) As a general rule, those union members, like the coal miners, who can isolate themselves from community racial and social pressures probably exhibit less racial bias than union members who are closely identified with their communities.

The preoccupation with the attitudes of union members and white manualists could lead to the conclusion that racial harmony might be achieved through education campaigns to change the attitudes of union members. However, union experience seems to support the conclusion that circumstances are more important determinants of attitude than attitudes are of circumstances. In other words, a biased union leader or member will be more likely to acquire more favorable attitudes toward Negroes if he finds himself in circumstances which require him to practice equality (need to appeal for black votes, pressure from employers or government agencies) than he would if he were favorably disposed toward racial equality and found himself in circumstances which made it difficult to practice racial equality (need to appeal to racists to get elected or to keep a job). For example, Lubell found racial attitudes of white Southerners to be somewhat more favorable toward various civil rights practices in 1968 than they had been in 1961, undoubtedly in part because whites had been forced by legislation and black pressures to do things they would not have accepted in the 1940s and 1950s.[6] As a consequence, it may be concluded that purely racial preferences are of marginal significance for behavior, which is more likely to be influenced by political, economic, physical, or moral power considerations. Long-term racial attitudes determine the direction of behavior within the framework of these constraints.

Other Factors Influencing the Relation

Community race relations have a profound influence on the attitudes of white union members toward race relations within unions, especially when prevailing sentiment is embodied in legislation. One of the main influences of law is to establish moral authority for various practices. Even when it is not vigorously enforced, civil rights legislation is important because it establishes a positive influence for racial equality—just as segregation laws tended to establish segregation as morally correct. Although law does not automatically change conduct, it certainly causes a shift in the direction of the sentiments expressed by the legislation.

In spite of the positive influence of legislative authority, the law will be undermined if it is incompatible with underlying political reality or fundamental concepts of justice. For example, while a majority of white workers were and are convinced that people should not be economically disadvantaged solely because of their race, they clearly disagree with Negroes over the extent to which racial discrimination is responsible for the black workers' economic disadvantages. To some extent, this is a problem of semantics. When white workers use the term "racism" or "discrimination," they are likely to mean specific overt acts of discrimination because of race. For blacks, on the other hand, racism is less likely to mean specific overt acts than institutionalized behavior patterns which make it difficult for blacks to upgrade themselves. The tendency to blame white racism for the Negroes' plight has therefore generated hostility among whites who might concede that the Negro faces institutionalized segregation but do not consider themselves personally responsible for the black man's disadvantages. Indeed, to feel a sense of guilt for racial discrimination probably requires a high level of abstract sophistication, such as that possessed by liberal intellectuals. Manualists are much more likely to be concerned with concrete facts and circumstances than with such abstractions.

Some unions have been able to avoid social pressures for or against segregation because they are relatively isolated from community pressures. We noted this in the case of the United Mine Workers, whose geographical isolation gave them a degree of social immunity. In other cases, unions acquired a degree of immunity in the South by keeping inconspicuous certain racial practices which violated prevailing moral sentiments. For example, some Bricklayers' locals have practiced racial integration in the South for years but in the greatest secrecy.

Outside the South, race relations have been less structured, but racial discrimination has been no less real. To some extent, racial discrimination outside the South has been an ethnic phenomenon. As various ethnic groups immigrated to the United States and settled in Northern communities, they tended to form close-knit units in order to protect their interests or to perpetuate their identities. It was common, for example, for local unions to be made up of particular language groups who defended their jobs from all outsiders. In craft locals, ethnic job control could be accomplished through control of the supply of labor through the union. Ethnics in industrial unions have less control over the supply of labor because the employers do the hiring, but ethnics sometimes perpetuate their control over jobs by controlling the union. As successive waves of immigrants entered various industries, they challenged those who had controlled the jobs and the unions. Indeed, in many industries the occupational hierarchies reflect the sequence in which various immigrant groups entered the industry.

As a consequence of these developments, conflicts developed between various ethnic and racial groups which sometimes were subtle and sometimes not. As a general rule, the stronger the identification of particular ethnic groups with geographic neighborhoods, the stronger the resistance to outsiders. Identification, on the other hand, was determined by the degree of homogeneity in the particular ethnic group. This undoubtedly explains why Jews, in spite of some anti-Semitism in black communities, usually show high levels of tolerance for blacks. The Jew's identification is more abstract and less with particular geographic areas, at least in the United States. Jews have therefore maintained an identity which apparently does not feel threatened by demands for equality. Moreover, since Jews have themselves been discriminated against, they have a vested interest in establishing the concept of equality of opportunity. Of course, one reason for anti-Semitism among some blacks is the conviction that blacks and not Jews should lead the civil rights movement. Finally, and possibly most significantly, many blacks are hostile to those Jewish landlords and merchants who cater to ghetto markets.

Because of their attachments to both their neighborhoods and their unions, some ethnic groups have demonstrated what may appear to be the inconsistent behavioral pattern of strong pro-Negro attitudes on the job and in the union and strong anti-Negro attitudes in neghborhoods. This results from different sets of forces determining behavior in each circumstance. Good trade unionism requires equality of all workers on the job regardless of race or creed. If the union's objectives require political allies, there is all the more reason to champion racial job equality. On the other hand, a strong attachment to the neighborhood might cause conduct designed to keep outsiders with a different culture from encroaching on community institutions or undermining property values.

The positive role of authority embodied in legal pronouncements can thus be counteracted by community forces, especially when the laws, or their administration, are considered to violate fundamental concepts of equity held by whites. The radical pronouncements of black leaders have undoubtedly lessened the willingness of white unionists to support black militant causes. Radical movements are incompatible with the values of patriotism, hard work, and law and order held by most white manualists. Moreover, demands for "affirmative action" which imply ignoring qualifications for entry into skilled trades and upgrading on industrial jobs are considered to be unfair by workers who feel that they have property rights in their jobs. Interestingly enough, whites seem to feel that they have "earned" rights to their jobs even when they have not met the qualifications they impose on outsiders. Of course, this comment could also be made about various professional groups. It is not too surprising, and even might be defensible, that people attempt to upgrade the standards for their jobs.

Economic considerations also are very important determinants of the racial practices of white union members. White unionists naturally are concerned about their jobs and can be expected to resist measures which threaten their job security. Moreover, there seems to be an inverse relation between labor market conditions and resistance to job demands by blacks. Negroes therefore are likely to make their greatest progress during periods of tight labor markets. This is not to argue that tight labor markets are sufficient for black economic progress. There is considerable evidence that some groups benefit very little from tight labor markets. Much depends on whether or not people are able to take advantage of job opportunities as they become available. Tight labor markets operate much faster to change the demand conditions than they do to generate supplies of labor to meet the demand. Therefore, unless training and other manpower measures are taken to enable blacks to meet the qualifications to fill jobs, a tight labor market will not necessarily lead to employment changes to soak up underemployed or unemployed black workers. Tight labor markets and job guarantees are particularly important in overcoming white resistance to black employment in industries like contract construction, where there is considerable job insecurity and where workers are not attached to particular employers.

The conflict between blacks, intellectuals, and white manualists is infused with considerable *class prejudice.* The conflict over job equality is partly a conflict over job status. Those white manualists who are likely to show the greatest resistance to blacks in their occupations are those who consider their jobs to have higher status than public opinion generally affords them. These tend to be manualists whose crafts are just below the technical and professional level. This is one of the reasons for the resistance to blacks by members of building, printing, and railroad crafts, who have felt that accepting Negroes into their unions would lower the status of their jobs.

But the class implications of this problem are not limited to manualists. To some extent, intellectuals and middle-class whites are likely to exhibit stronger biases against manualists than they do toward blacks, from whom they are insulated by lower-class whites. Intellectuals are likely to romanticize blacks as abstractions, much as they romanticized workers at an earlier time. (Indeed, intellectuals ignored racism in unions during the 1930s—and even denied that it existed in the CIO.)

People who are not immediately involved in a conflict are likely to make up their minds about it on moral grounds, but those immediately involved are more concerned with physical, economic, or political considerations. Since middle-class people can restrict the actual conflict to lower-class whites and blacks and thus are not immediately involved in a race conflict, they are free to take a moral approach which condemns white manualists and sympathizes with blacks, who are the underdogs. Since many middle-class intellectuals are not immediately involved with the manualists, they tend to emphasize the importance of racial discrimination and to ignore the fears and frustrations of the white manualists. The news media are likely to dramatize the racist statements of white manualists who may not be representative of the whole membership. In their zeal to take a moral position, many middle-class observers ignore the complex set of forces causing white workers' attitudes and behavior.

Class prejudices assert themselves in middle-class and journalistic reactions to the white workers' defense of their standards and qualifications. Middle-class whites often see no inconsistency between their defense of four-year requirements for B.A. degrees, longer requirements for law and medical degrees and for Ph.D.'s, and their condemnation of plumbers or electricians for requiring four-year apprenticeships, most of which are actually spent working. Middle-class critics are convinced that it does not take four years to become a plumber or an electrician, even when few of them know anything about the jobs they are criticizing. They know only that manual jobs have lower status than professional occupations and therefore should require less formal preparation. These kinds of class prejudices, which permeate black and white communities, make it difficult to recruit qualified blacks to enter manual occupations even when the unions agree to lower their racial barriers.

Union structure and objectives also have important implications for racial practices. As noted earlier, craft unions have the ability to limit employment to particular racial or ethnic groups, while the ethnic or racial composition of industrial unions is determined mainly by employer hiring practices.

Moreover, membership control over their union's affairs may promote racial prejudices; if the internal union political forces are balanced, a small racist group can prevent the leaders from taking equalitarian measures. One of the problems in overcoming racial discrimination by unions has been the strong membership control in craft locals which have no Negroes in them and have been able to control the supply of labor sufficiently to restrict black competition for jobs. This can be done if Negroes are denied access to better training and job experiences.

On the other hand, if there are large numbers of Negroes in the work force or potential work force, as there were in most of the industrial unions, the union will have to take pro-Negro positions in order to win bargaining rights or force the employer to sign a contract. Unions could not have been established in most of the basic industries during the 1930s if they had not appealed to the Negroes who were employed in those industries.

The unions' racial policies also are influenced by the scope of their objectives and their visibility. The more conspicuous a union organization, the greater the pressure on it to adopt whatever racial position prevails in the geographic area in which it operates. Because racial equality is the prevailing moral sentiment in the United States, international unions and federations must take an equalitarian stand. Of course, equalitarianism is good unionism, but many of these organizations could not take equalitarian positions before the 1950s and 1960s because of counterpressures from their members. The authority of legal pronouncements beginning with World War II freed many national union leaders from these counterpressures because they could shift the blame for equalitarian measures to the government.

Equalitarianism is good unionism for political as well as economic reasons. The unions are minorities and therefore cannot accomplish their political objectives without allies. By promoting pro-Negro causes, national unions can gain Negro and liberal political support. Local unions, on the other hand, have narrow political interests and therefore do not see the value of appealing to Negroes on political or economic grounds.

Population shifts have strongly influenced the relations between black and white manualists and unions. Indeed, these are among the most significant factors at work in race relations. As Negroes moved out of the rural South and into urban areas, North and South, their demands for job equality and civil rights increased. Blacks could not live in urban areas with sharecroppers' incomes and educations. At the same time, rising aspirations were accompanied by increasing power to change conditions.

Although the Negro's position improved materially as he left the rural South, many factors contributed to new frustrations. For one thing, the incongruity of his aspirations and his ability to satisfy them increased, and urbanization caused a deterioration in the Negro's control of his own institutions. Political and ideological considerations also have played a role in intensifying conflict between black and white workers. The failure of traditional civil rights approaches to produce rapid or perceptible changes in the lives of many Negroes encouraged the adoption of more militant rhetoric by some blacks and their white radical allies. This rhetoric justified violence, and subsequent reaction of many public officials only encouraged the view that violence would create more progress than the steady day-by-day attention to details which is likely to be the only way for individuals to produce lasting changes in their conditions. But militant rhetoric, publicized by the news media, gives whites a warped impression of blacks, who are also overwhelmingly opposed to violence. These developments have encouraged some white workers to prepare for violence and to stiffen their resistance to black demands on their unions.

Black-power rhetoric, when coupled with physical violence (which probably had other and unconnected causes), has stimulated group identification by various white ethnics and stiffened white resistance to further advances in the fight against poverty and racial discrimination.

CONCLUSIONS

We do not know how much racial factors have contributed to the alienation and frustration evidenced by white manualists. Nor do we know the extent to which the mood of union members differs from that of white nonunion manualists.

Nevertheless a number of conclusions would undoubtedly survive careful documentation. Whites are likely to put up very little resistance to further advances by blacks on the job, if programs developed to equalize job opportunities for blacks recognize the fears and interests of white manualists. Government programs which ignore these fears and interests are likely to cause considerable resistance, especially if quotas or preferential treatment to compensate for past discrimination results in hiring Negroes with less than minimum required qualifications ahead of better-qualified whites.

Regardless of its short-run consequences, this kind of preferential treatment will in the long run clearly perpetuate inequality. No better statement of this point can be made than the following comment by the noted psychologist Kenneth Clark:

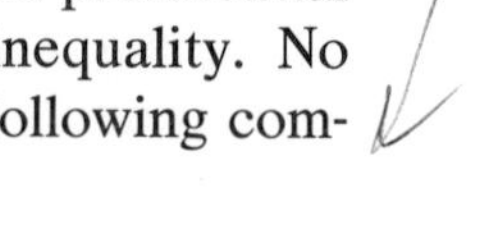

> I cannot express vehemently enough my abhorrence of sentimentalistic, seemingly compassionate programs of employment of Negroes which employ them on Jim Crow double standards or special standards for the Negro which are lower than those for whites.
>
> This is a perpetuation of racism—it is interpreted by the Negro as condescension, and it will be exploited by them. Those who have been neglected and deprived must understand that they are being taken seriously as human beings. They must not be regarded as peculiar human beings who cannot meet the demands more privileged human beings can meet. . . . I suspect that the significant breakdown in the efficiency of American public education came not primarily from flagrant racial bigotry and the deliberate desire to create casualties but from the good intentions, namely, the sloppy sentimentalistic good intentions of educators to reduce standards of low income and minority group youngsters.[7]

This, however, is not an argument against *special* programs that make it possible for blacks to meet the same entry-level qualifications and performance standards required of other workers. These special programs to overcome the effects of racial isolation can do a great deal to overcome the effects of institutionalized discrimination.

Measures which give greater recognition to and encouragement of the dignity of manual occupations undoubtedly would help moderate the hostility of white manualists. Perhaps these measures would require greater attention to opportunities for upgrading, but this need might be exaggerated. Surely the importance of upgrading varies considerably among occupations, depending on such factors as age and sex of workers and the wages of the occupation. Many workers, black and white, apparently are not so much interested in opportunities to upgrade themselves, which probably exist to a considerable degree, as they are in protecting their jobs and raising their wages.

Public officials and other opinion molders can moderate conflict between black and white manualists by recognizing a number of realities. First, racism, whether black or white, must consistently be challenged. Second, programs must be mounted which carefully recognize the legitimate interests of the various groups involved while counteracting racially motivated demands. Third, many of the fears and frustrations of racial and ethnic groups are based on myth. The myths, it is hoped, can be overcome by factual evidence, but appeals to the racist attitudes of blacks or whites should be avoided at all times. No matter how superficially well motivated, it is extremely shortsighted to assume that the nation's domestic problems can be solved by playing off one group of workers against the other.

Because public attention swings from one problem area to another, there is perhaps some danger that the present concern over white manualists might cause us to ignore the interests of minorities. Policy makers now realize that in concentrating on the problems of blacks and other disadvantaged persons during the 1960s we sometimes ignored the problems of white manualists. Indeed, in the South, many programs had difficulty attracting whites because they were regarded as "black" and therefore "inferior" programs. Legislatures also ignored the white manualists by failing to reform the tax system, to take measures to provide better law enforcement, or to protect working-class neghborhoods from "block busting." Even those who saw the need for black pride and identity were not concerned about ethnic pride and identity.

We were correct in giving priority to black employment problems, because this was and is our most disadvantaged group. But public programs for the disadvantaged erred in not considering the legitimate concerns of white manualists, whose resistance to human resource development programs could seriously impede the development of much-needed programs in this area. Of course, it is unnecessary either to ignore the white manualist or to adopt preferential treatment and quotas for blacks. Proper attention to program design can provide remedial efforts for all manualists similarly situated without threatening whites or taking a condescending attitude toward manual occupations. To fail to adopt these programs is to risk unnecessary racial conflict and to generate serious obstacles to social progress.

NOTES

1. Booker T. Washington, "The Negro and the Labor Unions," *Atlantic Monthly,* June 1913, p. 756.
2. Ray Marshall, *The Negro Worker,* Random House, New York, 1967, p. 38.
3. Samuel Lubell, *The Hidden Crisis in American Politics,* Norton, New York, 1970, p. 98.
4. Dietrich C. Reitzes, "The Role of Organizational Structures: Union vs. Neighborhood in a Tension Situation," *Journal of Social Issues,* 1953, pp. 42–43.
5. Louis Ferman, *The Negro and Equal Employment Opportunities,* Praeger, New York, 1968, p. 98.
6. Lubell, op. cit., p. 175.
7. Kenneth Clark, "Efficiency as a Prod to Social Action," *Monthly Labor Review,* August 1969, pp. 55–56.

9. MAKING THE GOOD LIFE: WORKING-CLASS FAMILY AND LIFE-STYLES

by Lee Rainwater

WORKING CLASS OR MIDDLE CLASS?

Perhaps the major success story of the post-World War II decades has been the steadily increasing level of prosperity and security of the average American workingman and his family.[1] Although there is no evidence of significant redistribution of income from the top to the bottom half of the population, the working class's share of the rapidly rising GNP has resulted since 1947 in a near doubling of family income in dollars of constant purchasing power. A combination of government policy and individual family choices has resulted in an investment of much of that dramatically increasing purchasing power in a similarly dramatic increase in home ownership and suburban dwelling among the working class.

This good news has been celebrated all along the way by governments, by business, by the party in power ("you never had it so good"), and, not least, by working-class people themselves, who have always been ready to testify as to how much more comfortable and secure their lives are than their parents' were.

The increases in income experienced by the working class and the investment of these increases in a wide range of mass-market products have also led from time to time to premature celebration of the "middle classification" of the working class. Commentators representing business and government perspectives have time and again pointed toward the gradual disappearance of differences between blue-collar- and white-collar-based groups. For example, at the end of the Eisenhower years, the Labor Department celebrated the disappearance of the distinctive working-class way of life, arguing that "the wage earner's way of life is well nigh indistinguishable from that of his salaried co-workers."[2] In fact, however, studies by sociologists of the life-styles of the stable working class during the late 1950s and into the 1960s suggest that for all the tremendous change in life wrought by affluence, urbanization, and suburbanization, working-class life-styles continue to be relatively distinctive compared to lower-middle-class life-styles. For one thing, working-class people do not want to be carbon copies of the lower middle class that they know. Moreover, the lower middle class itself has changed so that even when working-class people adopted life-style traits characteristic of the lower middle class, the latter had shifted enough in life styles to retain class distinctions.

The invention of the Silent Majority made working-class world views, attitudes, and political action an issue of establishment concern. The results of public-opinion polls and the apparent auguries from various recent elections suggested that somehow the American economic miracle of working-class affluence and security was no longer believed in by its beneficiaries. No doubt from the late 1940s through the early 1960s working-class people had thought of themselves as the beneficiaries (to be sure, by dint of their own hard work) of the great American nation, which, through its democratic genius and technological creativity, was managing to pay off most handsomely for the average man. Now it seemed that the working class (and not they alone) had begun to feel that the American golden goose was losing its touch. Somehow it was no longer able to make things work right, and therefore the Democratic, Eastern-dominated establishment that had been in charge of the goose should be replaced by political forces that might get the country back on the right track again.

Our concern in this chapter is not to describe this process of disenchantment, if in fact it exists, or to provide a quantitative description of the demographic and economic characteristics or the attitudes and opinions of the working class, for these are detailed fully in other chapters. This chapter seeks to provide a portrait of the working-class way of life to show how the constraints of working-class reality may work upon that way of life to produce the social and political attitudes that have lately become a source of concern to liberals and of joy to rightists.

COMFORT AND SECURITY FOR THE FAMILY

The central life goal of the stable working class is the creation of a comfortable and secure place for oneself and one's family. Once this is achieved, there is then room for efforts to make life more and more pleasurable by engaging in activities which are more playful and less earnest than those directed to assuring family comfort and its continuation.

This goal of making the good life has both positive and negative referents. The negative referents are perhaps the more powerful. Working-class couples are centrally concerned with getting away from or staying away from the disorganized and frightening world of poverty and the slums. For many working-class people who moved out of such a world either in adult life or as they were growing up, the morally frightening and socially degrading lower-class world is an ever-present centrifugal reference point. Others have not known that world personally but view it as a possibility, perhaps more mythical than actual, representing "what could happen" if economic sufficiency somehow failed.

A less prominent but nevertheless important negative reference point—particularly as working-class families move above what might be regarded as the minimum level for sustaining a working-class life-style—is the quieter and more constrained circumstance of just managing to get by, of having so little in the way of resources that one can just barely feed, shelter, and clothe one's family. This image of penury also haunts many working-class people who know of it from personal experience, from growing up in depressed families, or being told and retold family stories about the Great Depression. Here the danger is not that of moral survival as in the slum's threat to family respectability, but rather the survival of a fully human rather than stunted spirit. As we will see, working-class people are constantly aware of the need to exercise great self-control and care in spending their money; but they see a world of difference between the self-control needed to maintain a comfortable and gratifying standard of living, and the desperate control and care needed just to keep body and soul together.

The life-style of the working class, then, is constructed to ward off such negative but realistic possibilities. In addition, of course, the central strivings that motivate the working-class life-style have positive elements that involve a reaching out for known or imagined positive potentialities. Working-class people are deep believers in the possibilities of (though not overly sanguine about the inevitability of) a personally gratifying and meaningful existence. They tend to define these potentialities in terms of the amenities which a productive, technological society can provide, and in terms of the round of life that can be constructed with those amenities as the building blocks. The operating imagery of the good life is "the mainstream." Working-class people construct from many sources (people around them, more-favored relatives, mass media, advertising) a conception of a standard package of consumer goods and services which allow one to operate in, consider himself a part of, and be considered by others a part of the mainstream of American life.[3] Living in the mainstream reassures you both that you have escaped the moral threat and human constriction of poverty and the slums and that you are enjoying a fair share of the good things that your world has to offer. One of the reasons that working-class people do not become "middle-class" as their standard of living rises is that they reinterpret the mainstream consumer package in terms of their own goals and values. When they are able to afford a given object, they do not necessarily buy it for the same qualities that had attracted the middle-class people who were the former principal users of it. For example, while a middle-class woman is likely to value a dishwasher so that she can get out of the kitchen more quickly, a working-class woman is more likely to value it for the time and effort it allows her to invest in some other kitchen activity, or just for the lesser effort she will have to expend on her housewifely chores. Owning a dishwasher does not make her more interested in becoming a clubwoman like her middle-class sister.

The social capital needed to make the good life is, in working-class logic, perfectly straightforward. In order to enter the mainstream, you simply make a family by combining a man who is a good and faithful provider with a woman who is a sensible, responsible, and loving housewife-mother.[4] All other things (such as economic conditions and personal health) being normal, this combination and the children the man and the woman have are assumed to produce a family that enjoys the good American life by dint of applying hard work and good sense. Children in this imagery are relatively passive objects, more products than subjects of the family unit. More emphasis is placed on what the parents can do for and to children in forming them into eventual adults like themselves than on what the children contribute to the family's life. This construction of what the family is all about is simpler than in the middle class. Middle-class parents are more likely to emphasize the children as interacting units in a whole family system which together establishes its particular style of life. The tendency to see children either as passive products of well-intentioned parents or, when something goes awry in that plan, as destructive and uncontrollable ("bad seed") makes for an inevitable conflict between the parents' definition of children as passive and their children's, particularly adolescents', natural assertiveness; this is traditionally handled by segregating children's activities from adult surveillance and by a tacit agreement of adults not to pry too fully into what adolescents are doing. Intensive media attention to the rebellious activities of youth has shattered this fiction of youth's passivity. Traditionally, these conflicts within working-class families and neighborhoods were minimized because young men and women terminated adolescence at a much earlier age than today by going to work. Now that working-class youths leave school later, their parents are under increased pressure to accommodate to "youth culture."

WORKING-CLASS WORLD VIEWS

The working-class family's method of achieving the good life reflects several characteristics of their orientations toward themselves and the world around them. Working-class men and women resolutely regard themselves as middle-class. When given the option of designating themselves as working- or middle-class, the great majority of them choose the former label. They recognize the distinction in life station between white-collar and their own blue- or gray-collar worlds; yet they are often ambivalent when contemplating their own or their children's chances of moving into such a world.

They tend to regard their own class as generous and kindly compared to the selfishness of those above or below them in status. People of superior status are seen as selfishly devoted to their own ends or to their own small social circle. To them, the price of striving after career success is a loss of the comfortable virtues of family devotion and shared time with wife, children, and relatives. They view the lower classes as selfish in a different way: "not caring," being involved in personal pleasures to the detriment of one's responsibilities, and unwilling to work hard in order to support and care for a family. Thus, the selfishness of the lower classes stems from "weakness of character"; that of the higher classes is an unfortunate vice bound up with an otherwise admirable "strength of character." One of the reasons working-class people are often uninterested in moving up to middle-class status is that they believe the price to be that of accepting a more formal and self-controlled way of life. This formality tends to be strongly disliked; there is often the feeling that a secure working-class life provides for an optimally comfortable and interpersonally easy existence.

The group sees itself, then, as the backbone of the nation. In pre-World War II days the working class tended to define itself as "poor but honest folks." The rapid increase in affluence since World War II has dropped the self-conception as "poor." On the other hand, working-class people find it hard to conceive of themselves as affluent since they still have a sense of effort and struggle to achieve and maintain the standard American consumer package. At the same time, that package itself is so impressive that they know they are not poor.

The central roles in the good life are those of the husband as provider and the wife as mother-homemaker. The conjugal tie generally receives less emphasis in the stable working-class family than in the middle class; more emphasis is placed on the spouses' roles as operators of a family than on the affective demands between them. Thus there tends to be a sharper division of labor between the husband and wife, and less sharing of interest in leisure time and activities. The deep family orientation of the working class is perhaps its principal characteristic. And the family is imbued with such heavy responsibility that sometimes pleasure (as opposed to meaningfulness) hardly seems compatible with it. Working-class men experience a sharp discontinuity between their premarital and early marital roles. Before marriage, the greatest meaning in their life comes from being one of the boys in the extended adolescent to youth peer group. Their relations with girls tend to be fairly distant and either constricted or exploitative. With marriage they must not only come to terms with conjugal relations with a "stranger," but also give up irresponsible ways and irresponsible peer group activity and settle down and become a provider of the good-life consumer package. Since early adulthood is also a time of low stability and earnings, the combined pressures of personal, interpersonal, and economic adjustment threaten the early years of working-class marriages. When the marriages survive, the husband and wife often have a sense of weary triumph over both themselves and adverse external circumstances.

Traditionally the working-class family orientation included a very heavy involvement with kin, extending over a wide generational range in working-class communities where there has not been a great deal of geographic mobility. Very likely, much of what has been heralded as the ethnic quality of working-class life is more properly regarded as simply an extended family orientation. With greater geographical mobility—particularly as the working class is more and more suburbanized—the kin-based social network tends to be attenuated. Working-class men and women often lament the fact that large family gatherings seem much less frequent than they used to be. Since much of the sense of social security that working-class people have traditionally felt has come from being enmeshed in a network of ties based on blood, it may well be that one of the prices of affluence and modernity is a greater sense of isolation and social anxiety.

Working-class people have no clearly established place for ties that reach wider than those of family or close friends toward whom one adopts a kinlike relationship. The middle-class emphasis on community roles and responsibilities sits very uneasily in working-class identities. Working-class women are concerned mainly with their homes, and by some small extension perhaps with the school or church. They belong to few voluntary associations, because they are not sure that it would be right for them. Husbands are concerned with the outside world, but the only concern that is really taken for granted has to do with the world of work. Working-class men do not generally have much interest in assuming community roles or participating in civic activities. On the other hand, they have a strong sense of loyalty and patriotism to country, and they know that within their family it is their job to be concerned and informed citizens. It is they who must shoulder the burden of fighting wars, because they are in fact the backbone of the nation at such times, as they are in the area of economic production.

But the preferred world of the stable working class is one in which the individual minds his own business and avoids larger entanglements than those of work and family. They feel that the challenges and the energy required for working and family life are more than enough to ask of any man or woman. And what more can a nation ask of its citizens than that a man work and be productive and that men and women together raise a next generation that is also productive and responsible?

Middle-class and working-class perspectives on a family's life cycle across the decades show a striking difference. Whereas the middle class tends to see family circumstances as progressively better as the breadwinner matures and progresses in his career, and as the family's position is consolidated socially, working-class couples tend to view life in the future as essentially a replica of life in the present. They perceive a plateau—with the ever-present danger of things getting worse, not better. The middle-class family typically expects to be considerably better off in the later family stages than in the earlier ones by virtue of increased earning power of the husband (and wife, if it is a two-career family). The working-class family sees itself better off in the future only by virtue of what it may have accumulated and constructed for itself—by saving their money or increasing the number of hours worked (though there is some acknowledgment also that wages for all tend to rise with time and therefore the future should be somewhat better than the present).

The plateau conception subtly affects the working-class conception of later family years. Working-class men tend to look forward to the possibility of retiring at an age which middle-class men would regard as the time for just getting into the full swing of a career. If they begin their families in their late teens or early twenties and their children finish high school and perhaps a little college, and get married by the time the parents are in the mid to late forties, it makes good sense to want to retire and enjoy life at that time. If one's way of life has been modest, if a good deal of the expensive consumption which husband and wife have struggled so hard to afford has been for the benefit of "the family" (that is, the children), then early retirement—perhaps in a better climate—can be a well-earned reward.

While working-class families have always wanted to do well by their children, to bring them up to be respectable but at the same time to find some enjoyment in life, their child-rearing orientation has apparently shifted over the last two or three decades in a direction that would previously have been regarded as middle-class. That is, working-class families now frequently orient themselves toward "giving" their children the good things of life. They still want to do well by them, but they also want them to enjoy themselves as they are growing up. This is a relatively new conception of parental responsibility for the working class. It accompanies a more suburbanite orientation and a greater involvement of the husband in the home as opposed to his own male peer group. Working-class people themselves often comment on the change, contrasting their own behavior with their parents' more standoffish and removed style when they were growing up. Very likely this trend follows upon the greater equalization of roles of men and women which Goode has observed is characteristic of industrialized and industrializing societies.[5] (The views of American working-class fathers and mothers on this score are parallel to views expressed by German parents contrasting their own behavior to their parents rearing of them in the 1920s and 1930s.)

STYLES AND GOALS OF CONSUMPTION

If establishing, nurturing, and enjoying a family is what life is all about for the working-class man and woman, then earning and spending money are the two principal instrumental activities through which this central goal is accomplished.

The lion's share of the income of the working-class family, particularly in the family-building years, is spent for things that in one way or another can be regarded as devoted to the well-being of the family as a whole. The standard consumer package which concretizes the good American life-style allows only as the last frosting on the cake expenditures that are seen as personally indulgent of only one member of the family. Most expenditures are either directly for the family or fairly easily rationalized as for the family, even though one person may enjoy them more than others, as in the case of the purchase of a boat, which the husband may enjoy for fishing and which can be justified as allowing the whole family to spend some leisure time together.

Most of the expenditures that make up the standard package are of course for food, the house and its furnishings, and the automobile. As the working class has become more affluent, it has eaten more and more expensively. The working-class wife, along with her lower-middle-class sister, defines her success as a housewife mainly by her kitchen performance. It is not surprising, therefore, that she has upgraded the quality of her family's diet as incomes have gone up. There is always room for more steaks or more desserts, and at the more mundane level, more meat loaves and fewer macaroni casseroles. The relativity of the standard package is perhaps most sharply apparent in the case of food. After all, working-class families have eaten three meals a day for many decades; and during all this time working-class housewives have concerned themselves with whether they are doing a good job as cooks, whether they are feeding their families well. Working-class wives have prided themselves on how well they fed their families during times when half as much money was spent on food as is presently spent. Yet the modern working-class housewife would feel that the family was not living as well as it should, because it was not eating as well as it should, if she had to make do on the food budget out of which her mother proudly fashioned a reputation as a good cook.

How well the family eats, then, is a day-in, day-out indicator of whether or not they are in the mainstream. Because eating is the central ritual of family indulgence, it is not surprising that food prices are the most sensitive indicators working-class housewives and their husbands have of the threat to their standard of living that any period of rapid inflation brings.

The house and all that it contains is a much more complex and forward-looking symbol of the good life. Being able to plan confidently to buy a home, to buy that home sometime in the future, to have actually bought one, are perhaps the central acts that give one a purchase on the good American life-style. Working-class people, like other Americans, believe that buying a house gives you a better chance to have exactly the kind of home you want, as well as a heightened sense of independence and of escape from the treadmill of contributing to someone else's equity. Therefore more thought and planning and hoping probably go into the young couple's efforts to acquire a home than into any other single act of their family life. The wish to buy a home and furnish it brings the couple most forcefully to the problem of capital and the relation of their monthly income to the monthly costs of maintaining the standard package. It is in connection with the home more than anything else that the sense of squeeze comes.

Husbands and wives are deeply and jointly involved in the decision to buy a home and in the discussion of how they can put together the money to do so. Once that is accomplished, the wife tends to be in charge of the family's finances. The division of labor that sits most comfortably with the working-class style is one in which the husband earns the money and the wife spends it. Not that she does so without regard to his wishes and interests—she usually knows him and his wishes well enough to spend the money wisely in terms of joint standards—but it is she who struggles with the day-in, day-out tasks of making ends meet. Interestingly, once the husband has made the commitments that assure a particular income flow, his wife's handling of family budgeting and spending serves to protect him somewhat from concern over the extent to which the family's consumption may be pressing or outstripping his earnings. Since, as we will see, many working-class husbands extend themselves to the utmost in order to maximize the flow of income to the family, it is not surprising that their wives should seek to protect them from any sense of inadequacy as providers.

The extent to which young working-class couples are helped by their families in the initial period of married life is unknown. As most working-class couples describe this period of their family life, one gets the impression that they receive little help from their families—perhaps a few pieces of furniture plus wedding presents. Few working-class men and women have much savings when they marry because that is simply not the American way of marriage. (The wife may work early in the marriage, and her income may be saved toward the purchase of a home. Since they tend to marry quite young, however, there is often a honeymoon period of simply enjoying themselves and no savings are made.) The wife typically becomes pregnant fairly soon in the marriage (in perhaps a quarter of the cases, she is pregnant at marriage), and by working-class standards she should not work until all her children are in school. At the same time, the husband's income at this period is often nowhere nearly adequate to the couple's desire to move rapidly into the mainstream—in which, increasingly, they have grown up. The husband may seek to cope with this problem by working long hours. He generally cannot expect to progress very rapidly in his work or to earn significantly more money in three or four years from now than at present. Both husband and wife realize that the pace of their consuming will increase much faster than his income if they are going to build their family the way they want. This leads to a complex of second jobs and chasing after overtime at this period. Wives sometimes recount incredibly demanding work schedules on the part of their young husbands—schedules that involve 10 to 14 hours of work a day at two different jobs. In this way, a young man who is able to command only two-thirds the median family income level on a single job may be able to lift the family's income above the median. Given the impermanence of some of these jobs, the family's income over a two- or three-year period may average around the median or somewhat less, but in any case the money provided by the second job can make the difference between a marginal working-class life and incremental approximation of a mainstream life.

For the couple near the median income, firm exercise of the discipline of making ends meet allows over time for the construction of a standard package appropriate to the family's stage in its life cycle. For the family with an income significantly below the median, all kinds of compromises and second-best approximations to that level have to be made. When the family lives far enough away from the median, there is always the question of whether in fact they can make it in terms of the going standards, or whether instead they will have to consider themselves out of the mainstream—and no longer upper-working-class.

The various cost-of-living budgets compiled by government and private agencies give some aura of objectivity to these standards; but it is much more likely that a consensus of the subjective evaluations of families themselves better locates the minimum possible resource base for a viable working-class style of life. In this connection it is useful to consider the results of various Gallup surveys over the years which have asked the question, "What is the smallest amount of money a family of four (husband and wife and two children) needs each week to get along in this community?"

Table 26 shows the average judgment by Gallup samples of the annual income needed from 1937 to 1969. Table 27 shows some of the variations in judgments of annual income needed, depending on the respondents' own income and region. If the respondents understood by "getting along" a level of living that would place one at least on the edge of the mainstream, then we can say that an income equal to something more than 60 percent of the median family income is necessary to begin to play the mainstream game.[6]

The mainstream package can be had at a more or less luxurious level, and working-class families show little inclination in this early family building stage to rest on their laurels. Even men who are earning close to the median family income on their primary job will often seek to supplement income by overtime or second jobs. With the extra money they buy perhaps slightly better than average houses, or they invest more in fixing up those houses, thus perhaps providing a harbinger of what the mainstream standard a few years hence will be when real incomes have risen to the more currently privileged working-class family's level.

The central core of the standard package, then, relates on the one hand to eating, and on the other hand to shelter and the complex of activities pursued within that shelter. The automobile adds a third element to the consumer package—an element about which there

TABLE 26
PUBLIC JUDGMENTS OF MINIMUM ANNUAL INCOME NEEDED BY A FAMILY OF FOUR TO GET ALONG

	Annual income needed		
Year	*In current dollars*	*In 1969 dollars*	*Percent of median family income*
1937	$1,560	$4,030	Over 100%
1947	2,236	3,720	73
1957	3,744	4,920	75
1964	4,213	5,060	64
1967	5,252	5,810	66
1969	6,240	6,240	66

SOURCE: Various Gallup polls.

TABLE 27
VARIATIONS IN JUDGMENTS OF MINIMUM ANNUAL INCOME NEEDED FOR A FAMILY OF FOUR TO GET ALONG, BASED ON RESPONDENTS' INCOME AND REGION

(1) Variations by respondents' income in minimum needed, based on the 1964 sample

Respondents' income	*Minimum needed*	*Proportion of median family income ($6,600)*	*Proportion of median income of 4-person families ($7,700)*
Less than $3,000	$3,796	58%	49%
$3,000 to $4,999	4,056	62	53
$5,000 to $6,999	4,160	63	54
$7,000 to $9,999	5,148	78	67
$10,000 or more	5,148	78	67

(2) Region, from the 1969 sample

Region	*Minimum amount needed*
East	$6,552
West	6,552
Midwest	6,240
South	5,252

has been considerable ambivalence over the past decade. In the postwar period and into the 1950s, a great deal of romance was attached to the automobile; having a nice car and taking pride in it seemed to be one of the outstanding characteristics of mainstream life. This romance with the automobile seems to have declined over the last decade; attitudes toward the car have become more utilitarian. While the prosperous unmarried or newly married and childless worker may enjoy investing in a snazzy automobile, the worker who is putting together the family standard package is likely to regard automobile expenditures as an enemy of that goal, and to seek to prolong the life of whatever car he owns. When he must replace it, he is likely to invest in a respectable but inexpensive new car or, even better, a used one. In keeping with the heavy focus on family and home, it seems wasteful to put a lot of money in an object primarily to get the husband back and forth to work, and the husband and wife back and forth to the shopping center or to a relative's house.

Working-class couples strictly evaluate expenditures in terms of the activities they will facilitate; they are less interested in style or the social appropriateness of the expenditure per se. Part of not wasting money is not spending money in ways that give you nothing to show for it. This standard lies behind the reluctance of working-class couples to invest in services rather than goods unless they absolutely have to; it is much used as a rationale to do work yourself rather than have "professionals" do it. Working-class men think of themselves as good with their hands, but in addition doing one's own work around the house is regarded as simply good sense. Even if one is not skilled at a particular task, it pays to learn how to do it. Many working-class wives will learn a skill rather than pay a tradesman to do the work. Thus, a couple may buy a house which is not adequate but can be fixed up over time—by expanding to make more room as the family grows or by remodeling to bring the house up to proper standards of function and luxury. It is a fortunate working-class couple who are in a position to swap labor with others—as when an electrician rewires his neighbor's house in exchange for plumbing work on his own—or can get such labor free within the rules and obligations of exchanges among kin.

Similarly, working-class couples will avoid expenditures on services (including vacations), preferring to spend their money on items which seem extravagant; for example, a woman remarks that by not investing money in baby sitters (and therefore not being able to go out with her husband) the family was able to afford a color television set which everyone can enjoy night after night. In short, the working class wants something to show for its money and not just a memory gained or labor saved. Perhaps one of the reasons working-class people resent medical expenses so much is that after the fact there is nothing to show for the money, and yet they cannot afford to take the risk of treating medical care for serious ailments as a do-it-yourself project.

As the standard package begins to shape up (and particularly as time passes and initially burdensome mortgage payments consume a smaller proportion of income), the husband and wife can add some of the finishing touches to their particular version of the standard package by introducing elements that reflect their own personal adult interests, and also perhaps by indulging their older children, who are developing interests of their own. At this point, then, there is room for hobbies. Often these hobbies consume quite a lot of money, but interestingly in such cases, the hobby—a husband's photography, for example—is likely to be converted into something of interest to all members of the family. Everyone can take pleasure in the pictures the husband takes, the guitar playing of the teen-age son, or the piano playing of the daughter. Or the choice may be for hobbies which, like camping and boating, involve all or most of the members of the family.

WORKING-CLASS MORALE

The outside observer, depending upon his mood, standards, and ideological ax to grind, can look at the life-style of working-class people and see several things. In the past many commentators, impressed by the well-being of the working class, have tended either to celebrate the affluence and ease of their lives or to lament the *embourgeoisement* of the workers. In the last few years as working-class men and women have given unmistakable political indications that they are not very happy about the state of the world, it has become fashionable to stress the struggle and frustration that go into making a prosperous working-class life. But these are fashionable observer stances and in all likelihood do not reflect the real conditions of working-class life.

The working-class way of life has its costs and rewards. Anxiousness and isolation are probably the principal costs perceived by working-class men and women. The anxiety is constantly present because the working-class couple do not know whether they will be able to sustain the income they need to remain in the mainstream. Unemployment and ill health are frightening dangers because there is little margin against them in the form of savings, pension rights, or insurance.

Less obvious, but more pervasive, is the effect of social isolation. The pursuit of the good life, by concentrating energies heavily on the family, tends to increase working-class people's isolation from the community around them. The husband who has two jobs in order to make enough money to launch his new home is not likely to be very much interested in what goes on at either workplace. The wife, for her part, is often isolated both physically and psychologically. Psychologically she is deeply committed to her children and her homemaking, and she regards other commitments as distracting and potentially dangerous because they may reduce her effectiveness at home. And when the working-class family manages to acquire the house in the suburbs, the wife finds herself physically isolated. The family can afford only one car, and a surprisingly large number of working-class women do not know how to drive anyway. Thus the wife may not be able to get away from the house during the day unless a relative or neighbor drives her. She does her shopping with her husband in the evenings and on weekends. All she sees is her house, her yard, and a little bit of the neighbors' houses and yards. With her family she visits relatives and sees their familiar houses. For the most part this is the way she wants life to be, but the sameness haunts her from time to time; and she has the feeling of being trapped, of being so much of service to others that there are no time and resources left for her own pleasures.

If working-class people have occasion to examine their lives, most of them can find reasons for joy or sadness, gratitude or recrimination, comfort or frustration. Working-class people generally prefer to look at their lives with measured and pragmatic optimism. They prefer to recall how well things have gone and how much they have accomplished; by reflecting on this, they sustain their optimism about a future of which they are never quite certain. They believe that one's chances of having a good life, of being successful, are compounded of (1) strictly individual events and (2) the odds for all people such as they. In the post-World War II period the working class's assessment of their odds has tended to be quite positive. Despite threats of unemployment on the one hand and inflation on the other, the general sense of prosperity and security in contrast to the pre-World War II period has sustained an optimistic view of the chances for achieving a good life. In the working-class logic it then rests with the individual whether he in fact achieves such a life. His own chances are maximized by working hard and having a little bit of luck. You can have bad luck by getting sick or having an accident. A woman can have bad luck if her husband turns out unaccountably to be an alcoholic. A man can have bad luck if his job disappears while employment is generally good for everyone else. But these are personal problems requiring individual adjustment and the assistance of the people around you. Similarly, good luck may improve upon the achievements of hard work—if one is lucky enough to fall in love with and marry a girl whose father is a housebuilder who presents the couple with a house for a wedding present, or if one finds his way into a high-wage union-protected job. Such good luck merits enjoyment but must not go to one's head.

When, however, being sorely pressed by one's situation is interpreted as an indication of a turn for the worse in the odds for people in similar circumstances, then the basis for a nonindividual (political) interpretation is present. In such a situation, the traditional bread-and-butter issues of working-class politics—unemployment, wage levels, inflation—become salient.

Working-class morale is also affected by one's estimate of whether one's children can live a more prosperous mainstream life. Even when working-class parents are reasonably satisfied with their participation in the mainstream, they may be anxious about whether their children will be able to continue that participation. Much of this anxiety seems to center around the role of education in achieving economic status. Working-class people fear that the educational price of admission to mainstream jobs is going to increase so that their children will not have a decent chance unless they go to college. Thus, college would become not just an avenue to mobility, but a necessary path to staying where the parents are. Because working-class people feel intimidated by the financial demands of college and are not sanguine about their children's desire to go to college, they are doubly worried. Working-class people feel pressured by the rest of society, which continually emphasizes the value, the desirability, the moral superiority of college education. They would prefer a situation in which high school graduation plus hard work would merit participation in the mainstream, and they are confused by the middle-class emphasis on college for the masses. But if events decree that college is necessary to compete for those mainstream jobs, then they are prepared to encourage their children to go to college and, reluctantly, to bear some of the costs. Until now they have regarded college as for the mobile young man. Working-class people are no longer surprised that many persons from their group attend college. It is just that they prefer a world in which college education is not necessary for a decent life. In the context of these varied issues, the tremendous anger which working-class people have recently expressed toward youthful rebellion and exhibitionism can be understood. The anger accompanies anxiety that their children, too, may be weaned away by the dramatic and obviously gratifying, if immoral, activities of college kids. The most direct impact of youthful immorality upon their lives has to do with the apparent widespread use of drugs in high school (and now in junior high school)—a problem which for all their brave self-assurance that their children would not participate cannot but concern the working-class parent. Drugs stand as a near-at-hand symbol for all the other kinds of immoral activities into which their sons (and less likely, their daughters—college education for girls is not regarded as particularly valuable) might be seduced should they go to college. In a singularly dramatic and nightmarish way, college attendance—the former mark of an upper-middle-class existence—now represents to the working-class parent the same moral danger that his children would have faced had the family not been able to escape the slums.

Inflation is the most immediate pressure working-class couples feel—an endemic pressure which in the past few years has been raised to a much higher level. Working-class women are especially alert to inflationary surges, since they have to pay keen attention to how they spend their money. Whether or not the issue is being played up by the media or in political contests, they see inflation in the grocery store and (less regularly) at other stores. They convey their concern to their husbands, and before long the husbands are concerned too. Whereas unemployment is a disastrous threat to the relatively few people whom it affects, inflation affects all families in this class. The bread-and-butter issues of inflation and unemployment are by far the most potent political issues in the lives of the working class because such problems threaten in a direct and unambiguous way the central life goals of these families.

POLITICIANS, ESTABLISHMENTARIANS, AND THE WORKING CLASS

The currently fashionable diagnosis of working-class conditions, however, addresses itself not to these traditional economic issues but rather to a mood of social alienation and a rightward swing that some argue is characterizing middle America. The present analysis, however, suggests that anger over what Scammon and Wattenberg have called "the Social Issue," to the extent that it characterizes the working class these days, is a fairly superficial concern, probably reflecting more the dynamics and pathologies of politics and the mass media (amplified by the frustrating economic situation over the past three years) than any deep rightist trend.[7] At the base of the white working-class reaction to crime, racial turmoil, and campus unrest is probably a sense of unwarrented invasion of the tranquillity of their private lives. That is, working-class men and women assume a stance of detachment, if not outright ignorance, toward the larger social-political scene. Somehow, the events and the politics of the last five years have conspired to force working-class people to pay more attention to politics than they would prefer, a fact which may anger them even more than their disapproval of what is going on in the ghettos, on the campuses, and in the streets.

The fashionable diagnosis discovers an alienation of the working class from the establishment, but this alienation has always been present, and indeed properly so. The working class would be foolish not to be alienated from a group which possesses power and uses it in terms of its own interests and not necessarily in terms of the interest of the working class. Given their desire to ignore larger social and political issues, working-class suspicion of the powers that be represents one of the few defenses they have against those powers, even though it may not be a particularly effective one. It is a typical error of fashionable commentary to exaggerate the degree of alienation of the working class, much as the same fashionable commentary exaggerated the degree of militancy and alienation of poor blacks who, for all the misery of their existence, continue to be strongly committed to the central values of American society (a fact that will continue to embarrass those who seek to lead the black community in a revolutionary direction).

But working-class men and women have had to pay attention to a great deal that is going on in the larger world in the last few years. They have had to pay attention to a war which they do not understand and which they support (when they do) out of a sense of patriotic duty that wears thinner and thinner as time goes on. They have had to pay attention to riots and rising crime rates, consistently coupled with race problems by the mass media and by politicians.

While working-class people have a great deal more sympathy for the disadvantages suffered by poor blacks and whites than they are usually given credit for, their values tend to emphasize the virtue of fortitude more than rebellion; coupled with their deep fear of blacks, this has meant that they have felt that the rioting and the lawlessness must be stopped before any improvement in the situation of blacks can take place.

Much the same kind of ambivalence—support for the legitimate demands of the disadvantaged but anger and puzzlement over those who "take the law into their own hands"—is apparent in working-class attitudes toward strikes by public service workers. Surprisingly, although they feel pressed by inflation, working-class people often concede that public service workers such as teachers and postmen deserve more pay, and feel that such demands are legitimate because they have been long denied. At the same time, they are bothered when public service workers strike despite laws that say they should not. In the end they tend to side with the workers for, despite the unlawfulness, the tactic is recognized and the demands are just. Because public service workers provide essential services to the public, working-class citizens feel that they as members of the public must be prepared to pay for the value received.

It is the particular tragedy of the race and poverty issues that the working class perceives no direct value received from the changes argued on behalf of these disadvantaged groups. The initial effort at sympathy that many working-class people were willing to extend toward the poor and (more grudgingly) toward blacks was reversed as the 1960s wore on. Originally, the working class assumed that these groups were simply trying to shift the odds so that they would have a better chance to achieve a mainstream existence. They further assumed that this existence would be achieved by the same combination of personal hard work and good luck that they feel operates for themselves. These assumptions have shifted as a result of the liberal and radical rhetoric by which the establishment has argued the cause of the poor and the blacks, as well as of the great drama of the riots. Though few would really argue that the odds are fair for those at the bottom of society, working-class people have the impression that the established are proposing to remove the necessity for hard work and personal luck and simply "give" the disadvantaged the advantages of the good life. They quite properly perceive that this is impossible, and they also feel that it is not moral. As time has passed, they have gotten the idea that they are supposed to be so guilty about the situation of the poor and the black that they will accept such policies. The effort to make the working class feel guilty has boomeranged because working-class people have plenty of reasons to feel sorry for themselves. They ward off self-pity by their measured optimism most of the time, but the moment comparisons of how badly the world treats them are made salient, they do not find it at all difficult to concentrate on all the troubles they have and to adopt the attitude that at least they work for what they have, which is precious little. Then, too, the attack on the system which accompanies the effort to change things on behalf of the disadvantaged tends as it becomes more and more personalized (particularly in New Left rhetoric) to make working-class people feel that they have to make a choice between their country and something else. At that point the simple virtues of patriotism and sticking to their own take over.

In the face of these challenges, the normally high morale of working-class people is no longer a social psychological asset. If things are better and better for a person, then he ought to be responsive to demands that he sacrifice something for people who are less well off. A moral threat comes from accepting the definition of his stratum in society as lucky and affluent. Feeling sorry for himself and pointing to all his troubles is a way of warding off the demands of other people. This course is particularly easy if those issues come to the fore during a period of rapid inflation which does press a great many working-class families quite sorely.

As policy makers have become aware of some of these issues, they have tried to find areas in which the working class has not been equitably dealt with. It is argued that the working class believes that they are being ignored and that their just demands are being passed over in the interests of less deserving lower-class folk. Yet the sense of being ignored is probably a secondary issue, more responsive to the need to defend against the unpleasantness occasioned by lower-class demands than representing a genuine belief of there not being enough "programs" for middle Americans. Aside from the issues of health, disability, and unemployment, which have been issues for a long time, working-class people do not have a particular sense of an unfinished New Deal agenda. They are really better Keynesians than that, tending to count on the growth of the economy and the greater affluence of society as a whole as the source of continued progress for people like them. It is probably futile for governments to seek out programs (again aside from the three mentioned above) which somehow "reduce the alienation" of the working class.

It is hard to escape the judgment that the revolt of the alienated middle American (to the extent that it has any reality at all) is principally the result of an establishment becoming enmeshed in its own rhetoric, ambitions, and incompetence rather than of any newly revealed conflict of vital interests between militant poor and black classes and an overly bourgeois working class. In their all too apparent haste to placate the newly assertive black community during the 1960s, those in power succeeded only in making many promises and fostering a pseudoradical rhetoric that angered and insulted the working class, while at the same time delivering no more than symbolic resources to black people. (It should be noted that black working-class attitudes in this area are in many ways not different from white ones, although not infused in the same way with racial feeling. That is, black working- and middle-class people can be as vehement and angry in their denunciation of "criminals" and "welfare chiselers" as the white working and middle class can.) Now a wide middle range of the population deeply believes that many things are being "given to" the poor and the blacks who are not required to work to earn them, while in fact nothing of value has been given to the black masses or the poor (although a new bureaucratic cadre has been created which provides some work and leadership possibilities for representatives of those groups). As the failure and dishonesty of those tactics became increasingly apparent in the late 1960s, opportunities for political aggrandizement were opened for those who wished to capitalize on the myths of the revolutionary militants, and of a gigantic giveaway to the undeserving lower orders.

For the future, however, it may be of some value to try to identify the basis by which working-class people might favorably evaluate initiatives designed to improve the conditions of those at the bottom of the social scale. It will be useful to distinguish here between goals, policies, and programs.[8] Initiatives directed toward increasing equality in society, which is the only meaningful way of improving life for those at the bottom of the social scale, can be divided into equalitarian goals, equalitarian policies, and equalitarian programs. There is no evidence that working-class people will not support equalitarian goals. Working-class people repeatedly say that they believe in a society in which no one has to be below the mainstream level. One has either to believe that they do not mean what they say or to accept what they say as the statement of an ideal that they are willing to support. This does not mean, of course, that working-class people, any more than others in society, can be expected to make great sacrifices for the achievement of an ideal by which they do not see themselves to be particularly advantaged. However, their acceptance of equalitarian goals does suggest that at least under certain conditions it would be possible to elicit working-class support for a movement toward these goals.

Equalitarian programs, on the other hand, are much more problematic. The tendency of government to try to deal with each problem of disadvantage by establishing a program that somehow directly gets at it is not only often self-defeating but politically inflammatory. Thus many of the equalitarian programs of the late 1960s had the appearance of giving people something for nothing, of not being contingent on the recipient's willingness to earn his way in the mainstream. For equalitarian programs to be successful and to receive broad and continuing support, they need to make sense to working-class people. These programs cannot be seen as violating the central values of earning what you get and of not asking for more than you are entitled to. To a very large extent, this is a matter of how the programs are presented, but it is probably also true that many of the problems of the lower class and disadvantaged cannot be attacked directly by programs that do not have this self-limiting quality. Thus, working-class people might be willing to support a very low guaranteed income on humanitarian grounds, but they would hardly support one that is high enough to put families within striking distance of the mainstream if it is not tied to work.

The way out of the rhetorical dead end of equalitarian programs lies with equalitarian policies, that is, standards of government operation which are informed by a commitment to equalitarian goals. All government policies should be systematically evaluated in terms of their contribution toward bringing about a society in which all able-bodied members can earn participation in the mainstream. Policies would be oriented toward bringing about the conditions which facilitate equalitarian goals in terms of the common values of the society. Such policies could limit the areas in which equalitarian programs are necessary to clean up the messes in the form of dependency and social pathology left by an inequalitarian society.

The working class should prove to be a strong source of support for equalitarian policies that offer the twin payoffs of achieving equalitarian ideals and at the same time using the productive potential of the poor to contribute to the welfare of everyone through the products of their labor.

In the long run, it is likely that the working class and much of the lower middle class will prove responsive to political programs along these lines rather than to the current rash of rightist rhetoric with which the group is being courted. Working-class people are much too tough-minded to see their enjoyment of respectable rightists such as Vice President Agnew and George Wallace as other than a small self-indulgence justified by how sorely tried they feel by these times. They do not see such political leaders as people who will protect their vital interests or who foster the social and economic policies necessary to sustain them in the mainstream. In the long run they are much more available to political leaders like the late Robert Kennedy, who are able to cut through rhetorical and mass media provocations to deal instead with the basic facts that the working class and blacks and others of the underclass share essentially the same life goals and have a common interest in governmental policies that facilitate the achievement of those goals by the broadest range of citizens.

NOTES

1. The present article is based in part on current research into working- and lower-middle-class life-style supported by National Institute of Mental Health Grant 1-P01-MH15567.
2. See U.S. Department of Labor, *How American Buying Habits Have Changed,* 1959.
3. David Riesman and Howard Rosebourough, "Careers and Consumer Behavior," in N. Bell and E. F. Vogel (eds.), *A Modern Introduction to the Family,* Free Press, New York, 1960.
4. There is a great deal of consensus between the lower and stable working classes on the requisites for living the good life. See, for example, Lee Rainwater, *Behind Ghetto Walls,* Aldine, Chicago, 1970, pp. 47ff.
5. William J. Goode, *World Revolution and Family Patterns,* Free Press, New York, 1963.

6. George Gallup, "Poverty by Consensus," in Herman P. Miller (ed.), *Poverty American Style,* Wadsworth, Belmont, Calif., 1966; and George Gallup, "Poll Finds Family Needs $120 a Week," *Boston Sunday Globe,* Jan. 25, 1970.
7. Richard M. Scammon and Ben J. Wattenberg, *The Real Majority,* Coward-McCann, New York, 1970.
8. Daniel P. Moynihan, "Policy vs. Programs in the 1970s," *The Public Interest,* Summer 1970.

10. CAN WORKERS TRANSFORM SOCIETY?*

by S. M. Miller and Martha Bush

DIVERSITY OF BLUE-COLLAR WORKERS

American workers are described in a variety of ways, depending on the purposes of the commentator. They have been viewed as hard hats and fat cats, complacent in their affluence, raging in their racism. Some new and old leftists continue to see them as a class-conscious, potentially revolutionary proletariat, the only hope of revolutionary change in capitalist society. Others of the old and new left have lost hope in the working class as a revolutionary group: they regard workers as co-opted beneficiaries/victims of the welfare state or as dwindling remnants of an earlier technological era. Still others, perhaps the bulk of the liberals and ex-old left, regard workers and their unions as unworthy of concern and support. Workers are regarded as anti-intellectual, racist, authoritarian. Far from promoting positive change, they are seen as rearguardists, hostilely competing for resources that should go to the poor and discriminated.

In opposition to this view, a determined but beleaguered band of liberals retain faith in a resurgence of the New Deal liberal-labor

*We are indebted to the following for comments: Nat Goldfinger, Robert Schrank, R. D. Corwin, Sumner Rosen. We have utilized Basil Whiting's reworking of recent census data on income. Marsha Kroll has helped us to clarify the exposition. None bears responsibility for the present formulations.

coalition. This coalition is severely threatened: Republican politicians seek the blue-collar vote on the basis of social rather than economic issues; indeed, Labor Day in 1970 moved from a street demonstration of solidarity and demands to a White House lawn party.

What an extraordinary range of views! It is hard to believe that analysts are talking about the same group of workers. Perhaps they notice only particular kinds of conditions, or they have contrasting ways of judging behavior.

Heterogeneity

One of the major difficulties in generalizing about workers is their considerable heterogeneity. We can center on workers who display impressive union militancy in a General Electric or General Motors strike. Or we can concentrate on a union like the International Ladies' Garment Workers' Union, which economically regulates its industry and whose officers display virtually the same ethnic character today as 40 years ago, despite an enormous change among the membership. One can talk as though all workers were skilled, highly paid members of strong construction unions, or as though they all shared the conditions of low-paid, unprotected migrant workers. Many commentators have yielded to the temptation to select a particular slice of contemporary history and generalize from that or project a major trend from a minor event.

We never agree on whom to include among workers. Richard Hamilton has argued that it is more sensible to exclude foremen from studies of income and attitudes because their basic situation and outlook differ from those who constitute a manual population. Others believe that the circumstances of many technicians are very similar to those of workers and that they should be included in any discussion of workers. Others argue for the exclusion of low-skilled, low-pay workers because their conditions and possibilities differ so much from those of skilled and semiskilled workers.

For the purpose of this chapter, all manual workers except foremen are included. Every statement about workers should be interpreted as saying "some workers" or "many workers," for a recognition of the heterogeneity among workers is basic to any analysis.

Numbers

How one foresees the future size of the manual workers' grouping affects one's estimate of their importance. Despite the announcements of the coming of a "service economy" or a "postindustrial society," blue-collar work is not dwindling. True, overall occupational trends show that white-collar work is increasing much more rapidly than blue-collar. This relative decline does not mean that blue-collar employees are decreasing in absolute numbers; the great drop absolutely and relatively has been in agricultural employment. (The 1969 total of 27.3 million blue-collar workers is the largest figure ever for that type of employment. To this number should be added most of the 9.7 million service workers.) Furthermore, if one looks only at male workers, it turns out that blue-collar work has not been even relatively reduced: in 1940, 45.6 percent of the male labor force was in blue-collar work; in 1969, 47.2 percent.

Thus, although blue-collar workers are not a majority of all the labor force, they are not an insubstantial number. Misleading notions about the contraction of blue-collar workers partly stem from the assumption that they once predominated in the economy. They never did. Manufacturing employment never exceeded a third of the labor force and was usually considerably lower.

Some of those who deprecate the significance and attitudes of workers foresee the emergence of a revolutionary "new working class" of technicians and technocrats. That these occupational slots are rapidly growing is partly due to the low absolute base from which the computations start. The professional and technical category in 1969 constituted only 14.3 percent of the total labor force; almost four of ten in this category are women, many of whom are in low-level para- and semiprofessional occupations and are not likely to become radicalized.

Frequently, the figures for all white-collar work are confused with data about the professional-technical classification. Almost half of all white-collar workers are in low-level clerical and sales occupations, and another fifth are managers and small businessmen; thus only three of ten white-collar workers (or one-seventh of the labor force) are in professional and technical work. The slice of radicals in this group is not presently large.

Stressing the size of the manual categories and minimizing the size of the professional-technical categories should not lead to the simple notion that the venerable thesis of a proletarian revolution is tenable. Neither numbers nor outlook makes that prediction probable. But, as we shall discuss later, an effective movement for change cannot write off a large group like workers.

Income

The fat cat view of workers centers on those who earn at least $12,000 a year; the counterview focuses on those who barely make the minimum wage. Obviously both situations exist, but the more important issue is not the range (and therefore the heterogeneity) of incomes among workers but the fact that the median earnings of white workers are almost $2,000 less than the $10,000 that the Bureau of Labor Statistics considers a modest standard of living for an urban family of four.

Undeniably, the absolute incomes of workers have advanced markedly since World War II. But expectations regarding what is an adequate level of living have also changed in 2½ decades. Frequently workers' incomes are judged by the standards of 1945 while the incomes of those better off are evaluated on the basis of contemporary levels and styles. Many workers—especially those with young families and without a second wage earner—surely feel neither that they are doing well on their $8,000 income nor that they have much discretionary income. Their hopes for the future cannot be substantial since, after the age of 25, workers' income varies little with increasing experience, unlike that of professional and managerial employees. Nor do they have the fat cat's comfortable feeling that they don't have to worry about money—a freedom from fear and risk that is the ultimate luxury.

This luxury is now part of the standard of living of many families. This situation indicates the growing spread in income between manual workers and upper-middle-class income groups in society: in 1960 white blue-collar workers, born between 1926 and 1935, had 82.7 percent of the mean family income of professionals and managers; in 1970, they had 69.8 percent of the latter's income.

But even at an absolute level an important change has occurred. From the 1950s through the mid-1960s there was a growing confidence in the continuing expansion of real income; wages would increase more rapidly than taxes and prices. In the late 1960s this confidence disappeared as many factory workers discovered little if any gain in their real income. (Take-home pay—weekly gross earnings less Social Security and federal income taxes but without deducting state and local taxes—was no greater in terms of purchasing power in 1969 than in 1965 for a worker with three dependents. Between 1960 and 1965 there had been a real gain of 11 percent.) This experience shocked many. The confluence of this leveling of real income and the turmoil of the black and youth rebellions may have precipitated the irritability and volatility of many workers. Without the ending, at least temporarily, of the expectation of constant improvement, it is unlikely that worker unrest would have been strong.

Racial Attitudes

Although many workers accept the racist attitudes which are widespread in our society, their attitudes are not a complete rejection of blacks. While they may resist blacks' moving next door, they work alongside them in the plant. While they object to (black) people on welfare whom they see as being supported in indolence, they support full employment programs which would guarantee jobs for both blacks and whites. While furious over rioting and looting, they "do not want Negro repression."[1] While they think blacks have gotten away with too much, they don't believe that a return to the past situation of black subjugation is possible or desirable.

What should we make of those complicated statements? It has been suggested that many workers have strong antiblack feelings, as many other Americans do, but these are not fixed or unchanging. As Samuel Lubell says, they seek racial peace, not racial change. They are willing to make accommodations if "peace" would follow and if the burden of change were shared by others and not concentrated in their neighborhoods, schools, and jobs. They see the rest of society as saying that it is uninterested in their fate as long as blacks advance and better-off whites are left untouched by improving black opportunities. The resentment is not only against blacks but also against those whites who seem to disdain workers and their interests.

They do not always welcome the advance of minorities; they resist it when it seems to hurt them. But they are not unmovable on the race issue. Their racist attitudes were not the major obstacle to black advancement in this country; the elimination of their racist attitudes will not solve the racial problem in this country. Workers and their unions should and can do better on this issue; so should all of us. Thus, racial attitudes of workers do not seem to be an impossible barrier to joint action on issues. On the other hand, they are not likely alone to fashion a just society.

Culture

In the 1950s and 1960s many believed that affluence wiped out class differences. Rising standards of living and mass communication were thought to have drawn workers into a homogenizing melting pot: the pleasures of affluence erased outworn class attitudes and molded a universal middle-class outlook. Harold Wilensky described workers as part of a "middle mass": others saw them as "bourgeoisified," exhibiting the few virtues and many deficiencies of the bourgeois middle class.

Richard Hamilton[2] in this country and David Lockwood[3] and John Goldthorpe in England have questioned the contention that advancing incomes have resulted in workers' developing middle-class attitudes. On many issues, workers' attitudes differ strongly from those of many of the middle class. Wildcat strikes indicate an attitude which is not common among middle-class employees. Indeed, what seems to be happening to some extent is that many white-collar employees, especially in the civil service, recognize that their conditions are not altogether different from those of factory workers and begin to behave in the more militant fashion of organized workers. Thus, not only have workers not easily absorbed middle-class attitudes, but middle-class employees have assimilated many working-class attitudes.

To assert that class is still important does not mean that workers are class-conscious. It is not class consciousness which is important, but the notion of *equity:* that whatever differences exist among groups must make some sense and seem functional. For example, one group should not benefit while others suffer from inflation. When workers' normative sense of what is right is violated, they become irritated and angry. This anger sometimes has the force of a direct class consciousness. Most of the time it is a narrow *economic* consciousness expressed in terms of clear cut bread-and-butter issues rather than concern with broad issues of economic and political power. While "them" and "us" are the terms sometimes used, the argument is over concrete economic gains rather than sharing political power or seeking the revolutionary transformation of society—as implied in the term "class consciousness." Simple fairness rather than profound redistribution is the issue in equity.

Viewing workers as an imminent revolutionary proletariat is therefore unsound. Only a large-scale war or a cataclysmic, prolonged depression could produce revolutionary unrest among workers. The avoidance of a major hot war (despite the past intensity of the cold war) provides strong hope that we will continue to escape a highly destructive war. The prediction that internal economic contradictions would cause a major depression has been largely supplanted by the view that the ending of neoimperialism will cause economic crisis for the United States. This occurrence is unlikely despite its central position in new left thought. This is not to argue that Keynesian-tamed capitalism produces high growth with price stability, more equitable distribution of income and power, a cleaner or more satisfying nation, and a less status-ridden society. But dissatisfactions with some of the outcomes of managed capitalism are not likely to produce revolutionary discontent.

PERSPECTIVES

Disappointment is an important source of many liberals' and radicals' rejection of workers. The hopes of the 1930s for deep and basic changes in society have been frustrated, and workers and unions are regarded as major villains or willing accomplices in this failure. Many expected the organization of workers into unions and the development of national policies to advance their economic conditions, not only to improve the immediate lives of blue-collar workers but also to result in more basic change in the United States. These hopes have been largely unrealized. It is not that workers are not much better off than they were before. They certainly are; but society has not been drastically changed by these measures. Just as the intervention of government in business and economic affairs, roundly attacked by business for many decades, resulted in benefiting corporations to an unimaginable extent in terms of growth and profits, the organization of workers into unions—again denounced by business—has not deeply modified society or business. True, the authoritarian character of the employer-employee relation has been considerably reduced, but this shift has not substantially affected other parts of society or the central core of business practice.

As a consequence of frustrated hope, many liberals and radicals castigate workers for becoming middle-class, bourgeoisified, willing to benefit from society, and complacently or even jingoistically accepting that society if they are not hurt by it. Once the embodiment of the dream of a better society, workers are now decried as the violators of this dream. Romance breeds disillusion, and the disillusion may be as remote from reality as the original hope was.

The naïve expectation that workers and their unions alone could transform society does not mean that the desire for transformation is ill-founded or that workers have no important role in changing society. The criticisms of contemporary society cannot be adequately met by "fine-tuning" the economy to produce a little more growth or a little less inflation, or by passing more or less revenue or responsibilities to state and local governments. The issues that the United States faces will push workers as well as others to become more interested in transformational issues—the basic distribution of income rather than just getting "more"; the transfer of power to new groups away from narrowly based elites and establishments; deep-seated shifts in the relations between power wielders and citizens; the respect for all kinds of work (and leisure); the decline in the concern for "success" defined mainly in prestige terms and the development of humanistically satisfying values; the concern for the quality of social and family relations rather than the quantity of gross national product. Those concerned with transformation will be disappointed again if only the widely advocated but limited set of liberal reforms is enacted.

Contemporary programs offered to improve the situation of workers do not meet the objectives of this transformational agenda. They treat symptoms rather than promote profound change. They are valuable planks, but it is important to look beyond these immediate demands to a more transformational program. Coalition politics should be viewed not only in terms of immediate electoral objectives, but also in terms of long-range needs. Consequently, we will first review many of the currently recommended programs in order to show the limits of their possibilities. This critique will pave the way for the following sections, in which we outline some components of a deeper program and some reasons for believing that workers might support it.

SHORT-RANGE CHANGES

One way of examining these policies is in terms of their potential effects on income, assets, services, education and mobility, power, status, and satisfaction.[4]

Income

A policy of high employment would increase the income of blue-collar workers by reducing periods of unemployment and pushing up wage rates and hours worked. But high-employment policies lost many adherents in the 1960s as concern grew about high prices, which were a product of tight labor markets. Consequently, most of the recommended programs have a narrow focus. For example, the income supplementation provisions in the Family Assistance Plan would affect only the poorest of blue-collar workers. Unionization of low-paid workers is another suggestion, again benefiting those only at the lower level of manual work. A high national minimum wage would benefit more. A reduction in taxes, if carried out on a grand scale, would make a sizable difference.

But it is clear that a national consensus does not exist for either a sizable increase in real wages or the means of achieving it. There is only limited awareness that the basic question is what the general contours of the income profile of the country should be: what share of national income should go to labor, and within that group to white- and blue-collar workers, is not overtly at issue in current debates about income and economic policy, although these are the fundamental decisions, as we shall discuss later.

Assets

In the area of assets, the major issue today is adequate housing at feasible cost for blue-collar workers (and for others). The curtailing of housing construction because of credit stringency and the skyrocketing of sales prices both have to be overcome. No adequately financed program is on the horizon.

In addition to the question of an adequate housing supply and its cost is the question of desegregation. How can we increase the supply without increasing the strong tendency toward resegregation in suburbs and white depopulation of big cities? We are not even addressing ourselves to this issue.

Also important are the questions of sharing the burdens of change. Workers, as we have said, are more likely than those better off to run the risk of declines in real estate values as neighborhoods desegregate. In the process of desegregation, public expenditures on schools, sanitation, and amenities decline rather than increase to meet greater needs. Older homeowners lose out.

The housing difficulties of blue-collar workers can be alleviated somewhat by decreasing interest rates and giving other forms of subsidies. But even if these gains were achieved—an unlikely outcome—the basic problems of the production and desegregation of housing cannot be resolved without a comprehensive national housing policy. Tactical steps, such as insuring against loss in real estate values because of changing racial composition of neighborhoods, can be effective only if there are national policies which make it possible for minority individuals to locate in new communities and which promote desegregation of existing areas.

Generally, the restricted activities which are immediately likely on the housing front do not form a cohesive policy which would effectively deal with the problems. Rather we are likely to get limited and short-range answers which lessen some of the obvious difficulties but do not drastically change or resolve the problems.

Services

There is clear need to expand the range and availability of services to workers. In the 1960s, several kinds of services for poor people were introduced, such as Head Start and legal aid. Not only the poor could benefit from such amenities, which need to be universalized. It is unclear what the gains and losses are in treating services as "free" (uncharged) goods or imposing a user fee for those above the poverty line. But even with some charges, public services such as day care will be expensive to provide. As a consequence, only limited gains are likely. More important, even if the quantity and reach of the services were radically expanded, they would lessen life's burden but not change society. Day-to-day existence would be easier; there would be more time for the individual, and other services would be readily available. However, there would be no inevitable changes in power and social relations.

Education and Mobility

Schools in working-class areas are frequently charged with poor performance. Some contend that these schools have deteriorated sharply in the last decade. Therefore, many advocate increased funds for schools in workers' areas and government financial aid to parochial schools which enroll many students from blue-collar families. Though added funds may be important in raising performance level—and even that is questioned, they are not sufficient to achieve change in attitudes necessary to transform society. Increased funds will not necessarily teach students how to share in decision making or involve them in the goals of education. They will not enable people, especially blue-collar workers, to respect themselves or others. At best they would leave schools only a little better than they have been—not a notable objective.

Mobility is chiefly conceived of as intergenerational: the occupational advance of sons compared to fathers. There is very little concern for promoting the occupational advance of individuals during their work lifetimes. For many, the clank of the factory gate signifies the ending of the possibility of moving into higher-level jobs in the economy. Blue-collar workers hit a low job ceiling at an early age. Horizontal mobility is seen as unstable job hopping, not as a sensible way of getting variety in work. Education is still regarded as the major vehicle for upward mobility, even though many find it a very difficult road and little related to what jobs require. As a consequence, even inter- and intragenerational mobility rates are lower than they can or should be.

In the contemporary discussion of education for workers and their children, there is little concern for overcoming the anti-intellectual bias, which is a large source of the reactionary attitudes of many workers today. Obviously, economic change will affect these attitudes but not eradicate them. Any program which tries to eliminate this anti-intellectual bias must also remove the reciprocal bias of the intellectual toward workers. These reciprocal attitudes of distrust limit the possibilities of coalitions as well as the long-term development of workers.

Power

Workers have begun to feel they are not getting attention and have little power. Their resentment is manifested in their anger at apparent neglect at the hands of city government, their rejection of union contracts, and their hostility toward students.

Politicians obviously are responding to these angers. The Nixon administration is reaching out to labor leaders, and blue-collar stories now fill the mass media; these are responses to workers' growing political insurgence. As of 1970, however, few significant changes have occurred.

In some localities, neighborhood groups of ethnic workers are organizing for power over government, such as community control of schools in New York City; sometimes, too, they have organized to resist racial change. But little is taking place that is comparable to the events of the 1930s: the breakup of the company town, the sudden importance of the union vote in many industrial towns, the offsetting authority of unions in many plants. What seems to be occurring today is a limited response by government to recent worker activism, but no great transformation which redefines power and power relations.

Status and Satisfaction

Blue-collar work is still little esteemed—perhaps less now than before. Many young workers see their jobs as a sentence rather than an opportunity. Basic attitudes toward blue-collar work are not likely to be changed by gimmicky recommendations. On the contrary, the 1970 United Auto Workers' negotiating proposals for new work arrangements to promote greater job enjoyment and for an educational fund to support training for workers indicate an increased awareness of the problem. General working conditions—greater security, lessened time pressure, more autonomy, improved physical condition—are becoming increasingly important collective bargaining issues. The attitude toward manual work is one of the ingredients of management's slowness in meeting these issues.

The breaking down of the negative stereotype of blue-collar workers is necessary but unlikely. This stereotype is often promoted by the communications industry: it is easier and more sensational to focus on hard hats and fat cats than on the majority of workers or the issues which produce strong responses.

Even if the approaches outlined in the preceding pages were implemented on a large scale, they would not remold society. Workers' economic gains would provide better amenities but not necessarily a society with different social relations. Nor is it enough to transfer some power. For transformation to occur, the relations between power wielders and citizens must change drastically. Transformation must include changes in institutions as well as changes in fundamental attitudes and values. We must visualize the problem of blue-collar workers as a long-term concern rather than a crisis issue which can be resolved by a few ameliorative programs. Therefore, we turn to a consideration of the broader long-term issues facing blue-collar workers and some of the changes necessary to meet them.

LONG-TERM CHANGES

Many liberals and radicals have called for profound changes in the society. Some demand greater equality; others emphasize greater participation both in the community and in work; others envision remaking of the ways people get into jobs and develop. These goals or, perhaps more accurately, these efforts to instill new goals for our society often have a rather romantic and uncertain base. They appear utopian because they do not emerge from the pressing needs of our society as demonstrated by economic malfunctioning. They develop more from a perspective of what is good for individuals and society than from an examination of the probable trends in society. They appear as an unlikely escape from contemporary society rather than as a realistic effort to move that society in better ways. We feel, however, that attitudinal changes now occurring and the economic challenges of the next 10 years are likely to make these broad goals much more realistic politically than they have been.

Attitudinal Shifts

The rising educational level of workers has exposed them to wider ranges of experience, thus causing at least the younger ones to become more and more dissatisfied with the often narrow, menial, and routine tasks they are asked to perform. Workers feel that blacks made economic gains in the 1960s because once invisible men agitated and confronted. Workers want a piece of the action too and are willing to struggle for it. The mass media have seized upon the worker as the new headline and present an image of the worker as discontented, occupationally blocked, victimized—differing from the 1950s' notion of the affluent, complacent worker. Civil rights, blacks, students, and peace are passé; they are no longer "news." Workers, and women, are.

These experiences are leading workers to a new image of themselves and their role in society. Various spokesmen for the workers are beginning to voice strong interest in their history. They see workers as ethnics—a part of the melting pot of America; as a cornerstone of the American labor movement; and as the builders of America—the homes, factories, roads, and bridges; and as the last stronghold of the American dream.

It is paradoxical that workers and their critics seek the same goals—democracy, freedom, equal opportunity, and peace. Just as students and blacks began to feel a sense of powerlessness and frustration, so do workers. Like blacks and students, they will most likely look beyond narrow bread-and-butter issues.

Pushing this development will be the economic turbulence that will mark the 1970s. The character of work will change importantly because of technological and demand changes. Policy discussions will force out some of the underlying tensions of work, choice, productivity, and legitimacy.

Work

Profound shifts in the nature of work are likely. Contemporary industry in the United States, as Peter Drucker has written, is still largely a result of turn-of-the-century development.[5] The great industries are still steel and automobiles; their technologies are essentially rooted in the nineteenth century. Indeed, most large-scale industries were developed technologically in essentially their contemporary form by the beginning of this century. Recently, however, a new technology typified by computer operations is beginning to be important in this country. It will become much more pervasive and will lead to more emphasis on technical skill, training, and adaptability. These changes may not reduce blue-collar work as much as increase the numbers of technical workers whose conditions and outlook do not differ much from those of blue-collar workers.

The structure of domestic and foreign demand is likely to change in the next decade as well. Communications, professional, trade, repair, and other services are likely to grow more rapidly than other industries. Traditional jobs will decline as new tasks expand; continued redevelopment and shifting of workers will be required as new industries and firms replace old.

Economic Policy Choice

Economic policy also will be unsettled because it is faced with conflicting goals. The desire for high growth rates and high employment competes with the effort to limit price increases and prevent foreign trade imbalances. Unless Friedmanite monetary policy turns out to be more effective as an across-the-board panacea for the economy than we can now expect, it seems inevitable in the next years that wage and price controls (in the European phrase, an "incomes policy") will have to be instituted if both growth and price stability are to be achieved.

In general, the prospect is for more governmental regulation of the economy rather than less, as the Friedmanites and Nixonites would like to believe possible. Both American consumers and Zurich bankers have exacting requirements for the operation of the American economy, and their pressures will result in continuing efforts to balance the economy between its competing goals. The calm, settled, predictable growth procedure outlined by the Friedmanite approach of moderate monetary expansion will not be sufficient to accomplish all that is required of an economy that is constantly evaluated by its participants and its bankers.

The long-run consequence will be increasing rather than declining control over the economy. For not only is more expected of the economy, but policy makers are believed to be capable of delivering more if they are judicious. Poor national economic performance is charged to politicians' and administrators' poor decisions rather than to bad luck or "natural" economic forces. Accountability will promote intervention in the economy, and the politicalization of economic issues will become stronger and more controversial.

Productivity

Basic to economic growth is increasing productivity. While technology obviously is the basis of productivity, there are increasing soundings which indicate that the human factors in productivity should not be ignored. Reports abound of absenteeism, poor workmanship, lack of responsibility, and the reluctance of workers old and young to endure hard work. These problems will not be fully met by improving wage rates or personnel practices or by inventive plans which tie wages to output. They will require development of greater legitimacy for and commitment to work processes, the workplace, and the nation. Narrow economic incentives will not be enough, especially if puritan work attitudes continue to erode rapidly.

Legitimacy

These pressures will also lead to the questioning of legitimacy and loyalty. Partly because so many of the conditions which will be faced are policy results, it will be necessary to win loyalty and to gain legitimacy for institutions and their functions. The process of being socialized as an American will not automatically produce acceptance of and commitment to work, or to educational and governmental agencies. New institutions and practices will be necessary to hold society together; reforming the old will not be enough.

These issues in technology, economic control, and productivity will lead to widespread physical uprooting and breakdown of social ties. People will have to change jobs a great deal, move from one geographic area to another, experience a great variety of human relations, ingest more and a greater range of information. In other words, expect the unexpected and learn to cope with it.

TRANSFORMING POLICY

Four such changes—in education, economic equality, participation, and status—will serve as examples of the deep-seated transformations toward which the United States is moving and which directly engage workers.

Education

The flexible educational policy that is needed would radically shift our ways of developing skills and individuals. Schools will no longer be the quasi-monopolistic training ground for individuals, nor will individuals be expected to complete their development or training in their first 18, or 22, or 26 years. Rather, an extensive system of continuing adult education will be constructed. (The Swedish government of Prime Minister Olof Palme has set this as an important objective and has invented a new term for it: "recurrent education.") This will make it possible for individuals to change jobs at various points in their life and to acquire new kinds of information and training. The new system will be predicated on the assumption that people have continuing capacity for development—much more capacity than is now believed to exist. Dead-end jobs may still exist, but there would be fewer dead-end people. The concern for mobility will grow: new sets of educational institutions will emerge, more oriented to developing people than to processing them.

Futurity does not imply an automatic unfolding. Only as people—workers, nonworkers, the poor, and their children—become aware of and fight for these changes will substantial restructuring of education occur. These transformations are not inevitable: neither the technocrats' "professionalization of reform" nor the revolutionists' "locomotive of history" adequately describes social change. But drastic improvement of the educational and vocational future of workers, along with meeting the needs of emerging industry, requires deeper changes than spending more money on schools in working-class areas. Workers are likely to be an important part of the struggle to produce more than a modest reformation of schools, for they will increasingly be questioning why they should be restricted throughout their lifetimes to limited or dead-end jobs because they did not effectively manage the educational system when young.

Equality

Price-wage policy will be necessary in order to combat inflation. A workable price-wage policy requires people to have some loyalty or commitment to their society. This will be increasingly difficult to achieve because there is no readily agreed-upon basis for maintaining or reducing current wage differentials. Why should someone else suffer less from inflation than I? The principle of equity—assumptions about what is a fair set of differentials—will be in constant tension with the pressure toward equality because individuals are jointly immured in the difficulties of the economy. Price-wage policies might perpetuate present differentials or even accentuate them, but it is hoped they might decrease inequalities. What occurs will be clearly a result of policy and not of invisible market forces. Income is a clearly controllable product. But why should the increased controllability of income go in the direction of equality?

One hope for decreasing inequality rests in the need for obtaining support for the legitimacy of economic policy. "Why should I accept not getting as much as I could when others are getting so much more?" A workable price-wage arrangement requires to some extent a feeling of mutual sharing.

In addition, there is increasing recognition that much of what happens to individuals economically is due not so much to their particular merit or effort as to their fortuitous position within the economy. If luck, connections, and political clout, as well as skill and capital, determine income, the purported rationality in wage differentials and income distribution disappears. The uncovering of the shallow basis for the present distribution of income will weaken support for the maintenance of inequalities.

Participation

Greater participation in the workplace is one way of developing the loyalty and involvement that may build higher productivity. Participation in work will require more than the superficial activities of suggestion boxes or committees; actual deep-level participation in basic decisions will be necessary. Management may often take the lead where unions are reluctant to extend their scope; but more and more unions will feel compelled by members' pressures to extend the range of bargaining issues as governmental and corporate policies produce a highly turbulent economy of technological change, balancing and fluctuating policies, and geographic shifting. Unions' roles will expand as they become vehicles of greater participation. The forms are uncertain, though profit sharing and representation on boards are two possibilities. But the important issue will be whether worker and union participation will be marginal and symbolic or powerful and far-reaching.

Status

Greater participation alone does not ensure higher status or respect for workers. The low relative status of workers in an inegalitarian society influences their productivity. Feeling unimportant and disregarded, low-status workers are unlikely to invest much of themselves in the job; they will do what they have to rather than what they should do. To obtain a great change in workers' productivity will require different attitudes toward them. The result may be concern to build greater job satisfaction and to accord more respect to those who have not gone to college or do not work in offices. The problems obviously are not simple, but it seems increasingly evident that productivity is limited by human factors and that better technology and personnel divisions cannot do the job as well as a big jump in commitment, participation, and status. The issue is workers' membership and participation in the larger society as well as in the immediate factory. Thus, workers' status and power relations with other groups in the society will be central.

COUNTERPRESSURES

Outlining these possibilities runs the danger of converting preferences into predictions. The indicated trends are not inevitable, but they are probable. These changes depend to a large extent on how militant and far reaching unions are, how intelligent and accommodating businesses are, and how effective liberal and radical political organizations are. Many events could inhibit these developments. For example, economic tensions could be handled in ways that are contrary to these directions. Counterpressures against the outlined trends might prevent deep seated change; they have to be overcome if a forceful coalition is to be developed. These pressures are twofold: intraclass conflict and interclass conflict.

Intraclass conflict includes the struggle and tension between black and white workers as well as between skilled and unskilled workers. Increasing tension in many factories is reported. As the numbers of black workers expand, they will insist upon obtaining and defending their rights as they define them. Seniority systems may be upset and promotional procedures changed. In many unions there will be pressure for black leadership. As black workers become more numerous and more important, the militancy of workers in and out of unions may intensify; ethnic as well as economic class issues may fuse to produce a militancy which has not characterized the unionized working class in this country for some time. But racism is an important divider, and the conflict between black and white workers is not certain to abate even though many white workers are intimate with blacks on the job (but not off the job). As Brendon Sexton has contended, their relations on the job have greater intimacy than the general relations of whites and blacks in the upper middle classes.

There is no easy way to ease black-white tensions. A basic requirement is high rates of economic growth in which white workers improve their absolute situation while blacks improve theirs both absolutely and relatively. Without economic policies which promote improvement, the prominence of the race issue for workers is not likely to diminish. Workers' economic gains do not ensure the abatement of overt racism, but without gains little is likely to be accomplished. Also essential to any change is reeducation around the issue of race.

Interclass conflict refers to the conflict between workers on one side and students and professionals on the other. While lower white-collar and upper blue-collar workers live near to each other, cross-class relations between workers and professionals and managers are rare. There is no current discussion of overcoming cross-class social gaps.

The open, experimental style of students does not appeal to workers. This is partly because students are free from work. Workers who plug away at unsatisfying and regimenting jobs resent those who can dispense with working; and blue-collar workers cannot understand or accept student sacrilege of the American dream as manifested in "disrespect" for the flag, use of obscenities—especially those directed at authority, use of drugs, "dirty" appearance, freedom in sex, and an overall questioning of accepted goals and values.

Resentment of the condescending ways of professionals and academics needs to be interpreted in light of the value system which has grown up in America and affects both workers and professionals. This value system includes a growing disdain for manual labor and an increasing respect for mental work and higher education credentials. While the anti-intellectual attitudes of the workers need to be overcome, the intellectualism and condescension of intellectuals also require elimination. A large part of the effort must come from professionals and intellectuals who recognize the importance and problems of workers.

Tensions among these various groups can severely retard the possibilities of joint action. The conflicts are not, however, insuperable; they require open-mindedness from both workers and other groups.

JOINT ACTIONS

The profound changes that are required can be accomplished only by the joint action of a sizable majority. This will require the moving together of blue-collar workers, blacks and other minorities, youth, and a large segment of professional and managerial groups, as well as some of the lower white-collar workers. Since each of these potential members of a coalition is internally split, many groups must be involved to have power. These coalitions would be temporary at first, formed around specific issues in which all members have a stake.

For instance, one state has recently begun to construct a new expressway that will cut through several neighborhoods, damaging them extensively. These neighborhoods include a black neighborhood and a white ethnic neighborhood as well as a well-to-do suburb. Each of the individual neighborhoods has organized itself around this issue and is protesting the building of the highway. Perhaps more importantly, however, these individual neighborhood organizations have formed a coalition to protest the construction of the highway. This collective action is valuable not only in the immediate issue, but also in establishing a foundation of trust among these diverse groups. Other issues might be equality of income; housing policies; guaranteed income; transportation, sanitation, and consumer affairs services; educational opportunities, mobility, and continued individual development; distribution of power; and job satisfaction.

On issues of *economic policy* there seems to be a high degree of convergence among these groups. Economic expansion and government policy to produce high growth and high employment attract all these groups. These are the kinds of issues on which joint action could develop.

Foreign policy is a question that has separated these groups. One may hope that with the ending of the Indo-Chinese adventure and the realization in practice rather than in rhetoric of the Nixon doctrine of a "low profile" in the world, foreign policy will become a less salient and divisive issue. Thus, one of the important conflicts between workers on one side and many professionals and youth on the other may be reduced.

What about unions? Are they not a major obstacle to change? Even now they are not completely so. The AFL-CIO is the major force "for a broad range of progressive national economic and social issues," as contended by its chief economist, Nat Goldfinger; examples are the AFL-CIO's importance in fighting for economic expansion and improved medical, welfare, and Social Security programs. After the present generation of leaders retires, important changes that they have retarded may begin to surface. The issues facing workers and unions will require more comprehensive and penetrative policies and actions. Oppositional groups in their unions will proliferate and compel new programs to win support. Many unions will move beyond their limited agendas in collective bargaining and in national policies to wider objectives. Workers have problems and will continue to have them—undoubtedly accentuated. They are not inevitably a radical group, but they might be.

Can efforts to change the long-term position of workers transform all of society? Of that one cannot be sure. Those liberals and radicals (often despising each other) who believe that little can be gained from a concern about workers underestimate some changes while overestimating others. They have overestimated the importance of the new working class of technicians, managers, and professionals while underestimating the continuing significance of workers. Many continue to view workers from the scornful and distorting perspective of disappointed lovers. And they have ignored the significance of the problems which will unfold for workers in the decade of the 1970s.

Workers should be viewed as part of a potential although loose coalition which can produce important changes. These changes could go beyond the New Deal social reforms, important as they were for their day, to the large scale *structural* changes which are beginning to shape the outlook of Western European radical parties.

Instant change—instant success—is not a likely result of liberal or radical movements. Nor is the effort to achieve large scale change in this society likely to be more than ephemeral unless it links itself with workers and their unions. This linkage will not be easy to obtain or maintain, but its importance should not be obscured by attractive slogans about vibrant new classes and weary old ones. If we cannot have the high hopes of the 1930s, our chagrin should turn us not toward neglect or condemnation but toward a search—even if wary—for the possibilities of joint action.

NOTES

1. Samuel Lubell, *The Hidden Crisis in American Politics,* Norton, New York, 1970, p. 77.
2. Richard Hamilton, "The Income Differences between Skilled and White-Collar Workers," *British Journal of Sociology,* vol. 14, no. 4, pp. 363–373, 1963.
3. David Lockwood, "The New Working Class," *European Journal of Sociology,* vol. 1, no. 2, pp. 248–259, 1960.
4. S. M. Miller and Pamela A. Roby, *The Future of Inequality,* Basic Books, New York, 1970.
5. Peter Drucker, *The Age of Discontinuity,* Harper, New York, 1969.

« PART THREE »

Programs and Future Directions

Turning from attitude surveys and speculations about the desirability of overhauling American society, Part 3 explores how blue-collar workers or middle Americans are treated in American society. The areas considered are taxes, income maintenance, education, and availability of opportunities for upward mobility.

Few comparative data are available on blue-collar participation in government programs because public-sector programs rarely identify families on the basis of income source. The tax collector is normally concerned not with the occupation of the taxpayer but with his income, and Social Security payroll taxes are based upon clearly defined earning levels, which in turn determine benefits. Educational opportunities are open to all and indeed, until a prescribed age, are compulsory, but beyond that age they are voluntary; exclusionary policies, frequently based upon ability to pay, are practiced in the private sector. And even when higher education is provided "free," it does not follow that different occupational groups benefit equally.

Chapter 11 is devoted to an examination of the impact of our tax system, not because it is necessarily better to give than to receive, but because various levels of government together take, in taxes, 30 percent of total income. Stiff as the tax bite may be, Dick Netzer finds that, overall, the tax system is mildly progressive and is not, therefore, a reasonable basis for alienation and discontent on the part of blue-collar workers. Because people do not necessarily react on the basis of what is reasonable, however, Netzer is careful not to reject the claim that the tax system is a basis of blue-collar discontent. More than two-fifths of the average blue-collar worker's increments in earnings between 1965 and 1969 were taxed away. Inflation eroded most of the balance, leaving only a sixth of the total increase in spendable real income.

Short of cutting government expenditures, an unlikely development, Netzer sees no likelihood of alleviating the tax burden of lower-middle-class families. The facile solution of "soaking the rich" may be a good slogan in some places but offers a very limited source of revenue. Even if the entire income of all those earning more than $50,000 were confiscated, it would account for only about a tenth of total government tax collections. To ease the tax burden of the lower middle class without cutting total government revenue would require raising taxes of those with earnings above $10,000 or $15,000 a year (depending upon one's definition of lower middle class). There is no evidence, however, that the American upper class would agree to assume a higher share of the total rising tax burden; and even if the tax system were to become more progressive, equity might dictate that priority be given to reducing taxes of the poor rather than of the lower middle class.

A rounded appraisal of the tax system requires information not only about the incidence of the tax burden but also about how the revenue from the taxes is distributed. Possibly the two most important areas of government activity outside defense are income maintenance and education. Together these two activities account for more than a third of total government outlays. There is little question that most income maintenance programs are as strongly supported by blue-collar workers as by anybody else. This does not necessarily apply to public assistance programs whereby the recipient receives income without prior contributions from earnings. Although public relief programs have been increasing in importance, they still account for less than a fifth of total public income maintenance outlays. Because Social Security benefits are heavily weighted in favor of lower earners, Worth Bateman and Jodie Allen question the equity of requiring lower-middle-class workers to carry the brunt of supporting the Social Security system; they favor government contributions from general revenues to the upkeep of the system. But in the final analysis, they conclude that the Social Security system is not a significant contributor to alienation of blue-collar workers. On the contrary, it helps to include them in the mainstream of American economic life.

Education has traditionally been considered the surest way for upward mobility of the American working class. According to Robert Schrank and Susan Stein, children of manual workers have accounted for much of the recent increase in college enrollment; this reflects an emphasis during the past generation on expanding the opportunities for higher education to children of the lower middle class as well as of the poor. The growth of community, junior, and four-year colleges has brought technical or higher education within the reach of blue-collar families; expanded federal assistance programs for college students have subsidized the education of many children from blue-collar homes.

The persuasive though partial evidence gathered in this volume suggests that the position of the blue-collar worker has not deteriorated, but neither has it caught up with the image of an evolving American laboristic society, to use the late Sumner Slichter's phrase. In the last few years, there has been no improvement in the standard of living of many, if not most, blue-collar families. That the American working class faces no impending doom, however, does not justify ignoring efforts to improve their lot. Jerome Rosow presents a series of programs which would significantly assist workers. Not all of these can be realistically achieved in the next few years or even by the time this nation celebrates its bicentennial, but a democratic society can do no less than strive to achieve the goals laid down by Rosow.

Fred Harris proposes a liberal legislator's agenda, which focuses on a better distribution of the economic pie. He suggests that the blue-collar worker will remain a progressive as long as he shares in the progress.

The final chapter draws on the previous discussions in an attempt to assess the seriousness and consequences of the "blue-collar blues." Sar Levitan and Robert Taggart question the oft-repeated themes that the assorted woes of blue-collar workers are due to their inflexibility and that the pervasive changes undergone by American society have been particularly inimical to blue-collar workers. After having examined the problems facing the latter, the authors conclude that the burden of change has not fallen excessively upon manual workers and that political and economic mechanisms have helped them adapt to recent transitions. While specific problems of blue-collar workers deserve attention, Levitan and Taggart find no persuasive evidence that blue-collar workers feel particularly imposed upon, let alone that they are facing a crisis.

11. THE VISIBLE TAX SYSTEM

by Dick Netzer

RELATIVE TAX BURDENS

It is hardly surprising that blue-collar Americans, like others who are a good deal richer, are painfully aware of taxes. For one thing, unlike the poor, they are directly exposed to taxation: they have incomes that exceed exemption and deduction levels and thus have positive income tax liabilities; most of them are homeowners and thus are highly conscious of local property taxes; and they have some discretionary income to spend on automobile ownership and operation, appliances, home furnishings, apparel, and liquor—all of which are favorite objects of consumption taxation by federal, state, and/or local governments. Moreover, taxes for all Americans have been rising faster than incomes. Total tax collections were 26 percent of gross national product in 1960, but exceeded 30 percent by the end of the 1960s. Federal income and excise tax rates are on balance lower than they were 10 years ago, but payroll taxes have risen sharply, and rising incomes have pushed people into higher tax-rate brackets. Meanwhile, state and local governments have been busily increasing property, sales, and income tax rates and adopting new taxes at a rapid clip.

Nevertheless, the conventional wisdom among scholars in the field of public finance long has been that lower-middle-income Americans are *relatively* less harshly treated by the tax system than other income groups, that is, their tax burden as a percentage of income is lower than the corresponding percentage for both lower- and higher-income groups. Thus our target group should have less, not more, to complain about in connection with taxes, provided of course that the taxes collected are expended in ways that give blue-collar Americans a fair shake.

But is the conventional wisdom a sufficient answer? This chapter addresses a series of further questions designed to reconcile the traditional scholarly statements with the evident sense of outrage about taxes among lower- or middle-income urban families. First, are the statements about relative tax burdens an accurate description of the current situation? Second, have the objective circumstances of relative tax burdens changed in very recent years? Third, even if the conventional wisdom was right in the past and continues to be true at present, do blue-collar people really perceive it to be a fair description of their experience?

The analysis of the distribution of the tax burden by income groups is complicated by both statistical and conceptual difficulties. Only a few elements of the tax system, like the federal individual income tax, involve easily procured data and little argument about who really bears the burden of the tax. The incidence of several other major taxes is not in much dispute, but elaborate statistical manipulations are necessary. For example, most observers agree that the retail sales tax and excises on liquor, automobile ownership and operation, and tobacco tend to be shifted forward from the manufacturer or retailer (who actually remits the tax to a government tax collection agency) to the consumer who purchases the goods or services at higher prices reflecting the tax. Similarly, property taxes on homeowners are generally held to be a burden on the homeowners and no one else. But a good deal of work, leading to somewhat differing statistical results from each new study, must be done to associate the appropriate income group with purchases of the taxed items or ownership of houses of varying values.

Beyond this, there are some major taxes, including nearly all taxes on business profits, purchases, and payrolls, whose incidence has been hotly disputed for years. Some observers hold that all or most of such taxes tend to be shifted forward in the form of higher prices on business output; others aver that most of such taxes tend to be a burden on the owners of business enterprises; others hold that a large share is shifted backwards in the form of lower prices for business purchases, especially labor; and still others hold a rather eclectic view. The choice of assumption about the shifting of business taxes can make a good deal of difference in the final outcome.

In addition, the appropriate income measure for analysis of tax burdens is not self-evident. Are we concerned with taxes relative to income before or after the tax payments are deducted? Should we include, in addition to earnings from wages, salaries, and property holdings, other income such as government transfer payments, erratic items like gifts and capital gains, income in kind, and imputed portions of undistributed corporate profits? Is the appropriate measure this year's income, or income averaged over several years or even a lifetime?

The issues may be unresolved among scholars, but tax policy is continually being made by legislators and elected officials, in part on the basis of suppositions about the distribution of relative tax burdens among income groups. In the past 20 years, a large number of statistical studies of relative tax burdens have been made, often as part of official tax study commission research projects, to assist in forming tax policy. The detailed findings of these studies differ a good deal, but their approaches and general conclusions amount to a consensus that can be considered the conventional wisdom.

That consensus is as follows: If all tax payments, whether made by businesses or individuals, are allocated among family income classes—on the basis of assumptions about the shifting of the individual types of taxes—the federal tax burden rises faster than income rises. That is, the federal tax structure is progressive. In contrast, state and local government tax burdens, as percentages of income, decline steadily as income rises; they are distinctly regressive. Since federal taxes in the aggregate have been roughly twice as large as state-local taxes during the past decade, the progressive component of the tax system is dominant, and the overall shape of the American tax structure is somewhat progressive, though not consistently so.

There are two principal exceptions to the generally progressive character of the system. First, at the extreme low end of the income scale, deep in the poverty zone (incomes below $2,000 in 1970), the typical tax burden as a percentage of income is quite high and well above that for families next up on the income scale. Second, for incomes ranging from $4,500 to nearly $15,000, the tax burden remains about the same proportionately.[1]

What does this mean for the relative position of blue-collar Americans? It suggests that they are somewhat less heavily taxed than the small population group in extreme poverty and a good deal less heavily taxed than the larger group, which can be considered reasonably affluent, with 1970 family income before taxes of more than $15,000. They are more heavily taxed than families whose income is right around the poverty line. But despite the overall progressivity of the tax system, they are not significantly better off than the income group immediately above them. That is, the tax burden amounts in 1970 to as large a fraction of income in the $7,000 to $10,000 income range as in the $10,000 to $15,000 range.

This, then, would seem to afford some basis for a sense of grievance; if a family is able to make its way out of the poverty group, its relative tax burden rises fairly significantly. But the white-collar college-educated groups with income just above the characteristic blue-collar level do *not* have a higher relative tax burden. This could strike many as inequitable.

VISIBLE TAXES

However, it seems highly unlikely that ordinary people perceive tax burdens in this way because the total tax burden outlined above includes allocations of major taxes whose burden is largely invisible to them. All transfers of funds from the private sector to governments ultimately must result in reductions in the income or wealth of *some* families and individuals, just as all government expenditure ultimately enriches *some* people. But for some taxes, the path through which the economic effects are traced to family economic status is a highly indirect one. Prices may rise, wages may fall, or assets may decline in value, but only after an adjustment process that is not at all obvious. Therefore, few people may be able to ascribe the ultimate results to a specific tax instrument or tax policy change. This is very much the case with most taxes on business profits, business property holdings, and purchases by businesses from other firms, and for the employer share of payroll taxes for Social Security and unemployment insurance. It is less true of other elements of the tax system: personal income taxes and employee payroll taxes, which are shown on paycheck stubs; retail sales taxes, which are almost always separately stated when purchases are made; liquor, tobacco, and gasoline taxes, which amount to such large fractions of the retail prices of the taxed items that the taxes are fairly obvious even if not separately stated; and property taxes on housing (in the United States, largely owner-occupied housing) and automobiles. It is *this* group of taxes that is likely to be considered relevant by people—blue-collar or otherwise—when the fairness of the tax system is at issue. Another reason for excluding consideration of the less visible taxes is that their economic consequences are very much in dispute.[2] Indeed, the argument is so intense and the evidence so unsatisfactory that the incidence of these taxes can be said to be unknown and perhaps unknowable. Therefore, the remainder of this chapter focuses upon the more visible portion of the tax system.

In 1969, the taxes classified here as elements of the visible tax system yielded $185 billion, about two-thirds of total tax revenue for both the federal and the state-local tax systems (Table 28). In turn, two-thirds of the visible tax systems' revenues were produced by personal income and payroll taxes (largely federal); one-fifth by taxes on retail sales, liquor, automobile ownership and operation (mostly state-local taxes), and tobacco; and close to one-tenth by property taxes on housing (entirely state-local).

The visible tax system is, in general, rather progressive in its incidence (Table 29). The progressive income, death, and gift taxes provided over half of tax revenue in this system in 1969. Less than one-fourth of the revenue came from taxes that appear to be distinctly regressive in incidence. To understand this, it is worth exploring more fully the characteristics of the major tax forms.

Generally Progressive Taxes

Taxes on transfer of property by gift or bequest are obviously progressive in incidence in the sense that they are borne entirely by relatively affluent people. To be sure, there are all sorts of devices for minimizing death taxes, and the richer one is, the more actively employed these devices are. However, the exemptions provided in the federal law and in most state laws are so high that few people

TABLE 28
AMERICAN TAX SYSTEM IN 1969: TAX REVENUE OF FEDERAL, STATE, AND LOCAL GOVERNMENTS*
(IN BILLIONS)

Type of tax	*Total*	*Federal*	*State and local*
Total	$281.4	$197.2	$84.2
I. The visible tax system	184.8	129.5	55.3
Personal income taxes	102.2	92.2	10.0
Death and gift taxes	4.6	3.6	1.0
General sales taxes	14.6	....	14.6
Liquor and tobacco taxes	10.2	6.8	3.4
Taxes on automobile purchase and operation	11.8	4.4	7.4
Nonbusiness property taxes (largely on housing)	16.0	....	16.0
Personal contributions for social insurance (largely payroll taxes on employees)†	25.4	22.5	2.9
II. Other taxes	96.6	67.7	28.9
Corporate profits taxes	42.7	39.2	3.5
Business property taxes	16.0	....	16.0
Employer contributions for social insurance (payroll taxes on employers)‡	21.7	21.7	§
Other	16.2	6.8	9.4

* Excludes all identifiable nontax payments. Taxes shown net of refunds.
† Excludes contributions for veterans' life insurance.
‡ Excludes government contributions to government employee retirement funds, which cannot be considered the equivalent of taxes, by any definition.
§ Less than $50 million.
SOURCE: Department of Commerce and author's estimates.

in the bottom three-fourths of the income distribution are ever exposed to death and gift taxes.

The federal individual income tax presents a parallel situation. The well-advertised preferences and loopholes permit many very rich people to reduce (or sometimes even eliminate) tax liability. However, these tax advantages are of relatively little use to nearly all taxpayers with incomes below $50,000, that is, to more than 99.5 percent of all American households. If we ignore the very rich one-half of 1 percent, however distasteful their tax advantages may be, the federal income tax *is* fairly consistently progressive in impact. The very poor pay no tax at all, especially after the 1969 revisions of the tax law; tax liability rises steadily with income to a maximum approaching 70 percent of taxable income.

The federal income tax accounts for 90 percent of all personal income tax collections. In 37 of the 50 states, there are also generally applicable state personal income taxes, and in 8 of these 37, some local governments impose income taxes as well. In addition, Ohio and Pennsylvania, which lack a state income tax, have widespread municipal income taxation. Because state and local income taxation is not uniform, roughly 60 percent of the United States population live in areas with a state income tax, 10 percent in areas with both a state and a local income tax, and another 10 percent in areas with only a local income tax. Only in Connecticut, New Jersey, Texas, Florida, and seven smaller or less urban states do residents confront only the federal tax.

All the state income taxes have some degree of progressivity. Only four states do not have graduated tax-rate schedules, and all have personal exemptions (usually higher than the federal exemptions) which, quite apart from graduated rates, tend to make the

TABLE 29
GENERALIZED INCOME DISTRIBUTION CHARACTER OF THE AMERICAN VISIBLE TAX SYSTEM IN 1969
(PERCENTAGE OF TOTAL TAX REVENUE)

Type of tax	*Total*	*Federal*	*State and local*
All visible taxes	100	100	100
1. Generally progressive taxes (personal income, death, and gift taxes)	58	74	20
2. Generally regressive taxes (general sales, liquor, tobacco, and nonbusiness property taxes)	22	5	61
3. Other visible taxes, more or less proportional to income (auto taxes and personal contributions for social insurance)	20	21	19

SOURCE: Derived from Table 28.

taxes progressive in the lower part of the income scale. To illustrate, a 2 percent flat-rate tax on net incomes of $4,000 or more after personal exemptions works out to these percentages of income before exemptions:

Income	*Percent*
$4,000	0.0
$5,000	0.4
$7,500	0.9
$10,000	1.2
$15,000	1.5
$25,000	1.7

A number of state income taxes have additional credit devices, tending to increase their progressivity further. Then there are the graduated rates. Most often, the top rates are not high, typically 5 to 7 percent of taxable income contrasted with the 70 percent rate in the federal tax; but eight states have top-bracket rates in excess of 10 percent. Because rate brackets for state income tax often are narrower than for federal tax, the top-bracket rates are reached relatively quickly, in half the cases at family gross income below $20,000. This means that the state income tax is likely to appear quite progressive in the middle-income ranges, at least in those states, like New York, Hawaii, Minnesota, Oregon, and Wisconsin, that rely heavily on the tax and thus have high effective rates. A married couple with two children and an income of $10,000 in such states is likely to pay a state income tax of $300 or more, while a $5,000 income family pays $100 or less.

Unlike the federal and state income taxes, local income taxes are often not progressive at all. Usually, as in Ohio, Pennsylvania, and Kentucky, they are low flat-rate taxes (often 1 percent) applied to gross earned income, with no exemptions or deductions. Because the proportion of income from interest, dividends, rents, and capital gains rises as income levels increase, such taxes tend to be roughly proportional to income up to income levels of about $15,000, and then somewhat regressive at higher income levels. In contrast, the income taxes imposed by Michigan cities, Maryland counties, and New York City have a generally progressive nature, since they are similar to state income taxes with regard to coverage, exemption, and rate structures.

Generally Regressive Taxes

The general retail sales tax is the single most important revenue source for American state governments. It is used by 45 of them; of the 5 holdouts the largest is Oregon, and together they account for only 2 percent of the country's population. In addition, the retail sales tax is used widely by local governments in 13 states (one of them, Alaska, has no state sales tax) and by some local governments in 8 other states. A very large fraction of all Americans confront combined retail sales tax rates of 4 percent or more.

For years, the sales tax has been held to be highly regressive, in large part because of an important oversimplification. Although higher-income groups are able to save an increasing proportion of their income, in low-income groups total expenditures for current consumption exceed money income but decline steadily as a percentage of income as income rises. Therefore, it is generally concluded, a tax whose base is consumer expenditure in general must be regressive with respect to income: if consumer expenditure is twice as much as income in the lowest-income class (approximately the findings of surveys of consumer expenditure), then a 1 percent tax on all consumer expenditure will absorb 2 percent of the incomes of the very poor but only 0.5 percent of the incomes of the very rich.

But no American sales tax covers the *entire* range of consumer expenditure. Nowhere does the sales tax cover as much as two-thirds of total consumer spending, for it excludes housing—the single most important object of consumer expenditure—as well as spending for medical care, education, public transportation, and most personal-care services. Effectively, the common tax is one on spending for food and beverages, house furnishings and household equipment, clothing, and automobiles, plus a range of other items that together amount to only 10 to 15 percent of the tax base.

Some of the general exclusions like housing, public transportation, and medical care make the tax a good deal less regressive than it would otherwise be, since these are items that are far more important in the budgets of poor families than in high-income budgets. A partially offsetting factor, however, is the exclusion of other kinds of spending for services like personal care (such as in barber and beauty shops), private schools and higher education, and travel abroad, all of which rise in relation to income as income increases.

In general, the more a state's sales tax covers services (aside from housing), the less regressive it will be.

The sales tax in its most common form is thus not nearly as regressive as the data for total consumer spending would make it appear. Nonetheless, it does remain a regressive tax, with its tax burden relative to income declining steadily as income increases. However, this is true only where the tax applies to purchases of food for home consumption, which is the case in two-thirds of the sales tax states. But the 15 states that exempt food sales (aside from restaurant sales) include 8 of the country's 10 largest. About 55 percent of the people who live in sales tax states are covered by taxes that exempt food. Where food is exempt, the sales tax burden is roughly proportional to income for all households up to a 1970 income level of $20,000 or so.

The sales tax, then, takes two different forms: one that is regressive and is the basis for the data presented in most studies (Table 30), and a second that is not regressive in any important respect. This lack of regressivity may help to explain the fact that the sales tax is perhaps the least unpopular of broad-based American taxes, even among blue-collar union members whose leaders have denounced sales taxes in season and out since they first appeared on the scene at the depths of the Great Depression.

Taxes on alcoholic beverages and cigarettes are unequivocally regressive in incidence. Expenditure for these items increases rather slowly as income rises, and what is more, this increase is only partly reflected in increases in tax payments. This is because most alcohol and tobacco taxes are levied on the basis of physical volume—gallons of beverage or number of cigarettes—rather than dollar value; if the increase in expenditure as income rises takes the form of switching to more expensive types and brands (for example, from the cheapest blended whiskey to name-brand Scotch), rather than increased drinking or smoking, there may be no increase in tax payments at all. All this is fairly obvious. What may not be obvious is the singling out of liquor and tobacco taxes, since there is no income group for which total spending for liquor and tobacco amounts to as much as 4 percent of money income. However, the tax rates imposed on alcohol and tobacco are extremely high. Generally, combined federal, state, and local taxes of one type or another account for well over half the retail price of cigarettes and distilled beverages. The taxes thus constitute a significant element

TABLE 30
VISIBLE TAXES AS PERCENTAGES OF MONEY BEFORE TAXES, 1961

Type of tax	Family income class*			
	All classes	*Less than $5,000*	*$5,000 to $10,000*	*More than $10,000*
All visible taxes	25.1%	21.4%	24.8%	32.7%
1. Generally progressive taxes	13.7	8.2	12.7	23.5
Personal income	13.0	8.2	12.7	20.8
Death and gift	0.7	....	....	2.7
2. Generally regressive taxes	6.0	7.5	5.9	4.7
General sales	1.4	1.6	1.4	1.1
Liquor and tobacco	2.0	2.4	2.0	1.7
Nonbusiness property	2.6	3.5	2.5	1.9
3. Other visible taxes	5.4	5.7	6.2	4.5
Personal contributions for social insurance	2.7	2.8	3.2	2.4
Automobile purchase and operation	2.7	2.9	3.0	2.1

*Income class limits are expressed in money income after personal taxes, the basis used in the underlying statistical data for the Tax Foundation study.
SOURCE: Adapted from Tax Foundation, *Tax Burdens and Benefits of Government Expenditures by Income Class, 1961 and 1965* (1967).

of the total tax burden, even though the total spending for these goods is a minor element in family budgets.

The most important of the taxes classified as generally regressive is the set of state-local taxes described in Table 28 as "nonbusiness property taxes." Principally these are taxes on housing, though in a few states they embrace other taxable property owned by households rather than businesses. Property taxes on housing, in turn, can be divided into two classes for present purposes: taxes on owner-occupied housing and taxes on rental housing. The first is much the larger component, since ours is overwhelmingly a society of homeowners rather than renters; moreover, owner-occupied housing is usually a good deal more valuable per housing unit than rental housing is.

Taxes on homeowners clearly impose burdens on homeowners and no one else. These burdens are distributed, within any political jurisdiction with a common tax rate, in proportion to the value of owner-occupied housing. But the value of houses is not the same at all income levels. In the lower-income ranges, the house value is likely to be three or more times as high as family income; twice as high in the middle ranges; and 1 to 1½ times as high in the upper ranges, according to the 1960 *Census of Housing.* Thus, the tax burden is regressive with respect to current income.

Over longer periods, consumer decisions on housing closely reflect long-term income prospects and experience. Elderly families with low incomes often occupy houses that were purchased and paid for earlier, when their incomes were higher; lower-middle-income families may strain themselves to buy a relatively costly house on the basis of future income prospects; and other families whose incomes have recently risen substantially may still be occupying the houses they bought when their incomes were much lower. Over a long period of years, then, the property tax on owner-occupied housing may not be so regressive. Still, in any given year when the tax is increased, the immediate distribution of the burden of the tax increase is apt to be highly regressive, and tax policy decisions necessarily must give greatest weight to the near-term consequences of those decisions.

The conventional wisdom is that the largest component of the taxes on rental housing is shifted forward by property owners to tenants in the form of higher rents. To the extent that this is the case, the distribution of this tax burden is even more regressive than that for owner-occupied housing. The ratio of rent to income is very high for low-income households and declines sharply as income rises. To some extent this is related to shifts in the form of tenure, from rented to owned housing. The higher one's income, the easier it is to elect home ownership rather than renting. Thus, at higher income levels the renter population is likely to be dominated by those who have found such rented housing so attractive financially that they chose not to buy a house, or by those who simply rate housing low in their order of preferences. In either case, the result is a low rent-to-income ratio.[3]

A dissent from this line of argument holds that the tax on rented housing, like the rest of the property tax, is a tax on capital whose burden is borne by the owner in proportion to the value of the property. Since owners and occupants are identical for owner-occupied housing, the distinction is not important for that part of the tax, and of course for that major fraction of lower-middle-class Americans who live in such housing. But for renters, the distinction is important. To the extent that the heterodox view is right, the tax on rental housing is progressive, not regressive, since ownership of rental property is presumably concentrated among the rich. Alternatively, the tax on rental housing could be considered a largely invisible tax, like other business taxes, and not part of the collection of taxes which ordinary people perceive. This is not entirely defensible, since property taxes on small rental properties, like two- to four-family houses with resident owners, are indeed visible to *some* ordinary people, notably the lower-middle-class owners of such properties.

Moreover, even the dissenters agree that some part of the tax on rented housing is shifted forward like other excise taxes, notably in such high-tax areas as old central cities. If this is so, and if some account is taken of the owners' share of taxes on rental housing owned by individuals rather than corporations, the overall property tax on housing continues to be a somewhat regressive one, although less so than the conventional approach suggests.

Other Visible Taxes

The two other major elements of the visible tax system have similar income distribution characteristics. Both tend to impose a heavier relative burden in the middle-income ranges than on either lower- or higher-income groups. Personal contributions for social insurance, largely Social Security payroll taxes, are relatively low at the bottom end of the income distribution because so many people in those groups are not employed or are employed only casually, and instead receive their meager incomes from transfer payments and other sources not subject to Social Security taxes. The tax burden rises in the middle groups, where nearly all income comes from earnings subject to the payroll taxes; but it falls again at higher levels, where much income is from interest and dividends, rather than earnings, and where salary levels exceed the ceilings on the individual annual earnings to which the payroll taxes apply.

Taxes related to automobile purchase and operation follow a similar pattern, but for a different reason. The relative tax burden is low for the poor simply because so many poor households do not own cars. When we reach the middle-income groups, car ownership becomes close to universal, and thus the relative tax burden rises for the average household in the group. However, the relative tax burden for those poor families that do own cars is undoubtedly higher still. Among the rich, there is the usual consumption pattern: expenditure for automobiles and their operation increases, but not as fast as income. Richer households may own two or more cars, but each vehicle will not be used as heavily as that in a single-car family, and thus taxes (like those on gasoline) related to the extent of use will not rise proportionately. Moreover, richer families are heavier users of air transportation for long-distance travel, thus reducing their relative auto use and the concomitant taxes.

The Statistical Evidence

The incidence pattern for the visible tax system, based on the conventional wisdom concerning tax shifting and statistical results in a study of the situation in 1961, is shown in Tables 30 and 31. These are *average* tendencies, with large deviations around the average. Income and payroll tax payments will differ for households with the same income, depending on family composition, personal deductions, and source of income. Property, sales, and excise tax payments will differ still more because they depend upon consumption choices—whether a family spends above-average or below-average amounts for such heavily taxed goods and services as housing, liquor, tobacco, and gasoline. In addition, there are geographic variations because one-third of the revenues of the visible tax system comes from state-local taxes that vary considerably in level and composition.

The national averages in Tables 30 and 31 reveal a distinctly progressive visible tax system, more so than the tax system including the less visible taxes. Our target group is presumably the lower part of the $5,000 to $10,000 income range, that is, the $5,000 to $5,999 and $6,000 to $7,499 classes. The income classes in the tables are for 1961 and are expressed in terms of income after income taxes paid. (The equivalent before-tax income classes for 1969 would be

TABLE 31
INCIDENCE OF THE TOTAL VISIBLE TAX SYSTEM, 1961

*Family income class**	*All visible taxes as percent of money income before taxes*
All classes	25.1%
Less than $2,000	14.7
$2,000 to $2,999	16.8
$3,000 to $3,999	20.1
$4,000 to $4,999	23.1
$5,000 to $5,999	23.7
$6,000 to $7,499	24.5
$7,500 to $9,999	25.2
$10,000 to $14,999	26.1
$15,000 and over	39.2

* See Table 30, footnote.
SOURCE: Table 30.

roughly $7,600 to $9,299 and $9,300 to $11,800.) As the tables show, those groups do have significantly higher visible tax burdens than the groups at the bottom of the income distribution, and much lower tax burdens than the rich. However, our target group has relative tax burdens which are only slightly below the tax burdens of the groups immediately above them in the income distribution, groups dominated by white-collar occupations. This seems to be explained by two factors: the generally regressive taxes continue to be high in the $5,000 to $7,499 (1961) income groups; and the generally proportional automobile and Social Security taxes are at their highest levels for these groups.

Is the Evidence Reliable?

Since the statistical evidence depends upon a set of assumptions about tax shifting, some of which are disputed, it is worth considering the consequences of different assumptions. It was noted earlier that one important dispute concerns the property tax on rental housing. In the computations underlying Tables 30 and 31, it was assumed that this element of the tax system is shifted forward to renters. The extreme opposite assumption would be that the tax is entirely borne by landlords. Let us examine the effects of several alternative assumptions:

Original: The tax is borne by renters.

Alternative I: The tax is borne by landlords and is part of their visible tax burdens.

Alternative II: The tax is borne by landlords but is not considered part of the visible tax burden at all.

Alternative III: One-third of the tax is shifted forward to renters; one-third is borne by landlords as personal owners of buildings and included in their visible tax burdens; and one-third is borne by landlords indirectly through corporate property ownership and is not part of the visible tax system.

How do these alternative assumptions affect relative tax burdens? The figures below indicate the results, with the relative burden for each income group expressed as an index number, the ratio of its tax burden to that of all income groups:

	Assumption			
	Original	*I*	*II*	*III*
All groups	100	100	100	100
Less than $5,000	85	81	81	82
$5,000 to $9,999	99	98	100	100
$10,000 and over	130	135	133	133

Clearly, the overall incidence pattern is very little changed, especially when we move from the original results to the intermediate position expressed by alternative III. The system is somewhat more progressive, but hardly enough to alter the general conclusion. Moreover, the blue-collar lower-middle-income group is virtually unaffected.

This outcome is paralleled by the results of changing the assumption underlying the sales tax incidence calculations, which (in Tables 30 and 31) is that food constitutes part of the tax base everywhere. If instead we assume that food is excluded everywhere, the visible tax system becomes more progressive but only slightly so, and the relative position of the target group is little changed.

A second qualification is that the data apply to 1961, and the composition of the system has changed since then. Largely because of the adoption of new taxes at the state-local level and/or increases in the rates of existing taxes, the state-local sales and income taxes and federal Social Security taxes make up a larger proportion of the total visible tax system now than in 1961. Most other taxes have declined in relative importance, especially the liquor, tobacco, and automobile taxes, which are measured by physical quantity rather than value. On balance, the system has shifted slightly in the direction of greater progressivity. If everything except the composition of the tax system had remained the same during the 1960s, the following change in tax burden index numbers would have occurred (the 1961 figures are for the original set of assumptions, those underlying Tables 30 and 31):

	1961 visible tax system	*1969 visible tax system*
All groups	100	100
Less than $5,000	85	83
$5,000 to $9,999	99	99
$10,000 and over	130	133

GEOGRAPHIC DIFFERENTIALS

A much more significant qualification of the evidence presented here stems from the variation in state and local tax systems. In effect, the United States has 51 distinct subnational tax systems, one for each state and the District of Columbia. The states vary widely in the extent to which they rely upon each of the major tax forms—property, sales, and income taxation. The character of each of these taxes also differs according to the classes of property taxed, whether food is exempt from the sales tax, and the rates and exemptions of the income tax. Moreover, within each of the 50 state systems, there are significant local variations in the levels and composition of the property tax base and the use of local taxes on sales and income.

One important differential relates to the overall height of the state-local tax burden. State-local tax systems tend to be regressive; at the very least, they are substantially less progressive than the federal system. Therefore, the lower the level of state and local taxes, the less regressive will be the visible tax system for residents of that state. According to calculations made by the Advisory Commission on Intergovernmental Relations, state-local "direct personal taxes," a category roughly equivalent to our "visible tax system," averaged 8 percent of personal income in 1968, but ranged from 5.5 percent in

TABLE 32

CHARACTER OF THE VISIBLE STATE-LOCAL TAX SYSTEM, SELECTED STATES, 1966–1967*

(PERCENT DISTRIBUTION OF TOTAL REVENUE FROM THE VISIBLE TAX SYSTEM)

State	*Total*	*Generally progressive taxes*	*Generally regressive taxes*†	*Other visible taxes*
Oregon	100%	41%	34%	25%
New York	100	34	55	11
California	100	11	64	25
Texas	100	2	58	40
Florida	100	1	67	32
New Jersey	100	4	77	19

* Classification of taxes according to regressivity/progressivity is that shown in Tables 29 and 30 above.

† In the five states (other than Oregon) with a retail sales tax, food is exempt from the tax.

SOURCE: Adapted from U.S. Bureau of the Census data.

Texas to 11.5 percent—or more than twice as high—in Hawaii. In 11 states, the tax burden differed by 1.5 percentage points or more from the national average.[4]

The other dimension is the composition of the state's tax system. Property taxes provide, on the average, slightly more than 40 percent of total state-local tax revenue, but the range is from less than one-fifth to more than two-thirds. Sales taxes can make up as much as 38 percent of state-local tax revenue or as little as 6 percent in the states employing the tax; the range for personal income taxes is from 6 to 31 percent, and for automobile taxes from 6 to 22 percent of total tax revenue.[5]

The consequence for the income distribution character of visible tax systems is shown for selected states in Table 32. The selected states illustrate some general state-local tax system combinations. They are ranged in descending order of progressivity, but note that none is predominantly progressive in effect. Oregon, at the top of the scale, has a high and steeply graduated personal income tax, no retail sales tax, low use of liquor and tobacco taxes, and above-average use of automobile taxes. New York also has high progressive personal income taxation, but it also has a sales tax, very high cigarette tax, and the lowest automobile taxes in the country, resulting in a tax system that is more regressive than that of Oregon.

In California, the personal income tax is somewhat lower than in New York or Oregon, the sales tax is high, and automobile taxes are high. As in New York and Oregon, residential property taxes are high. The combination produces a rather regressive system. The other three states—Texas, Florida, and New Jersey—have still more regressive tax systems. None of them employs a personal income tax on residents, all use the sales tax, and all rely relatively heavily on liquor and tobacco taxes. But New Jersey shows up as most regressive of all, because the residential property tax amounts to over half the visible tax system, compared to roughly one-third in Oregon, New York, and California and only one-fourth in Florida and Texas.

In general, states with relatively regressive tax systems tend to have low levels of taxation overall; states with more progressive systems tend to have higher levels of taxation. Thus, Texas and New Jersey, of the six states presented, are well below the national average in tax burden and have distinctly regressive tax systems; other such states include Ohio, Pennsylvania, Illinois, and Connecticut. In contrast, New York and California have more nearly progressive systems but high overall tax burdens, as Wisconsin, Minnesota, and Hawaii do. If this relation between progressivity and overall level were a perfect one, then the nationwide averages in Tables 30 and 31 might not be misleading. In this case, the progressivity of the federal tax system would be offset only to a small degree in states with very regressive but low state-local taxes, and to a similar small degree in states with high but less regressive taxes. However, the relation is by no means perfect. The relatively progressive Oregon system is below average in level, and the regressive Florida system is above average. There are numerous similar departures from the general rule.

Moreover, intrastate as well as interstate differentials exist. In general, local taxes are low outside metropolitan areas. Within a single metropolitan area, the levels of residential property tax rates vary widely among individual units of government. In some metropolitan areas, residential property tax rates tend to be higher in central cities than in suburbs; in others, there is little difference between central city and suburb, but substantial variation among suburbs. Most large central cities impose other kinds of personal taxes as well (for example, retail sales or personal income), typically resulting in an overall personal tax burden that is higher than in the suburbs.

On balance, state-local tax systems *within* central cities are likely to be even more regressive than the statewide tax systems. In part, this reflects tax system composition. Local governments in central cities rely more on locally raised revenue to finance their budgets (and have higher levels of expenditure to match) than do other local governments, for whom state and federal aid is relatively more important; local tax sources tend to be more regressive than state ones. But in part the explanation is simply that statistical aggregation understates regressivity.

I have discussed this elsewhere for the residential property tax; the argument would seem to apply equally to a sales tax with food exempt:

> Aggregation tends to reduce the regressivity of the principal local revenue, the property tax, by combining high-housing-consuming suburbanites with low-housing-consuming city dwellers, the former with high incomes and the latter with lower incomes. Effective property tax rates are usually higher in the larger central cities, but these differences are not reflected in the aggregate studies which apportion property taxes in some relation to housing consumption. In any case, the evidence suggests that the property tax is far more regressive within individual cities than it is on a statewide or nationwide basis.[6]
>
> In any event, the few existing studies of the incidence of taxes within large cities suggest a substantial degree of regressivity of the *local* portion of the combined state-local tax system. Unless this is offset by highly progressive *state* government taxes, the overall result will be very regressive. Thus, the combined visible state-local tax system is indeed highly regressive for residents of Chicago, Cleveland, and Philadelphia, is a bit less so in Los Angeles and Detroit, and tends to be progressive in New York and Minneapolis, where there are steeply progressive state income taxes.[7]

THE OBJECTIVE EVIDENCE REVIEWED

Despite the geographic variation in state-local tax systems, the weight of progressive federal taxation means that there is virtually no place within the United States that is not characterized by a combined federal-state-local visible tax with a fair amount of progressivity. A more important variable in assessing the evidence concerning the relative tax position of the lower-middle-income blue-collar group seems to be the viewing angle. If the Target Group is compared to those who are poorer, then the Target Group is indeed more heavily taxed—only slightly so if we are considering residents of Chicago and Cleveland but appreciably so in the case of residents of Detroit, New York City, and Minneapolis, for example. This may be considered unfair if the jump in relative tax burdens is construed as an undue penalty for "making it on your own." If the comparison is with the income group just above our Target Group, the latter group's tax advantage is rather small. If the comparison is with the upper 15 to 20 percent of the income distribution, the Target Group does seem well treated, especially in the places with less regressive state-local tax systems. But there is an important ingredient missing from these comparisons. To examine only the tax side of the budget in an analysis of fiscal equity is to assume implicitly that the public services bought with tax payments are provided equally to all income groups. If this is indeed the case, then the objective evidence on tax equity suggests on balance that the lower-middle-income group does *not* have a strong case for claiming unfair treatment. On the other hand, if public services are provided as many blue-collar people seem to assert—mainly to poor people and neighborhoods with low tax payments and to articulate white-collar neighborhoods occupied by people with tax burdens only marginally above those of the blue-collar group—then there may be real fiscal inequity. Therefore, the tax evidence by itself is inconclusive.

PERCEPTIONS VERSUS REALITIES

It is, of course, entirely conceivable that a tax system which objectively is more than fair to lower-middle-class Americans is perceived by them as harsh and oppressive. Appraisal of one's own economic circumstances is relative. Others may be even worse off, but that is usually cold comfort as long as one feels that one's taxes are becoming increasingly onerous over time.

There are several bases for such perceptions. Tax payments, of course, rise with money income. This is true of all major personal taxes because most consumption expenditures and housing values increase along with money income; but it is especially marked for progressive income taxes, with their exemptions and graduated rate structures. As money income rises above exemption levels and into higher tax-rate brackets, income tax liability increases substantially more rapidly than income.

A conventional rationalization for progressivity in taxation is that the sacrifice entailed in surrendering a given percentage of income declines with rising income. That is, income has a diminishing marginal utility. This is perhaps true of *real* income. However, it is highly unlikely that increases in money income that largely reflect rises in price level have this characteristic. And, of course, a large fraction of recent income increases is attributable to increases in prices. Thus, a progressive income tax can involve increasing, rather than constant or decreasing, sacrifice over time.

Let us examine a hypothethical but concrete example: the circumstances of a white husband and wife family headed by a wage earner falling within the "craftsmen and operatives" Census occupational classification. The median earnings of such heads of households in metropolitan areas in the North and West were roughly $8,800 in 1969, an increase of 30 percent over 1965. Because of secondary wage earners and nonwage income, median family income was undoubtedly significantly higher. Thus, such a family with a $7,700 income in 1965 and $10,000 in 1969 would not be atypical. To illustrate the effects of progressivity in state-local income taxes, as well as the federal income tax, let us locate the family in New York City but in an owner-occupied single-family house in the City's outer reaches. Assume further that the family has two dependent children and average consumption patterns, deductions, and the like.

Had income tax rates and other tax law provisions remained unchanged between 1965 and 1969, income tax payments would have risen from $708 to $1,191. That is, an increase in income of $2,300 (30 percent) would have produced an increase in income taxes of $483 (68 percent); income tax payments would have risen from 9 to nearly 12 percent of income before tax. Payments of other major visible personal taxes—the sales tax, the Social Secur-

TABLE 33
DISPOSITION OF HYPOTHETICAL 1965–1969 INCREASE IN MONEY INCOME FOR A TYPICAL NEW YORK CITY BLUE-COLLAR FAMILY*

Increase in money income before taxes		$2,300
Less:		
Absorbed by increased tax payments, assuming constant tax rates:		
Income taxes	$483	
Other major visible taxes†	109	592
Absorbed by tax-rate increases:		
Income taxes	119	
Other major visible taxes	251	370
Absorbed by price-level increases		1,060
Increase in after-tax real income (in constant 1965 dollars)		278
As a percent of 1965 after-tax income		4.4%

* See text for description of the characteristics of the family.
†Sales tax, Social Security payroll tax, and property tax on the family's house.

ity payroll tax, and the property tax on the family's house—also would have increased, but a good deal less than income (from $728 to $837, or 15 percent).

But, in reality, tax rates did not remain constant. By 1969, the 10 percent federal income tax surcharge had been passed and a city income tax had been imposed. The sales tax rate was increased, and the Social Security tax, for this family, more than doubled. Income taxes rose 85 percent and the other taxes 49 percent, combining the effects of income increases and tax law changes; thus, increased taxes absorbed $962 of the $2,300 increase in family income. In effect, the combined marginal tax rate was close to 42 percent.

High as this was, it might have appeared tolerable if the remaining $1,338 increase in money income were translated into an increase in living standards. However, four-fifths of the increase in after-tax income was absorbed by the rise in the consumer price level (Table 33). The real after-tax income available would have provided an increase of less than 5 percent in the family's standard of living, which is surely not in keeping with expectations in 1965. And even if tax rates had not risen at all, real after-tax income would have increased less than 10 percent.

Moreover, some families with these characteristics no doubt view themselves as even more harshly affected by the tax system. This is especially true of the large group, aged 45 to 60 in 1970, that married, had their first children, and bought houses in the years around 1950, shortly after World War II. In blue-collar families, the early postwar babies are no longer dependents and thus not exemptions on their parents' income tax returns. If our hypothetical family had experienced this transition during the 1965–1969 period, income tax payments would have increased more than $300, thus entirely eliminating any increase in after-tax real income. To be sure, the financial independence of children on balance makes parents a good deal better off; but the increase in tax liabilities can add to the general sense of grievance.

For many blue-collar families, the property tax on housing is a major source of grievance. Again, some of this feeling can be traced to actual changes in the objective circumstances, including the frustration of common expectations. Another source of grievance has to do with changes in the visibility of the tax rather than in its actual burden. One example of the latter applies to the early postwar home buyers: if they still live in the house they then purchased, the 20-year mortgage may have been paid off. If so, after years of paying property taxes as part of monthly mortgage payments, they are now faced with the necessity of making large annual or semiannual payments directly to the tax collector, surely an unpleasant and unwelcome shock.

More generally, property taxes on housing, whatever their true incidence, are virtually invisible to renters and highly visible to homeowners. Despite the slow pace of new single-family house construction during the 1960s, the percentage of home ownership among households with incomes in the $7,500 to $10,000 range (at the end of the decade) has been rising and now exceeds 70 percent. At least 500,000 households in this income group that were tenants at the beginning of the decade were homeowners by mid-1969, and newly aware of the existence of the property tax.

But there are more objective reasons. Evidence from the *Census of Governments* suggests that average property tax levies on a single-family house rose about 80 percent in the decade of the sixties. Personal income per household rose about 68 percent for the entire population, and median earnings for craftsmen and operatives in metropolitan areas outside the South only about 60 percent. Thus, rising property taxes on housing have been absorbing an increasingly large fraction of personal income in the past decade.

Moreover, the increases have been most marked in the two kinds of geographic areas in which the blue-collar population is heavily represented. One area includes the larger central cities in the North and West, where rapidly rising local government expenditure has combined with slowly growing property values to produce sharp increases in effective tax rates in many cases. This has been exacerbated in some instances by changes in assessment practices. Traditionally, the large old American cities have tended to underassess, in relation to other property types, one- and two-family owner-occupied houses, especially older ones in white ethnic, blue-collar neighborhoods. Judicial decisions, legislative enactments, and fiscal reform movements have attacked this systematic but extralegal nonuniformity; and during the past decade or so, numerous reassessments have resulted in substantially heavier relative property tax burdens on owner-occupied housing in the central city.

Even more widespread and painful have been sharp increases in the tax rates in hundreds of lower-middle-income suburban communities, the kinds of places for which blue-collar Americans leave the central city. Property tax rate increases have been especially marked, and shocking, in such communities, in part because many of these places experienced virtually overnight conversion from farms (with characteristically low rural property tax rates) to moderate-priced suburban housing tracts. The first of the immigrants to the new tracts typically have had the experience of actually paying the low rural-stage tax rates at the outset.

However, this changed quickly, largely because of the very high ratio of school-age children to population in new suburban communities. The new tracts at the edge of the metropolitan area are occupied by young family heads. Families move to new suburban communities when they can afford to buy a new house and when their children are numerous enough and old enough to require a substantial increase in the size of the housing unit. Couples with one or two preschool children are generally too young to meet the income criterion, and their space needs are not so severe. When there are more and older children, however, space needs become severe, and usually income and savings rise. Thus, they arrive in the new suburban tract with one or more school-age children, with younger children closely following.

This has an obvious effect on school costs and on property tax rates, because the house values are not high in the new tracts. As time passes, those families whose income does rise substantially will be able to buy higher-priced houses in richer suburbs and will thus be moving out when their children are nearing the end of their public school lives. They are likely to be replaced with younger moderate-income households with children just beginning the school cycle. Thus, the pattern of high school enrollment and school taxes is perpetuated. And most blue-collar households early reach a peak in earning capacity and are unable to escape to more affluent suburbs with more moderate tax rates.

CONCLUSION

Thus, the tax complaints of blue-collar Americans have some basis, in subjective responses if not in objective evidence. However that may be, it is difficult to rectify the situation. *Someone* must pay for government; indeed, almost everyone must pay to some extent when the public sector amounts to 30 percent of the economy. It is highly unlikely that an appreciably larger proportion of the tax burden can be shifted to the relatively rich, say, to the 0.4 percent of American households with money income in 1969 above $50,000. They account for roughly 3 percent of total money income and perhaps 8 percent of the total tax burden; there simply is not enough income in the aggregate among these households.

If blue-collar Americans in lower-middle and near-poor income classes ($7,500 to $14,999) are to get tax relief, more of the tax burden must be shifted to upper-middle ($15,000 to $24,999) and near-rich ($25,000 to $49,999) income classes. The latter two groups include only 16 percent of all households but account for about 38 percent of money income and perhaps 43 percent of the total tax burden at present.

There is no conceivable way that this shift can be accomplished except by increasing the role of progressive personal income taxation vis-à-vis other taxes in our total tax system. But personal income taxation is already more important in the American tax system than in most other countries. Perhaps more to the point, progressive income taxation is not at all popular with *any* income group that is subject to it, least of all the lower middle class. Moreover, the required shift in tax burdens requires substantial economic sacrifice on the part of 10 million of the country's most articulate and influential households. However desirable to egalitarians or to those concerned with cooling discontent, it seems a most unlikely prospect.

NOTES

1. Based on Tax Foundation, *Tax Burdens and Benefits of Government Expenditures by Income Class, 1961 and 1965,* New York, 1967, with results converted to 1970 income levels. This study is representative of the conventional wisdom referred to below.
2. Peter Mieszkowski, "Tax Incidence Theory: The Effects of Taxes on the Distribution of Income," *Journal of Economic Literature,* December 1969, pp. 1103–1124.
3. Dick Netzer, *Economics of the Property Tax,* The Brookings Institution, Washington, 1966, chap. 3.
4. Advisory Commission on Intergovernmental Relations, *State and Local Finances: Significant Features, 1967 to 1970,* 1969, table 1-A. The standard deviation was 1.23.
5. These figures refer to the total state-local tax system, not just the visible tax system. They are derived from U.S. Bureau of Census, *Compendium of Government Finances, 1967 Census of Governments,* vol. 4, no. 5, 1969.
6. Dick Netzer, "Federal, State and Local Finance in a Metropolitan Context," in Harvey S. Perloff and Lowdon Wingo, Jr. (eds.), *Issues in Urban Economics,* Johns Hopkins, Baltimore, 1968, p. 439.
7. Dick Netzer, "Tax Structures and Their Impact on the Poor," in John P. Crecine (ed.), *Financing the Metropolis: Public Policy in Urban Economics,* Sage Publications, Beverly Hills, 1970, pp. 474–476.

12. INCOME MAINTENANCE: WHO GAINS AND WHO PAYS?

by Worth Bateman and Jodie Allen

DOES INCOME MAINTENANCE CONTRIBUTE TO ALIENATION?

Has blue-collar alienation increased? Have income maintenance programs been a significant factor accounting for the rise? If so, what action, if any, should be taken?

If, as George Meany asserts, the gut issue behind blue-collar alienation is the pocketbook issue, then the alienation of this class from the rest of society would be nothing more novel than a recasting by the media, the sociologists, and the journalists of the time-honored gripes of the workingman: taxes too high, government too big, and upstarts too noisy. Behind its public facade, alienation may simply be the shortsighted contrariness of a major segment of society called upon to shoulder a major share of the burden of carrying out programs which, from a more disinterested and enlightened perspective, most would agree are in the public interest. If so, blue-collar alienation is not a new phenomenon, but a more or less unavoidable condition which has simply been relabeled and given prominence by a society which has become highly sensitized to the conflict of class interests.

On the theory that the voice given to the meanness of the human spirit is importantly related to the burden of taxes on income, the share of the levy returned in one form or another in fairly immediate and tangible benefits, and the share which goes to others who are disliked, distrusted, or both, then alienation, in this sense, has probably increased in the last few years.

Assuming this to be the case, however, what mandate emerges for public policy? Should taxes be reduced for this class? Increased for others? Should they receive a higher share of the benefits? Not necessarily. Taking a clear-cut stand on any or all of these options for reducing blue-collar alienation would not be easy. Undoubtedly, higher-income groups would resist mightily any attempt to shift a larger burden to their tax bill; liberals would oppose any attempt to cut back the hard-won measures aimed at a greater degree of social equity, as would those to whom the legislation was directed; and unless some or all were willing to see their taxes increased, cutting in blue-collar workers for a larger share of some benefits must mean cutting back benefits for someone else somewhere along the line—a move virtually guaranteed to upset everyone.

In this chapter, we shall examine the evidence of whether there are reasonable grounds to assume that income maintenance programs contribute to increased blue-collar alienation. Since no objective measure of alienation exists, we cannot, in fact, know whether it has increased, declined, or stayed the same over the last few years, but it is possible to examine changes in factors which may be correlated with alienation. Our purpose is to discover whether the evidence supports claims by the blue-collar class for corrective action.

Finally, we shall look at some possible options which might reasonably be selected for dealing with the particular problems of this group. We recognize, of course, that a disgruntled blue-collar class may not be a phenomenon linked only, or even importantly, to income maintenance programs. War protesters, the breakdown of law and order, the generation gap, the Black Panthers, the yippies, hippies, and women's lib—the events and people who are challenging "our official sense of what America is"[1]—are probably much more crucial in accounting for the revolt of America's common man.

Other things equal, we assume that blue-collar alienation resulting from income maintenance programs varies inversely with the ratio of benefits received to contributions made by blue-collar workers and directly with the proportion of total current blue-collar worker income earmarked for the support of income maintenance programs.

It seems likely, however, that the degree of class hostility to income maintenance programs is not merely a function of the actual amount of benefits which are being transferred away from that class. Some clearly redistributive programs seem to have a high degree of acceptability among all income classes. Sixty-eight percent of Americans at every economic level expressed support for the generous McGovern food stamp proposals. Seventy-nine percent support a guaranteed work plan although such a plan would imply subsidizing wages up to a level of $3,200 a year.[2]

The degree of alienation resulting from a change in either of the two variables noted above thus appears related to at least three additional factors. First, the greater the proportion of benefits going to non-blue-collar beneficiaries who are viewed as fundamentally different from the "typical" blue-collar worker, the greater the degree of alienation. If the "typical" blue-collar worker is white, male, married, and a full-time worker, then a shift toward programs whose beneficiaries are predominantly families which are black, female-headed, and nonworking is going to encounter greater resistance than a shift, say, to retired workers. In addition to racial or class antagonism, this difference in attitude may stem in part from a difference in the blue-collar worker's perception of the likelihood that he himself will be a recipient of the program. For example, beneficiaries of retirement programs are characteristically much older than the blue-collar worker and nonworking, but a favorable shift toward this group may be virtually unopposed by the blue-collar worker if he feels that ultimately he too will benefit.

Second, blue-collar alienation will diminish if eligibility for benefits is perceived to be contingent on prior or current work effort. It is not surprising that the blue-collar class which relies so heavily on employment income for its own support should feel that others should not be getting "something for nothing." Public-opinion polls provide strong evidence of the strength of this attitude. In a national opinion poll, only slightly over 30 percent of adults in families with incomes in the $5,000 to $10,000 range and 24 percent of families with incomes of $10,000 or more expressed approval of a plan to guarantee a minimum income of $3,200 a year. By contrast, over

80 percent of the first group and 76 percent of the second expressed support for a plan to guarantee sufficient work for all employable wage earners to bring their family income to a comparable level.[3]

Finally, the degree of alienation will depend on the method by which the program is administered. Relatively impersonal programs, such as the personal income tax and Social Security programs, are preferred by the middle class when they are the clientele. The opposite is true when members of other classes are the primary recipients of benefits, as in the case of public assistance programs. Hence, middle-class preference for in-kind programs, such as food stamps, commodity distribution, and social services for the poor, and insistence on rigorous investigation of cash benefit recipients. This attitude seems to reflect both a distrust of the lower classes' ability to manage their money resources in a socially acceptable manner and a desire to make recipients "pay" for their benefits by accepting some degree of inconvenience and stigma.

The benefits of public and private income maintenance programs have grown apace in the last 20 years. Total benefits have risen from about $9 billion in 1950 to nearly $59 billion in 1969. Benefit payments tripled in the period 1950–1960 and more than doubled in the period 1960–1969 (Table 34).

The most striking growth has been in Old Age, Survivors, and Disability Insurance (OASDI), or, popularly, Social Security. This program, which accounted for only about 10 percent of total benefits in 1950, claimed more than 45 percent of total benefits in 1969—by far the lion's share. Other highlights are: (1) government employee retirement programs accounted for the second largest share in 1969 and also had very rapid growth during the last 19 years, particularly the period since 1960; (2) public assistance accounted for the third largest share of total benefits in 1969, although the share of total benefits was about half that of 1950 with little or no change in the share in the last 10 years; (3) private pensions accounted for the fourth largest share and also had a very rapid rate of growth; (4) taken together, the remainder of the programs—unemployment insurance, temporary disability benefits, workmen's compensation, veterans' pensions, and railroad retirement—have declined from about 50 percent in 1950 to 20 percent in 1969; (5) overall, the effect of these changes has been a shift away from those programs which are financed with general tax revenues (59 percent

TABLE 34

CASH PAYMENTS UNDER PUBLIC AND PRIVATE TRANSFER PROGRAMS, 1950, 1960, AND 1969

(IN MILLIONS OF DOLLARS)

	1950		*1960*		*1969*	
Total	$9,025.7	100.0%	$27,559.0	100.0%	$58,884.0	100.0%
Public retirement and survivors programs	4,301.2	47.6	17,725.4	64.3	38,766.7	66.1
OASDI	961.1	10.6	10,676.6	38.7	24,208.6	41.1
Railroad retirement	298.1	3.3	942.4	3.4	1,525.5	2.6
Public employment retirement	784.6	8.7	2,597.8	9.4	7,861.0	13.4
Veterans' pension and compensation	2,223.8	24.6	3,436.9	12.5	5,154.2	8.8
Other lump sum	33.6	0.4	71.7	0.3	117.4	0.2
Private pensions	370.0	4.1	1,750.0	6.4	5,730.0	9.8
Disability payments	532.4	5.9	1,796.4	6.5	4,934.6	8.4
OASDI	......	.....	568.2	2.1	2,542.2	4.3
Workmen's compensation	415.0	4.6	860.0	3.1	1,720.0	2.9
Temporary disability	117.4	1.3	368.2	1.3	672.4	1.2
Unemployment benefits	1,467.6	16.3	3,024.8	11.0	2,423.0	4.1
Public assistance money payments	2,354.5	26.0	3,262.4	11.8	6,889.7	11.7

SOURCE: U.S. Department of Health, Education, and Welfare.

in 1950 versus 34 percent in 1969) and toward those financed with payroll taxes (41 percent in 1950 versus 66 percent in 1969).

The remainder of this analysis will be focused on the contributions which changes in these programs might have made to blue-collar alienation and what might be done about it.

IS SOCIAL SECURITY A GOOD BUY?

Social Security is far and away the largest as well as the most socially acceptable income maintenance program. Numerous studies have been made of whether Social Security is a "good buy."[4] It is clear from these analyses that Social Security has been an unparalleled bargain for virtually all beneficiaries. Because of the relative newness of the system, no beneficiaries have made contributions over a full lifetime of work, although their benefits are calculated as if they had. The Chief Actuary of the Social Security Administration estimated that the average Social Security beneficiary retiring at any time during the life of the system up till now has paid in at most 10 percent of the value of the benefits he stands to receive.[5]

Many workers "blanketed in" under extensions of the 1950s have experienced even greater windfalls. Moreover, benefit levels have been periodically increased by Congress for all beneficiaries so that a person retiring in 1940 would, were he still a beneficiary in 1968, receive a monthly payment 23 percent greater in constant dollars than that he received in 1940.[6] He typically would have made no additional contributions to the program during this period.

As a class, blue-collar workers have probably not made out quite so well. They have been in the system since its beginning. As a result, they were not the primary beneficiaries of the "new start" provisions which extended benefits in the 1950s and 1960s to farmers, farm and domestic workers, professionals, and the self-employed. The importance of this differentiation will, of course, fade as coverage approaches universality and the system matures. The relatively great weight given to recent earnings in computing retirement benefits also favors workers with incomes which continue to rise over their entire working careers. Because less-skilled blue-collar workers typically peak in earnings in their late thirties or early forties, they are at a disadvantage compared to skilled and

TABLE 35

CHANGES IN SOCIAL SECURITY BENEFIT FORMULA AND WAGE DISTRIBUTION OF COVERED WORKERS: AVERAGE MONTHLY WAGE, PRIMARY INSURANCE AMOUNT, AND AVERAGE WAGE REPLACEMENT RATE BY WAGE CLASS, 1940, 1958, AND 1969

	1940			*1958*			*1969*[c]	
Average monthly wage	*PIA*[a]	*Wage replacement rate*	*Percent of workers below average monthly wage*[b]	*PIA*	*Wage replacement rate*	*Percent of workers below average monthly wage*[b]	*PIA*	*Wage replacement rate*
$ 50	28	56%	11.39	33	66%	1.86	64*	128%
$ 100	35	35	41.52	59	59	6.98	82	82
$ 200	49	25	87.07	84	42	19.96	117	59
$ 300	60†	20	96.35	105	35	36.26	147	49
$ 400	60	15	98.55	127†	32	56.79	176	44
$ 500	60	12	99.36	127	25	75.89	204	41
$ 600	60	10	99.54	127	21	86.55	234	39
$ 700	60	9	d	127	18	d	251†	36
$1,000	60	6	d	127	13	d	251	25

* Minimum payment.
† Maximum payment.
[a] Assumes 40 years of coverage with $200 or more of wage credits a year. The 1939 benefit formula increased PIA by 1 percent for each such year up to a maximum PIA of $60.
[b] Full-year male workers covered by Social Security only.
[c] Covered wage data not available for 1969.
[d] Data not available on distribution of workers above the maximum covered wage.

SOURCE: Derived from Robert J. Myers, *Old-Age Survivors, Disability and Health Insurance Provisions: Legislative History, 1935–67,* Social Security Administration, January 1968, and *Social Security Bulletin: Annual Statistical Supplement, 1968.*

professional workers. The benefit formula also favors late entrants into the labor market because they are taxed for fewer years. These are typically college or advanced-degree graduates, not blue-collar workers.

Nonetheless, the blue-collar class, like all Social Security beneficiaries, has had little to complain about thus far. Taxes have until recently been low, and returns more than generous. This happy situation cannot, of course, last forever. As the system matures, more workers will be contributing over a full working lifetime, and unless benefit levels are increased (and of course financed in turn by higher lifetime payroll contributions by those newly entering the labor force), benefit-contribution ratios will decline—according to some calculations, quite drastically. Analyses by Aaron and Brittain indicate that for the average worker in the long run, Social Security will be comparable to a private savings program in fixed-yield investments.[7] This is a far cry from the 10 to 1 returns cited earlier.

If Social Security becomes less of a good buy for the "average" worker, it will be far less of a good buy for some than for others because of the way Social Security is financed and its redistributive benefit structure.[8] The redistributive structure of the Social Security system is seen most clearly in Table 35, which shows for selected years the relation between the average monthly wage (AMW), the primary insurance amount (PIA, the corresponding monthly benefit at retirement),[9] and the ratio of the two, the wage replacement rate. The table shows that the low-income worker receives a much higher portion of his monthly contribution in monthly benefits than the high-income worker does. Furthermore, a minimum benefit (raised during the 1935–1969 period from a level of $10 to $64) is payable to any covered worker whose average covered wage was insufficient to establish entitlement to that amount.

Despite the highly redistributive benefit structure of Social Security, changes in this structure *alone* have probably not been a major cause of increasing blue-collar alienation. Changes in the benefit structure between 1939 and 1969 (as measured by the ratio of wage replacement rates in 1969 to those in 1939) have uniformly favored workers at higher wage levels. In 1939 the wage replacement rate of workers with an AMW of $100 was about 3.5 times the rate of workers with an AMW of $600. In 1969 the ratio had fallen to about 2 to 1. For the period 1958–1969, the picture is more or less the same in broad outline except for a relatively large increase in the wage replacement rate of those eligible for the minimum payment (Table 35).

Furthermore, the growth in money wages during the 1939 to 1969 period has been such as to maintain a relatively stable replacement rate for the "typical" worker. In 1940 the median wage of covered workers was somewhat over $100 a month, and the wage replacement rate at that level was around 35 percent. By 1968 the median wage had risen to almost $600, and the replacement rate at that level was again about 35 percent.

If changes in the redistributive aspects of the benefit structure, looked at alone, seem unlikely to have increased blue-collar alienation, several other factors may have worked to this end. Until recently, the typical worker may have been only dimly, if at all, aware that Social Security has strong redistributive elements. Far from viewing Social Security as a government handout, most Americans have regarded the program as something they do for themselves.[10] However, the increased political attention given to the redistributional aspects of the system may have changed this view. For example, it was an explicitly stated goal of the 1967 Social Security amendments that Social Security be made a more effective antipoverty device.

More importantly, the OASDI tax itself has become hard for the worker to ignore. The tax rate has risen precipitously over time and is likely to continue its climb. Under current legislation, the combined OASDI tax is scheduled to rise from its 1970 level of 8.4 percent to 10 percent by 1973.

These high tax contributions combined with rising wage rates and a redistributive benefit structure have placed more and more workers in income classes in which taxes appear high in relation to benefits. For the average covered worker (whose monthly wage rose from about $350 in 1958 to $540 in 1969), the ratio of monthly benefits to contributions in 1969 was only 64 percent of what it was in 1958, while his tax contributions were almost 300 percent higher. For the low-income worker earning $50 or less in AMW, the ratio of benefits to contributions was about 10 percent *higher* in 1969 compared to 1958, while his tax contributions were only about 100 percent higher. Although the benefit-contribution ratio has deteriorated for both groups, it has been far worse for the average worker (Table 36).

In effect, the redistributive benefit structure, coupled with rising wages and proportionally larger increases in tax contributions, has caught many workers in an increasingly tight benefit-tax squeeze. In particular, this squeeze has been felt the most by workers with the following characteristics: (1) *Families with individual workers with earnings at or near the maximum covered wage.* Workers below that level receive higher returns on their contributions; those above that level pay a smaller proportion of their total earnings in taxes. (2) *Families with working wives or other secondary earners.* For example, a family with two earners each making the maximum covered wage of $7,800 would pay combined Social Security taxes of $749; a single-worker family with the same total family income of $15,600 would pay only half that amount. Furthermore, under the current law, the additional contributions would net benefits for the first which are only one-third greater than the second. Families with wives earning smaller amounts would receive even less return on the taxes paid by the wife.[11] (3) *Families relying on wages or salaries for all or most of their income* since OASDI taxes will take a larger proportion of their total income than that of families with substantial amounts of payroll-tax-exempt income.

Blue-collar families tend, disproportionately, to have one or more of these "unfavorable" characteristics. The result is to place a relatively high burden on the blue-collar class as compared to the rest of the population (Table 37). In 1971, blue-collar families will pay an average of 3.7 percent of their total family income in OASDI taxes, a rate 33 percent higher than the average rate for non-blue-collar families. A tax rate differential of 0.93 percent (1.86 percent if we assume that the employer's share of the tax is shifted back to the worker in the form of lower wages) may not appear of great importance in itself; but, as we shall see in a later section, it is not greatly different from the average blue-collar workers' contribution to public assistance redistribution; as taxes go, it is not an insignificant bite.

This tax burden could be eased significantly and the redistributive aspects of Social Security more equitably shared by moving toward more progressive methods of taxation. The Social Security tax is the most regressive tax associated with any of our major income trans-

TABLE 36

OASI COST-BENEFIT RATES, 1940, 1958, AND 1969

	1940			*1958*			*1969*			
Average monthly wage	*Primary insurance amount (PIA)*	*Tax contribution**	*Advertised rate of return (PIA/tax)†*	*PIA*	*Tax contribution*	*Advertised rate of return (PIA/tax)*	*PIA*	*Tax contribution*	*Advertised rate of return (PIA/tax)*	*1969 rate of return/1939 rate of return*
$ 50	$28	$1.00	28.0	$ 33	$ 2.00	16.5	$ 64	$ 3.73	17.2	0.61
100	35	2.00	17.5	59	4.00	14.8	82	7.45	11.0	0.62
200	49	4.00	12.3	84	8.00	10.5	117	14.90	7.9	0.64
300	60	5.00	12.0	105	12.00	8.8	147	22.35	6.5	0.54
400	60	5.00	12.0	127	14.00	9.1	176	29.80	5.9	0.49
500	60	5.00	12.0	127	14.00	9.1	204	37.25	5.5	0.45
600	60	5.00	12.0	127	14.00	9.1	234	44.70	5.2	0.43
700	60	5.00	12.0	127	14.00	9.1	251	48.43	5.2	0.43
1,000	60	5.00	12.0	127	14.00	9.1	251	48.43	5.2	0.43

* Combined employer-employee tax for survival and retirement benefits assuming entire employer tax is shifted to employee. On the opposite assumption of no backward shifting, rates of return would be multiplied by two, but ratio of 1969 to 1939 would be unchanged. The extent to which the entire burden of redistribution is borne by covered workers depends upon the judgment made as to the ultimate bearer of the 50 percent of the payroll tax initially levied on the employer. In a perfectly competitive economy it is likely that the entire burden would be shifted to the employees in the form of lower wages. Even in less than purely competitive situations, there is a presumption among most economists that a substantial proportion is backward-shifted and that most of the remainder of the tax is shifted forward to the consumer in the form of higher prices, in which case the employee again shares in the tax in proportion to his consumption expenditures. The disability portion of the tax added in 1957 is excluded from the computation since it buys for the worker an additional type of protection not reflected in the retirement benefit.

† By "advertised" rate of return, we mean the benefit in relation to the workers' current contribution which, in a given year, the Social Security Administration tells the worker he will receive if he lives to collect it.

TABLE 37

INCIDENCE OF SOCIAL SECURITY TAX, 1971

Total family income	*Blue-collar families**		*All other families*	
	Percent of families in income class	*Social Security tax as percent of total family income†*	*Percent of families in income class*	*Social Security tax as percent of total family income†*
Total	100.00	3.73	100.00	2.80
Less than $1,000	0.71	‡	2.08	‡
$ 1,000 to $1,999	1.22	3.59	5.13	1.57
$ 2,000 to $2,999	2.40	3.79	10.27	1.27
$ 3,000 to $3,999	3.15	3.96	9.60	1.50
$ 4,000 to $4,999	4.98	4.37	7.43	2.25
$ 5,000 to $5,999	6.29	4.34	5.71	3.04
$ 6,000 to $6,999	8.44	4.43	6.00	3.51
$ 7,000 to $7,999	6.93	4.40	5.07	3.69
$ 8,000 to $8,999	8.69	4.32	5.23	3.88
$ 9,000 to $9,999	8.80	3.98	4.64	3.81
$10,000 to $10,999	9.53	3.72	4.76	3.60
$11,000 to $11,999	7.25	3.64	3.91	3.60
$12,000 to $12,999	6.65	3.55	4.05	3.39
$13,000 to $13,999	5.63	3.52	3.85	3.30
$14,000 to $14,999	4.61	3.41	2.83	3.23
$15,000 to $19,999	11.26	3.37	10.57	2.95
$20,000 to $24,999	2.62	3.25	4.74	2.50
$25,000 and over	0.82	2.97	4.13	1.50

* Includes craftsmen, operatives, and nonfarm laborers.

† The Social Security tax rates used include only the employee share of the OASDI tax (health insurance taxes are not included), which is currently scheduled to rise to 4.6 percent on the first $7,800 of earnings in 1971.

‡ Estimates of tax burden in this class are biased by the presence of families with negative total income or large self-employment income losses relative to wage and salary income.

SOURCE: Special tabulations prepared by the Urban Institute.

fer programs. Unlike personal income taxes, the ratio of taxes paid to total income does not increase as total income increases. Instead, the OASDI tax (8.4 percent at present shared equally by employer and employee) remains proportional to earned income up to the maximum covered wage, currently set at $7,800, practically the midpoint of the income range of blue-collar workers.[12] Other income and earned income above that amount are not taxed at all, with the result that wealthier individuals in general are subject to a lower average tax rate than those with total income from earnings below the $7,800 wage cutoff. Individuals in uncovered occupations or dependent for their support on property or transfer income do not contribute at all, no matter what their income position.

Given the far greater progressivity and the broader base of the personal and corporate tax systems, shifting the redistributional burden away from the payroll tax base would clearly be more equitable. Social Security could be put on a purely contributory basis, with benefits proportional to contributions and the redistributional aspects handled through a separate system financed through general revenues. The alternative is to leave the redistributional aspects of the system alone and move toward general revenue financing and away from payroll tax financing. In either case, the aim would be to shift the tax burden for redistribution from payroll taxes to broader-based taxes which are more progressive.

Explicit separation of the insurance and welfare elements of Social Security would, of course, remove the protective shield from the latter. But given current growth trends in the coverage and benefit levels of our explicitly redistributional public assistance programs, the net value of the redistributional benefits of Social Security is diminished, and the inequity of shifting part of the welfare burden from the general taxpayer to the wage-earner class is sharpened. To some extent, the redistributional provisions of Social Security are already anachronistic. Many Social Security beneficiaries are recipients of Old Age Assistance. Because welfare benefits are normally reduced dollar for dollar against Social Security benefits, the latter in most cases result in no net income improvement for the very poorest among the aged. The effect is to reduce public assistance costs which would alternatively be borne by the general taxpayer. The provisions of the Administration's proposed welfare reform package would establish a nationwide minimum Old Age Assistance monthly benefit of $110 per person, an amount almost equal to the current average Social Security payment for retired workers of $117 and far superior to the minimum Social Security payment of $64. The minimum Social Security benefit will thus raise incomes only for those who have other sources of unearned income sufficient to disqualify them for welfare benefits (or who are willing to suffer considerable loss of income to avoid the stigma of welfare).

This last consideration points to the fact that, apart from any inequities or potentially disruptive economic side effects associated with payroll tax financing, fighting poverty through a general social insurance system is inefficient since, without an explicit means test geared both to need and to *total* resources (not just, as in the case of Social Security, earned income), any rise in minimum benefits will also be dispersed among the nonpoor. Considering the financing and benefit distribution facets together, it is not difficult to conclude that the blue-collar worker, as well as society in general, would be more equitably and efficiently served through an income redistribution system financed through the progressive income tax and distributed through an explicit program of need-related transfers.

To summarize: to date the Social Security program has deserved its popularity among the working classes. It has been an unparalleled bargain for almost all its beneficiaries, and it will continue to offer incalculable advantages over private pensions in terms of continuity of coverage, shortness of vesting period, broad spreading of risk, and consequent minimum requirements for the maintenance of reserves. On the other hand, if present trends in the direction of raising minimum benefit levels at the expense of steeper payroll taxes continue, Social Security will not continue to be a good buy for the average worker, and by some estimates it may become a very bad buy indeed. One might indeed conclude that the self-interest of the blue-collar worker dictates that he support a broadening of the explicitly redistributional welfare programs which he has traditionally opposed.

PUBLIC ASSISTANCE: SOMETHING FOR NOTHING?

The public assistance money payment programs would probably win hands down in any governmental program unpopularity poll taken among blue-collar workers or, for that matter, among the general public. No one, it seems, likes welfare—not even the recipients.

Public antipathy to the welfare system has grown along with the increasing size and consequent visibility of its programs. Between 1960 and 1969, public assistance money payments more than doubled from $3.2 billion to $6.9 billion and are estimated to be almost $8 billion in 1970. (If medical assistance payments are included, the 1960–1969 change is increased by an additional $4 billion.) But public assistance money payments in 1969 still constituted only some 13 percent of all public income maintenance transfers and less than 3 percent of total federal, state, and local government expenditures, and it is not clear that the blame for the programs' unpopularity among the public should be laid solely or even primarily on the associated tax burden. For example, in a recent survey of attitudes toward welfare programs, only 4 percent of respondents mentioned the tax burden at all in response to an open-ended question on favorable and unfavorable aspects of the current public assistance programs. Furthermore, there appears to be general acceptance of the need for a welfare program of some sort. In this particular poll, only 2 percent of respondents condemned welfare programs out of hand; in a 1969 Harris poll, respondents rejected by 65 to 25 the notion that "money spent on welfare in cities is just wasted."[13] It thus appears that it is the particular structure of our current welfare system which has won its dubious reputation.

Nonetheless, the extent of the actual welfare-associated tax burden on the blue-collar class is still of interest. Since public assistance (PA) is financed out of federal, state, and local general revenues rather than a payroll tax, the tax base for public assistance is considerably broader than that for Social Security. However, almost half of the public assistance burden is borne by state and local governments. Since sales and excise taxes are a major source of state and local revenues, and these taxes tend to be regressive, the result is a pattern of incidence by income class which, while not plainly regressive, is not notably progressive. Bridges estimated that in the 1960–1961 period, the $3.3 billion of PA taxes comprised sales and excise taxes (33 percent), federal personal income taxes (30 percent), corporate income taxes (18 percent), property taxes (11 percent), state and local personal income taxes (5 percent), and death and gift taxes (3 percent). This mixture produces a pattern of tax rates by income class which is regressive at the lowest-income classes and almost flat across the middle-income range. Across this range, Bridges estimates the average tax rate at a relatively low and virtually constant 0.8 percent of income. Above incomes of approximately $13,600, the tax rate rises only slightly, to 0.9 percent, reflecting the greater importance of progressive income taxes at this level.

Examined alone, the growth in public assistance has not significantly increased the tax burden for the blue-collar worker. In an unpublished report, Bridges estimates that total taxes as a percent of personal income have risen from about 32 percent to about 36 percent in the 1960–1969 period; this would raise the average PA tax from about 0.8 to 0.9 percent of blue-collar income. The shift in the proportion of benefits paid for by state and local governments (from about 41 percent in fiscal year 1961 to about 45 percent in fiscal year 1969) also tended to shift the burden of financing to the lower-income worker. On the other hand, the low growth in state-financed general assistance programs compared to federally assisted programs during this period has worked in the opposite direction.

These calculations suggest that although the average public-assistance-associated tax at each income level has probably increased somewhat since 1960, the tax as a proportion of income in each income class has probably not changed very much; and the magnitude of the change—one-tenth of 1 percent—suggests that this change could not have caused a significant rise in blue-collar alienation.

But if the public assistance tax burden is not a source of growing alienation among the blue-collar class, other features of the program clearly are.

The fact that public assistance helps some and excludes others who are equally poor is one major problem. Few blue-collar workers, poor or not, are either current or potential beneficiaries of public assistance programs simply because they are excluded by the current system. Over 95 percent of the benefits in federally assisted programs go to the aged, the blind, the disabled, and female-headed families with children (Aid to Families with Dependent Children: AFDC). In half the states, benefits are also available to families in which the male head is employed less than 30 to 35 hours a week (Aid to Families with Dependent Children—Unemployed Father: AFDC-UF). This last program does provide potential coverage to unemployed blue-collar workers whose unemployment benefits have been exhausted; but participation in the program has been low in relation to estimated need because of complex eligibility criteria and low publicity given the program by states fearful of the potential cost implications. At present, no federally supported income maintenance program provides coverage to full-time male workers with chronically low incomes relative to their needs, and only New York State provides such coverage at its own expense.

The categorical distinctions in these programs clearly create horizontal inequities among equally needy families. From the viewpoint of blue-collar alienation, they also increase the perceived gulf between the blue-collar and the welfare class. Although the poor are significantly different socially and demographically from the middle class, the categorical exclusions in the welfare program have created a class of recipients considerably different from the poverty population as a whole—and even more different from the blue-collar class, many of whom are close to, if not below, the poverty line.[14] This effect is most pronounced for the AFDC program, which accounts for most of the dollars (56 percent in April 1970) and recipients (67 percent) of public assistance. While both blue-collar and non-aged poor families are predominantly male-headed, white, and working, families receiving benefits under the AFDC program are heavily female-headed, nonwhite, and nonworking (Table 38).

As these programs have become more visible, it is reasonable to assume that the perception of these differences between the two groups has become a major factor in the alienation of the blue-collar worker. In the case of public assistance programs, this animosity is intensified because public assistance benefits are not in any sense "earned" by prior work—they relate only to current need. If this were not so, public assistance would not serve its purposes.

However, the "antiwork" image of public assistance goes beyond the question of how entitlement is established. In the opinion of many nonrecipients, at least, public assistance programs have offered little or no reward for work effort, since federal law, until recently, allowed welfare benefits to be subtracted dollar for dollar from earnings. This "100 percent tax" on earnings created a power-

TABLE 38

CHARACTERISTICS OF AFDC FAMILIES, POVERTY POPULATION, AND BLUE-COLLAR FAMILIES, 1969

	Percent of families and unrelated individuals who are:					
	Male-headed	*Female-headed*	*White*	*Nonwhite*	*Employed*	*Mainly unemployed*
AFDC families	18.2	81.8	50.5	49.5	19.4	80.6
Poverty population	62.9	37.1	72.1	27.9	47.6	52.4
Blue-collar families	93.7	6.3	86.8	13.2	92.6	7.4

SOURCE: U.S. Department of Health, Education, and Welfare, Social and Rehabilitation Service, National Center for Social Statistics, and special tabulation prepared by the Urban Institute from the March 1969 *Current Population Survey*.

ful disincentive to work. The 1967 amendments modified this anti-work bias somewhat by liberalizing provisions for retention of earned income (the first $30 per month and one-third of income above that are disregarded in the calculation of benefits) and by creating the Work Incentive Program for training and placing non-aged adult welfare recipients in the job market. Neither amendment has yet had much impact either on the aggregate work effort of welfare recipients or on the popular view of welfare recipients as a group of willing idlers. This opinion is particularly strong among blue-collar workers.[15]

The only feature of public assistance which probably scores high with the blue-collar class is its method of administration. Public assistance benefits, unlike Social Security benefits, have never been considered a matter of entitlement. Eligibility criteria have been strict, and in many jurisdictions recipients have been subjected to demeaning investigations and judgments of "moral worth." However much this situation is decried by recipients and "liberal" observers, it is probably true that this is the way middle America likes it. The two most frequently cited criticisms of the welfare system, according to a recent poll, were that stricter requirements were needed and that more investigation was needed to prevent cheating. And yet, ironically, by insisting upon this stigmatizing method of administration, the middle American has erected a barrier to even potential personal benefit from these programs by creating a system in which he would be loath to participate, however great his need. Moreover, the image of the system in his own mind virtually guarantees his opposition to "welfare" reforms which would radically alter the structure of income maintenance programs and, by doing so, erase some of the causes of his own alienation.

To the extent that the features of present public assistance programs have contributed to blue-collar alienation, the administration's proposed Family Assistance Plan (FAP) and similarly structured alternative proposals would seem to move in precisely the right direction. FAP would provide coverage to the same demographic, if not financial, category as the blue-collar worker; i.e., working male heads of families, particularly those with low earnings and large families. If FAP passes, estimates indicate that some 560,000 blue-collar families would be eligible for payments. If the federal floor of $1,600 for a family of four were to increase over time at a rate in excess of wage increases, more and more blue-collar workers could expect some benefits.

Family Assistance should help in other ways. The extension of coverage to the working poor would change the profile of the population aided by income-conditioned programs to conform more closely to that of the poverty population as a whole and to the blue-collar class. Presumably, such alteration in the characteristics of the recipient population could make these programs more acceptable.

FAP would also shift the welfare burden from state governments to the federal level. Initially, this would come about primarily through injection of substantial amounts of new federal dollars into the system rather than from large-scale assumption of current state obligations by the federal government. (Current estimates show about $1.5 billion in new federal obligations for transfer payments as against about $700 million in state savings.) But the trend toward federalization of welfare payments would be set, and it is likely that further increases in the welfare burden will be financed through the federal treasury. To the extent that state tax systems are more regressive than the federal structure, this would tend to reduce middle America's relative share in public assistance redistribution.

FAP would also strengthen work incentives; indeed, this has been the administration's major selling point for the plan. It would seem, therefore, that if Congress passes the FAP, welfare may take a turn for the better from the blue-collar point of view. How far it is possible to go with such schemes is really the subject of another paper. However, it might be useful to sketch out the main issues here.

Negative tax schemes, such as FAP, have two main features: (1) basic benefits scaled to family size and (2) benefits reduced fractionally as other income increases in order to preserve incentives for increased work effort, as well as for vertical equity. Depending on the basic standard and the reduction formulas actually chosen, the effect is to extend coverage into the lower-middle- and middle-income ranges. For FAP, with a $1,600 guarantee for a family of four and a 50 percent tax on earned income above the first $720, the income at which benefits are phased out is $3,920. For an intact family with five children, the cutoff point is $5,720.

To some extent, these two features of negative tax schemes define the limit of their practical extension. At some point, increases in benefit levels or reductions in marginal tax rates, or both, lead to steeply rising program costs and heavy redistribution of income from small to large families in the same income class. For example, a plan such as that supported by the National Welfare Rights Organization, with a $5,500 guarantee and a 50 percent marginal tax rate, would cover some 37 million families and 132 million people (well over half the population). Its net federal cost in 1971 would be a staggering $67.6 billion, including some $20 billion of federal income tax loss. Thus less than half of the population would provide direct transfers to the other portion as well as assume the positive tax burden previously borne by the latter. In addition, a significant percentage of the costs would represent intra-income-class transfers from small to large families. It seems very unlikely that a plan involving such a massive reshuffling of income in the middle- and upper-income ranges would be either politically acceptable or economically feasible.

UNEMPLOYMENT INSURANCE AND WORKMEN'S COMPENSATION

In earlier sections, we have looked at programs which either serve the blue-collar worker only as a part of the total labor force or serve him hardly at all. In this section, we will look briefly at those transfer programs which by design have him as their primary beneficiary.

The two largest public income maintenance programs serving the blue-collar worker are the nationwide unemployment insurance program (UI), which provides cash benefits to unemployed workers; and the workmen's compensation program, the nation's oldest social insurance program, which provides benefits to workers injured in employment-connected activities. Both are insurance programs designed to provide wage replacement for some portion of the worker's prior salary. These government programs have been supplemented by a variety of private and public programs. In addition, there is a separate program for railroad workers administered by the Railroad Retirement Board, and two others, for federal government employees and for unemployed ex-servicemen, administered by states as federal agents and financed from general revenues. The regular unemployment insurance program was temporarily amended in 1958 and 1961 to extend the benefit period for workers who have exhausted their regular benefits during recessions.

The 1970 employment security amendments established a permanent new program of extended benefits which is automatically triggered within a given state when unemployment in that state exceeds a specified level.

Unemployment insurance for covered workers has been further supplemented in certain industries by private supplementary unemployment plans. About 700 of these programs cover about 2.5 million workers (half of whom are in the automobile and steel industries). These are generally designed to improve upon the wage replacement rate afforded by regular UI benefits, and in most cases they also provide allowances for workers' dependents, a feature included in only 11 state UI programs. Automobile industry workers are further protected by a guaranteed annual wage program which, since 1967, provides 95 percent of normal pay for 31 weeks to workers with 1-year seniority and for a full year to workers with 7-year seniority.

To these programs must be added the vast number of employee benefit plans which provide income maintenance payments to replace earnings lost by death, accident, sickness, or retirement. More than 28 million workers (over 45 percent of the private wage and salary labor force) were covered in 1968 by private pension plans which paid out benefits of over $5 billion and took in contributions of over $10 billion. About half of these plans were products of collective bargaining, and many of them were multiemployer plans. Virtually all were entirely employer-financed, and most of them were integrated with Social Security benefits under Treasury Department regulations, which were substantially revised in 1968 to require a more even distribution of benefits among workers at all salary levels. Private temporary and long-term disability plans paid out $1.8 billion in 1968 (up 23 percent from the previous year) and collected some $2.2 billion in employer contributions.[16]

Since most of the privately supplemented programs are the result of collective bargaining agreements and hence may be considered as the blue-collar workers' private business, we will concentrate on the two nationwide public transfer programs—unemployment insurance and workmen's compensation.

The perspective for evaluating blue-collar reactions to these two major transfer programs is considerably different from that for Social Security and public assistance. In this case, there is little question of extragroup transfers. Both programs have had as their primary, if not sole, target group the blue-collar class itself; in fact, much of the criticism leveled at them comes from their service of this group to the exclusion of such other working groups as agricultural and domestic workers. If the burden of the employers' tax is borne entirely by the covered employees, these programs simply redistribute income among blue-collar workers. If some of the burden is borne by consumers and profit recipients, blue-collar workers become net beneficiaries.

These programs are of interest to us primarily from two viewpoints: first, because a considerably warped picture of the overall redistributive effect of income maintenance programs would result from omitting programs of such magnitude (in 1969, unemployment insurance transferred some $2.4 billion to covered workers, and workmen's compensation some $1.7 billion, for a combined total of nearly 8 percent of all income maintenance transfers); and second, because the relative deterioration of these programs compared to their previous position may have led the blue-collar worker to conclude that in a prosperous society with increasing concern for the welfare of at least some of its citizens, he isn't "getting his."

Neither program has been without its critics. The most familiar criticism of both programs has been inadequacy of coverage: whereas about 70 percent of the labor force is covered by UI, 64 percent of unemployment in 1968 was uninsured. (The recently passed 1970 UI amendments will extend coverage somewhat to certain agricultural workers and a few other small groups.) While about 80 percent of the labor force is covered by workmen's compensation, the industry with the second highest work-related death rate, agriculture, is not covered. But with the exception of new labor-force entrants or marginal workers, blue-collar workers have not suffered from such discrimination and, in the absence of a high degree of philanthropy on their part, we may assume that they are not unduly worried about these restrictions.

But other features of these programs may well sadden even their star customers. Both programs are employer-financed (only in three states do employees still contribute to unemployment insurance), state-supervised systems. As a result, there has been little consistent pressure to improve benefits and great variation in both program adequacy and administrative practice. In the case of unemployment insurance, overall standards are established by the federal government and a small proportion of employer contributions (0.5 percent out of a maximum tax of 3.2 percent) is earmarked for a federal trust fund to cover state and federal administrative costs. However, the states retain considerable discretion over the level and duration of benefits, the minimum earnings criterion for eligibility, and the duration of employment needed to establish benefit rights. Workmen's compensation varies even more because there is neither a federal law establishing standards nor a federal administrative or financial mechanism. Each state establishes its own minimum standards; and in all but six states, which run their own exclusive state insurance fund, employers may (or in two states must) self-insure upon proof of financial ability or purchase qualifying insurance from private carriers.

Given this multiplicity of programs, judgments about their adequacy become difficult for any geographical area or industry, or even for a specific case, let alone for the national level. Nonetheless, it seems safe to conclude that benefits in both programs have kept pace neither with improvements in other money transfer programs nor with rising living standards.

The unemployment insurance tax rate has remained virtually unchanged from its 1939 level of 3 percent of the first $3,000 paid to workers. (In 1961 the tax was raised to 3.1 percent. The 1970 amendments raised the federal portion of the current tax 0.1 percent, bringing the total tax to 3.2 percent, and provided for raising the taxable wage to $4,200 in 1972.) In 1939 the $3,000 taxable wage limit covered 98 percent of all wages paid in covered employment; now it accounts for only 50 percent.[17] Furthermore, the program incorporates a "merit system," allowing tax reductions to employers with relatively low unemployment experience, with the result that few, if any, employers pay the full 3.1 percent tax. In 1968 the average UI tax, nationwide, was only 1.6 percent.

Workmen's compensation has done somewhat better in maintaining the ratio of contributions to payroll. In 1940 workmen's compensation costs represented 1.19 percent of covered payroll; in 1968 they were 1.08 percent although the recent trend has been steadily upward from a low of 0.89 percent in 1950.

From the worker's point of view, this failure of revenues to keep pace with economic growth has resulted in a considerably lower level of self-protection. The best summary measure, and perhaps the most relevant indicator of program adequacy, is the ratio of weekly benefits to average weekly wage; i.e., the replacement rate. The generally accepted principle with regard to unemployment insurance has been that benefits should replace about 50 percent of wages, and workmen's compensation about 67 percent, the discrepancy being justified by the need to maintain work incentives for the unemployed workers. The unemployment insurance program has fallen increasingly short of this goal, largely because of the maintenance of relatively low statutory maxima on benefits and, with rising wages, the increasing number of eligible claimants receiving these maxima. In 1939 the mean ratio of maximum benefits to average weekly wages across states and other covered jurisdictions was some 67 percent with a range of 45 to 98 percent. By 1968 it had declined to about 45 percent with a range of 31 to 61 percent. Furthermore, by 1967, 47 percent of all eligible claimants were affected by these maxima (and hence received less than 45 percent of their prior wage) whereas in 1939 only 26 percent were.

No comparable time series data are available for workmen's compensation. (In fact, it appears that very few published data of any sort are available on this mysterious program.) However, in 1965 the ratio of maximum weekly compensation benefits to average wages of injured workers was estimated at 66 percent nationally. Inasmuch as injured workers tend to be those in lower-paying employment, the ratio of maximum benefits to average covered wages would be considerably lower. Severely disabled workers may, of course, also receive benefits under the disability insurance portion of Social Security. However, replacement rates (calculated in a similar fashion to retirement benefit rates) are low for all but the lowest-paid workers and are offset dollar for dollar against workmen's compensation to the extent that the sum of the two entitlements exceeds 80 percent of the worker's prior wage.

The adequacy question, of course, has other dimensions. Because both systems are primarily or exclusively employer-financed, employers naturally resist any relaxation of eligibility criteria or raising of benefits. As noted, these incentives have been further reinforced in the case of unemployment insurance by the use of the merit rating system, which reduces employer taxes as a function of their actual unemployment experience. Many employers apparently retain consultants who automatically challenge every employee claim in the hope that either this will discourage workers or they will find new jobs before the claim is settled. The low tax base for unemployment insurance also discourages hiring of low-wage workers, since the tax is a relatively high proportion of their wages and tends to encourage reliance on overtime by employers in lieu of new hires.

The efficiency of the unemployment insurance program in serving its clientele is also impaired by the fact that it is a state-run system and consequently each state must maintain its own separate reserve fund. Higher total reserves must thus be maintained than if the risk were to be pooled over the entire population. Overly cautious actuarial principles have also been followed in developing the current total reserve fund of $11 billion in state funds plus some $0.5 billion in an emergency federal loan fund. This amount is sufficient on a national basis to cover almost twice the benefit costs that would occur in a 12-month period were the worst recession of the last 10 years to be reexperienced, even assuming that no additional revenues were accumulated during that period.[18]

For workmen's compensation, it is hard to generalize on the question of benefit adequacy and administrative efficiency. But the absence in 21 jurisdictions of provision for lifetime benefits for permanent disability, the failure to update payments under past settlements to reflect rising living costs, and the lack of coverage for occupational diseases seem obvious defects. The most obvious indictment of the workmen's compensation program, nonetheless, seems to be its staggeringly high rate of overhead. From 1940 through 1960, for every $3 paid to beneficiaries, $2 went for lawyers' fees, commissions for insurance salesmen, and other administrative costs.

Some of the problems with these programs concern their relation to other transfer programs. Assuming burdens which should properly be placed elsewhere may restrict the ability of UI and WC to serve their legitimate roles. For example, some observers feel that the unemployment insurance system's ability to serve its goals of countercyclical stabilization and adequate income protection against involuntary employment has been eroded by its overuse in covering predictable (seasonal) and structural unemployment—two problems which might properly be served by general income maintenance and manpower programs financed from general revenues.

As both programs have evolved, they have also incorporated more or less explicit redistributional features. Replacement rates for workers earning the average wage or better have declined considerably. The programs do continue, however, to provide relatively adequate replacement rates for lower-paid workers who do not suffer from the low maxima. This effect is increased in unemployment insurance, which, in many states, provides higher replacement rates for lower-wage workers and, in 11 states, variations in benefits with the number of dependents. The suitability of including such "welfare" elements in purportedly insurance-type programs may be questioned; but given the extreme regressivity of the unemployment insurance tax as a proportion of individual wages, the net redistributional impact of these provisions is probably not large.

Despite their failings, do these programs give blue-collar workers their money's worth? If not, what prevents improvement? The question of getting their money's worth may not at first glance seem relevant because the initial incidence of the costs of both programs is on employers and not employees. But for payroll taxes of all sorts, most economists agree that at least half of the tax, and probably more, gets shifted back to the employee in the form of lower wages. To the extent that it is not shifted backward, it appears to be shifted forward to the consumer in the form of higher price. But with the relatively high ratio of consumption to income in the income range with which we are concerned, the blue-collar worker again picks up a good chunk of the tab.

This hard fact of working life means that the blue-collar worker must make a choice. Payroll taxes are already high. Adding the combined OASDI tax projected for 1972 (10.4 percent) to the recently legislated unemployment insurance tax (3.2 percent on wages up to $4,200) and the current average workmen's compensation tax (1.07 percent), we come to a total payroll tax in 1972 of over 13.2 percent on a salary of $7,800 and of 14.7 percent on a salary of $4,200. Leaving aside the question of the unfavorable economic side effects of such a high level of payroll taxation, we may fairly ask whether the blue-collar worker wants to trade more of his current consumption for further protection. Of course, many workers might be said to have already so opted, as evidenced in the growing importance of private supplementary unemployment insurance, retirement, and other fringe benefit plans. One might further question the extent to which the rank-and-file worker is explicitly aware of the choice he must make between further protection and higher current wages, but there is no reason to doubt that the unions which represent him are keenly conscious of this trade-off.

Certain obvious steps could be taken to improve the efficiency of these programs, such as federalization of the unemployment insurance trust fund or establishment of a national workmen's compensation program with uniform standards and, it is hoped, cheaper if not better administration. But any major improvements in benefits will increase costs, much of which is likely to come from blue-collar workers.

One might also question whether it is sensible to consider reform and expansion of these programs as separate entities within our overall income maintenance system. Both the unemployment insurance and workmen's compensation programs already overlap significantly in coverage and purpose with two other major programs discussed earlier. The disability insurance segment of Social Security could, in theory, displace the workmen's compensation program entirely. In fact, replacement rates under DI are usually not competitive with workmen's compensation benefits, although since 1967 they may supplement such benefits up to a level of 80 percent of prior wage. Furthermore, Social Security disability criteria have been so restrictive as to exclude in 1969 all but 1.3 million of an estimated 17 million disabled workers from benefits. Nonetheless, both coverage and benefits under the DI program will probably continue to improve over time, with the overlap between the two programs becoming more significant. Although substituting DI for WC would essentially replace one payroll-tax-financed program by another (to which, furthermore, the employee must contribute directly), the blue-collar worker should gain a net advantage from such a displacement. It is to be hoped that the overhead on benefits would be reduced; in any case, the net redistributional position of the blue-collar class should be improved because the tax base for the DI tax is spread to white-collar and other working groups having lower disability rates.

The opportunity for shifting the unemployment insurance burden is also apparent. For many states, the "unemployed fathers" welfare program (AFDC-UF) provides comparable and, in some cases, superior benefits to workers with medium to large families; and of equal importance, these benefits, unlike UI payments, have no fixed time duration. This competitive advantage is offset somewhat by the general distaste for welfare. Moreover, most states require AFDC-UF claimants to exhaust first their UI benefits, whether superior or not, before establishing welfare eligibility, and to meet asset tests and eligibility criteria not related to need. The equity of the first provision is questionable. A trend toward relaxation of peripheral welfare eligibility criteria is clear. Furthermore, during the current recession, more and more workers (both blue- and white-collar) are apparently swallowing their pride and entering the welfare rolls. As unemployment increased in 1969 and 1970, AFDC-UF rolls rose even faster—from 61,500 families in July 1969 to 157,000 in December 1970. In the hard-pressed state of Washington, the flood of unemployed workers into welfare offices has forced the state to rescind its policy of supplementing unemployment insurance benefits for workers with multiple dependents. Having once had a taste of welfare, many blue-collar workers may question the efficacy of financing, from their own pockets, programs which might easily be displaced by other programs supported progressively by all income and demographic classes.

SUMMARY

The attitudes of a given class toward income maintenance programs is related to the benefits distributed by the program and the burden it places on the resources of the class. The actual relation, however, is not so simple. Attitudes of blue-collar workers toward income maintenance programs are significantly affected by the perceptions of fundamental differences between themselves and the major recipients of the program, and popular mythology about how the programs are operated and financed.

The largest of our income maintenance programs, Social Security, enjoys a high degree of acceptability among all segments of society, both because of its image as a self-protective rather than a welfare program and because of the wide dispersion of its clientele among all ranks of society. The Social Security program is, however, a significantly redistributive program whether looked at as a transfer at a point in time from the non-aged worker to the aged retiree or an insurance program through which individual workers set aside earnings against the risks of disability, death, or old age. Moreover, since Social Security is financed through payroll taxes falling most heavily on low- and middle-income workers and on multiearner families, the blue-collar worker contributes heavily to this redistribution. Serious consideration should be given to financing the redistributive aspects of Social Security through more broadly based methods of taxation.

Public assistance programs have not as yet constituted either a large or a growing burden on the blue-collar tax dollar. Hostility toward these programs is nonetheless high, not only because of their avowedly redistributional purpose, but because they tend to emphasize the socioeconomic and demographic distinctions between their beneficiaries and the working class. Currently proposed reforms should improve the acceptability of the public assistance system to the blue-collar class.

There are a number of programs which are specifically addressed to the workingman's income maintenance needs. These include the variety of public and private programs which provide compensation to the regular worker in the event of involuntary unemployment, work-related injury, or retirement. These programs are significant both because they increase the payroll tax burden and because the failure of the two largest programs, unemployment insurance and workmen's compensation, to improve benefits commensurately with economic growth may lend strength to blue-collar claims of public neglect of their interests. However, the fact that taxes for these programs are levied on employers rather than employees has probably muted demands for their improvement, for many workers are probably not aware that a major part of the financing burden falls ultimately on them through lower wages or higher prices.

Although income maintenance programs, as a large and growing part of public expenditures, may well contribute to discontent arising from a tax squeeze, the actual amount of redistribution—as opposed to self-protection which the blue-collar worker is currently called upon to support—is still not large in comparison either to his income or to the net benefits he receives from all public and private programs looked at together. Nor does it seem either practical or desirable to blanket middle America in a gigantic income support program related to needs. Most of our income maintenance programs, both public and private, are already designed to provide protection not to those who for one reason or another participate only marginally in the work economy, but to those with stable records of earnings and employment. Since blue-collar workers constitute one-third of the wage-salary labor force, they may be presumed to be major beneficiaries of our income maintenance system. Furthermore, there is no reason why the blue-collar class as a large and relatively affluent part of our society should not contribute its "fair share" to helping those in greater need.

Nevertheless, the predominance of payroll tax financing among our income maintenance programs and the significant and growing overlap among the purposes and coverage of the various programs suggest that both social equity and blue-collar interests would be served by attempts to rationalize our income maintenance system and to shift the burden of redistribution between income classes to more broadly based and progressive taxes. A sensible program of income maintenance reform cannot proceed from a narrow analysis of the interests of a single class, but from broader considerations of public welfare.

NOTES

1. Peter Schrag, "The Forgotten American," *Harper's,* August 1969, p. 28.
2. *New York Times,* Apr. 20, 1969, and Jan. 5, 1969.
3. *New York Times,* Jan. 5, 1969, p. 44.
4. Henry Aaron, "Benefits under the Social Security System," in Otto Eckstein (ed.), *Studies in the Economics of Income Maintenance,* Brookings, Washington, 1967, pp. 61–72; George A. Bishop, "Issues in Future Financing of Social Security," in Joint Economic Committee, *Old Age Income Assurance,* part III: *Public Programs,* 90th Cong., 1st Sess., 1967, pp. 21–71; John Brittain, "The Real Rate of Interest on Lifetime Contributions toward Retirement under Social Security," in Joint Economic Committee, *Old Age Income Assurance,* part III: *Public Programs,* 90th Cong., 1st Sess., 1967, pp. 109–132; and

Elizabeth Deran, "Income Redistribution under the Social Security System," *National Tax Journal,* September 1966, pp. 276–285.

5. Cited in Bishop, op. cit., p. 49.
6. Social Security Administration, *Social Security Programs in the United States,* 1968, p. 9.
7. Aaron, op. cit., pp. 49–70; Brittain, op. cit., pp. 109–132; and Joseph A. Pechman, Henry J. Aaron, and Michael K. Taussig, *Social Security: Perspectives for Reform,* Brookings, Washington, 1968, pp. 231–250. This assumes the following roughly stated conditions are met: Real wages and the size of the labor force continue to grow; benefit levels are periodically increased; and the ceiling on maximum taxable earnings is raised accordingly.
8. Pechman, Aaron, and Taussig, op. cit., p. 249, and Deran, op. cit.
9. The Primary Insurance Amount is the monthly benefit—not including dependent allowances—to which a worker entering the system now would be entitled at retirement, if he worked at a given average wage in the interim and if benefit schedules were not changed in the interim. The actual amount a household receives is a function also of the number of dependents and the limitation on maximum family benefits.
10. Robert M. Clark, *Economic Security for the Aged in the United States and Canada,* Queen's Printer, Ottawa, 1960, vol. I, p. 155.
11. Under the current law, the wife of a retiree is entitled to a monthly benefit equal to 50 percent of her husband's benefit. If she has earned an entitlement of her own, she must choose between it and her spouse's benefit. At worst, a woman whose own entitlement is less than half her husband's receives no incremental benefits at all for her contributed taxes. At best, even if her separate entitlement exceeds her spouse's dole, the net return on her lifetime payroll taxes is slight when compared to the benefits received by a wife who has not worked at all.
12. Benjamin Bridges, Jr., "Current Redistributional Effects of Old Age Income Assurance Programs," in Joint Economic Committee, *Old Age Income Assurance,* part II: *The Aged Population and Retirement Income Program,* 90th Cong., 1st Sess., 1967, pp. 95–176.
13. William E. Bicker, *Public Attitudes towards and Opinions of the Current Welfare System and Major Components of the Proposed Family Assistance Plan,* unpublished findings of a study undertaken for the Department of Health, Education, and Welfare, University of California, Berkeley, July 1970, p. 12; and *The Philadelphia Inquirer,* Jan. 27, 1969.
14. According to an occupational definition of blue-collar worker which includes craftsmen, foremen, operatives, and nonfarm laborers, an estimated 1.1 million blue-collar families (5.6 percent) were classified as poor in 1969 by the U.S. Bureau of the Census.
15. In a recent analysis of public attitudes, the belief that most people are on welfare because they are lazy was found to be most common among those with middle income ($7,000 to $15,000) and high school or less, both archetypical characteristics of the blue-collar class. This, as the study notes, is typically the class who has worked hard and is working hard to make it, and its intolerance of those whom they think haven't is not surprising, if not completely admirable. Conversely, as one might expect, the belief that most welfare recipients would work if they could is most prevalent among the very lowest income classes, who may be presumed to have experienced the difficulties of obtaining work, and among the upper-income education classes who can perhaps afford to take a more tolerant view of other people's habits. Bicker, op. cit., pp. 17–27.
16. Walter W. Kolodrubetz, "Employee Benefit Plans in 1968," *Social Security Bulletin,* April 1970, pp. 35–49; and Social Security Administration, *Social Security Programs in the United States,* 1968, pp. 115–116.
17. Saul J. Blaustein, *Unemployment Insurance Objectives and Issues: An Agenda for Research and Evaluation,* W. E. Upjohn Institute for Employment Research, Kalamazoo, Mich., 1968, pp. 20–21.
18. Ibid., p. 19.

13. YEARNING, LEARNING, AND STATUS

by Robert Schrank and Susan Stein

WHAT'S BOTHERING THE BLUE-COLLAR WORKER?

The American dream—a life blessed with consumer products, healthy, good-looking kids, respect from the community, a good job, and your own home—is the hope of many blue-collar workers. This is a dream of material well-being, economic security, and status in the community; in a word, "success." Many Americans in blue-collar jobs believe they can best achieve this dream by moving up the occupational ladder, either into more-skilled blue-collar work or into white-collar positions. In either case, education is considered a key to this upward mobility.

We are interested in the kinds of educational opportunities that might assist blue-collar families in gaining mobility, the extent to which these opportunities are used, and the implications this utilization has for national policy. In this connection, we will review broad social trends affecting working-class attitudes toward education; blue-collar enrollment in high schools, the peripheral education system, and colleges; and the ways in which the education system equips the blue-collar family to deal with new expectations and demands.

A blue-collar family, by our definition, is one headed by an employed craftsman, operative, or laborer whose annual income ranges from $5,000 to $15,000. Within this range, there are differences in skill level, educational attainment, home ownership, and spending power, to name only a few. There are as many differences among blue-collar workers as there are among ethnic groups, nationalities, ages, and sexes. However, we have attempted to generalize, on the basis of what we see as strong common factors.

There seems to be a consensus that something—what it is, is unclear—is bothering the blue-collar worker. Indeed, a great many Americans, not just blue-collar workers, are discontent because of racial, environmental, and income issues. Thus, the blue collars' discontent is part of a more general dissatisfaction. That the present administration may deem the blue collars' problems more critical because of their political clout certainly does not render less legitimate many of the gripes. Nevertheless, it may be advantageous to those in office to raise blue-collar expectations so that the working class will identify with the current administration.

The varied attempts by the news media to interpret the causes of blue-collar malaise have been singularly devoid of hard data. Most consisted of open-ended interviews with "alienated" assembly-line workers, militant hard hats, and other blue-collar personalities. One gathers from the reports only an ill-defined impression of what troubles the working class.

The economic squeeze, rising consumer expectations, and inflation are clearly important elements in the discontent. However, data on income and occupations suggest that blue-collar families have done as well economically as other major groups of workers. Although the average white, married, blue-collar worker enjoyed a 15 percent increase in annual earnings (after adjusting for changes in cost of living) between 1965 and 1969, and a gain of about 25 percent—approximately the same as that for other white workers—between 1959 and 1969, much of the gains has been eroded by rising taxes, and expectations have outpaced real gains. We do not agree, however, that this income-expectation gap accounts for the variety and intensity of woes recounted by blue-collar workers in recent interviews. It certainly does not account for their vehement street demonstrations against students and for the President.

Since income cannot account for all the malaise, at least some of the reasons for the restiveness must be elsewhere. While there may be many factors contributing to blue-collar blues, as well as to "the rest of us" blues, two reasons may account for a large portion of their particular discontent.

First, manual work is increasingly regarded by Americans as degrading. Second, many blue-collar workers believe the educational route to upward mobility is under heavy fire from students and intellectuals. This threatens their hopes for their and their childrens' future.

Blue-collar work orginally involved, at the top, old immigrant craft traditions which gave it prestige and character. These traditions are now being replaced by technology. Knowledge, not skill, is the critical factor in modern technology. For example, a craftsman who can square off a piece of steel with a hand file may be a true artisan; but his artisanship is useless on a numerically controlled machine tool which needs someone who understands a system.

The worker with traditional job skills has been replaced by a worker with the specific technical skill required to operate a complicated piece of equipment. The machine no longer acts as an extension of the artisan; it has absorbed him. As a result, much of the manual work that remains is routine and unchallenging. This trend of advances in machine technology accompanied by the elimination of skills is likely to continue, resulting in further loss of status for blue-collar workers. The effects are likely to be distributed unevenly, but the general rate of change will probably accelerate in the years ahead. There simply will not be any turning back to the simple life of the wooden plow.

A recent study of the impact of technological advance on the work force illustrates the effects of this change.[1] It found the most decisive factors in job dissatisfaction were monotony, decreased chances for learning, and less need for exercising judgment. On the other hand, workers on automated equipment showed a higher rate of job satisfaction because they felt they were making decisions. The status discontent of blue-collar workers, which will probably continue to grow, can be found among lower-level and assembly-line blue-collar workers whose jobs involve a series of undemanding tasks. These workers see themselves lagging behind as the new class of "technocraftsmen" becomes more evident in the plant. This new class consists of blue-collar workers who operated logical-control machines and combine traditional skills with programming *expertise*. These technocraftsmen are considered the "smarts" and, therefore, a growing threat by the traditional craftsmen.

Education has long been regarded a key ingredient in getting ahead. Strains of this sentiment can be traced from Ben Franklin to Horatio Alger and James B. Conant. Few American presidents have failed to exude some rhetoric on the subject. Many blue collars who regard the educational system as the route to higher-prestige white-collar jobs, see this route being threatened by three occurrences of the last decade. These threats constitute another cause of blue-collar malaise.

First, the nation's schools and colleges have recently become battlegrounds over the issues of desegration, community control, the war in Vietnam, Defense Department contracts, and radical attacks on "the system" and on "irrelevance" in the schools. The blue-collar worker feels extremely threatened by these attacks. He and many other Americans previously regarded the schools as "neutral turf." The new school conflicts mean that another institution has been converted into a battlefield for warring social factions.

The blue-collar worker does not see the substantive issues at all. For him, the attack on the schools is a threat to his or his children's chance to "make it." Many blue-collar families see themselves putting in years of hard work, saving and sacrificing to enable their children to go to college. This threat to their beliefs is now compounded not only by attacks on the schools and colleges but by those who openly disdain the traditional goals of money, success, steady work, and credentialism. The reaction is virulent. In these instances what the blue-collar worker perceives as being under fire is a basic belief in an open-opportunity system, not "the establishment" that the radical students think they are attacking.

Second, a vocal antieducation tradition has appeared and is challenging the educational system. Members of this group suggest that the American educational process is self-defeating, producing increased failure and discontented citizens. A quick view of a university bookstore will show literally dozens of these critiques. Although blue-collar workers may not read these books, television interviews with authors and angry students ensure that blue-collar workers at least hear about the nature of such complaints. These ideas must be particularly devastating to people who may be pinning their hopes for the future on the educational system. Part of the blue-collar anti-intellectualism may stem from this perception of the intellectuals as constant detractors of the education mobility process.

Third, threats to the proper functioning of the educational system for blue-collar workers come from the civil rights movement, from the 1954 Supreme Court *Brown* decision, all the way through the compensatory education, training, bussing, and legal aid programs of the 1960s. National legend taught Americans that if a man was sober, wise, diligent, and a little lucky, he "had it made." Natural selection would assure that the most capable received the rewards they deserved. Many blue-collar families perceived that the rules of the game were changed by antipoverty efforts which gave poor and minority members a boost up the ladder at the expense of blue-collar opportunity. Also, the civil rights movement and these special programs created an advocacy voice for the poor and the minorities; on the other hand, the advocates for blue-collar workers, the unions, were not involved in the social programs of the sixties.

Although a great variety of factors undoubtedly cause the blue-collar blues, two elements closely related to education play a particularly important role. The declining respect for craftsmanship creates pressure to get out of the crafts and into technocraft or white-collar work. "Getting out" means working with the head and not with the hands, which in turn means going to school and getting a credential. At the same time, however, chances for mobility are impaired because the opportunity system embodied in the schools is being challenged and tinkered with. While educators and behavioral scientists may be in great pain over the poor job being done by the schools, the blue-collar worker sees the school only in terms of its credentialing function. He has little or no concern as to whether or not the schools are educating the whole man.

Blue-collar blues or anomie seems, therefore, to result from rising expectations of status and mobility and the apparent inability of the system to deliver. In other words, there seems to be a widening gap between what blue-collar families would like out of life and what they think they have a chance of getting. Blue-collar workers have never been class-conscious, but they have always been mobility-conscious. They have traditionally pinned their aspirations on "the system." Their aspirations are now threatened by what they consider leapfrogging via compensatory programs and attacks on the school system. Nothing is quite so disturbing to aspiring persons as a threat to their routes for mobility.

Education is still a major pathway to higher socioeconomic status in this society. All evidence indicates that education tends to qualify one for higher-paid jobs and brings prestige to its recipients. Further, effective education can bring challenge and status to the life of a student. National educational policy is therefore an important part of what the blue-collar workers see as their opportunity structure within the society.

There are grounds for optimism about social change in this country. While glaring inequities remain between the affluent and the very poor, the minorities and the whites and so on, there is evidence that things have gotten better—particularly for the working class.

The working class is not essentially discontented or revolutionary. On the contrary, we view this group as basically conservative and aspiring toward "success" within the traditional fabric of society. While others may hope to bring broad transformations to the society, the blue-collar worker wants to "make it" in the present system. His discontent is partly an impatience with those who threaten what he hopes are stable routes to upward mobility.

EDUCATION AND MOBILITY: RISING LEVELS OF EDUCATION

Educational opportunities have expanded tremendously in the last decade. Between 1960 and 1970, annual expenditures for higher education rose from $6.0 billion to $21.5 billion. Capital outlays for higher education grew from $1.7 billion to $3.1 billion.

A longer view shows that between 1890 and 1950 the number of students attending American colleges and universities increased about seventeenfold, and the number of persons in academic employment increased about thirteenfold. During that time, the population increased only 250 percent. New types of educational institutions, such as two-year colleges, are growing at a rapid pace. In 1947 there were 480 two-year colleges with about 220,000 persons enrolled. In 1969 the Office of Education estimated that there were 886 such institutions with nearly 2 million students. The greatest portion of this increase has been in public community colleges. These two-year vocational and academic institutions are now opening at the rate of one per week. Gains in educational attainment of the work force reflect this greater educational opportunity (Table 39).

The blue-collar work force benefited from the national educa-

TABLE 39
EDUCATIONAL ATTAINMENT OF CIVILIAN LABOR FORCE 18 YEARS OLD AND OVER, 1952 AND 1968

	1952	*1968*
Median school years completed	10.9	12.3
	Percent of labor force	
4 years high school	27	38
1 to 3 years college	8	12

SOURCE: Bureau of Labor Statistics.

tional upgrading. The change is particularly striking in the last decade. In 1960, 26 percent of white and 14 percent of black craftsmen and operatives had completed four years of high school. By 1969, the percentages were 41 and 28 respectively. Much of this change comes from the postwar baby-boom children who entered the labor force in the mid-1960s, having benefited from the increasing investment in education made between 1950 and 1970. These younger workers have completed significantly more years of school than their older coworkers. Blue-collar workers between the ages of 25 and 44 have completed 12 years of school compared to 10 years for those aged 54 to 64. By 1975, it is expected that the median number of school years completed by the labor force between the ages of 25 and 34 will be 12.6 years.

SIGNIFICANCE FOR BLUE COLLARS

What is the significance of recent and projected educational gains for blue-collar workers? First, "the undereducated worker" has been redefined. In the 1940s and 1950s, those with a high school diploma were in a good competitive position in the labor market, being well above the median. Today, they are considered to have average qualifications for blue-collar work.

This change in relative status results in part from changing job requirements. Ivar Berg's studies suggest that during the 1960s many employers raised minimum job qualifications to high school graduation for blue-collar work and at least two years of college for white-collar jobs. He indicates that the shift upward was not based on any demonstrated superior capability of high school graduates compared with nongraduates, or college graduates compared with high school graduates. Rather, management simply believed that those who "stayed with it" were more reliable. In other words, criteria in the sifting process were raised.[2]

What is the impact of this more-educated work force? In many instances, blue-collar workers are moving up to technician or what might be called white-collar plant jobs or technocraftsman's jobs operating blue-collar machines. That trend is likely to continue. In the face of rising job requirements, increasing educational attainment, and increasing desire for upward mobility, what chance does the present blue-collar worker have for returning to school to obtain at least a high school diploma or, more importantly, a college degree? The high school diploma and college degree not only will qualify him for better jobs but will also bring him increased income (Table 40). Clearly, the significant jump occurs at college graduation.

AVENUES TO UPWARD MOBILITY

Although some blue collars become disillusioned because their first educational experience does not improve their status, many still look for upward mobility through part-time education and training. Few blue-collar workers have sufficient resources to support a full-time return to college or technical training. We need, therefore, to consider the part-time avenues for blue-collar upward mobility.

The blue-collar worker generally has three possible approaches

TABLE 40
EDUCATIONAL ATTAINMENT AND EXPECTED LIFETIME INCOME

Years of school completed	*Lifetime 1966 income (age 18 to death)*
1 to 3 years high school	$284,000
4 years high school	341,000
1 to 3 years college	394,000
4 years college	508,000

SOURCE: Bureau of Labor Statistics.

to upward mobility: (1) upgrading on the job, (2) training for another specific job, and (3) college education. Available data suggest that only the last of these alternatives could move blue collars into prestigious white-collar jobs.

Most studies of employee training indicate that on-the-job training usually occurs informally with no guarantees of advancement. Howard Rosen reports that according to a national survey made in 1963 of the vocational education of 52 million workers between 22 and 64 years of age who had less than three years of college, only 15 percent had been trained by employers in a formal training setting. Most had received casual instructions from coworkers or had been enrolled in high school vocational courses. Another study found that, of those who had formal training, most took only a single course or program during their career.[3]

A further study of companies offering training found that only medium-sized and large firms conducted any significant amount of training.[4] A 1969 study found that industry training in Cleveland is sporadic and geared only to specific plant requirements. Many of the skills taught by companies do not significantly enhance a worker's competitive position.[5] Thus, while many blue-collar workers may eventually be upgraded via this route, few can look to this as a certainty. Not many can expect to move out of blue-collar work through employer-sponsored programs.

The manpower activities sponsored by the federal government offer another choice. In 1970 these programs enrolled more than a million persons at an estimated federal outlay of $3 billion. These programs have been used heavily by minority groups. The publicity surrounding the programs has convinced many people that the minorities were receiving special consideration. However, the education and training was for entry into "first-rung" jobs and had little or no effect on those already higher up the blue-collar ladder. In fact, a major criticism of these programs by minority organizations has been that they are training people for jobs they would have obtained anyway.

Traditional vocational education probably has the greatest impact on blue-collar families, for a large proportion of blue-collar children and adults are educated in vocational classes. About 7 million persons enrolled in vocational education programs offered in 1970.

While the federal government is active in manpower and training, few of its efforts assist the blue-collar worker to move upward, particularly into technocraftsman slots or white-collar work. In fact, the blue collar could argue that he gets a disproportionately small chunk of federal training and occupational mobility money.

Education, particularly college or high-level technical training, is the blue-collar adult's most promising alternative. He must first get support for this education or training, for it is unlikely that his employer will underwrite his school fees. Very few companies have plans for tuition reimbursement for blue-collar workers, usually reserving these benefits for their white-collar staff.

To speculate on the assumptions behind this distinction is interesting. It suggests that white-collar jobs are viewed as requiring the judgment and responsibility that, employers believe, results from some form of higher education. They are also seen as the jobs of the future—the source of future supervision and management. That blue-collar work does not offer such opportunities tends to support the blue-collar worker's sense that his job is dead-end, undemanding, and lacking in status.

Self-supported continuing education is another option for blue-collar workers. They can turn to the traditional school system or to the "peripheral institutions." This latter group consists of proprietary schools, correspondence schools, all instructional television associations, church-sponsored education, and all other organized, nonrecreational learning which occurs outside the traditional and accredited school system.

A large number of American adults continue their education outside the regular, or core, system. Indeed, if evidence is needed to verify the learning, education, go-to-school syndrome in America, the peripheral system is living proof. We estimate that 35 million people are in this system, including 8 million blue-collar workers, most often in nonaccredited vocational courses which give them an extra skill or improve their performance on the job they held at enrollment. Blue-collar participation might be considerably higher if such education were both more available and subsidized. The cost per course usually ranges from $5 to $300; some of the very specialized and technical courses run as high as $1,000.

Current population surveys bear out the claim that blue-collar workers are entering the learning force in ever-increasing numbers. Adult blue-collar participation is an important indicator of interest in upgrading and mobility. Perhaps if steps were taken to facilitate blue-collar participation in peripheral and higher education, a significantly greater number would enroll.

At the present time, there seems to be a conflict between the established accredited schools and the peripheral adult education system. While the former are anxious to retain control of credentialing, the latter are providing a growing number of educational services to the public. Clearly, many of the millions of Americans learning outside the formal system are gaining useful knowledge and in many cases are being taught with new methods. Their learning experience, although currently scorned by the established school system, could represent a significant source of innovation and effectiveness. Consideration should be given to broadening the scope of the school system to include a number of these other learning institutions.

Much of the problem of who gets credit (or a credential) for what in schools is based on class. For example, to get a degree from a college to qualify for professional work, an individual may be required to take folk dancing, archery, fencing, or hygiene. All these courses contribute to the final credential. In contrast, people in the peripheral education system can take advanced physics and be denied credit because it is not a matriculated course or not offered by a recognized school. It would seem reasonable to substitute for this a lifetime approach to education in which students would collect credit for all courses taken and schools attended regardless of whether they were in the periphery or the core. Blue-collar workers could then begin to build credits which would later qualify them for entry into higher-prestige work.

The nation's growing number of two-year colleges provide another avenue for post-high school education for adult blue-collar students. While participation is still small, these two-year institutions are increasingly used by the adult, part-time student. In the fall of 1969, one in ten of all two-year college freshmen were adults (over 21), compared to one in fifty in four-year colleges. More than 60 percent are part-time students. Many of these adults enroll for a series of courses (particularly in business or technical areas), seeking not a degree but preparation for white-collar jobs. A study of a sample of workers shifting from blue- to white-collar jobs suggests that this kind of specific post-high school education is particularly critical for those becoming professionals, electrical and electronic technicians, tool and die designers, and draftsmen.[6]

From this review of alternative routes to adult blue-collar upgrading, it seems that existing job training opportunities are unlikely to lead many to high-level technical or white-collar jobs. The other main mobility factor, education, is increasingly used by adult blue collars; however, the educational opportunities for adults are limited.

One is led to question why unions have been negligent in winning greater educational opportunities for their membership. The few educational programs sponsored or promoted by unions are related to leadership training within the union. They are of short duration and unaccredited. Generally, unions continue to look upon education as someone else's business. This attitude stems from traditional union attitudes. First, anything that encourages members to move out of the bargaining unit is seen as a threat to union power. This somewhat myopic outlook ignores the growing group of technocraftsmen who operate "blue-collar machines" and are potential members. Second, a few of the old-style union leaders tend to view education as irrelevant to work. Skill training and learning a trade are still considered the most important types of preparation. While the younger membership may regard education and training differently, the older leadership still hold to traditional attitudes.

This analysis leads us to conclude that, more often than not, the blue-collar workers' aspirations to educational mobility may be realized through the next generation. It is probable that many blue-collar adults accept their own achievement and look for upgrading through their children's education and eventual employment. If this is so, we need to consider how blue-collar children fare in the educational marketplace and what preparation they will need in the future to find jobs offering personal fulfillment and mobility.

LABOR MARKET PROJECTIONS AND EDUCATIONAL REQUIREMENTS

There are any number of sources for economic, industrial, and social projections for the coming decades. A general survey of the future gazers suggests that rapid growth and strong public interest

TABLE 41

OCCUPATIONAL DISTRIBUTION AND EDUCATIONAL REQUIREMENTS OF CIVILIAN LABOR FORCE, 1968 AND PROJECTIONS FOR 1975

Occupational groupings	*Occupational distribution for 1968*	*Projected distribution for 1975*	*Median years of school completed, 1968*	*Minimum educational requirement projected for 1975*
Total	100%	100%		
Professional and technical	14	15	16	17
Managers and proprietors	10	10	13	13
Clerical	17	17	13	13
Sales	6	6	13	13
Craftsmen and foremen	13	13	12	13
Operatives	18	17	11	12
Service (except household)	12	14	*	*
Farmers	5	4	*	*
Laborers	5	4	10	11

* Not available.
SOURCE: Bureau of Labor Statistics.

are likely to center around the fields of education, health, research, and transportation. Within the first three areas, the growth is expected to be largely in white-collar and technical jobs. In transportation and to a lesser degree in housing, urban, and natural resources development, expansion could open new blue-collar opportunities.

The service occupations provide a good example of growth and employment opportunities in the decade of the 1970s. The Bureau of Labor Statistics estimates that these areas will continue to expand by two-fifths between 1970 and 1980, or more than 1½ times the expansion for all other occupations combined.

By 1975, white-collar workers are expected to outnumber blue collars by three to two. By 1980, white-collar employment is expected to reach 48.5 million; it was 35.6 million in 1968. Professional and technical workers will outnumber skilled craftsmen. Table 41 outlines these broad occupational changes and suggests what may be the implications of the shifts for education.

The projections suggest that most of the middle- and higher-level white-collar technical jobs will soon require at least four years of college work. Lower-level white-collar jobs will need high school or two-year-college graduates. The largest number of new jobs will occur in occupations requiring the most training and education.

A recent study of technology and industry suggests that many of the most glamorous and rewarding jobs in the next decade will involve new machine technology.[7] They will also be in areas of rapid technical change. The computer industry has been a good example of this in the recent years; its glamour and sophisticated technology have attracted many who actually have little idea of what computer work comprises. These new glamour jobs will most likely be filled by the better-educated.

What, then, are the chances for blue-collar children to meet the high minimum educational requirements for white-collar employment and the new prestige jobs?

BLUE COLLARS AND HIGH SCHOOL

Studies of high school drop-out rates suggest that the principal wage earner ranks lower on the occupational scale in a dropout's family than in that of a student who stayed in school. Coleman's and

Sexton's studies make a similar correlation between dropping out and low family income.[8] They argue that students from families in the lower socioeconomic groupings tend to have lower reading and verbal skills, to be taught by less-qualified teachers, to fail more often and be held back, and eventually to drop out of the schools. Recent data indicate that the lower socioeconomic groups continue to get the least from the educational system.

However, Bowman and Matthews found in 1960 that socioeconomic groupings need to be scrutinized carefully to gauge the effect of class on drop-out rates.[9] They argue that drop-out rates become significant only in the lowest socioeconomic categories and that lower-middle-class students (many of whom would be from blue-collar families) had graduation rates above their representation in the sample.

Socioeconomic class	*Percent of sample*	*Percent of graduates*	*Percent of dropouts*
Lower middle	25	31	10
Upper lower	38	27	41
Lower lower	27	20	47

Further, it was noted above that, in 1970, 41 percent of blue-collar men had completed high school. It is generally agreed that the level of education attained by a father most often sets the minimum to be attained by the majority of his progeny. In the past, the process of educational escalation by generation has occurred in this way, as can be seen in surveys of school retention rates over several decades. If this trend continues, we can expect an ever-increasing number of high school graduates in blue-collar families.

It is interesting to speculate why there is a greater proportion of high school graduates today than in the past. Several elements may account for this improved retention. First, increasing employer demands for more education have kept many students in school for the few critical extra years. Second, changing assumptions about education, particularly among working-class Americans, may also be important. Many immigrant families attached little or no importance to formal schooling per se. Now there seems to be a growing belief in the American educational ethic among children and grandchildren of immigrant families. The later generations have absorbed more of the American value system which regards education as a very useful commodity. While the high school continues to act as a sifter, there is growing pressure from families, employers, and the general public to retain the students longer and to devise ways of improving their learning. These methods include the growth in new curricula, textbooks, and programmed instruction. Although it is extremely difficult to measure the effects of these efforts on performance, it is clear that they are keeping greater numbers of blue-collar students in school for longer periods of time.

BLUE COLLARS AND COLLEGE

Many blue-collar families hope to provide college education for their children, though they experience difficulty in getting their children into college and paying for the education. The argument is that most blue collars have limited savings and that their incomes tend to level off just as their children would enroll in college. This income squeeze is said to keep many blue-collar children out of college and to account for their low representation on campuses today. However, the data do not entirely support these arguments. As a matter of fact, working-class parents have managed fairly well to enroll their children as both full- and part-time college students (Table 42).

TABLE 42
COLLEGE ENROLLMENT BY FAMILY INCOME AND OCCUPATION IN 1969 FRESHMAN CLASS

Family income or occupation	*Percent of 2-year-college freshmen enrollment*	*Percent of 4-year-college freshmen enrollment*	*Percent in population, 1969*
Blue-collar father	34	26	30 (approx.)
Less than $4,000	7	6	16
$4,000 to $9,999	46	38	44
$10,000 to $14,999	28	29	25
$15,000 and over	19	27	15

SOURCE: American Council on Education and U.S. Bureau of the Census.

The Census Bureau's figures on the percentage of college-age children who go to college show, by income group, the same fairly high level of blue-collar participation. The participation rate of college-age blue-collar children varies from 32 to 50 percent (Table 43).

Although schoolteachers, clerical sales personnel, and other non-blue-collar workers account for some of the families in the $7,500 to $9,999 category, a significant number of blue-collar workers have dependents attending college full time.

Although middle- and upper-level blue-collar families are represented on college campuses about proportionately to their representation in the population, the lower-income groups—primarily those with incomes below $5,000—are not well represented. The places which children from these families might have occupied seem to be filled instead by children from the $15,000 plus grouping, who are overrepresented in the college classroom. The higher-income groups get proportionately more than their share, and the lower groups less; the middle-income groups get approximately their share. In a study of California's higher education system Hansen and Weisbrod noted the same effect when they considered costs paid for and benefits received from education. The benefits increased with income; for example, the average family with an income of $8,800 received a $40 net benefit from taxes and subsidies whereas the family with a $12,000 income received a net benefit of $790.[10]

TABLE 43
FAMILIES WITH DEPENDENT MEMBERS 18 TO 24 YEARS OLD AND PERCENTAGE WITH DEPENDENTS ATTENDING COLLEGE FULL TIME, BY FAMILY INCOME, OCTOBER 1968

Annual family income	*Number of families with dependent members 18–24 years old (in thousands)*	*Percentage of families with dependents in college full time*
$5,000 to $7,499	1,600	32
$7,500 to $9,999	1,501	41
$10,000 to $14,999	1,876	50
$15,000 and over	1,194	63

SOURCE: U.S. Bureau of the Census.

While this represents a significant inequity in the distribution of educational resources, it does not seriously affect a large number of blue-collar workers, whose income usually falls in the $7,000 to $15,000 group. The two-year junior or community college, particularly the publicly supported institution, has accounted for much of the new blue-collar college enrollment. The number of these schools has doubled in the last 10 years, and their average enrollment increases at the rate of 6 percent per year.

The two-year college seems to attract students of average academic achievement and socioeconomic level, many of whom could neither qualify for nor afford a university or four-year college education. It rarely enrolls a large proportion of the poor or minorities in the community. Many two-year-college students aim not at a baccalaureate but at an associate degree or a series of specialized courses. Many of the new technocraftsmen have received this shortened kind of higher education. Most of these students say that vocational or professional training is their immediate goal.

The two-year colleges are interesting, as well, from the viewpoint of social and occupational mobility. A survey of California's community colleges found that while 32 percent of the students came from "professional or managerial" families, 64 percent, or twice that number, aspired to this occupational level. In the four-year colleges the discrepancy between family background and student aspiration is smaller. Thus, it seems that the junior college is regarded as a stepping-stone by many blue-collar children.

The federal government has four main college assistance programs which are available to needy students. Of the 7 million students in college in 1968, 2 million received some federal assistance in the form of loans, stipends, or grants. In four programs, the majority of the funds go to persons whose family income is below $9,000 (Table 44). Thus, these programs are of greater assistance to the lower-level blue-collar worker than to his more highly paid coworker.

Other formidable obstacles may prevent blue-collar families from enrolling their children even in the two-year-college system. Cost is the main item. Surveys of students' financial status indicate that blue-collar students and students in two-year colleges receive smaller percentages of loans, scholarships, and fellowships than white-collar or four-year-college students do. Among two-year-

TABLE 44

DISTRIBUTION OF FEDERAL ASSISTANCE RECIPIENTS BY FAMILY INCOME LEVELS, 1968

Federal program	*Number of recipients (in thousands)*	*Percent of families with incomes*		
		Below $6,000	*$6,000–$8,999*	*$9,000 and over*
National Defense Education Loan	455	49	28	23
Coop Work-Study Payments	367	61	26	13
Equal Opportunity Grant	255	69	26	5
Guaranteed Loan Program	922	33	24	43

SOURCE: U.S. Office of Education.

college students, 24 percent are assisted by loans, grants, and scholarships; 39 percent of four-year-college students use these financial aids. Certainly the fact that many two-year colleges usually cost less than $1,000 per year and four-year colleges more than $1,000 influences the use of these financial aid programs. However, the fact remains that for many blue-collar families even the two-year-college costs are a strain. Thus, part-time work and student savings accounts seem to cover a larger portion of fees for blue-collar or two-year than for white-collar or four-year students.

Additional educational subsidies and opportunities for blue-collar workers are needed. Current suggestions for increased loan and grant programs, open enrollment, and tax relief for education expenses are among others which should be considered. These changes could have significant impact on blue-collar college enrollment.

ADAPTING THE EDUCATIONAL SYSTEM TO NEW NEEDS

The last decade saw tremendous increases in educational enrollments, expenditures, teachers, and administrators. The diversity of the student population increases annually: various age, economic, occupational, and racial groups are represented in expanding numbers. These changes argue for adjustments to increase the ability of the system to meet varied needs.

The 1950s and 1960s saw two important educational developments: first, a reassessment of educational objectives and performance in the sputnik scare; and second, a series of compensatory educational programs based on the notion that "equality of opportunity" consisted in specialized programs for the special needs of minority groups and poor. The civil rights movement was largely responsible for establishing the latter notion in the school system. Until that time, the main distinctions made between educational needs were between the very slow and the very bright. In many cases, the slow were routed to the vocational education system while the bright went further up the academic ladder. Now, as participation increases among diverse groups, there is an even more pressing need to widen the types of educational programs. The slow and the bright, the minorities and the poor, represent only a tiny sample of specialized needs—as the new ingroup, the "alienated" blue collars, do.

Blue collars may indeed be alienated; but there is evidence that youth, minorities, college students, white-collar managers, and elderly people are, too. Blue-collar deprivation should be examined critically in relation to the problems of the very poor, who are still the most in need of educational benefits. The new blue-collar limelight must not be used to turn the public conscience from the most serious national inequities.

However, blue-collar educational needs are valid and deserve attention along with the special needs of other groups. The educational system needs to broaden its focus to include programs that meet the modern multiplicity of demands. Peter Schrag noted in a recent article that "if we want to understand why the schools have failed, we have only to state the criteria of success. The schools achieved their reputation when they did not have to succeed, when there were educational alternatives—the farm, the shop, the apprenticeship—and when there were other routes to economic and social advancement."[11]

We have been educating with two general curricula—vocational and academic—in a fairly uniform system of instruction and school organization. The system may need to be broadened to include educational paths such as those which now exist and are utilized on the outside. The modern equivalents of Schrag's farming, shop, and apprenticeship should be brought into the system.

Such changes would operate on three levels: the educational institutions themselves, the curriculum, and the students. First, the peripheral institutions should be drawn into the accredited school system. Many of the nonaccredited schools have high-quality educational programs worthy of accreditation. Many are small and have flexible schedules to accommodate day and night, employed and unemployed students. The large numbers enrolled in peripheral institutions are a testimony to their growing importance in the nation's social and educational activities.

These schools presently serve diverse income and occupational groups who choose not to reenroll in the traditional schools. In the past, the established school system has scorned the courses of "peripheral institutions" as "below standards." As noted above, this distinction may be shortsighted and somewhat class-biased, for the "outside" educators are an important source of educational opportunities for many Americans. The past effort to exclude the peripheral institutions is most likely an attempt to cut the educational pie into as few pieces as possible.

Established educational institutions should also open their doors further to admit the continuing-education student. The increasing pace of technical change, increased leisure time, and ongoing respect for education as a good in itself all argue for keeping educational entry open throughout a person's lifetime rather than viewing it as a preparatory step.

There is a need to integrate more effectively general technical and academic education. Specific occupational training may be more efficiently handled by industry. The rapid pace of technological change makes it difficult for vocational schools to keep up with changing skill, equipment, and instructional requirements. A more reasonable role for schools is to provide broad technical and academic knowledge and leave job training to the employers. If there is still a need for some skill certification and testing, schools and colleges could fill this role as a service to industry.

The community colleges are a likely place for experimentation with an integrated curriculum. Their students usually seek both academic and vocational education. Owing to their newness, the two-year colleges also have the fewest years of academic habit and tradition to overcome in designing experimental programs. They could begin to develop a higher-education equivalent of the comprehensive high school.

On the student level, experiments with vested or voucher educational funds are to be encouraged, allowing students a sum of money to spend in any educational institution at any time. Such a system could open the educational options of a student to the full range of educational facilities that now exist. Again, certification of some sort could be provided by an outside authority.

Education might also be useful as an issue in collective bargaining, especially since unions seem to need new collective bargaining issues. Continuing education could fill this gap. Companies now pay health and welfare costs on the theory that in return they get a more productive work force; workers could begin to argue for the extention of this policy to educational benefits. This would provide a new agenda, in which unions could involve themselves and redevelop their former advocacy role. It would give the unions a source of new sophisticated leadership. They need this, first, because technocraftsmen will assume an increasingly important role in plant operations. Unions need to develop ways to involve this new class of workers in their affairs. Second, the world is becoming even more complex, and unions need to be involved in learning about the complexities if they are to play a key role in a changing society. For example, the issue of "participation" will continue to grow. Unions need people who understand how participatory schemes can fit into huge organizations like General Motors or U.S. Steel. Third, private enterprise is moving into education, and if for no other reason than assuring their advocacy role for union membership, unions ought to be involved.

The rising educational attainment of the work force is a factor for disruptive but positive change. When higher educational levels are not met immediately by greater opportunity and challenge, increasing demands and restlessness should be expected in the workplace. The constant rise in turnover rates, absenteeism, and lateness have all been analyzed by industrial and human-behavior specialists as symptoms of dissatisfaction with the job. "People want more meaningful work" has almost become a slogan of industry.

It seems evident that at least some of the new demands come from the better-educated work force. This can be viewed as positive effect. Education is preparing workers for more advanced jobs and stimulating them to demand more meaning in the jobs they have already. The educational system should continue this role. However, if it is to meet the more and more varied needs of the student body, it must move away from the notion that equality of opportunity is synonymous with uniformity of opportunity. The 1960s saw some progress in this direction with compensatory programs. A greater variety of educational institutions, curricula, and financial aids would better meet the different and unequal needs of students in the seventies.

NOTES

1. Eva Mueller, *Technological Advance in an Expanding Economy,* The University of Michigan, Institute of Social Research, Ann Arbor, 1969.
2. Ivar Berg, *Education and Jobs: The Great Training Robbery,* Praeger, New York, 1970, p. 59.
3. Howard Rosen, Director, Office of Research and Development, Manpower Administration, U.S. Department of Labor, "Findings of Manpower Research: Relevance to Training," presented at American Society for Training and Development, Twenty-sixth National Conference, May 12, 1970, Anaheim, Calif.
4. Ibid.
5. John L. Iacobelli, "Training Programs of Private Industry in the Greater Cleveland Area," unpublished doctoral dissertation, University of Texas at Austin, June 1969.
6. William M. Smith, "White-collar Pay in Private Industry," *Monthly Labor Review,* April 1970, pp. 59–62.
7. Mueller, op. cit.
8. James Coleman, *Equality of Educational Opportunity,* Government Printing Office, Washington, 1964; and Patricia Cayo Sexton, *Education and Income: Inequalities in Our Public Schools,* Viking Press, New York, 1969.
9. Paul Bowman and Charles Matthews, *Motivations for Youth for Leaving School,* University of Chicago and Quincy Youth Development Project, Quincy, Ill., September 1960, p. 24.
10. W. Lee Hansen and Burton A. Weisbrod, "The Distribution of Costs and Direct Benefits of Public Higher Education: The Case of California," *Journal of Human Resources,* Spring 1969, pp. 176–191.
11. Peter Schrag, "End of the Impossible Dream," *Saturday Review,* September 1970, p. 68.

14. DIRECTIONS FOR ACTION

by Jerome M. Rosow

Awareness of both the validity and the significance of a national problem is a necessary precondition to any effective response. Chapter 3 presented the diagnosis that is necessary though not sufficient in facing up to that problem. We have tried to lay a factual base that demonstrates the scope and intensity of the problems facing lower-income workers. Because these problems are shared and deeply felt by such a large slice of the American labor force, they should command the attention of policy decision makers at all levels—government, business, community leaders, and concerned citizens generally.

It would certainly be a mistake to assume that the federal government has either some exclusive concern over, or some special capability to handle, these problems. Of course, many key actions can be taken at the federal level. National economic policy has a major role to play in creating conditions which contribute to economic relief for this group. The Nixon administration has steered a course designed to reach an effective balance between the twin objectives of stemming inflationary pressures and maximizing employment opportunities. These objectives will remain in the forefront of the administration's priority list. Moreover, national legislation in the areas of crime and public disturbance, revenue sharing, environment, consumer protection, and health will all have positive impact on our entire society, but perhaps it will go even further in meeting the needs and grievances of those in the lower-middle-income group. Comparable legislation at the state and local levels will, of course, be helpful.

Employers and unions also have special responsibilities. Some will argue that a worker's general welfare is not a proper or necessary concern of his employer. The argument neglects the fact that an employer's economic interests are usually affected by a worker's total life pattern. A nerve-racking journey to the job may adversely affect a worker's patience and performance on a particularly tedious job chore. Workers victimized by crime in the community may be compelled to miss work altogether. Job dissatisfaction is often expressed in low product quality, visits to medical departments, and high turnover. It is no concession to paternalism to suggest that employers must consider the worker's environment and life-style, for these seriously affect on-the-job productivity.

It should also be made clear at the outset that any new programs or policies should not be at the expense of the poor. Nor should attention to the workingman be construed as favoritism for whites; there is a heavy concentration of racial minorities in the same occupational and income groups. Reform and policy should reflect sensitivity to the problem of the lower-middle-income worker, not insensitivity to other groups.

The problems facing this group might be addressed in a variety of ways, and what follows is not intended as an exhaustive list. Some of the suggestions would require new legislation; others require administrative action by public authorities. Some are proper concerns at the collective bargaining table; others imply changes in action and attitude by every citizen. Many of the suggestions address more than one of the three general forms of pressure identified in Chapter 3. Most of them are a proper responsibility of a wide band of institutions and individuals, public and private employers, unions, and social and political leaders at local as well as national levels. But they all stem from an underlying conviction that the matter is of such importance to the health of our society that every significant area of new activity of our public and private institutions should take into consideration its effects on this group and its problems.

1. Education. The development of a strong system of continuing education in the United States holds one of the best hopes not only for increasing earning power but for easing other problems: the availability of adult education can minimize the dead-end feeling that results when a worker lacks the education necessary to move up the job ladder, develop the political awareness that makes it more possible to control one's destiny in a democracy, and help to establish, at community colleges or adult extension courses, the common meeting ground that often lessens the impact of racial and ethnic stereotypes.

The higher-education legislation proposed by President Nixon would provide material help to this income group by directing funds to postsecondary technical and career training and channeling both grants and loans specifically to children of families making below $10,000 per year. Additional funds and increased authorities through the Adult Education Act of 1965 and the Vocational Education Act of 1968 will also help to broaden the opportunities for employees to increase their salability in the job market.

Special efforts are needed to link industry training efforts with adult education. State programs under the Adult Education Act are often planned independently of labor market and workers' needs. Such planning should be related more closely to instruction available in plants, to skill shortages, and to workers' schedules. Furthermore, it should be based on more realistic credential requirements for both teachers and students. A strong formal link between education and manpower planning agencies would help accomplish these goals.

Television has great, but as yet barely tapped, potential educational benefit for the workingman. Through this medium, residents of remote and depressed areas can be exposed to job opportunities. Demand projections for occupations can be targeted to youth. An immediate visual description of working conditions in various industries and urban conditions in different cities can help workers make intelligent decisions about a job and a place to live. Educational television can also provide adult education and training both in the evening for the husband and during the day for wives who can't attend formal training classes because of economic constraints or family responsibilities.

2. Upgrading. Employer-sponsored training and education designed to add to the existing skills of employed individuals are one of the key ways of drawing upon untapped capabilities and permitting people to work out of dead-end jobs. The Department of Labor has sponsored programs to stimulate greater private-sector activity in this area and has funded a nationwide program in the public sector as well. The road is all uphill, however. Basically, management does not tend to view upgrading as a necessary component of sound management, and many first-line supervisors are hostile. Such success as has been enjoyed by the Labor Department's upgrading programs is often attributed to special efforts to overcome supervisors' low estimation of low-level workers' potential, their inability to train workers, and the threat posed by upwardly mobile subordinates.

Upgrading of skills, coupled with job redesign and development of career ladders, should play a more significant role in the collective bargaining process. The state Employment Services also can be helpful in determining which industries should be selected for special assistance, linking schools with employers to develop supplemental job-related training, and stimulating and aiding employers to train supervisors.

3. Employment Service Reforms. More timely information about jobs will be a great boon to those seeking better employment. A national program of job banks to cover major labor market areas is now being instituted, and the results should be evident in the years to come. Employment Service offices could be kept open at night and on Saturday to serve millions of employed people who find it difficult to spend any significant time searching for a job during working hours.

4. Part-time Jobs. More youths and women want to enter the labor force. The models of full-time housewife and student become more obsolete as housework is increasingly automated and as youths, regardless of family income, seek both work experience and the personal freedom that is often equated with economic independence. The number of industries that tend to use part-time workers is expected to grow, but there is need for additional concentrated efforts to break down the traditional resistance of unions and private and public employers to this practice. Part-time work offers many advantages to both the employer and society as well as the individual. More part-time jobs can help alleviate morning and evening traffic jams. Part-time workers may also increase the productivity of a firm; a student, housewife, or older worker who does not view his part-time job as a career and whose work hours are limited should be less alienated by the routine or repetitive jobs that often cause boredom and inferior production. Employers could tap the part-time labor market, probably at lower wages, to increase productivity and lower turnover.

5. Sex Discrimination. A forceful attack on discriminatory wages, hiring, and promotion practices for women is needed to open up opportunities for women of all income levels. Discrimination against educated women for managerial jobs seems to have a depressant effect on all women's wages, since it forces many college-educated women to settle for jobs that really could be filled by less-educated women. Such restrictive practices are counterproductive and frequently reflect obsolete standards and value judgments.

6. Child Care. The Nixon administration's Family Assistance Plan would provide free child-care facilities for welfare and "working poor" mothers who work. Child-care facilities available on a partial-fee basis to slightly higher-income groups would increase earning power and mobility by enabling many more mothers to work and reducing the burden of child-care costs on those now working. Tax relief for child care is now limited to families earning less than $6,900; this figure could be raised to $10,000. Deductions could be increased from $600 to $900 for the first child and from $900 to $1,200 for two or more children. This change could be made with minimum revenue loss. With passage of the FAP, pressure for extended child care will probably mount. These measures would open an enlarged supply of labor which industries can tap, especially with the forecast growth of government and service sectors of the economy.

7. Tax Policy. The Tax Reform Act of 1969 reduces taxes for families earning $5,000 to $10,000. However, additional measures need to be considered: for example, the possibility of increasing the amount of tax exemption for older children in families with incomes below $10,000. It may be hoped that President Nixon's revenue-sharing program will gain further support, for it will tend to help this group by raising taxes through the progressive federal tax system rather than through the often regressive local and state systems. Overall tax policy decisions at local and state levels should also become more sensitive to these lower-income groups.

8. Transportation. Mass transit will go far to meet the pinch caused by automobile expenses, a major cost item for these and all other workers. Without access to such public travel modes, two cars for the $5,000 to $10,000 income family are not a luxury but a necessary condition of economic survival.

9. Workplace Conditions. The Occupational Health and Safety Act will respond to a prime area of improvement needed by workers. Some 14,000 workers are killed on the job each year, and time lost from accidents costs five times as much as labor strikes. Beyond that, both the public and private sector need to examine the work environment in terms of current conditions and reasonable expectations. The formation of employer consortiums might make it possible to extend health and other benefits to employees not now receiving coverage. New attempts should be made to develop modern temporary disability insurance and workmen's compensation systems.

The results of pioneering efforts to relieve monotony by job redesign or job rotation and to increase morale by participation in decision making indicate dramatic improvements. In fact, such experiments have shown profit increases. Training that increases supervisors' sensitivity to worker expectations can reduce one of the major blue-collar complaints: dissatisfaction with treatment by supervisors. Improvement in the way first-line supervisors relate to subordinates or handle grievances will have a positive influence on both individual worker morale and total plant production. Employer concerns with the workplace need not be altruistic. Workplace conditions affect morale, turnover, product quality, absenteeism, and labor costs. The University of Michigan survey findings should alert industry to look inward and relate working conditions to profit goals.

10. Incentive Systems and Thrift Plans. Increased attention should be given to offering blue-collar workers the kind of opportunities more often limited to middle management and executives. Profit sharing, the highly effective Scanlon system of sharing cost reductions, and employee thrift plans are constructive ways to relieve the economic pressures and the dead-end feeling that affect lower-middle-income workers.

11. Housing. Action has been taken to pump more mortgage money into the housing market; this should increase the houses available to low-income workers and reduce their cost. The most significant potential for reducing housing costs is probably in Operation Breakthrough and other efforts to increase productivity in construction. At the same time existing housing legislation can be more effectively applied and related to the housing needs of lower-income families ($7,500 or less). The administration has turned its attention to this objective. Interest rate subsidy programs directed to this group have already grown dramatically.

12. Recreation Facilities. Recreation and vacations, a major problem for the lower-middle-income worker and his family, should be made more available through vest-pocket parks, more development of public lands near metropolitan areas, and mortgage guarantees for low-income recreation facilities.

13. Job Status. It is a tragic by-product of the proliferation of higher education that individuals without college or advanced degrees have lost status. This has lowered the dignity of blue-collar workers more than that of their white-collar income equals. Not everyone wants to or should go to college, and not all jobs require a college education. We must find a way to recapture the traditional pride associated with working at a necessary job—no matter what the educational requirements of the job. Improvement of the work environment is critical in this respect. National awards for craftsmen will make a contribution. More effective job guidance and counseling by secondary schools are also necessary. This is not an easy problem to solve, and innovative measures will be needed. If workers became actively involved with vocational guidance, spending a few hours a week, on the employer's time, to bring reality into the schools and involve themselves in the mainstream of community concerns, they might help change the aspirations of young people and improve their own job performance.

14. Model Public Employers. We have just begun to explore what the federal government can do for its own employees. It should go farther than the announced policy of wages comparable with private employment. On nonwage matters, it should become a model employer by careful attention to such things as upgrading possibilities, subsidized child care, part-time employment for women, and perhaps partially subsidized recreation and vacation facilities for low-income federal workers. State and local governments would do well to set a similar example.

15. Pensions. Private pension reform is an area with great potential for lower-income workers, and it should be a major agenda item for both unions and management. Higher-paid executives often enjoy pension privileges not available to lower-income workers, many of whom are not covered in any plan at all. For those who are covered, the benefits are usually inadequate, and the period of time they must stay with the individual employer to qualify is excessive. Legislation to tighten the fiduciary responsibilities of pension-plan administrators has already been placed before the Congress, and it should be followed by legislation to ensure that covered employees are vested with pension rights after a period of no more than 10 years of employment.

The above list of proposals, as indicated at the outset, is only tentative and exploratory. It suggests the breadth and variety of constructive actions that can be taken to relieve the problems of this group. Much work needs to be done in moving beyond the proposal stage to concrete action; and at the federal level that process is already well under way. But these suggestions are not revolutionary: they do not challenge or wrench apart existing institutions of our society; nor do they discriminate against any social or economic group in order to aid the lower-income worker. They are, above all, "doable."

At the same time, the breadth, depth, and duration of the problems facing this group suggest some limitations on the speed and the effect of any remedial action. Americans are famous for their propensity to list problems and target solutions on the first calendar at hand. The road to disappointment is quickly paved by such glibness, notwithstanding the best of intentions. In recent years the federal government has been all too ready to promise the moon. In this case, we should recognize in advance that we are looking at a long-range problem. Moreover, these various possibilities will obviously need to be examined in the context of other competing programs, policies, and national needs, in the search for the best and most balanced achievement of national goals. At the very least, we have added the lower-middle-income worker to the active list of national goals; at the best, the private and public leadership of our country at all levels will deliver improvements for these workers in a manner which will advance the cause of our entire nation.

These caveats should not, however, be an excuse for inactivity. Both the well-being of American society as a whole and simple justice for millions require a constructive response to the problems of lower-middle-income workers. These frustrated individuals, caught in a situation from which they see no escape, are likely to vent their feelings in actions harmful to both themselves and society. Beyond that, our system of values signals that something is very wrong when conscientious, able, and hardworking people cannot make it. Our response should be in proportion to the seriousness of that charge.

15. HOT UNDER THE BLUE COLLAR

by Fred R. Harris

"What do those people want?"

That was a question my father asked me when I was embroiled in the controversy surrounding the findings and recommendations of the Kerner Commission. We had reported on the causes and prevention of the kinds of terrible urban riots which had flared up in the night skies above the black sections of so many American cities during the explosive summer of 1967.

My father lives on—and lives from—a very small farm in southwestern Oklahoma. There is great satisfaction for him in the fact that he now owns (together with the mortgage company) the first place he lived on in Oklahoma as a small boy, after his parents left Mississippi in the early 1900s and came out West as sharecroppers. He has worked hard all his life because he has had to. He kept food on our table by working at various times as a mechanic, a truck driver, a sharecropper, a day laborer, a roughneck, a carpenter's helper, a mule skinner, a cattle buyer, a bus driver, a custom wheat harvester, and a farmer.

"What do those people want?" he asked, puzzled and put off by the harsh rhetoric of freshly militant blacks, no longer willing to accept compromises and delays.

"They want what you want," I answered.

Today, I am often asked what men like my father want. The answer is the same. "They want what you want." They want more power. They want to feel more important. They want a better slice of the pie.

A great deal has been written about the breaking up of the old progressive coalition in America. Kevin Phillips wrote what I think is an immoral book, *The Emerging Republican Majority,* asserting in effect that Republicans need not fool with the complaints of poor people and black people and those who live in the central cities, since these groups are a part of the natural constituency of the Democratic party. Continued identification of the Democratic party with these troublemakers, he said, would drive blue-collar workers and "middle Americans" into the Republican party in increasing droves.

Richard Scammon and Ben Wattenberg wrote what I think is an amoral book, *The Real Majority,* declaring that the "social issue"—race, crime, dope, and related matters—had come to be dominant in the thinking of the machinist's wife in Dayton. Find the middle, they told politicians, and get there as fast as you can.

The blue-collar worker is not as dumb as some think. Nor is he as evil as some would have us believe. The Dayton housewife voted Democratic in 1970. CBS reported that the Wallace voter of 1968, more often than not, became a Democratic voter in 1970. Indeed, surveys show that the guy in Queens may be less racist than the Westchester County commuter. Agnew's "soft on crime" attacks on the "radical liberals" mostly backfired. Nixon's suspect confrontations with young people probably cost his party votes.

Members of the old coalition have not left home, but they would like to hear "I love you" now and then. Old coalitions never die; their people just quit talking to each other.

The blue-collar worker has legitimate complaints, but too often he feels no one is listening to him. The tougher complaints are those of powerlessness and lack of self-worth and the absence of a sufficient sense of community. There is evidence that black people and Chicanos and American Indians and young people are, as is said these days, getting it together. Members of these groups have developed, or are developing, a kind of "soul," a zestful life-style, pride in group, and heroes. People listen to them and emulate them. The blue-collar worker increasingly wants more of these things for himself. He has legitimate complaints, and his *economic* complaints are the easiest to answer—if we will act.

It is a public outrage that there are men out of work when there is plenty of work that needs to be done. It is a scandal that there are short work weeks and idle plant capacity when legitimate needs for goods and housing go unsatisfied. People, most of all, want to work. We have taught them that. "Make your own way," we have said. But telling a man that work is the only way to achieve dignity, and then denying him that chance for dignity, is indefensible.

For President Nixon to have promised near-full employment by 1972 is to admit the assertion of one noted economist that "Republicans seem only to worry about people being out of work in even-numbered years." My father, who never had a high school education, was not far wrong when he said, "Things always get better at election time."

When you think about it, it is almost unbelievable that grown men would say that some men have to go jobless or with fewer working hours as the neccessary and inevitable cost of bringing down prices. I am reminded of my old fundamentalist grandmother's suspicion that God would have given us wings if he had intended for us to soar the heavens. The trade-off between inflation and unemployment is not predestined.

There must be a strong wage-price income policy—with temporary freezes when necessary—to hold increases within justifiable limits. Adam Smith never reckoned with the fact that some wages and prices can be administered in modern America, without regard for market pressures. Steel and automobile prices were raised, not lowered, in times of decreased demand. Lost volume was made up for in increased unit prices. Despite an idle work force, some wage increases were nevertheless inflationary where labor was sufficiently powerful. Big bankers ought to be embarrassed to say that across-the-board high interest rates and tight money are necessary to bring inflation under control, without regard for regional differences and social goals. "Please don't make us have to charge more for the money we loan, in order to save the nation's economy," they seem to entreat us. President Nixon and others should be ashamed to have supported them.

President Nixon announced an "expansionary budget" in 1970.

That is a euphemism for deficit spending—the kind of deliberate deficit spending he has always attacked heretofore as Democratic extravagance and irresponsibility. But this Republican deficit, conservatively estimated at $16 billion, was different from Democratic deficits. It resulted not from overspending, but from decreased tax collections in a deliberately slowed economy. We would have had at least $16 billion more in federal revenues—think what could have been done with that—if unemployment had been 4 percent instead of 6 percent.

Despite rising unemployment, the President vetoed an important bill which would have paid for new and needed public service jobs. The Reverend Jesse Jackson of Chicago has said, "I don't blame that white trade unionist for not wanting a black man to get his job, and I don't blame the black man for wanting to get that job; I want to see a policy under which they can both have jobs!" That is the kind of common sense that progressive coalitions are made of.

But the assertion that everyone will be happy if only the pie to be cut up keeps getting larger has been proven false. There must be a better division of the pie, whether large or small. Divide the nation's income groups into fifths, and you find that each fifth—top, bottom, and those in between—has about the same share of the nation's wealth and income that each had before the advent of New Deal programs. Maldistribution of wealth and income is still a decided and glaring feature of the American economic panorama. With all our talk about slicing things up a little more fairly, things are about the same, or maybe slightly worse.

Changes in the tax system and higher levels, and broader coverage of minimum wage laws, will help to even things up. Taxes are not fair for the blue-collar worker. He is paying more than his share. State revenues, typically, are too dependent on sales and property taxes, rather than on ability to pay, and there are too many privileges for the special interests.

The federal income tax system also falls short of the progressive mark. A stiffer minimum income tax on people with large incomes, capital gains taxes at death, and other reforms were dropped by the wayside in 1969 after the much-heralded and justified "taxpayers' revolt" of that year was blunted by minimal changes. The tax-reform cause and the potential public support for it still exist.

Tax reform means not only taxing those who pay far less than their fair share, but at the same time providing relief for those who pay more than they should. There's no question that middle-income Americans pay more than they should, not just in federal taxes but in state and local taxes as well. We ought to understand the anger of a man with an annual income of $10,000 who perceives that his taxes are paying for social and welfare services for poor people, and that some rich people are getting by with a lesser tax rate.

Ralph Nader has recently identified another tax inequity which is particularly inequitable for middle-income industrial workers, and he is organizing to do something about it. Nader has found that many industries pay far less than their fair share of local property taxes, mainly through local laws designed to grant incentives to industry to locate or stay in a given area. In highly industrialized areas where industry occupies a relatively large proportion of urban land, lower industrial property tax rates inevitably require proportionately higher tax rates on individual property owners—a rather large number of whom turn out to be blue-collar workers employed in the industries which are undertaxed.

The federal Social Security tax system is even worse than the income tax system. Its burden falls heaviest on the lower-level wage earner. Each worker pays a flat rate, whatever his income. There is no graduation. Moreover, there is an upward limit—$7,800 before the new law in 1970—of annual wages subject to the tax. That is why needed increases in Social Security payments and medical benefits must be financed more and more from federal general-revenue funds. While income taxes are not as progressive as they should be, they are still collected much more on the basis of ability to pay than are the payroll taxes which presently sustain the Social Security system.

The workingman and -woman are paying more than their fair share in other ways. They bear a disproportionate part of the social costs of racial integration. It is most often their jobs which are threatened, their neighborhoods which are changing, their schools where tensions are growing. The special anxieties which result from these changes are real. To say that we understand how it is would be more helpful than most of the moralizing and preachments blue-collar workers hear. To compensate for these extra burdens when we can would be even better. Schools in integrating neighborhoods, for example, should have special funds—enough to make them model schools. They should have the best buildings, not the worst; the most accomplished teachers, not the poorest; the lowest pupil-teacher ratios, not the highest.

The blue-collar worker is frequently just a little too well-off to qualify for many federal programs which were basically designed, and properly so, to aid poor people. A member of the United Auto Workers Union in Tulsa, Oklahoma, recently told me that he lived in a $9,000 house—not a very good house in Tulsa—and that he could buy a new $15,000 house under a federal subsidized-interest program if he earned $1,000 less per year. Understandably, he does not think that program is the best one Congress ever passed, nor is he overly happy about helping to pay for it.

It seems to me there is a general remedy for this common defect in many of our social programs: we ought to amend the laws authorizing those programs to provide a graduated schedule of benefits instead of specifying one cutoff income level which qualifies someone for full benefits if his income is less than that level and completely disqualifies someone whose income is above the level. In that way, a family with $8,000 income might, for example, qualify to receive a 25 percent interest subsidy on a home mortgage, while the really poor family, with an income below $4,000, could get a full subsidy. Just that principle, of course, is incorporated into most proposals for welfare reform, where it is explained as a method for granting incentives for people to earn an income above their welfare payments.

Education has always been seen as the basic and fundamental means by which workers and their children can improve their lives and their income. I think a lot of new proposals ought to be considered and encouraged here. One promising idea is the plan Yale University intends to test, under which any student, regardless of income, can borrow money from Yale to get his degree by agreeing to pay Yale back a fixed percentage of his income for a specified term of years after graduation. I like the scheme very much because it allows students from poor families to go to college without putting impossible financial demands on their families; it also gets those who earn a high income after college to subsidize the college education of those who come from poor families and makes it easier for college graduates to decide to enter relatively low-paying occupations such as teaching, nursing, and other essential human-service jobs. There is possibly a role for the federal government in underwriting or insuring risks involved in this program.

Health is a major, critical area. My wife and I recently learned, for example, of a young working couple in a small Oklahoma town whose first baby was born with a serious birth defect. They incurred medical expenses of $3,000 in the first 48 hours of the baby's life. This burden of expenses is going to wipe them out. A relative of mine just died after many months of illness. In spite of the fact that he and his wife had worked as hard as they could all their lives—most recently running a little café in the town of 2,000 where I grew up—there was no way they could meet the medical costs which arose from his having suffered a stroke. That is outrageous in this richest, most medically knowledgeable country in the history of the world, and we ought not to stand for it. We've got to enact a universal health insurance and health service program in America which is available to all at nominal cost. In the main, I support the major health bill introduced by Senator Kennedy, but I also advocate some additional measures, including a much more rapid and larger increase in medical and paramedical personnel, incentives for group practices, and other means of bringing excellent medical care to people, including lower-middle-income workers and their families, who just aren't getting it.

I've been asked how I would rank such programs in order of importance, and I have refused to try to rank them, aside from stating that programs which increase real income are probably most important. I'm a legislator, involved daily in fighting for whatever we can get—lately it hasn't been much, and it isn't generally helpful to say that one program is more important than another. We have to fight on all fronts.

Health Care. President Nixon vetoed two health measures authorizing hospital construction and setting up a program to increase the number of family doctors. Congress overrode the hospital-construction veto.

Manpower Training. President Nixon vetoed, as already mentioned, a $9.5 billion manpower-training bill which would have reorganized manpower programs and established a public service program for the unemployed.

Education. President Nixon vetoed a $4.4 billion appropriation for federal aid to education. Congress overrode the veto.

Urban Development. The President vetoed the Independent Offices Appropriations Bill which would have provided increased funds for our cities.

Government Blue-Collar Pay Scales. The President approved a white-collar raise for civil servants and vetoed a blue-collar pay raise.

These were all bills which would have benefited a large percentage of blue-collar workers. While opposing them, the Nixon administration nevertheless pressed Congress to approve a multi-billion dollar antimissile defense system (ABM) and to appropriate hundreds of millions of dollars for an SST and a space shuttle. Congress also granted a $2.4 billion investment tax credit to big business.

I end where I began. What do the blue-collar workers want? They want the same things that other groups want—income, education, decent homes, jobs, health care, importance. This carries an important lesson for politicians. It means that political leaders have a special responsibility. They must take care to formulate popular grievances in ways that draw blue-collar workers and black people together, instead of driving them apart.

Experts like Irving Levine and Judith Herman have pointed out that if the country is to avoid political splintering, political leaders must engage in "bridge building" among the various groups of our society on a whole host of current issues. It can be done.

The blue-collar worker will continue to be a progressive so long as it is not progress for everyone but himself.

16. THE BLUE-COLLAR WORKER WEATHERS THE "ORDEAL OF CHANGE"

by Sar A. Levitan and Robert Taggart III

THE BLUE-COLLAR BLUES THEME

The litany of alleged blue-collar woes is lengthy and complex: the real spendable income of the working-class American in recent years has remained unchanged in the face of growing needs; jobs are becoming less attractive as expectations rise and some jobs become more mechanized; progress of the poor and the minorities has undermined the social and economic status of white blue-collar workers while the gains of the educated technical and professional class have left them further behind; changing cultural values have challenged their way of life, upsetting family cohesiveness, religious institutions, moral behavior, and consumption patterns; political parties have neglected their interests, alienating them from the rest of society; and the mechanisms for self-improvement have broken down because economic advancement is increasingly dependent on education that is beyond the means of blue-collar families.

Each of these problems subsumes a whole host of difficulties that have psychological, sociological, and political, as well as economic, ramifications. There are 70 million persons living in families headed by blue-collar workers, here identified as craftsmen, foremen, operatives, and nonfarm laborers, whose annual income is concentrated between $5,000 and $10,000. The troubles and anxieties of such an inclusive group understandably touch on every major institution in our society.

One common thread that seems to tie together the disparate problems and complaints of blue-collar workers is an apprehensive view of the future. A Gallup poll of middle Americans in September 1969 found that 46 percent agreed that the United States had changed for the worse over the past decade, with only 36 percent feeling that conditions had improved. Moreover, these citizens looked ahead with pessimism: 58 percent believed that things are likely to get even worse over the next decade, and only 19 percent disagreed.[1] Clearly, "the times, they are a-changin'" and the majority of blue-collar workers view the changes with misgivings.

But everyone faces change with apprehension. Blue-collar workers are not the only ones who are upset by shifting moral values or by the rapid pace of social and economic developments. The issue is not whether they have anxieties and adjustment difficulties as a result of change, but whether these are more deep-seated and pervasive than for others in the population or whether they are a source of potential disruption.

There are several plausible reasons why blue-collar workers might have been especially hurt by or unable to cope with recent changes. They might be on the whole less flexible and adaptive than others. Not as well educated as white-collar workers, they may not be able to understand or adjust to the rapid swirl of events, assuming that education fosters flexibility and adaptation. Their lives regulated by puritan ethics and confined by limited opportunities, they may be preoccupied with defending themselves against threats from below. It is also possible that change has had an especially adverse effect on the economic, social, and psychological well-being of blue-collar workers. They may be the ones who are challenged most by the progress toward racial equality, the ones who feel the constant threat of technological unemployment or erosion of skills, and the ones whose budgets are squeezed the hardest by rising taxes and rising prices. The normal mechanisms for adjusting to and cushioning the effects of change might also have broken down. The politicians, schools, and churches may be increasingly out of touch with blue-collar needs, no longer providing the solace and assistance which they gave in the past.

If blue-collar workers are in fact more inflexible, if recent developments have injured them more than others, and if the institutional and personal mechanisms for adjustment have broken down, then the consequences could be dire. Eric Hoffer, the working-class philosopher, has put it this way:

> When a population undergoing drastic change is without abundant opportunities for individual action and self-advancement, it develops a hunger for faith, pride and unity. It becomes receptive to all manner of proselytizing, and is eager to throw itself into collective undertakings which aim at "showing the world." . . . We are usually told that revolutions are set in motion to realize radical changes. Actually it is drastic change which sets the stage for revolution. The revolutionary mood and temper are generated by the irritations, difficulties, hungers and frustrations inherent in the realization of drastic change.[2]

The need to alleviate any "irritations, difficulties, hungers and frustrations" which will lead to social disruption is vital in the interests of a stable and orderly society. It is, therefore, imperative to ask whether these allegations apply to blue-collar workers. Have they, in fact, been left without an anchor in a world which is constantly adrift? Have they weathered the "ordeal of change," cushioning themselves from adversity and adjusting, albeit grudgingly, to the demands of a rapidly changing society?

The answers to such questions are necessarily equivocal. There are no standards to judge what is a "normal" adjustment or a "reasonable" burden of change. To complicate matters, different measures of the problems yield significantly different answers. Preferences expressed to the opinion survey interviewer may differ from those expressed in the voting booth. Objective measures may be misleading where the problems are subjective and the intensity of feeling cannot be judged. The seriousness of the blue-collar problem depends, therefore, upon subjective measures and standards used to evaluate its dimensions.

Much of the recent analysis of blue-collar conditions has been problem-oriented, focusing on the ways the system may work against the welfare of manual workers. This concern with dysfunction is selective and ignores the positive aspects of much that is satisfying in blue-collar life. Concentrating upon the troubles and frustrations which may plague manual workers, the analyses tend to gloss over the prevailing contentment, security, and successful adjustment to change.

An alternative way to assess the seriousness of blue-collar problems is to assume that society and the economy are functioning reasonably well. This hypothesis is supported by overwhelming evidence. The total net national product and real per capita income have continued to grow in recent years as the only recession in a decade was short-lived and the economic downturn brief. The educational attainments of the population are on the rise, and the leisure enjoyed is increasing. Nonetheless, the fact that society has undergone rapid and potentially disruptive changes cannot be denied. Manifestations of these changes can be found in support of third-party candidates, antiwar protests, student unrest, and the questioning if not rejection of long-held values and mores. The hypothesis examined in this chapter is that the working class is able to adjust to new developments under the assumption that the existing frustrations, anxieties, and difficulties are part of life's unavoidable travails. Operating under this hypothesis, one must analyze blue-collar problems to determine whether they are outside the limits of the tolerances built into the American social mechanism.[3] From this perspective, the relevant questions would be threefold:

First, is there evidence that blue-collar workers are more inflexible to change than other classes and inherently less capable of adaptation?

Second, is there any persuasive evidence that change has had unduly adverse effects on blue-collar workers?

Third, are there substantive indications that the institutional and personal mechanisms for adjustment have broken down?

This approach permits a balanced perspective for assessing the blue-collar problem. It does not deny the existence of difficulties or understate the need for ameliorative measures; rather, it tries to weigh the good with the bad so that problems and pathologies will not be overestimated. Quite clearly, this approach can tell us when there is, indeed, a threat of violent reaction to the ordeal of change.

IS THE BLUE COLLAR STARCHED?

Despite the wide diversity among blue-collar workers, there is also evidence of considerably homogeneity. With an income normally between $5,000 and $10,000 annually and with 11 to 12 years of education, blue-collar life-styles cannot differ very widely. Usually working at manual jobs for an hourly wage and in a factory setting, these workers are subject to similar disciplines and share many problems and satisfactions, frequently including common characteristics of ethnicity.

Attitudes and behavior are significantly affected by income, education, work, and ethnic backgrounds. Because manual workers have many such characteristics in common and because they differ in significant ways from other groups in the population, it is plausible that their viewpoints and patterns of action will be distinctive. The question is whether they are inherently less flexible to change.

Income and Adaptability

The "average" married blue-collar worker earned $8,000 in 1969, and one of every two supplemented family income by moonlighting or by his wife's earnings. His savings are meager, and home ownership is his major investment. In order to acquire desired goods, he must usually take on such a large burden of consumer debt that monthly payments eat up much of his income.

According to some analysts, these circumstances diminish the blue-collar worker's adaptability to change. He is viewed as hooked by his consumption patterns, running to stay in place on an economic treadmill. With all energies devoted to maintaining his standard of living, he is understandably upset by any distractions. Living at the margin where consumption keeps just ahead of earnings, he is haunted by the fear of economic change. Adjusted to circumscribed horizons, he views life as a zero-sum game, in which gains to others are a loss to himself.

This is a familiar but misleading scenario. By focusing on a supposedly "typical" family, it ignores the all-important variations in the income, size, age, and future prospects of blue-collar families. There are good reasons to doubt whether the earning and consumption patterns of the "typical" blue-collar worker make him especially rigid in his ways. He has personal (if few material) resources to help him adjust to change, and society has provided institutions to cushion its adverse impact. He is insulated by an increasing range of income maintenance benefits when idleness strikes. Moonlighting and job holding by his wife are ways of adjusting to temporary increased family needs. When children are grown and college expenses mount, the wife is needed less in the home and can seek full-time work.

In making such adjustments, manual workers are probably as sure of their future income prospects as most other groups because of established seniority pay scales and known advancement prospects. The assemption is, of course, that the United States has learned to avoid deep depressions; the post-World War II experience justifies such optimism. Middle-income workers can therefore rationally adjust their lifetime income to lifetime needs through borrowing, which in reasonable proportion is not necessarily a sign of impecuniousness. Workers whose earning capacities are limited tend to adjust to their circumstances. Everyone would like more, but we do not spend much of our waking hours chasing an elusive carrot.

The Effect of Education

Blue-collar workers have spent fewer years in school than professional, managerial, sales, and clerical workers. If added schooling improves one's flexibility, it could be assumed that the average clerical worker is more adaptive to change than the average blue-collar worker. Undoubtedly, exposure to a college liberal arts education can broaden horizons, but the contribution of an extra year of high school remains questionable. Whether education contributes to flexibility depends on whether or not it is applied productively, and the underutilized intellect may be more dangerous than the one that is underdeveloped. Though education affects attitudes and behavior, there is no way of knowing a priori whether it increases or diminishes the adaptability to change. It undoubtedly depends on the type of change under consideration, with increased education making some easier and others more difficult.

An Assembly-line Mind?

Blue-collar work also imprints its stamp on attitudes and values, but there is no way of knowing whether it makes a person more or less rigid. There is copious literature about the dehumanizing aspects of mechanization—how work on the assembly line dulls the mind and body. Rising rates of absenteeism and increasingly shoddy workmanship are alleged to be reactions to onerous working conditions. But these behaviors have many other causes. It is not just in blue-collar jobs that workers expect more and offer less. Many white-collar workers are subject to the same dissatisfactions and complaints as blue-collar workers. Though their jobs are usually less taxing physically, they demand a repetitive mental effort which may be equally exhausting. Even the prestige white-collar jobs may not be especially rewarding. Considering the education which is required, filling a tooth may be no more satisfying than putting a rivet in an auto body.

It is difficult to generalize in this area because of the wide range of both blue-collar and white-collar jobs. Skilled craftsmen may have prestigious working conditions and high rates of pay; they may find jobs challenging in every way. Laborers may toil in repetitive and physically demanding work. And whether manual workers as a whole are more or less satisfied with their jobs than other workers, there is no evidence that dissatisfaction leads to inflexibility. Indeed, the opposite might be the case.

Ethnicity and Adjustment

Ethnicity is a long-ignored factor that has recently been revived almost to the point of exaggeration. An estimated 40 million immigrants or children of immigrants live in the United States, not counting the many more third- or fourth-generation nationals who still identify themselves as "ethnics." In order of numerical importance, these include Italians, Germans, Poles, Russians, and the Irish. Immigrants initially concentrated in blue-collar work, and many ethnic groups are still overrepresented among manual workers.[4]

Conventional wisdom once assumed that immigrants were being rapidly assimilated into the great American melting pot;

today, many social scientists have discovered that the contents of the pot haven't entirely melted. According to Gus Tyler, "America is less a melting pot than a casserole with solid chunks of ethnic ingredients flavoring one another while holding on to their distinctive textures."[5] The recognition of the persistence of ethnicity has coincided with an increasing activism on the part of different ethnic groups, including some ethnic confrontations.

But it is misleading to associate legitimate ethnic problems with blue-collar difficulties. Though ethnics are overrepresented in blue-collar employment, they still constitute only a minority of blue-collar workers, and this minority is far from homogeneous, for its members hold diverse views on social issues. Germans tend to be more conservative than the Irish, and Jews are liberal on most social issues.[6] Many second- and even first-generation ethnics have broken their national and religious ties, but many third- and fourth-generation "immigrants" still have not shed their ethnic habits. Thus the whole concept of ethnicity is hazy, and there is little proof that it has had a recognizable impact on overall blue-collar attitudes and behavior patterns. To the degree that it does have an effect, ethnic identification may even serve as a "security blanket" which makes change easier. Traditionally it provided a support to those who were new on the shores; perhaps it still continues to serve as a vehicle to ease adjustments in the new country.

The rural origins of many blue-collar workers also must be considered. Migrants from the farm may find adjustments more difficult than ethnics.[7] They tend to be traditionalistic, work-oriented, and conservative. Many maintain contacts with their homes, and they are usually slow to change their values. Undoubtedly, they have contributed to elements of inflexibility among manual workers, but many white-collar workers share a similar background.

On balance, there is no reason to believe that blue-collar workers are inherently less capable of changing with the times than other groups, as long as they do not have to bear an excessive burden. On the contrary, if improved income and education are helpful in weathering change, then blue-collar workers should be growing more adaptive. The increasing distance from ethnic origins should have made them more and not less flexible if there is anything to the argument that ethnicity is an obstacle to adaptability.

THE BLUE-COLLAR BURDEN

The nation has undergone some massive economic and social changes over the last decade. It has been argued that blue-collar workers have had to bear an "excessive" share of the burdens and that they have been especially squeezed by rapidly rising prices and slowly rising income. Although taxes at all levels of government are increasing, it is often asserted that blue-collar workers have paid more than their share while receiving little in return in the way of improved government services. It is also assumed that the gains of blacks in recent years have come at the expense of white manual workers, who are threatened by the advances of minority workers.

The Pocketbook Changes

The evidence of an income squeeze is far from conclusive. According to the federal Bureau of Labor Statistics, the average weekly earnings of a factory worker, adjusted for federal taxes and rising prices, remained relatively constant between 1965 and 1971. However, these statistics are subject to many technical corrections and should be used with great care. The consumer price index used to deflate the money wage gains apparently overstates the real rise in costs. It is also misleading to equate higher taxes with lower wages. Blue-collar workers, like other groups, benefit from government expenditures and have a voice in determining the level of tax collections and how they are spent. Finally, the average real wages reflect an influx of "secondary" workers.[8] The proportion of female blue-collar workers rose from 15.1 percent in 1960 to 17.2 percent in 1970, and the proportion of male craftsmen and operatives who were family heads fell from 65.1 percent in 1960 to 59.4 percent in 1970. The stagnant average real wage was therefore in part explained by the entrance of lower-paid secondary workers and the changing mix of the work force.

Data for blue-collar family heads show that their real income has increased over the decade. The median annual earnings of white married blue-collar workers adjusted for change in consumer prices rose 25 percent between 1959 and 1969, about the same as for white professional, managerial, clerical, sales, and service workers. Because more wives worked, the family income of all groups, including blue-collar families, increased even more than the earnings of family heads. Thirty-three percent of the wives of white operatives and craftsmen worked in 1960; the proportion increased to 44 percent in 1969. As a result, the mean family income in real terms rose from $8,236 in 1960 to $10,731 in 1969, or 30 percent.[9]

A reasonable interpretation of these data is that white blue-collar workers have increased their real income substantially over the decade. Family heads, who are the most committed workers, have experienced noticeable earnings gains, while working wives have increasingly supplemented family income. It is difficult to see anything inimical in these developments. Those who feel there is a blue-collar economic crisis must rely on other arguments.

For instance, it is sometimes suggested that wives are driven to work by economic necessity and that this is a source of despair to the blue-collar male. Undoubtedly, some blue-collar workers resent the possible loss of "machismo" which comes with the wife's work, but the benefits seemingly outweigh the costs. The secondary income is a way of maintaining a higher standard of living, and it may offer desired independence to the wife. The lack of adequate child-care facilities for the children of working mothers does offer serious problems; institutional arrangements have not kept pace with the rapid increase of working mothers. It is likely that insistence that the government provide child-care facilities would result in needed funding of these services. Meanwhile, the families with working mothers benefit from the added income, though the costs of even inadequate care may be high.

Another rejoinder to the evidence of economic progress is the claim that despite their gains, blue-collar families are on the average unable to attain a "moderate standard of living." The Department of Labor estimates that an intermediate standard of living for an urban family of four required in 1970 an annual income of $10,664. Obviously, a majority of blue-collar families cannot attain this standard without the wife's earnings. The significance of this income deficit should not be exaggerated, however. The intermediate standard is based largely on the consumption patterns of a middle-income urban family, and roughly half of all four-member families will be below the standard. It would be a gross exaggeration to assert that families whose income is below the median are "deprived," and there is no proof that they are goaded by comparison with an arbitrary set of standards which are designed to be out of reach for half the families.

It is fairly clear, then, that blue-collar families have not been hurt in the pay envelope. Like everyone, they would prefer a larger income, but their earnings have apparently increased in real terms over the past decade, at least until the 1970 slump.

Rising Taxes and Government Spending

Some would argue, however, that the gains in earnings were illusory and did not translate into take-home pay. Federal, state, and local taxes have been taking an ever larger bite of income and earnings. In 1960, 29.6 percent of the net national product was collected in taxes, with 5.6 percent redistributed as transfer payments. By 1969, 34.9 percent was taxed away and transfer payments accounted for 7.5 percent. Certainly blue-collar workers feel the sting of the tax bite, but they share this complaint with every taxpayer. They also share control over the level of government expenditures and benefit from the goods and services that government provides. The issue is whether they have had to bear an increasing proportion of the tax burden or have failed to receive their "appropriate" share of benefits. Though the evidence is far from conclusive, it does not indicate that there have been any significant imbalances to justify blue-collar alienation.

The most recent and careful data attempting to treat the incidence of taxation suggest that on balance taxes are roughly proportionate. The aggregate rate of federal, state, and local taxes, which averaged 32 percent in 1968, fell from 40 percent for incomes under $2,000 and 33 percent for those between $2,000 and $4,000 to 30 percent at the $8,000 to $10,000 income bracket; they then rose gradually to one-third for those with an annual income above $25,000. But the government does not only take; it also transfers income by taking from Peter to pay Paul. When transfer payments are considered, the net incidence of the tax system becomes progressive. Families with an annual income of less than $4,000 actually come out ahead, and they receive more from transfer payments than they pay in taxes. The tax rises to 14.9 percent for the $4,000 to $6,000 income class, 25.4 for the $8,000 to $10,000 group, and 31.6 percent for those between $25,000 and $50,000. The net tax rate rises continuously with income, so that no income group pays a higher proportion in taxes than does another group with greater income.[10]

Different taxes have different incidence patterns. The income tax is progressive; the Social Security tax is mildly regressive (with the $4,000 to $8,000 income group paying the largest share); and state and local taxes are markedly regressive. There are no comparable data to indicate whether the aggregate tax rate has grown more or less progressive with increases in the separate taxes. Between 1960 and 1969, federal income taxes rose from 9.1 to 11.2 percent of net national product, or 2.1 percent, and transfer payments rose 1.7 percent, making for a more progressive tax structure. But Social Security and state and local taxes increased 1.8 and 2.0 percent of net national product, respectively, and these have had a regressive effect.

On balance, these changes most likely neutralize each other. The tax structure is only slightly, if at all, more regressive than it has ever been, and this could be perceived only by the most astute analysis. Blue-collar families have been adversely affected by rises in Social Security, state, and local taxes. When the total government tax impact is considered, however, blue-collar families have not suffered disproportionately.

An analysis of the reaction by blue-collar workers to governmental fiscal policies must also consider the distribution of expenditures. A redistribution of outlays for programs in which workers receive less than they pay proportionately in taxes might be the basis of a legitimate complaint, but this apparently has not been the case. Per capita governmental expenditures rose from $841 in 1960 to $1,414 in 1968, or 57 percent, with three-fifths of this increase going for defense, education, and Social Security. There is no way of knowing in any detailed way whether the share of blue-collar benefits in these areas has changed.

The main complaints presumably deal with increasing public welfare payments, especially to those who do not work, and with expanding manpower services for the disadvantaged blacks, which better equip them to compete for blue-collar jobs. Per capita public welfare expenditures rose 125 percent between 1960 and 1968, while total manpower outlays increased tenfold. Nevertheless, these welfare expenditures account for only a small share of total governmental expenditures. In 1968, per capita public welfare expenditures accounted for $56 and manpower for $11 out of the total of $1,414. Blue-collar workers would undoubtedly agree that a large proportion of these are warranted so that the incidence of benefits from government expenditure has apparently not shifted appreciably as a result of the growing welfare and manpower expenditures.

Perhaps more significant has been the 133 percent increase in Social Security and Medicare expenditures between 1960 and 1968. These programs are financed by a regressive payroll tax, falling most heavily on families in the $6,000 to $8,000 income class. In many of these families, two persons work and both make contributions to the family income. The OASDHI (Social Security) payroll tax may be especially onerous to younger workers, who will not benefit for a long time. Nevertheless, Social Security contributions are still a fairly good investment for the blue-collar families, especially those with low incomes who stand to get back more than they put in.

On the face of it, governmental expenditures ought to offer little cause for blue-collar alienation, though reliance on a more progressive method of taxation would obviously reduce their burden. Resentment by middle-income groups may build, however, as more workers qualify for benefits and as tax rates are boosted to keep Social Security payments dependent exclusively upon payroll taxes. But in the past decade, increases in the regressive Social Security tax have been balanced by boosts in progressive federal income taxes.

On the whole, then, blue-collar families have not been placed under an excessive tax burden, nor have they been slighted by governmental expenditures. Minor changes may have occurred, but they are marginal; even experts have difficulty identifying them. Blue-collar workers are probably disturbed by increasing taxes just as much as everyone else, but there is no adequate reason to assume that they are not willing to carry their fair share of the tax burden;

considering the overall tax and expenditure picture, they most likely recognize that they are not being hurt by change.

The Black Challenge

Another major change that is claimed to have threatened blue-collar workers is the improving social and economic status of non-whites. Viewed narrowly, the claim is that blacks are competing with whites for blue-collar jobs and are undermining the value of their investments in homes by moving into white blue-collar neighborhoods. On a broader scale, it is sometimes asserted that the blue-collar workers feel that their status is being eroded by the gains of Negroes as a group. The latter claim is difficult to prove or refute. White blue-collar workers generally favor black progress, especially where they consider it to be earned; they react adversely, however, if it affects or threatens their welfare.

That blue-collar workers are concerned about specific incursions of blacks should not be a surprise. It is a vast exaggeration, however, to claim that they alone bear the burden of Negro gains. They were probably the first to feel the effects as blacks moved into marginal blue-collar neighborhoods and marginal blue-collar jobs. But contrary to popularly held views, black gains on the job front have not been especially threatening to white blue-collar workers. The number of black men who are blue-collar workers increased 29 percent between 1958 and 1970, but white employment also rose 14 percent, and the number of white blue-collar workers increased 2.5 million while the number of blacks rose 0.7 million. It is a safe assumption that many of the blacks finding jobs could get them only because qualified white workers shifted to other employment, so that jobs were not being wrested away from those already employed.

It is especially noteworthy that Negro incursions have slowed noticeably over the last half decade. Between 1958 and 1964, the number of white blue-collar workers increased 6.8 percent compared with 15.2 percent for blacks; during the next six years, the white growth continued at about the same rate while the growth rate of black manual workers declined somewhat. This change is even more marked for craftsmen, among whom the number of whites was increased by a healthy 11.7 percent between 1964 and 1970. These data further support the hypothesis that the entry of blacks into blue-collar ranks did not involve discernible encroachments upon jobs held by whites, whose opportunities expanded while the blacks also made gains.

Though white manualists may resent the gains of nonwhites as a class, their objections are more likely to be influenced by direct personal contacts with black coworkers. If so, they should be no more upset by Negro income gains than other groups in the population. From 1960 to 1970, the median earnings of nonwhite male family heads who were craftsmen and operatives increased 42 percent; for those in all occupations, the gain was 60 percent. White blue-collar workers probably were faced with less of a "loss in status" relative to their black coworkers than whites in other occupations were.

There is little evidence, then, that blue-collar workers have been inordinately or adversely affected by measurable changes of the last decade, although some may be troubled by the fact of change. Not all manual workers shared in the rising real income because of meager earning gains and increasing prices. Those who are paying more taxes but are benefiting little from government expenditures may be alienated—for instance, the young blue-collar workers who are burdened by regressive Social Security taxes. Some workers are threatened directly by Negro competition for jobs which formerly excluded blacks, or they fear a decline in property values if blacks move into their neighborhoods. Such problems are always a part of social change; though they are real and deserve attention, they are not so widespread or severe that they have contributed to a blue-collar crisis. While blue-collar workers have been affected by recent change, they seem to have made the needed adjustments and adapted themselves to the new conditions.

MECHANISMS OF ADJUSTMENT

No matter how benign, the massive changes of the last decade would be overwhelming to some individuals if they had to face the transformation alone and without help. But every group has institutional and personal adaptive mechanisms to cushion the impact and to facilitate adjustment. For blue-collar workers, the union is one of the most important institutions, and it has a major role to play in helping the worker adjust to a changing labor market. Upward occupational mobility is a more personal mechanism, serving as a safety valve and offering a positive way to exercise the energies generated by change. Politics also play a role in the adjustment process, for government can affect the pace of change or provide assistance to its victims.

If these mechanisms did not function adequately, blue-collar workers would have extreme difficulty in coping with change. Some analysts have argued that the institutional mechanisms have not functioned effectively in recent years and have attributed the cause of the perceived "crisis" to these institutional failures. Unions, it is claimed, no longer represent their members or protect their interests. Upgrading opportunities are being undermined by technological change, while educational opportunities are not adequate to the needs. Democratic processes are supposedly insensitive to the blue-collar workers, ignoring their interests in an effort to woo other voters. If these claims are true, the blue-collar crisis would be real.

Are Unions Effective?

In protecting and furthering the blue-collar worker's economic interests, and to a lesser extent, representing his views in the political arena, unions are perhaps the major institutional mechanism for adjusting to change. More than three-fifths of operatives are organized, as are half of craftsmen and foremen and almost two-fifths of nonfarm laborers.[11] The union influence is pervasive among manual workers because collective bargaining affects wages and work conditions in nonunion as well as union jobs, while it protects the interests of workingmen in the political arena.

A recurrent theme of the blue-collar blues is the alienation of the rank and file from the union's "establishment" leadership. According to a 1968 Louis Harris survey, 40 percent of union members felt that their unions represented the wishes of a few leaders rather than those of the members. Analysts of blue-collar problems have also claimed that a growing minority of young unionists resent the domination of "old guard" members who prefer increases in the form of greater retirement, health, and other deferred benefits while the young want cash. It is also asserted that the unions are incapable of dealing with the new concerns of workers—their job dissatisfactions and their demands outside the workplace. In short, it is claimed that the unions have not done a good job of helping their blue-collar members adjust to change.

It is ironic that these arguments are being raised at the very time when the unions are flexing their muscles and demonstrating their power to protect worker interests even in slack economic conditions. This has brought on threats of direct wage and price controls by a Republican administration. If union leadership were unresponsive to the opinions of the rank and file, this concentration of power would be especially dangerous; but there is little evidence to support the claim that unions are undemocratic. The Landrum-Griffin Act was passed to guarantee the rights of union members and to prevent abuses so widely publicized by the McClellan hearings in the late 1950s. Progress has been made over the last decade, and unions are certainly no less democratic than other major institutions or political organizations. To guarantee the democratic rights of members, the Secretary of Labor is empowered to investigate all union elections. During fiscal 1968, evidence of misconduct was found in 18 out of some 20,000 elections.

Unions are not unresponsive. In recent years, the rank and file have been more vociferous in their demands to oust official members who they felt ignored their interests. Union members can also express themselves through referendums, though the participation rates on such issues are usually as low as they are in local political referendums. But, most significantly, the membership usually votes on the collective bargaining agreements reached by their leaders. More and more, they are rejecting these agreements. In settlements the Federal Mediation and Conciliation Service has participated in, the membership rejection rates rose from 8.7 percent in 1964 to 14.2 percent in 1967. This demonstrates that many union members are frequently dissatisfied with their leadership, but in many cases the rank and file can maintain control and reject the propensity of leadership to exercise its own judgments.

A different argument, one which is often juxtaposed, is that blue-collar workers are increasingly alienated because their minority views are not heard. In particular, unions are claimed to be unresponsive to the gripes of younger workers. Needless to say, leadership cannot please everyone, and as long as it is democratic, it will pursue the interests of the majority. There must be some accommodation of minority-group interests, however, and there is no reason to believe that the unions have failed in this regard. Unions, like other democratic institutions, can be moved to action by an active minority. When this fails, there is always the threat of decertification or withdrawal from the bargaining unit by a group of dissatisfied workers. Wildcat strikes are another way of expressing minority interests. Most importantly, compromise is a basic ingredient of the collective bargaining process. Union negotiations have to accommodate the initial demands of competing groups, balancing, for instance, wage hikes desired by younger workers against pension increases sought by the older ones.

To believe that unions are inflexible to the changing needs of their membership is to ignore the massive transformation of the collective bargaining process. The earliest agreements encompassed little more than wages and hours. Now the scope of bargaining has extended to unemployment provisions, the rate of technological change, pensions, health, and insurance. And possibly most significant is the protection that unions have provided members in the workplace.

Health care is a major example of what unions can accomplish where they have support of the rank and file. Expansion of the Blue Cross and Blue Shield systems was largely the product of collective bargaining. The unions then assumed leadership on the political front in support of Medicare, and they can claim much of the credit for its passage. Finally, their pressure has resulted in plans for universal health insurance which are likely to be adopted in the near future. Where the rank and file have been willing to forgo immediate gains, unions have been able to bargain in entirely new areas; these are likely to become more important in the future as blue-collar workers feel the force of current changes.

Horatio Alger Is Alive and Well

The rags-to-riches stories of American folklore exaggerate the extent of upward mobility in the past. It is a frequent assumption that economic concentration has reduced opportunities for advancement, but it is more likely that the improvement and expansion of public education have provided more people with a chance for substantial progress.

Despite the existence of many dead-end jobs that allow little exercise of independent judgment and provide little expectation of advancement, opportunities for upward occupational mobility are not foreclosed. A study of 11 major industries estimated that, of the 7 million workers employed, about 2.4 million were in relatively dead-end jobs, 2.0 million had moderate prospects for progression of three to five steps, and the remaining 2.8 million had craft or multiple-step progressions.[12] The conclusion was that those wanting to get ahead could do so through job changes if promotion were foreclosed on the job.

It is significant that the service (hotels and motels) and retail (department and variety stores) industries that were investigated provided little opportunity for advancement. The problem of unattractive and dead-end jobs is not restricted to blue-collar work. The rubber and steel industries, with large concentrations of blue-collar workers, had significant upgrading potential, but the mass-production automobile and apparel industries had very little. Obviously, wide variation in the opportunities for advancement is found in the industries blue-collar workers are concentrated in.

Adequate data are not available to provide clear insights as to whether opportunities for advancement have increased or declined. Few collective bargaining agreements have thus far made provisions requiring employers to finance college or technical education. Unions have generally shown little interest in upgrading programs or job restructuring, either because they are misreading the desires of their membership or because the average worker is not particularly concerned about his chances of moving up. The picture varies from industry to industry. In the case of motor vehicles, the entry-level worker is paid a high wage, and though he may not be satisified with his job, he balances the benefits against the costs, which include the greater chances of progress elsewhere. In the case of apparel, the largely female work force has only peripheral job attachments, and so it probably exhibits more concern over wages and hours than advancement opportunities. Conditions may need improvement in these industries, but it is misleading to generalize about the "dehumanizing" effects of the automobile assembly line and the alleged widespread discontent generated by such jobs.

Careful analysts have claimed that technological change is making most jobs simpler while it is creating others with high skill and education requirements. According to this thesis, the gap between the two types of jobs is increasingly difficult to bridge because of the lack of education among the unskilled and the lack of gradations through which they can acquire work experience in lieu of education. Despite the plausibility of this development, it has probably not had a noticeable effect on mobility in recent years. From 1964 to 1970, the number of craftsmen increased 12.8 percent and operatives only 4.2 percent. Since most blue-collar skill needs are filled by promotion, at least in unionized industries, there have undoubtedly been a large number of operatives moving up to become craftsmen. The lack of job mobility is probably not a contributor to blue-collar anomie, though it might become so if aggregate demand continues to be slack.

Within the blue-collar ranks, education is associated with earnings; and increased schooling is often a prerequisite for advancement, especially into white-collar jobs. At the same time, blue-collar workers are concerned about the prospects for their offspring. Those who are immobile can pin their hopes on their children. Blue-collar workers are concerned about the availability of "free" education not only because it opens personal opportunities for upward mobility but also because it offers a means to achieve a better status for their children.

It is misleading to view this justifiable concern as a source of dissatisfaction. On the contrary, educational opportunities for the blue-collar worker and his family are continually expanding. The educational attainment of the average blue-collar worker is rapidly increasing, owing to the influx of better-schooled youths, frequently his own children. The median educational attainment for male blue-collar workers was increased by nearly two years of schooling during the past decade, or double that of all other employed males.

It might be argued that some of the problems of the blue-collar workers stem from overeducation rather than from deficient schooling. Studies of job situations have shown that most workers are overqualified for their jobs. If the blue-collar worker is not challenged, his rising education may lead to work dissatisfaction.

Those who need additional skills or credentials have many options. An estimated 8 million blue-collar workers are pursuing some type of education outside the regular school system—enrolled in everything from a matchbook course promising "learning for earning" to complex technical training courses offered by community schools or private institutions. It is unlikely that, as some have claimed, this peripheral education is of little use because its credentials are not recognized by employers. It is doubtful that millions of blue-collar workers would be misled to undertake self-improvement courses without tangible rewards for their efforts.

Whatever the prospects for the blue-collar worker himself, there is little reason why he should feel that his children's chances have been reduced by any recent developments. Blue-collar children accounted in 1969 for 30 percent of college-age youth; they constitute 34 percent of freshmen enrolled in two-year colleges and 26 percent of freshmen in four-year institutions. The major expansion in higher education has been the impressive growth of two-year colleges, from which blue-collar children have benefited more than proportionately. It is true that the chances of attending institutions of higher education are significantly correlated with family income and that poor or near-poor blue-collar families (like others with meager earnings) have trouble sending their children to college. Changes which would provide truly equal opportunities for a college education might be welcome, and the expansion of federal assistance to college students will continue to benefit children from blue-collar families. It is unlikely, therefore, that a shortage of educational opportunities is perceived to be, or has in fact been, an impediment to blue-collar adjustment.

Can 25 Million Voters Be Forgotten?

Blue-collar problems were thrust to the forefront of public attention by political developments. In the Nixon-Humphrey-Wallace campaign of 1968, there were indications that the blue-collar vote was up for grabs. Observers were quick to project these circumstances into a trend, which politicians were equally eager to exploit. The direction of alleged change is by now familiar. Long ignored by the political parties and long silent as a political force, blue-collar workers were supposedly losing faith in the old Roosevelt coalition. Sick of social change and threatened by the gains of Negroes, they had shifted their sentiments to the right and they were ripe for third-party appeals or inroads by a right-of-center Republican party. Convinced that the traditional political machinery had been unresponsive to their needs, they had grown more reactionary under the pressure of social change brought about by the Johnsonian Great Society drive.

In retrospect, the events which were the basis of this interpretation seem more a temporary political aberration than the beginning of a trend. Hindsight is always better than foresight, but even at the time those who foresaw a realignment of blue-collar allegiances were basing their forecasts on rather tenuous grounds.

One basis was the presumed widespread appeal of Wallace's third-party movement in 1968, especially among hard hats and other union members. Blue-collar workers as well as other workingmen crowded to hear his exhortations, apparently delighting in his new blend of populism. Early public-opinion polls gave him as much as 21 percent of the electorate, with a substantial showing among blue-collar workers. But by Election Day much of this sentiment had ebbed as large numbers of Northern blue-collar voters returned to the Democratic fold. Fifteen percent of blue-collar workers voted for Wallace, compared with 13.6 percent of all voters. The largest proportion, 50 percent, voted for Humphrey, compared with 43 percent of the total population.

The initial popularity of Wallace among manual workers and his subsequent loss of ground in the election have been variously interpreted. The intense efforts of union leadership on behalf of Humphrey no doubt may have switched some votes. But considering the lackluster batting average of the unions in the 1968 elections, their influence should not be exaggerated. A more likely explanation is that the early expression of approval by blue-collar workers was not sustained at the "moment of truth" when they expressed their choice in the voting booth. Being in favor of Wallace was a way of saying "right on" to his free-swinging efforts and probably a way of letting off steam.

The fact that 15 percent of blue-collar workers voted for Wallace could be significant in itself, however. A swing of such magnitude could have changed the outcome of national elections; Presidents Kennedy and Nixon each won by less than a 1 percent plurality. If the Wallace vote could be shifted to the Republican party, a new and dominant majority party could be formed.

This was the theory of the Republican campaign in 1970, which appealed to the public on social rather than bread-and-butter issues.

The Democrats apparently neutralized the social issues and retained the support of blue-collar workers. A more likely explanation, however, is that Republican harvest of blue-collar support was aborted by the force of economic realities. When faced by inflationary pressures, the Nixon administration opted for policies intended to dampen inflation at the cost of rising unemployment. The AFL-CIO has strongly criticized the Nixon administration for its domestic policies during the 1970 campaign. The later suspension of the Davis-Bacon Act in 1971 and the increasingly hard line on union wage gains did not win many blue-collar adherents.

The most persuasive interpretation of recent political developments indicates no massive shift in voting patterns, and there is no evidence that lasting realignments are in the works. Some blue-collar voters strayed from the Democratic camp in 1968, but two years later they returned to their traditional alliances and concerns.

CHANGING WITH THE TIMES

A "Reasonable" Interpretation

Change is always difficult, and the last decade has encompassed more than its share. Most of the major developments of recent years have been long-sought social goals—the progress in combating poverty, and efforts to achieve greater equality of opportunity. However, these favorable developments have nurtured other problems, for adjustment to even the most constructive change is not easy. Everyone, including blue-collar workers, has experienced difficulties and dislocations while trying to adjust to new conditions and shifting rules.

The so-called "blue-collar blues" are basically a reaction to change—an expression of the anxieties and frustrations it has generated. Although there is no denying that these concerns are real and pervasive, they should not be equated with proof of deep-seated alienation or even a failure to adjust to the temper of our time.

Tested against the hypothesis that the social and economic system is functioning and that certain difficulties are to be expected, there is little evidence of a blue-collar crisis. Blue-collar workers do not appear to be especially inflexible to change; they have not been affected more than others by recent developments; and their mechanisms of adjustment have functioned and continue to function reasonably well.

The current developments which have been used as a proof of a blue-collar crisis can and probably should be interpreted in a more optimistic light. Rather than manifesting dysfunction in the social and economic system, they are an integral part of the process of adjustment. What is remarkable is the extent to which change has been accepted without reaction.

This is not to deny that blue-collar workers have new and pressing concerns. Health care has become a major issue because of spiraling costs and expectations. The Blue Cross and Blue Shield arrangements hammered out in collective bargaining are proving inadequate, and a substantial portion of blue-collar workers and their families are left without coverage. Likewise, education is perhaps becoming a greater worry as the college credential is more and more regarded as a *sine qua non* for upward mobility, and lack of day-care facilities is becoming a more acute concern as an increasing number of wives seek and find work.

While problems associated with the delivery of health care and education are growing more severe, the manifestations of blue-collar concern suggest that these are some of the areas where even greater attention is desired. There is nothing unhealthy about society's constantly shifting needs and concerns; the selective focus on certain problems is a way of making improvements. Health care has become a critical issue, and it is almost certain that a comprehensive medical insurance scheme will be effected sometime in the near future.

In a broader sense, most of the manifestations of alienation can be viewed as a means of drawing attention to the needs of blue-collar workers and obtaining an immediate response—in short, signs of strength rather than weakness. On the job, the rising absenteeism and sometimes shoddy workmanship have resulted in a greater effort on the part of management to improve the work atmosphere and rethink their methods of operation. It is naïve to think that only the world around the blue-collar worker is changing and that he must do all the adapting. His values, like those of everyone else, are undergoing a transformation, and other institutions have to do some adapting.

Blue-collar Politics

Politically it is not only naïve but disastrous to underestimate the power of the blue-collar workers. Though few blue-collar workers are active in politics or are joiners in many organizations, they carry a massive clout at election time. While many view the blue-collar third-party dalliance as an indication of massive shifts in political alliances, a more likely explanation is that the major parties temporarily misread the sentiment of the middle American and that the flirtation with a third-party candidate was a way of snapping the major parties back into line. The Republicans were the first to recognize and identify with the mood of the times, and they thereby eked out a narrow victory. In the 1970 elections, however, the law-and-order issue did not lead to major shifts. The Democrats were able to neutralize the early edge of the Republicans, and the stance of the parties has remained traditional despite the increased attention given to social issues. It is doubtful that the concerns of the Silent Majority were as substantive as some have interpreted them to be. They apparently wanted some rhetoric and recognition and perhaps a slight breather from the demands of social change. The important thing is that the parties reacted quickly (though the Democrats more slowly). The chances are that the two major parties will retain the allegiance of the blue-collar class. The group is too heterogeneous to shift en masse to the sirens of new promises. Though they may be relatively united on such an amorphous issue as law and order, they are divided on almost everything else. Older blue-collar workers may be helped by increased Social Security and medical insurance, but the younger ones may balk at increased payroll taxes that would be required for added benefits. Union members may resent wage and price controls, but others may prefer controls instead of rising prices. Any homogeneity on certain broad issues breaks down on specific questions. It is unlikely that any major issue will arise and unite the working class enough to overcome their disagreements on other issues and to sustain a third party. If one did arise, it would in all likelihood be adopted by the major parties.

We All Have Problems

We do not live in the best of all possible worlds. Blue-collar workers, like everyone else, have troubles and anxieties, most of which are the consequence of rapid economic and social change. But the recent developments have not been especially adverse, and on balance blue-collar workers have improved their circumstances. The institutional and personal mechanisms of adaptation have functioned reasonably well, and blue-collar expressions of dissatisfaction have in fact served as one of these mechanisms. Though blue-collar workers have a multitude of problems, there is no evidence that their difficulties represent long-standing broken promises and inattention or that they call for any substantial shift in priorities. The needs of blue-collar groups facing special problems must be provided for recognizing, however, that not much can be accomplished by equalitarian movements for those in the center of the spectrum. The best hope of the middle Americans lies in the advancement of the nation as a whole. All evidence points to the conclusion that the vast majority of blue-collar workers have successfully weathered the ordeal of change.

NOTES

1. "The Troubled Americans," *Newsweek,* Oct. 6, 1969.
2. Eric Hoffer, *The Ordeal of Change,* Harper & Row, New York, 1963, pp. 5–6.
3. Basil Whiting, "The Suddenly Remembered American," The Ford Foundation, New York, 1970, p. 38. (This paper is an excellent review of blue-collar problems.)
4. Irving M. Levine and Judith Herman, "The Ethnic Factor in Blue-Collar Life," American Jewish Committee, New York, 1970, p. 16. (Mimeographed.)
5. Cited in Whiting, op. cit., p. 11.
6. Andrew M. Greeley, *Why Can't They Be Like Us?,* Institute of Human Relations Press, New York, 1969, pp. 53–54.
7. Arthur Shostak, *Blue-Collar Life,* Random House, New York, 1969, p. 7.
8. George L. Perry, "Wages, Productivity and Profits," *The Conference Board Record,* March 1971, p. 43.
9. U.S. Department of Commerce, Bureau of the Census, *Occupations and Earnings of Family Heads in 1969, Current Population Reports,* ser. P-60, no. 73, September 1970, p. 25.
10. Roger A. Herriot and Herman P. Miller, "The Taxes We Pay," *The Conference Board Record,* May 1971, table 7.
11. Derek C. Bok and John T. Dunlop, *Labor and the American Community,* Simon & Schuster, New York, 1970, p. 45.
12. William Grinker, Donald Cooke, and Arthur Kirsch, *Climbing the Job Ladder,* E. F. Shelley and Company, New York, 1969.

Index

Aaron, Henry, 293, 316, 317
Abramson, Harold J., 118, 129
Accidents, workplace, 31
Advancement, 37–39
  unions and, 161
Advisory Commission on Intergovernmental Relations, 275–276
AFL (*see* American Federation of Labor)
Age, census data on, 58–64
Agnew, Spiro T., 18, 124, 126–127, 228, 352
Aid to Families with Dependent Children (AFDC), 301-302
Aid to Families with Dependent Children—Unemployed Father (AFDC–UF), 302, 314
Alienation:
  income maintenance and, 286–291
  manifestations of, 382
  political views and, 116–119
  taxes and, 287
  tolerance levels and, 146–150
Allen, Jodie, 257, 286
Amalgamated Meat Cutters Union, 157
American Airlines, 34
American Federation of Labor (AFL), 184
  race relations and, 177–181
American Federation of Labor–Congress of Industrial Organizations (AFL–CIO), 9, 99, 165, 184, 251
  leadership of, 128
    City Central Body representatives, 157
    Executive Council, 185
  Nixon criticized by, 381
American Federation of Labor–Congress of Industrial Organizations (AFL–CIO) (*Cont.*):
  politics and, 101
  race relations and, 183–187
    equalitarian position, 192
  social transformation and, 251
American Federation of State, County and Municipal Employees (AFSCME), 157
American Indians, 352
American Jewish Committee, 15
Anti-Semitism among blacks, 195–196
Antiwar demonstrations, 132, 148
Apprenticeship, 37–38, 188
Assets, changes in, 238–239
Attitudinal shifts, 243
Authority, respect for, 113
Automobiles:
  styles and goals of consumption and, 216–218
  taxes related to, 272

Banfield, Edward C., 8
Bateman, Worth, 257, 286
Bell, N., 228
Berg, Ivar, 324, 341
Bicker, William E., 317
Birth control, 28
Bishop, George A., 316, 317
Blacks:
  alienation of, 52
  anti-Semitism among, 195–196

Blacks (*Cont.*):
group pride of, 352
intraclass conflict with, 249
law-and-order issues and, 108–111
militant, 351
support for Democratic Party among, 126–127
(*See also* Nonwhite workers; Race relations; Tolerance levels)
Blau, Peter M., 35, 42, 46
Blaustein, Saul J., 317
Blue Cross, 376, 382
Blue Shield, 376, 382
Bok, Derek C., 75, 384
Bowman, Paul, 332, 341
Bricklayers' Union, 195
Bridges, Benjamin, Jr., 317
Brittain, John, 293, 316, 317
Brotherhood of Locomotive Firemen, 185
Brotherhood of Railway Trainmen, 185
Brotherhood of Sleeping Car Porters, 176, 181, 185
Bureau of Labor Statistics, U.S., 81, 85, 233, 331
Bush, Martha, 230

Catholics:
birth control and, 28
race relations and, 11, 136, 192
views on government of, 118
Wallace support among, 145
Census Bureau, data of:
age, 58–64
education, 64–67
geographic distribution, 55–58
industrial distribution, 67–68
limitations in use of, 71
trends in employment and earnings, 51–55
working wives, 68–70
Census of Governments, 282
Changes:
problems created by, 359–384
education, 364
ethnicity and adjustment, 365–367
improving status of blacks, 372–373
income and adaptability, 363–364
increase in real earnings, 367–369
mechanisms of adjustment to, 373–381
rising taxes and government spending, 369–373
working conditions, 365
"Chicago plan," 188
Chicanos, 352
Child care, 346, 368, 382
Children:
middle-class, 208
working-class, 212
economic squeeze and, 85–87
improvement for, 39–40
CIO (*see* Congress of Industrial Organizations)
Civil Rights and Opportunities Act (1964), 177, 187, 191, 192
Civil rights legislation, 109–110
Clark, Kenneth, 201, 203
Clark, Robert M., 317
Class conflict, 7–11
Class prejudice, 197–198
Clerical workers, 56
(*See also* White-collar workers)
Coleman, James, 331, 341
College education, 333–337
financial aid for, 335–337
Columbia Broadcasting System, 352
Commodity distribution, 289
Compulsory military service, 44
Conant, James B., 321
Congress, U.S., 16
civil rights legislation in, 109–110
Nixon vetoes overridden by, 357
Social Security benefits increased by, 291
tax legislation in, 358
Congress of Industrial Organizations (CIO), 181–183
Committee to Abolish Racial Discrimination of, 182
Consumption:
patterns of, 29
styles and goals of, 212–219
automobiles, 216–218
food, 213
home ownership, 213–214
moonlighting, 215
services, 218
Converse, Philip E., 152, 153
Conyers, John, Jr., 126
Cooke, Donald, 384
Craft unions, 182, 198
(*See also* American Federation of Labor; Unions)
Craftsmen (*see* Skilled workers)
Crecine, John P., 285
Credit, consumer, 29, 218
Croly, Herbert, 7–8, 19
Crosland, Anthony C., 16–17
Cultural diversity, 235–236

Davis-Bacon Act, 381
Death taxes, 263–264

Debts, 82–83
 (*See also* Credit, consumer)
Deficit spending, 354
Democratic party, *xvii–xx,* 3, 9–11, 380–381, 383
 constituency of, 352
 deficit spending and, 354
 desertion of, 101–103
 identification with, 121–122
 New Deal of, 104, 105
 support among blacks for, 126–127
Demonstrations, 132, 148
Dennison Company, 30
Department of Housing and Urban Development, U.S., 92
Deran, Elizabeth, 317
Diseases, occupational, 31
Draft, military, 44
Drucker, Peter, 243, 252
Duncan, Otis Dudley, 35, 42, 46
Dunlop, John T., 75, 384

Earnings (*see* Income)
Eastman Kodak Corporation (*see* Kodak Corporation)
Eckstein, Otto, 316
Economic issues, 105–108
Economic policy, long-term changes in, 244–245
Economic squeeze, 78–87
 methods of dealing with, 82–84
  debts, 82–83
  moonlighting, 83–84
  nonwage income, 82
  working wives, 84
 next generation and, 85–87
 taxes and, 84–85
 unions and, 157–60
  tax burden, 158–159
  working wives, 159–160
 wage-budget factor in, 78–82
Education, 318–341
 adaptation to new needs by system of, 337–340
 adult, peripheral system of, 327–328
 amount of, 22–23
 census data on, 64–67
 changes in, 240–241
 in college, 333–337
  financial aid, 335–337
 easing problems through, 244
 expansion in, 25–26
 Head Start program, 84
 in high school, 331–333
 immigrants and, 332
Education (*Cont.*):
 labor market projections and, 329–331
 mobility and, 39–40, 323–329, 378–379
  avenues to, 325–329
  significance of, 324–325
 public expenditures for, 44
 reforms needed in, 356–357
 respect for authority and, 113
 social transformation and, 240–241, 246
 union programs for, 329, 340
 veto by Nixon of bill for, 357
 vocational, 326–327
 workplace, 164–165
Eisenhower, Dwight David, *xvii,* 124
Electrical Workers Union (Local 3), 31
Emerging Republican Majority, The (Phillips), 352
Employment Service reforms, 345
Employment trends, 51–55
Environmental-psychological-sociological squeeze, 91–94
Expenses, reduction of, 15
Extended family, 210

Fair Deal, 105
Families:
 size of, 28–29
 working-class, 204–229
  comfort and security for, 206–208
  compared to lower-middle-class, 204–206
  styles and goals of consumption by, 212–219
  world views of, 208–212
Family Assistance Plan (FAP), 16, 84, 238, 304–305
 child care under, 346
Federal Mediation and Conciliation Service, 375
Ferman, Louis, 192, 203
First Bank of the United States, 8
Fletcher, Arthur, 188
Food consumption, 213
Food stamps, 288, 289
Ford Foundation Conference on Blue-Collar Alienation, 18
"Forgotten American, the", 8–9
Fringe benefits, 33, 77, 90, 160–161, 164, 171–174, 347–349, 374–376

Gallup, George, 191, 215–216, 229, 360
General Electric Corporation, 30, 231
General Motors Corporation, 29, 231
Generation gap, 162
Ginzberg, Eli, 3–4, 20, 46

Goldfinger, Nat, 251
Gomberg, William, 129
Gompers, Samuel, 177, 184
Goode, William J., 212, 228
Gooding, Judson, 94
Government pay scales, 358
Great Depression, the, 30
Greeley, Andrew M., 384
Grinker, William, 384
Groppi, James, Fr., 132
Guaranteed work plan, 288

Hacker, Andrew, 108, 129
Hamilton, Richard F., 97–98, 129, 130, 152, 231, 252
Hamiltonianism, 4, 7–8, 19
Hansen, W. Lee, 334, 341
Hard hats, 9, 10
Harrington, Michael, 102, 128
Harris, Fred R., 257, 351
Harris, Louis, 52, 75, 190, 191, 300, 374
Harvard University, 8
Hausknecht, Murray, 129
Head Start program, 84
Health care, 357
  unions and, 170, 376, 382
Herman, Judith, 358, 384
Herriot, Roger A., 384
Hickey-Freeman Company, 30
Hiestand, Dale L., 46
High school education, 331–333
Hill, Herbert, 185–186
Hillman, Sidney, 51
Hodgson, James D., 128
Hoffer, Eric, 361, 384
Home ownership, 106, 213–214
Hormel Company, 30
Hours worked per week, 30–31
Housing:
  styles and goals of consumption and, 213–214
  supply of, 238–239
  taxes on, 270–271, 282–284
  unions and, 170
Humphrey, Hubert H., 379–380
  supporters of, 122–124
  union leadership and, 128
Husband, role of, 209–210
Hyman, Herbert, 153

Iacobelli, John L., 341
Immigrants, 25, 27
  adjustment of, 365–367
  education and, 332
  socioeconomic origins of, 36

Income, 51–55
  age and, 58–64
  diversity in, 233–234
  education and, 64, 67
  levels of, 11–14
  means of increasing, 15
  median: changes in, 52–54
    geographic distribution and, 56–57
  nonwage, 82
  spread in, 22
  taxes and increase in, 280–281
Income maintenance, 286–317
  alienation and, 286–291
  public assistance as, 299–306
    (*See also* Public assistance)
  Social Security as, 291–299
    (*See also* Social Security)
  unemployment insurance as, 306–314
    (*See also* Unemployment insurance)
  workmen's compensation as, 306–314
    (*See also* Workmen's compensation)
Income tax, 354–355
  changes, 354–355
  federal, 264–265
  local, 266
  middle-class support for, 289
  state, 265–266
Independent Offices Appropriations Bill, 358
Industrial distribution, 67–68
Industrial unions, 181–182
  (*See also* Congress of Industrial Organizations; Unions)
Inflation, 353
Institutions, legitimacy of, 245
Intellectuals:
  class prejudice of, 197–198
  interclass conflict with, 250
Interclass conflict, 249–250
Intermarriage, 137, 138
Internal Revenue Service, 82
International Ladies' Garment Workers' Union (ILGWU), 47, 186, 231
Intolerance (*see* Tolerance levels)
Intraclass conflict, 249

Jackson, Jesse, 354
Jeffersonianism, 4, 7–8, 19
Jews, race relations and, 136, 192, 195–196
"Job consciousness," 9
Job equality, attitudes on, 136
    in the South, 142
Job security, 55
Johnson, Lyndon B., 114

Kennedy, John F., 380

Kennedy, Robert F., 228
Kerner Commission (National Advisory Commission on Civil Disorders), 108, 129, 351
Kirsch, Arthur, 384
Kodak Corporation, 30
Kolodrubetz, Walter W., 317
Kornhauser, Arthur, 94

Labor Department, U.S., 5, 52, 205
Labor market projections, 329–331
Labor Party, British, 17
Labor unions (*see* Unions)
Laborers:
  education of, 64
  median age of, 58
  seasonality and, 30
  tolerance levels of, 135
    in the South, 140–141
Landrum-Griffin Act, 375
"Law-and-order" issues, *xviii,* 108–113
  desegregation and, 108–111
  protest and civil disobedience and, 111–113
Levine, Irving, 358, 384
Levitan, Sar A., 258, 359
Lewis, John L., 51, 181
Liberals, world outlook of, 130–132
Lipset, Seymour Martin, 105, 129
Lockwood, David, 252
Lubell, Samuel, 102, 108–109, 128, 129, 189, 193, 203, 252

McClellan, John L., 375
McGovern, George, 288
Machinists Union, 177
Managerial workers:
  education of, 64
  geographic distribution of, 56
  income gains of, 57
  working wives of, 69
Manpower Development and Training Act (1962), 187
Manpower development programs, 326
  veto by Nixon of bill for, 357
Marshall, Ray, 98–99, 176, 203
Mass communications, 29
Matthews, Charles, 332, 341
Meany, George, 3, 9–11
  on alienation, 286
  on financial status of unionists, 11–13
  Vietnam war supported by, 99
Medicare, 371, 376
Michigan, University of, 347
    Survey Research Center of, 77, 82, 89, 102, 134, 136, 139, 144
Middle class, the:
  class prejudice in, 197–198
  families in: children of, 208
    life cycle of, 211
  income tax, personal, supported in, 289
  self-identification with, 105
  Social Security supported in, 289
Mieszkowski, Peter, 285
Miller, Herman P., 4–5, 47, 229, 384
Miller, S. M., 99–100, 230, 252
Miller, Warren E., 153
Mobility:
  changes in, 240–241
  criteria for, 35–40
    improvement for children, 39–40
    improvement over parents, 35–37
    occupational advancement, 37–39
  education and, 39–40, 323–329, 378–379
    avenues to, 325–329
    significance of, 324–325
  opportunities for, 376–379
  social transformation and, 240–241
  technology and, 377–378
  views on, 106–107
Model Cities program, 16
Moonlighting, 83–84
  styles and goals of consumption and, 215
Moynihan, Daniel P., 229
Mueller, Eva, 341
Murray, Philip, 51
Myrdal, Gunnar, 36

Nader, Ralph, 355
National Association for the Advancement of Colored People (NAACP), 181, 182
  AFL-CIO and, 185–187
National Labor Relations Act, 187
National Labor Relations Board, 187
National Opinion Research Center (of University of Chicago), 137–139, 142–143
National Urban League (NUL), 181, 182, 186
National Welfare Rights Organizations, 306
Negro American Labor Council (NALC), 185–186
Negroes (*see* Blacks; Nonwhite workers; Race relations; Tolerance levels)
Netzer, Dick, 53, 256, 259, 285
New Deal, 10, 104, 105, 182
Nixon, Richard M., 8–12, 15, 101, 241, 251, 352, 380–381
  bills vetoed by, 357–358
  campaign of, 379

Nixon, Richard M. (*Cont.*):
  economic objectives of, 342, 353
    child care and, 346
    deficit spending, 354
    education and, 344
    revenue sharing, 347
    unemployment, 354
  Family Assistance Plan of, 16
  supporters of, 122–123
Nonwhite workers, 23
  demographic patterns and, 24
  education of, 64
  geographical distribution of, 56
  income of, 13
    age and, 63
    gains in, 54–55
    median, 57
  industrial distribution of, 67
  mobility among, 36
  occupational distribution of, 27
  as operatives, 36, 371
  publicly employed, 170
  views on war of, 115
  working wives of, 70
  workplace squeeze and, 91

Occupational advancement, 37–39
Occupational diseases, 31
Occupational distribution, 54
Office of Education, U.S., 323
Office of Federal Contract Compliance, 188
Old Age, Survivors, and Disability Insurance (OASDI) (*see* Social Security)
Old Age Assistance, 298
On-the-job training, 326
Open-housing, 135, 136
  marches for, 132
Operatives, 23
  educational level of, 324
  nonwhite, 36, 371
  seasonality and, 30
  tolerance levels of, 135
    in the South, 140–41
  women as, 37
Opportunity to advance, 39

Palme, Olof, 18, 246
Parnes, Herbert, 37
Participation in the workplace, 247–248
Part-time jobs, 345–346
Pechman, Joseph, 317
Pensions, 33, 90, 173–174, 349, 374, 376
Perlman, Selig, 9
Perloff, Harvey S., 285
"Peronism," 105
Perry, George L., 384
"Philadelphia plan," 188
Phillips, Kevin P., 9, 101–102, 128, 352
Political views, 101–129
  alienation and, 116–119
  on economic issues, 105–108
  on law-and-order issues, 108–113
    desegregation, 108–111
    protest and civil disobedience, 111–113
  on political parties, 120–124
  realignment or retrenchment in, 101–105
  on Vietnam war, 113–116
Pollution, 169–170
Population shifts, 199–200
Powell, Adam Clayton, Jr., 126
Powell, Enoch, 17
Power, changes in, 241
Powerlessness, sense of, 146–150
Preferential treatment on the basis of race, 187–188
Prejudice:
  class, 197–198
  (*See also* Race relations; Tolerance levels)
Price-wage policy, 247
Procter & Gamble, 30
Productivity, human factors in, 245
Professionals:
  education of, 64
  geographical distribution of, 56
  income gains of, 57
  working wives of, 69
Protestants:
  race relations and, 111, 136, 192
  views on government of, 118
  Wallace support among, 145
Public assistance, 299–306
  administration of, 304
  Aid to Families with Dependent Children (AFDC), 301–302, 314
  "antiwork" image of, 302–304
  Family Assistance Plan of, 16, 84, 238, 304–305
  income maintenance, as, 299–306
  increased spending for, 371
  reforms needed in, 356
  taxes for, 300–301
Public employers, 349

Race relations:
  diversity in attitudes on, 234–235
  social transformation and, 247
  unions and, 176–203
    AFL, 177–181

Race relations, unions and (*Cont.*):
AFL-CIO, 183–187
attitudes of white workers, 190–194
CIO, 181–183
community, 194–196
economic considerations, 196–198
policy conflict, 187–190
population shifts, 199–200
present and potential conflict, 176–177
union structure and objectives, 198–199
working-class families and, 224–228
workplace, 162–163
(*See also* Tolerance levels)
Race riots, 180
Railroad Retirement Board, 306
Rainwater, Lee, 99, 100, 204, 228
Randolph, A. Philip, 181, 185, 186
Reagan, Ronald, 124
Real Majority, The (Scammon and Wattenberg), 352
Realignment, political, 101–105
Recreation, 163–164
Regressive taxes, 294–299
Reich, Charles A., 14
Reiter, Howard L., 97–98, 101
Reitzes, Dietrich, 189–190, 203
Religious affiliation, 119
(*See also* Catholics; Jews; Protestants)
Republican party, *xvii–xx,* 9, 10, 14, 381, 383
conservatism in, 379
constituency of, 352
deficit spending and, 354
"full dinner pail" of, 104
identification with, 121–122
social issues seen by, 231
support for, 101–103
wage and price controls and, 375
Retail Clerks Union, 157
Retrenchment, political, 101–105
Riesman, David, 228
Robinson, John P., 153
Roby, Pamela A., 252
Roosevelt, Franklin Delano, 8–9, 10, 100
Rosebourough, Howard, 228
Rosen, Howard, 326
Rosow, Jerome M., 5, 76, 257, 342
Rusk, Jerrold G., 153
Ruttenberg, Stanley H., 98, 99, 154

Sales workers, geographical distribution of, 56
Satisfaction, job, 241–242
Scammon, Richard M., 102, 128, 223, 229, 352
School integration, attitudes on, 136, 139
in the South, 143
Schrag, Peter, 316, 341
Schrank, Robert, 257, 318
Schuman, Howard, 152
Schwartz, Mildred, 153
Seasonality in employment, 30
Second Bank of the United States, 8
Seligman, E. R. A., 29
Seniority, 32
Service workers, 23
education of, 64
increase in numbers of, 331
median age of, 58
seasonality and, 30
tolerance levels of, 135
in the South, 140–141
women as, 37
Services:
changes in, 239–240
consumption of, 218
Sex discrimination, 346
Sexton, Patricia Cayo, 332, 341
Sheatsley, Paul B., 153
Shelley, E. F., & Company, 83
Shipbuilders Union, 157
Shostak, Arthur B., 129, 384
Silent Majority, 9, 11, 205, 383
Silk, Leonard, 3–4, 7
Skilled workers, 23
education of, 324
nonwhite, 36, 373
seasonality and, 30
tolerance levels of, 135, 136
in the South, 140
Slichter, Sumner, 257
Small business, 38
Smith, William M., 341
Social Democratic party, Swedish, 18
Social issues, *xviii,* 15
Social Security, 10, 33, 85, 257, 289, 315, 370–371, 383
income maintenance, as, 291–299
middle-class support for, 289
redistributive structure of, 293–294
taxes for, 271
increased, 294–299
redistributive structure of, 293–294
regressive, 355
unions and, 167, 174
Social squeeze, 165–171
Social transformation, 230–252
counterpressures on, 248–250
diversity of blue-collar workers and, 230–236

Social transformation (*Cont.*):
joint actions for, 250–252
long-term changes and, 242–246
perspectives on, 236–238
policy needed for, 246–248
education, 246
equality, 247
participation, 247–248
status, 248
short-range changes and, 238–242
Southern Railway, 35
Status, 241–242, 248
Stein, Susan, 257, 318
Strikes, wildcat, 376
Suburbs, move to, 56
Supplementary unemployment plans, 306
Supreme Court, U.S., school desegregation decision of, 322
Survey Research Center (*see* Michigan, University of)

Taggart, Robert, III, 258, 359
Taussig, Michael K., 317
Tax Foundation, 285
Tax Reform Act (1969), 346
Taxes, 259–285
alienation and, 287
burden of, relative, 259–262
economic squeeze and, 84–85, 158–159
evidence on, statistical, 272–275
geographic differentials, 275–278
kinds of: alcoholic beverage, 268–269
automobile, 272
cigarette, 268–269
death, 263–264
gift, 263–264
income, personal: federal, 264–265
local, 266
state, 265–266
property, on housing, 270–271, 282–284
sales, retail, 267–268
Social Security, 271, 293–299
regressivity of, 355
unemployment insurance, 306–314
workmen's compensation, 306–314
legislation in U.S. Congress, 358
perceptions versus realities, 279–284
policy for, new, 346–347
unfair, 354
"visible," 262–275
Technology:
impact of, 44
job dissatisfaction and, 320
mobility and, 377–378
"Techtronic" age, 155

Television as education medium, 344
Thurmond, Strom, 144
Tolerance levels, 130–153
alienation and, 146–150
candidacy of Wallace and, 143–146
contrary evidence on, 132–140
liberal world outlook and, 130–132
removal of sources of strain in, 150–152
in the South, 140–143
(*See also* Race relations)
Trade unions (*see* Unions)
Training, 164–165
on-the-job, 326
Transportation, 347
Treiman, Donald J., 152
Tyler, Gus, 47–48, 366

Unemployment, 354
Unemployment insurance, 306–314
adequacy of, 310–311
supplementary unemployment plans and, 306
taxes for, 309–310, 312–313
Unions, 23, 154–175
adjustment to change through, 374–376
economic squeeze and, 157–160
tax burden, 158–159
working wives, 159–160
educational programs and, 329, 340
expanding role of, 171–175
extent of membership in, 32–33, 105
gains made by, 51
health care and, 376, 382
Humphrey and, 128
job security and, 55
opinions of members of, 52
political views on, 106
race relations and, 176–203
AFL, 177–181
AFL–CIO, 183–187
attitudes of white workers, 190–194
CIO, 181–183
community, 194–196
economic considerations, 196–198
policy conflict, 187–190
population shifts, 199–200
present and potential conflict, 176–177
union structure and objectives, 198–199
Social Security and, 167, 174
social squeeze and, 165–171
health care, 170
housing, 170
pollution, 169–170
as vehicles of participation, 247–248
viability of, 154–157

Unions (*Cont.*):
working conditions and, 160–165
advancement, 161
education and training, 164–165
generation gap, 162
racial issues, 162–163
recreation, 163–164
United Auto Workers (UAW), 30, 241, 356
United Mine Workers (UMW), 178, 181, 195
United States Steel Corporation, 32
United Steelworkers, 157
Upgrading, 15, 39, 345
Upper middle class, tolerance levels of, 134–135
in the South, 140, 141
support for Wallace and, 145
Urban development, veto by Nixon of bill for, 357
Urbanization, 27–28

Van Arsdale, Harry, 31
Verba, Sidney, 129
Vietnam war, 10, 14, 71, 113–116
demonstrations against, 132, 148
employment during, 57
reaction to, 131
"Visible" taxes, 262–275
Vocational education, 326–327, 344
Vogel, E. F., 228
Voluntary associations, 118, 126

Wage and price controls, 375
Wages (*see* Income)
Wallace, George, *xviii,* 13, 17, 52, 122–124, 228, 352, 379–380
alienation and, 147–148
nationalism and economic populism of, 105
tolerance levels and, 143–146
union support for, 190–191
Washington, Booker T., 179, 203
Wattenberg, Ben J., 102, 128, 223, 229, 352
Weisbrod, Burton A., 334, 341
Welfare (*see* Public assistance)
White, Theodore H., 144, 152
White-collar workers:
geographical distribution of, 56
increased numbers of, 26
median age of, 58
Whiting, Basil, 384
Wingo, Lowdon, Jr., 285
Wives:
role of, 209–210
working (*see* Working women, married)

Wolfe, Arthur C., 153
Work, changes in demands of, 243–244
(*See also* Workplace squeeze)
Work Incentive Program (WIN), 84, 304
Working-class families, 204–229
comfort and security for, 206–208
compared to lower-middle-class, 204–206
morale of, 219–222
politicians, establishmentarians and, 222–228
race relations, 224–228
styles and goals of consumption of, 212–219
automobiles, 218
food, 213
home ownership, 213–214
moonlighting, 215
services, 218
world views of, 208–212
children, 212
extended family, 210
roles of husband and wife, 209–210
Working conditions:
improvements in, 31–32, 347–348
unions and, 160–165
advancement, 161
education and training, 164–165
generation gap, 162
racial issues, 162–163
recreation, 163–164
unpleasant, 90–91
Working women, 12–13
change in role of, 27
increased proportion of, 367
married, 22, 51, 368
census data on, 68–70
economic squeeze and, 84, 159–160
Social Security and, 295
mobility and, 36–37, 41–42
as operatives, 37
part-time, 345
views on war of, 115
Workmen's compensation, 306–314
adequacy of, 310–311
taxes for, 309–310, 312–313
Workplace squeeze, 87–91
job satisfaction and, 89
promotion opportunities and, 89–90
unpleasant working conditions and, 90–91
World War I, 179
expansion of union membership during, 180
World War II, 183, 199

Yale University, 356